Martin Guggenheim is a professor of clinical law and the director of Clinical and Advocacy Programs at New York University School of Law. He served as the staff attorney and acting director of the Juvenile Rights Project of the American Civil Liberties Union and as staff attorney for the Juvenile Rights Division of the New York Legal Aid Society. He has litigated many important cases involving children's and parents' rights. He has written numerous articles, contributed chapters for several books, and is coauthor of *The Rights of Parents, The Rights of Young People,* and *Trial Manual for Defense Attorneys in Juvenile Court.*

Alexandra Dylan Lowe advocates in the field of family law and adoption and has written about a wide variety of legal topics. A graduate of Harvard Law School she serves on the U.S. State Department's Study Group on Intercountry Adoption and currently advises adoptive parent support groups in the area of adoption and foster care reform.

Diane Curtis is an attorney at the Center for Reproductive Law and Policy. She is a recent graduate of New York University School of Law, where she was an Arthur Garfield Hays Civil Liberties and Civil Rights Fellow. A longtime advocate for reproductive rights, she was a cofounder of the national grassroots activist group WHAM! (Women's Health Action and Mobilization) and has previously published articles on self-help gynecological care and violence against lesbians and gay men.

ALSO IN THIS SERIES

THE RIGHTS OF
FAMILIES

The Authoritative ACLU Guide to
the Rights of Family Members Today

Martin Guggenheim
Alexandra Dylan Lowe
Diane Curtis

General Editor of the Handbook Series
Norman Dorsen, President, ACLU 1976–1991

SOUTHERN ILLINOIS UNIVERSITY PRESS
CARBONDALE AND EDWARDSVILLE

Guggenheim, Martin.
    The rights of families : the authoritative ACLU guide to the rights of
family members today / Martin Guggenheim, Alexandra Dylan Lowe, Diane
Curtis.
       p. cm.—(An American Civil Liberties Union handbook)
    Includes bibliographical references.
     1. Domestic relations—United States. 2. Human reproduction—Law
and legislation—United States. 3. Child abuse—Law and
legislation—United States. 4. Family—United States. I. Lowe,
Alexandra Dylan. II. Curtis, Diane. III. American Civil Liberties
Union. IV. Title. V. Series.
KF505.Z9G84   1996
346.7301′5—dc20
[347.30615]

ISBN 0-8093-2051-7   95-24832
ISBN 0-8093-2052-5 (pbk.)   CIP

The paper used in this publication meets the minimum requirements
of the American National Standard for Information Sciences—Permanence
of Paper for Printed Library Materials, ANSI Z39.48–1984. ∞

For Ellen
—D. C.

For my family
—M. G.

For Nicholas and David
—A. D. L.

CONTENTS

PREFACE

This guide sets forth your rights under present law and offers suggestions on how they can be protected. It is one of a continuing series of handbooks published in cooperation with the American Civil Liberties Union (ACLU).

Surrounding these publications is the hope that Americans, informed of their rights, will be encouraged to exercise them. Through their exercise, rights are given life. If they are rarely used, they may be forgotten and violations may become routine.

This guide offers no assurances that your rights will be respected. The laws may change, and in some of the subjects covered in these pages, they change quite rapidly. An effort has been made to note those parts of the law where movement is taking place, but it is not always possible to predict accurately when the law *will* change.

Even if laws remain the same, their interpretation by courts and administrative officials often varies. In a federal system such as ours, there is a built-in problem, since state and federal laws differ, not to speak of the variations among states. In addition, there is much diversity in the ways in which particular courts and administrative officials interpret the same law at any given moment.

If you encounter what you consider to be a specific abuse of your rights, you should seek legal assistance. There are a number of agencies that may help you, among them ACLU affiliate offices, but bear in mind that the ACLU is a limited-purpose organization. In many communities there are federally funded legal service offices that provide assistance to persons who cannot afford the costs of legal representation.

In general, the rights that the ACLU defends are freedom of inquiry and expression; due process of law; equal protection of the laws; and privacy. The authors in this series have discussed other rights (even though they sometimes fall outside the ACLU's usual concern) in order to provide as much guidance as possible.

These books have been planned as guides for the people directly affected: thus the question-and-answer format. (In some areas there are more detailed works available for experts.) These guides seek to raise the major issues and inform the nonspecialist of the basic law on the subject. The authors of these books are themselves specialists who understand the need for information at "street level."

If you encounter a specific legal problem in an area discussed in one of these handbooks, show the book to your attorney. Of course, he or she will not be able to rely exclusively on the handbook to provide you with adequate representation. But if your attorney hasn't had a great deal of experience in the specific area, the handbook can provide helpful suggestions on how to proceed.

NORMAN DORSEN, *General Editor*
Stokes Professor of Law
New York University School of Law

The principal purpose of this handbook, as well as others in this series, is to inform individuals of their legal rights. The authors from time to time suggest what the law should be, but their personal views are not necessarily those of the ACLU. For the ACLU's position on the issues discussed in this handbook, the reader should write to Public Education Department, ACLU, 132 West 43d Street, New York, NY 10036.

ACKNOWLEDGMENTS

This book would not have been written without the generous help of a large number of individuals. The authors gratefully acknowledge their assistance.

Marcia Lowry wrote the original draft for chapter 6.

Chapter 10 is based substantially on the work of Nan D. Hunter, Sherryl E. Michaelson, and Thomas B. Stoddard, who cowrote the chapter on family for the 1992 ACLU handbook *The Rights of Lesbians and Gay Men.*

Andrea Miller collaborated in the writing of chapter 11. Nina Loewenstein assisted in the writing of the "HIV and Pregnancy" section of chapter 11, and the "Right to Direct the Course of Pregnancy" section of chapter 11 is based substantially on the work of Kary L. Moss, "Liberty Rights During Pregnancy," in Susan Deller Ross et al., *The Rights of Women* (1993).

Peter Bienstock, Nancy Erickson, Dixie Hathaway, Carol Hogan, Joan H. Hollinger, Cindy Hounsell, Margaret Klaw, Paula Roberts, John J. Sampson, and Linda Silberman tirelessly reviewed drafts of portions of the book.

Harriet Newman Cohen, Linda Elrod, Joan Entmacher, Margaret Campbell Haynes, Ronald K. Henry, Susan Paikin, Ross Thompson, and Robert Williams patiently answered questions.

Rhoda Sandler, Henry Sandler, Charlotte Lowe, and Ray Lowe provided limitless encouragement and support.

Finally, Allison Armour, Christine Lehman, and Michael Neft provided invaluable research assistance.

INTRODUCTION

This book is about how families come into being and how they break apart. Had it been written a generation ago, it would have been much shorter and significantly simpler.

At an earlier time in this country's history, the courts and society in general had a clear, if narrow, conception of how a family was formed: men and women married and conceived children together. Divorce was relatively uncommon and required proof of marital misconduct. Children born out-of-wedlock had few if any rights. Women had little or no control over the bearing of children. Adoption was controlled by adoption agencies and was, in most families, a closely guarded secret. Gays and lesbians stayed in the closet. The right of children to be protected from physical abuse or neglect by their parents was barely articulated. In vitro fertilization, surrogate parenting, and other complex reproductive technologies were unheard of.

The last quarter-century has witnessed nothing short of a revolution in family law. Stepparents, adoptive parents, foster parents, single parents, grandparents, and gay parents have come forward to challenge the traditional definition of a family based on blood ties alone. Indeed, one of the oldest and most deeply rooted presumptions in family law—the idea that a child is best off being raised by his or her biological parents—is now repeatedly called into question. In contested private adoption cases, in custody disputes involving stepparents or grandparents, in child abuse or neglect cases where foster parents wish to adopt a foster child who has lived with them for a long period of time, and in visitation disputes involving gay or lesbian parents, courts are increasingly being asked to protect children's emotional ties to the people who have actually parented them, as opposed to their ties to the persons who are their parents in name only.

Over the same period of time, divorce has shed its social stigma and has become widely available without proof of marital misdeeds. New laws have been written to govern the distribution of property between former marital partners and the availability of alimony. And increased national attention has been focused on abuse and neglect of children in their homes.

Once the exclusive province of state courts and state legislatures, family law increasingly bears the national stamp of Congress and the Supreme Court of the United States. Beginning in the mid-1970s, Congress has enacted a series of broad new laws to boost child support payments to children whose parents no longer live together. During that same period, the Supreme Court ruled that pregnant women have a constitutional right to obtain an abortion; the Court continues to monitor the laws passed by various states to regulate the availability of abortions. Whole aspects of foster care and adoption law are now governed by mandates imposed by federal law.

This book is designed to help the reader understand today's family law and to give the reader some sense of where the law in this field might be headed over the next decade. The book first looks at the human and financial consequences of a married couple's divorce or the separation of unmarried partners. The chapters in this section, which describe the law in the areas of child custody, visitation, child support, property division, and alimony, were written by Alexandra Dylan Lowe.

The second part of this book looks at the law that applies when the state intervenes temporarily or permanently to protect children from harm by their parents. The chapters in this section were written by Martin Guggenheim.

The third part of this book looks at how families are formed, especially families that differ from the traditional nuclear family: adoptive families, single-parent families, families headed by a grandparent, and gay and lesbian families. This section also covers the rights associated with the choice of when and how to have children. Chapter 8 was written by Alexandra Dylan Lowe; chapters 9 through 11 were written by Diane Curtis.

It is worth noting that there are other important aspects of family law that are not covered here but are addressed by other publications in this series. The government benefits available to family members are considered in detail in *The Rights of Poor Persons*, which is currently under revision. The responsibilities of parents to control and discipline their children are addressed in *The Rights of Parents*. The "right to die" and other questions relating to the care of terminally ill family members are discussed in *The Rights of Patients*. Domestic violence and the legal rights of battered women are considered in *The Rights of Women*.

Finally, readers should be aware that one theme that runs throughout much of American family law is the right to be free from unjustified governmental interference. This is, in essence, a "hands off" view of family law, one that focuses heavily on a family's procedural rights. It is very different from other countries' conception of family rights, which reflect their society's commitment to the well-being of children and their families. Unlike the United States, many countries around the world believe that families need positive support in the form of paid childcare leave, national health insurance, subsidized day care, free universal preschool, child allowances, child support assurance, and free (or low-cost) higher education. The absence of such substantive rights for families in the United States is the subject of ongoing debate.

PART 1

Divorce and Its Consequences

1

Child Custody

Each year, over a million marriages end in divorce.[1] Thirteen million children—more than one-fifth of all children under eighteen—now live with a divorced single parent or in married stepfamilies.[2] As the divorce rate during the early years of marriage has grown, a higher percentage of divorces are now taking place among the parents of young children.[3]

At the same time, the focus of divorce law has shifted dramatically over the past twenty-five years. Divorce is no longer an exclusively fault-based ordeal, involving proof of cruelty, adultery, or other form of marital misconduct. Increasingly, "irretrievable breakdown" of the marriage, "irreconcilable differences," or living apart for a minimum period prescribed by law have become common grounds for divorce. Although only a few states have done away with fault-based grounds altogether, all fifty states have now added some form of no-fault provisions to their divorce laws.[4]

With the shift from a fault to a no-fault divorce system, attention has turned to other issues: Who will raise the children after the divorce? Is there a way for both parents to be involved in the children's upbringing when the marriage ends? Who will pay to feed, clothe, house, and educate them? How should the property that the couple accumulated during their marriage be divided? How will a long-married spouse who has never entered the job market make ends meet after the divorce?

This chapter takes a close look at the law's view of the relationship between parents and their children after a divorce. Many of the principles discussed here also apply in custody disputes between unwed parents involving nonmarital children. The two following chapters examine the dollars and cents issues of family law: the law of child support (which applies equally to the children of divorce and the children of unmarried parents), spousal support, and property division.

In a divorce, who decides where the children will live and who will care for them?

The parents, if they can agree. If they do not agree, a judge will decide for them. The vast majority of couples work out their custody arrangements by agreement. In some cases, there is no custody dispute at all because one parent does not want custody. In other cases, agreements are reached either by the parents on their own, with the help of a mediator, or through a process of attorney-assisted negotiations. Although the divorce court technically retains the power to review the agreement reached by the parents to make sure that it meets the best interests of the children involved, these agreements are commonly accepted by the court.

Some states provide that when the parents have entered into a written custody agreement, the agreement should be presumed to be in the child's best interests. Other states require the court independently to assess whether the agreed custody arrangement will be right for the child. The court may refuse to honor a custody agreement if it finds that it is not in the child's best interests.[5]

If the parents are unable to agree on a custody arrangement, the custody decision will be made by a judge, often with the aid of evaluations prepared by psychiatrists, social workers, or other mental health professionals. The court may award sole custody to one parent or joint legal and/or joint physical custody.

What types of custody arrangements are permissible?

Sole custody gives one parent, who is known as the *custodial* or *residential parent*, the power to determine the child's upbringing, including her education, healthcare, discipline, and religious training. The child lives with the parent who has sole custody and spends time, known as *visitation*, with the other parent.

Joint custody gives both parents legal decision-making authority over the major decisions affecting the child. *Joint legal custody* requires both parents to consult with each other and to make decisions jointly about the child's upbringing. At the same time, one parent has primary residential custody.

Where the parents agree to or are awarded *joint physical custody* (also known as *shared residency*), the child lives with each parent for a substantial portion of the year. Although joint physical custody does not require a precise fifty-fifty split of time between the two parents' households, it does require more than traditional visitation and calls for a stable schedule of regular contact with both parents. One common joint custody arrangement is for the child to spend the school year with one parent and summers with the other. Other parents who live near each other sometimes divide up the week, so that the children spend part of the week at one parent's home and part of the week at the other's.

During the 1980s, joint custody became the favored custody arrangement in many states.[6] Over forty states have laws authorizing the award of joint or shared custody.[7] Reflecting the public policy that children need maximum contact with both parents, some joint custody laws permit the court to award joint custody over the objection of one of the parents and require the judge to articulate clear and convincing reasons for not awarding joint custody if one parent requests it.[8] In states without an explicit statutory authorization, courts often have inherent power to grant joint custody if they find that it is in the child's best interests.

Joint custody laws have been hailed by fathers' advocates who believe that they ensure an ongoing, meaningful role for fathers in their children's postdivorce lives. Although the percentage of divorced parents involved in joint physical custody arrangements is small, there is evidence that fathers who share physical custody of their children are more committed to them and more likely to pay child support.[9]

At the same time, however, the notion of joint custody has been questioned by others. Shuttling children back and forth between two houses, two sets of friends, two sets of toys, and two different environments is seen by some courts and psychologists as a threat to the stability that is considered important for children's growth and development.[10] Doubts have been raised about the wisdom of imposing joint custody when the parties' personal animosity is so great that it spills over to the children.[11] Advocates for battered women have opposed both joint legal and joint physical custody because it forces the mother into continued contact with her abuser.[12]

Joint custody seems to work best when both parents are willing to cooperate on the children's behalf, are flexible, and live relatively near each other. Parents embarking on joint custody should work out a detailed parenting plan establishing the child's residence schedule, spelling out transportation arrangements and outlining who will be in charge of which kinds of decisions. They should also bear in mind that joint physical custody may well be more expensive than sole custody, since it costs more to maintain what amounts to two homes for the children.[13]

In a custody battle, is a woman automatically entitled to custody of her children if she is a fit mother?

Not anymore. A virtual revolution in child custody law that began in the 1970s has dramatically altered the legal framework governing child custody.

Until the nineteenth century, fathers were automatically entitled to custody of their children. From Roman times until the last century, fathers were viewed under common law as their children's natural guardian. Fathers had an inalienable right both to the child's physical custody and to all income earned by the child.[14]

Beginning in the mid-nineteenth century, courts deciding custody disputes began to forsake the notion of children as the exclusive property of their father and to focus instead on the child's needs for nurturing and care. By the early part of this century, it was generally assumed that children, particularly young children under the age of seven, were better off with their mother after a divorce. As recently as 1976, in more than thirty states the mother was to be awarded custody of her young children, as long as she was not unfit.[15]

By the 1970s, however, this legal rule, known as the "maternal preference" or "tender years" doctrine, had come under attack by fathers' rights advocates and some feminists on the grounds that it perpetuated sex-based stereotypes and violated the Equal Protection provision of the United States Constitution. Most states now specifically prohibit discrimination on the basis of sex in child custody cases and substitute a broader and vaguer "best interests of the child" test that requires judges to take into account a number of factors before making their custody decisions.[16]

In some states, the state legislature has spelled out the factors a judge must consider. Washington State's child custody law, for instance, which speaks in terms of "parenting plans" and "allocating parenting functions" instead of the more conventional notions of custody and visitation, requires judges to provide for the child's residential schedule based on:[17]

> 1. The relative strength, nature and stability of the child's relationship with each parent, including whether a parent has taken greater responsibility for performing parenting functions relating to the child's daily needs;
> 2. The agreements of the parties, provided they were entered into knowingly and voluntarily;

3. Each parent's past and potential for future performance of parenting functions;

4. The emotional needs and developmental level of the child;

5. The child's relationship with siblings and with other significant adults, as well as the child's involvement with his or her physical surroundings, school, or other sigificant activities;

6. The wishes of the parents and the wishes of a child who is sufficiently mature to express reasoned and independent preferences as to his or her residential schedule; and

7. Each parent's employment schedule (which the judge is required to accommodate).

In other states without specific statutory guideposts, courts have developed a set of standards for assessing the child's best interests that includes the emotional ties between the parent and the child; the parent's capacity to provide the child with love, affection, guidance, education, religious training, and the necessities of life; the length of time the child has lived in a stable environment and the desirability of maintaining custody with the parent who has provided that environment; the preference of the child, if of sufficient age and maturity; the willingness of the proposed custodial parent to foster a loving relationship with the other parent; and the mental, physical, and moral fitness of the parents.[18]

In a growing number of states, an important factor to be weighed in custody decisions is the determination of which parent is the child's primary caretaker.[19] The primary caretaker is the parent who generally attends to the child's day-to-day needs for physical care, nourishment, comfort, affection, and stimulation.[20] The primary caretaker doctrine is based on the belief that stability and continuity in the child's life are essential to a child's sense of security and happiness and that an award of custody to the primary caretaker will promote the child's well-being.[21]

The outcome of the "primary caretaker" test is often not all that different from the "tender years" doctrine, largely because women continue to shoulder the bulk of childrearing responsibilities and are the primary nurturers and caretakers of children in many marriages.[22] Indeed, one study found that among courts that favor the primary caretaker, mothers received custody in 80 percent of the contested cases and fathers received custody in the other 20 percent.[23] Nonetheless, in families where the father has assumed a large share of the caretaking responsibilities, the primary caretaker doctrine serves as a gender-neutral rule that gives him a chance to demonstrate his fitness to serve as the custodial parent.[24]

In most states, the primary caretaker is only one of several factors courts look to in determining custody under the "best interests of the child" doctrine. If one parent is better able than the other to fulfill the child's emotional and psychological needs, that parent may prevail over the primary caretaker.[25]

Yet another key factor is the time that a parent has available to spend with a child after the divorce.[26] Even in a contest between a working and a nonworking parent, the working parent is not disqualified simply because a child will be placed in day care if custody is awarded to him or her.[27]

In short, "the best interests" test is a highly flexible and indeterminate approach to child custody that forces judges to make predictions about the child's future welfare based on a wide variety of different factors, many of which are difficult to assess. A number of legal scholars have called on more states to adopt instead the gender-neutral primary caretaker standard, which is based on easily determined, verifiable facts about the parent's prior conduct and which would give parents and children alike a sense of greater predictability and certainty in disputed child-custody cases.[28] Others, including fathers' advocates, argue that the primary caretaker doctrine undervalues the way fathers most often nurture their children and stacks the deck against fathers seeking custody of their children.[29]

Is the noncustodial parent entitled to spend time with the child after a divorce?

Yes. A parent who does not have sole custody of a child is entitled to time with the child, which is known variously as *visitation, access,* or *parenting time.* A parent who opposes visitation bears the burden of proving that visitation would seriously endanger the child by jeopardizing his or her mental, physical, moral, or emotional health.[30] Otherwise, the law presumes that preserving a close parent-child relationship with both parents is in the child's best interests.

There are two common types of visitation orders. Some specify only that the noncustodial parent is to have "liberal and reasonable visitation," with the details of the schedule left to the parents to work out. While open-ended visitation provisions work well in some families, they are a source of ongoing conflict in others. Some states, such as Texas, favor highly structured visitation schedules, which spell out in detail definite times and places for visitation to occur.[31] Structured visitation schedules are also easier for the noncustodial parent to enforce if the custodial parent improperly interferes with visitation.

What recourse does the noncustodial parent have if the custodial parent interferes with visitation?

Most states affirmatively recognize that children need the love and affection of both parents, particularly in a situation as stressful for children as separation and divorce. In making custody awards or in modifying custody orders, courts are often required by their state's "friendly parent" provision to consider the extent to which one parent encourages or thwarts the child's contact with the other parent.[32]

Under these "friendly parent" laws, parents who are viewed by a judge as more cooperative with respect to visitation may obtain custody. If the custodial parent later interferes with visitation, the courts in some states are empowered to increase the noncustodial parent's visitation rights or, in extreme cases, to modify the existing custody order to transfer custody to the other parent.[33]

Unfortunately, the application of friendly parent laws may also have the unintended consequence of penalizing battered women who need to minimize or avoid contacts with the abusive spouse and who have raised legitimate concerns that joint custody or visitation with the noncustodial parent will be harmful to their children.[34] Kentucky recently passed a law that addresses this issue by prohibiting the modification of custody orders solely on the basis of which parent is more likely to permit visitation.[35]

As explained in the next chapter, courts do not view visitation and child support as reciprocal. It is therefore legally impermissible to suspend support payments in retaliation for the custodial parent's interference with visitation. The traditional remedy available to the aggrieved parent is to petition the court for modification of custody or visitation.

Some states have developed innovative court-sponsored programs to encourage and, if necessary, compel the custodial parent to provide the non-custodial parent with access to the child. In Michigan, for instance, an independent "friend of the court" investigates complaints of visitation interference and will try to resolve the complaint through a variety of means, ranging from informal consultation and mediation to contempt proceedings.[36] In Arizona, expedited visitation enforcement procedures are in place

to deal with visitation complaints. Program personnel are available to monitor scheduled visitation, and referrals may be made to a supervised visitation
program if a custodial parent has withheld visitation out of a legitimate fear
for a child's safety and well-being.[37]

What is mediation, and is it available for child custody disputes?

Mediation is an informal process by which a neutral third person known
as the *mediator* helps disputing parties to reach their own agreement. Mediation is available for child custody disputes. Most mediation programs focus
on custody and visitation, although some include alimony and property settlements too.

Thirty-six states have passed laws or developed rules of court authorizing divorce mediation.[38] In many states, these programs are offered as part
of the family court's services and are either free or assessed as court costs.
Other mediation programs are private or are offered through bar associations and other community programs. Private mediators charge fees that are
comparable to those of private therapists or attorneys.

Some mediation programs are voluntary, and the parties can choose or
decline to participate in a search for a mediated solution to their custody
dispute. Many states, however, now authorize judges to order the spouses to
attend one or more mediation sessions in an effort to resolve their custody
disagreements before going to trial.[39] Neither a court nor a mediator, however, can force the parties to reach a settlement.

Some states permit the spouses' attorneys to sit in on mediation sessions.
Others limit attendance to the divorcing couple or give the mediator power
to exclude their attorneys.[40] The mediator may also meet with the couple's
children and, in special cases, may involve the children's grandparents or
stepparents.

Mediation tends to result in a much higher proportion of joint custody
awards than court-ordered custody decrees. Only 20 percent of mediated
custody agreements, for example, provide for sole custody.[41]

Opinion is divided on the benefits of mediation. Proponents believe that
mediation allows couples to reach agreement on contested issues without
the hostility, psychological trauma, expense, and delay of a full-fledged custody battle. They argue that a good mediator helps the couple put aside their
differences and focus on the child's needs and best interests. When it is successful, mediation results in an enduring, child-oriented solution to the custody dispute.[42]

Opponents, including some women's advocates, assert that mediation is a "boon to the strong and a bane to the weak."[43] Many women, they point out, lack the equality of bargaining power with their spouses that is a prerequisite for successful mediation and have suggested that without the assistance and advice of an attorney, a woman who is fearful of losing custody of her children may, in the course of mediation, bargain away the right to an adequate property settlement in exchange for custody.

Domestic violence is often seen as jeopardizing the voluntariness of the mediation process and the equality of the spouses' bargaining power. Some states have therefore carved out an exemption from mediation for custody cases where there is evidence of domestic abuse.[44]

Do courts prefer to keep siblings together?

Yes. When a custody case involves more than one child, most courts will presume that brothers and sisters should remain together.[45] However, if a convincing case is made that the children's best interests call for a different arrangement, the court may make a split custody decision.

Who speaks for the child in a disputed custody case?

In many states, the court may appoint a guardian ad litem or an attorney to represent the child in a contested child custody or visitation case.[46] Such appointments, however, are rare. Most children, caught in the crossfire between their warring parents, have no independent spokesperson to present their concerns to the court.

When a guardian ad litem is appointed, the guardian's duty is to protect the child's best interests, which may or may not correspond to the child's wishes.[47] The guardian ad litem typically acts as an independent investigator, interviewing parents, teachers, and others to get a picture of the child's home life and family dynamics. The guardian ad litem may also review the child's medical and psychological records and evaluate the impartiality and competence of experts who have offered an opinion about the child. The guardian ad litem will usually then submit a report to the judge and to the parents' attorneys summarizing his or her recommendations for the child's custodial placement.[48]

Unlike a guardian ad litem, a court-appointed attorney for the child is expected to represent the child's expressed opinion if the child is old enough to have a reasoned opinion.[49] While some of the attorney's investigative responsibilities may overlap with those of a guardian ad litem, the attorney usually does not prepare a report but instead serves as an advocate and may present witnesses and other evidence on the child's behalf at trial if a settlement is not reached.

What weight is usually given to a child's preferences as to custody and visitation?

Forty states and the District of Columbia have laws requiring judges to take into account the preferences of children old enough to have an independent opinion.[50] Even in those states without specific statutory authorization, courts usually have discretion to consider the child's wishes.

The child, however, does not get the last word. The weight that judges give to a child's wishes usually depends on the child's age and maturity and on the judge's overall assessment of the child's best interests.[51] Court's may discount the child's choice if the judge believes that the child's preference is at odds with the child's welfare.[52] For instance, a child who wants to live with a parent whom the court considers unfit is unlikely to see his or her wish granted. Likewise, a court may order visitation with a parent even though the child is opposed to such visits.[53]

In many states, the judge may interview the child in his or her chambers out of the presence of the child's parents and their attorneys. In fairness to the parents, many states require that the interview be transcribed and made a part of the court record.

Is a parent's sexual activity relevant in awarding custody or visitation?

Yes. A parent's sexual activity is still a factor to be considered in awarding custody or visitation but most states have come a long way from the days when custody awards were used to punish one parent for marital misconduct or to reward the other "innocent" parent.

Nowadays, in assessing a parent's fitness to serve as the custodial parent, most courts take the view that an extramarital affair or nonmarital sexual conduct is relevant only if the parent's sexual conduct can be shown to adversely affect the child.[54]

In some cases, a court may award custody to a parent engaging in a sexual relationship but prohibit overnight visits from a lover while the children are present.[55] If there is evidence that the parent's lover has sexually abused his own children, the court may intervene to switch custody to the other parent.[56]

Homosexual parents still face an uphill battle in seeking custody against a nonhomosexual former spouse. A few states apply a hard and fast rule that a homosexual parent's exposure of the child to his or her "immoral lifestyle" renders the homosexual parent unfit as a matter of law.[57] Other states have held that a parent's sexual orientation is relevant only if it can be shown to adversely affect the child.[58] At the same time, some courts appear to take an expansive view of conduct that is harmful to the child and have awarded custody to the nonhomosexual parent to protect the child from taunts and rejection by other children.[59]

A parent's sexual behavior is also considered relevant to visitation. In most states, adultery, cohabitation, or homosexuality do not automatically disqualify a parent from visiting with the child. Most courts will prohibit overnight visitation with a sexually active parent only if there is a showing of adverse impact on the child. As with custody disputes, homosexuals parents often bear a greater burden, and some courts have restricted visitation to times when the homosexual partner is away from home.[60]

Does domestic violence affect custody and visitation decisions?

Within the past several years, a growing number of states have enacted laws to force judges to focus on the issue of family violence before awarding child custody. As state legislatures have come to recognize, violence often escalates after a divorce, and child custody and visitation may become the new forum for the abuse.[61]

Louisiana, for instance, passed a law creating a rebuttable presumption against an award of sole or joint custody to a parent who has inflicted physical or sexual abuse on the other parent or any of the children.[62] As of 1995, forty-four states and the District of Columbia have passed laws making reference to domestic violence as a factor to be taken into account in child custody determinations.[63]

State laws in this area tend to fall into one of several categories. In some states that have a statutory preference for joint custody or for making custody awards to the parent most willing to cooperate with the other parent, courts must consider domestic violence before joint custody is awarded. These laws run the gamut from a requirement that the court consider spouse abuse as one factor in the joint custody decision to a prohibition on awarding joint custody if there is evidence of abuse.[64]

Other states have incorporated the issue of spouse abuse into their "best interests of the child" test. Minnesota, for example, provides that one of the relevant factors a court should consider in determining custody is "the effect on the child of the actions of an abuser, if related to domestic abuse . . . that has occurred between the parents."[65]

Finally, several states have taken additional steps to protect the custodial rights of abused spouses. Colorado and Kentucky prohibit courts from drawing an inference that a battered spouse has abandoned her children if she left them with the abuser when she fled.[66] Some states provide that mediation of child custody and visitation disputes that is ordinarily mandatory is not required where there has been a history of family violence.[67] Other states have opened supervised visitation centers where staff members who understand domestic violence and child abuse can monitor the visitation.[68]

If parents separate and one parent moves out-of-state with the children before divorce proceedings begin, where will issues of child custody be decided?

Child custody cases that involve parents living in different states pose some of the most difficult legal questions in the family law field. Before reaching the heart of the dispute, a court handling an interstate child custody dispute must consider a threshold question: does it have the power (known in legal terms as *jurisdiction*) to decide the custody case?

The answer to this threshold inquiry is provided by two laws: the Parental Kidnapping Prevention Act (a federal law passed by Congress in 1980)[69] and the Uniform Child Custody Jurisdiction Act[70] (UCCJA), which has been enacted in some form in all fifty states and the District of Columbia.

The Parental Kidnapping Prevention Act (PKPA) gives priority to the child's home state (the state where the child lived with at least one parent for six months before the custody petition was filed).[71] If one parent moves with the child to live in a new state, the original state continues to be the home state for an additional six months after the move. The child need not be physically present in the original state for the child custody proceeding to be initiated there by the parent who has remained behind.

If the custody dispute involves an infant who is less than six months old, the child's home state is the state where the infant has lived since birth. Regardless of age, periods of temporary absence (for vacation or for medical treatment, for example) are counted as part of the six-month period.

The PKPA's preference for home state jurisdiction serves to protect the parent who remains in the home state after the other parent has taken the child(ren) to another state.[72] To take advantage of this protection, the parent who is left behind needs to act promptly and initiate a custody action within six month's of the child's departure from the state. However, if the left-behind parent waits too long and the child remains out-of-state for more than six months, the "old" home state will lose its home state status, and the new state will acquire jurisdiction to hear the case.[73]

If one parent moves out-of-state with the child and the other parent moves to a different state, neither state may be the child's home state if the child has lived in the new state for fewer than six months. Similarly, if the whole family moves to a new state and had not yet lived there for six months when the parents file for divorce, the new state will not yet have become a home state. In the absence of a home state with jurisdiction, the PKPA and UCCJA provide that a state that has significant connections to the child may exercise jurisdiction to decide the custody dispute.[74] Whether or not a state has a significant connection to the child depends on a variety of factors, including how much time the child and parent(s) have spent in the new state; the closeness of the child and parent's relationships to friends and family in the new state; their ties to schools and work in the new community; the availability of witnesses and the length of time the parent is likely to remain in the new state with the child.[75]

In the absence of an emergency, the mere physical presence of the child and a parent in a state is not enough to allow a court there to make a custody award. An "emergency" under the UCCJA and the PKPA is defined as a case where the child has been abandoned or is in danger of actual or threatened mistreatment or abuse.[76] Emergency jurisdiction is designed to permit a court to enter a temporary custody order that gives the parent seeking custody time to travel to the appropriate state to seek a permanent custody award.[77]

Can a custody order be modified?

Yes. In all states, custody orders can be modified by a court in order to further the best interests of the child. Usually, the parent requesting the modification must convince a judge that a substantial change in circumstances affecting the welfare of the child has occurred since the original custody order was entered.[78]

If one parent takes a child to another state and tries to modify custody there, which state will decide the case?

Because of the subjective nature of child custody determinations under the "best interests of the child" standard, historically there has been a strong incentive for a dissatisfied parent to "seize" the child and "run" to another state after losing a custody case. It was the prevalence of such seize-and-run cases that prompted the states to pass the Uniform Child Custody Jurisdiction Act and Congress to enact the Parental Kidnapping Prevention Act.[79]

Under the PKPA, the court that issued the initial custody decree has "continuing jurisdiction" over custody matters,[80] provided that three preconditions are met by the first state: (1) it entered its initial custody order in accordance with the Parental Kidnapping Prevention Act; (2) the child or one parent continues to live in the state; and (3) the state's own law allows continuing jurisdiction.[81]

If these conditions are met, a parent living in another state who wants to modify the initial custody arrangement must file the modification petition in the first state. A modification petition filed in the second state should, at least in theory, be dismissed.[82] Indeed, the UCCJA says that dismissal is mandatory where the noncustodial parent violates an existing custody order by refusing to return the child to the custodial parent at the end of the child's period of visitation and then asks the out-of-state court to modify custody.[83]

Neither the PKPA nor the UCCJA totally precludes the second state from ever modifying the initial custody order. The PKPA permits the second state to modify the initial custody provision if (1) the second state has jurisdiction to make a child custody determination and (2) the first state no longer has jurisdiction or has declined to exercise jurisdiction.[84]

In addition, even if a child has been wrongfully removed from the first state in violation of an outstanding court order, the court in the second state may intervene if intervention is required in the interests of the child.[85] This exception is especially significant for women who have fled with their children from a violent and abusive spouse and who seek to file an out-of-state petition to modify an existing custodial arrangement.[86]

When the noncustodial parent lives in another state, what can the parent do to ensure compliance with the custody order?

A parent wishing to ensure that the parent living in another state abides by the terms of the initial custody decree should be aware of several available tools. The parent may immediately obtain a certified copy of the custody decree and promptly file it with the court clerk in the state where the other parent resides so that the order can be enforced there.[87] If it becomes necessary to file an action in the other state, the UCCJA directs the court in the second state to communicate with the court in the first state in an effort to resolve any competing jurisdictional claims.[88] In addition, if the parent with a valid custody decree is forced to travel to the second state to enforce the custody decree there or to respond to a modification petition filed by a parent who has wrongfully removed the child, he or she may seek reimbursement for the attorney's fees, travel expenses and other costs incurred in litigating custody in the second state.[89]

What other recourse does the left-behind parent have in an interstate custody dispute?

Needless to say, the remedies available under the UCCJA are useless if the left-behind parent is unable to find the abducting parent and the child. For this reason, the PKPA makes the federal Parent Locator Service available to assist local police in locating the abductor.[90] The PKPA also provides that any state that treats parental kidnapping as a felony may enlist the F.B.I.'s assistance under the federal Fugitive Felon Act in locating the abducting parent, provided he or she has left the state.[91]

Once the child has been found, there are a number of remedies available to the left-behind parent. These include filing a petition for a writ of habeas corpus, asking the court in the state to which the parent has gone to issue a contempt citation, or seeking to recover damages based on a variety of tort claims, such as false imprisonment, negligence, civil conspiracy, intentional infliction of emotional distress, or custodial interference.[92]

A civil lawsuit for custodial interference permits the left-behind parent to recover, among other things, expenses incurred in searching for the child, including legal fees, but this remedy is unavailable in some states if the kidnapping occurs before a final custody decree has been entered or if the left-behind parent has joint rather than sole custody.[93] Some states do not permit civil custodial interference lawsuits at all on the grounds that they thrust children into the midst of their parents' lawsuit and further enflame family tensions.[94]

Is it a crime for a parent to kidnap a child?

Yes. In many states, parental kidnapping—also known as interference with parental custody—is a felony. In others, it is a felony if the child is taken from the state. However, in most states, there can be no kidnapping unless there is an existing custody order that the parent has intentionally violated.

Because many parental kidnappings take place before a final custody decree is entered, a few states have extended criminal sanctions to kidnappings that occur before the final custody decree.[95] Several states also permit the court to assess expenses incurred in returning the child against any person convicted of violating the state's criminal custodial interference law.[96]

Parents remain exempt from criminal sanctions under the general federal kidnapping statute.[97] International parental kidnapping, however, has become a new federal crime, punishable by a fine and/or imprisonment for up to three years.[98]

Are there steps a custodial parent can take to ensure that a child will be returned at the end of the visitation period?

Yes. If the custodial parent has reason to fear that the noncustodial parent will not return the child to the custodial parent at the end of the visitation period, there are several options. First, the parent may ask a court to require the posting of a visitation bond to ensure that a child removed from her home state for visitation is returned.[99] If there is a fear that the noncustodial parent may take the child out of the country illegally, the custodial parent may ask the U.S. State Department to add the child's name to its passport name check system and request that no new passport or travel document be issued for the child. Alternatively, the parent may ask the judge presiding over the custody case to include in the custody order a requirement that the visiting parent deposit his or her passport with the court or custodial parent whenever he or she takes the child for visitation.[100]

Under what circumstances may a custodial parent move away from the area where the noncustodial parent lives?

If a noncustodial parent learns of an impending move, he or she may seek to enjoin the custodial parent from moving or try to get custody.[101] Indeed, some states' laws now explicitly require the custodial parent to obtain the consent of the noncustodial parent or the permission of the court before making an out-of-state move.[102]

As usual, different states handle the issue of an out-of-state move differently. At one extreme are states that have a general presumption against allowing the custodial parent to move or that place a heavy burden on the custodial parent to demonstrate that relocation is in the child's best interests. Until 1996, New York, for example, required the custodial parent to make a "compelling showing of 'exceptional circumstances' or a 'pressing concern' warranting removal of the child to a distant locale."[103] New York, which has now relaxed its standard for relocation, formerly placed a high priority on vindicating the noncustodial parent's visitation rights, often with harsh results from the custodial parent's standpoint.[104]

At the opposite end of the spectrum are those states that give priority to the child's relationship with the custodial parent and presume that a custodial parent is entitled to move with the child to another state unless the opposing parent proves, by a preponderance of the evidence, that the move would significantly harm the child or is sought for the purpose of interfering with visitation.[105] If the noncustodial parent fails to make the necessary showing of harm, the custody order will not be modified, and the move will be allowed.

In between are those states that apply a balancing test requiring the custodial parent to show a sincere, good-faith reason for the move, such as a better job, proximity to the parent's extended family members, or the need to follow a new spouse to a new location. Once the custodial parent establishes a good-faith reason for the move, the move will be allowed, and custody will not be transferred to the other parent unless the noncustodial parent can show that the proposed move would affect visitation in a way that would prove harmful to the children.[106] It is interesting to note that although custodial parents (who are usually mothers) who wish to move may be constrained by their legal obligation to make the children available for visitation by the noncustodial parent, noncustodial parents (usually fathers) are typically free to relocate without interference from the courts, since visitation is treated as a legal right rather than as a legal responsibility.[107]

Are grandparents entitled to visit their grandchildren after a divorce?

Traditionally, grandparents had no legal right to visit their grandchildren over the objections of the children's parents. More recently, the trend has been toward expanding grandparent visitation as state legislatures and courts have come to recognize and value the benefits children derive from continued contacts with their grandparents. Indeed, in some divorces, grandparents may provide a crucial element of stability for the child and courts have shown a growing willingness to protect the child's right to continuity of that important relationship.

Over forty states now permit grandparents to petition the court for visitation when the parents divorce.[108] State laws vary in their authorized scope of grandparent visitation: some states permit visitation by any grandparent, while others grant visitation rights to the parents of the noncustodial parent.

In any event, grandparental visitation must be predicated on a finding that visitation is in the child's best interests.

In determining whether grandparent visitation is in the child's best interests, courts look to a variety of factors often listed in the statutes: the nature of the relationship between the grandparent and the child (i.e., the frequency of contact, as well as love and affection); the relationship between the grandparent and the child's parent; and the preference of the child, if the child is old enough and mature enough to express an opinion.[109]

Courts may take into account any deep antagonism between a grandparent and a parent over visitation.[110] Where the animosity between the petitioning grandparent and the custodial parent is so extreme that it undermines the parent-child relationship, a judge may deny the requested visitation.[111] Similarly, if the child might come into contact with an abusive parent at the grandparent's home, the request for visitation may be turned down.[112]

May a stepparent seek custody or visitation?

Historically, stepparents had no rights to custody of a stepchild outside of marriage. Reflecting the law's bias in favor of biological parents as the child's only legally significant parents, courts traditionally have ruled that divorce or death of the biological parent severed the legal connection between the stepchild and his or her stepparent.

As the number of stepfamilies has grown, there has been a slow evolution of the law in this area. While most states still do not permit a custody award to a stepparent after divorce unless the court first finds that the child's biological parent is unfit or has abandoned the child, some judges have looked for ways to preserve and protect the continuity of the child's relationship with a stepparent who has served as a significant caregiver.[113] Where the child has lived with the stepparent for a long period of time, a few courts will award custody to the stepparent if the stepparent can show that to be in the child's best interests.[114]

It is easier for a stepparent to obtain visitation than to win custody. The stepparent need not show that the biological parent is unfit. Some states' laws expressly authorize stepparent visitation in the event of death or divorce while others have laws that permit visitation by "other interested persons" if in the child's best interests.[115] In those cases where stepparent visitation is allowed, there is typically a showing that the stepparent and child have developed a strong, loving bond that should be preserved.[116]

What recourse does a parent have if the other parent abducts the children and takes them to another country?

The first problem facing a parent whose spouse has abducted the couple's child is to find the child. The U.S. State Department, in a useful publication entitled *International Parental Child Abduction,* recommends taking several steps to search for a child who has been abducted. First, the parent left behind should file a missing person report with the local police department and request that the child's name and description be entered into the missing persons section of the National Crime Information Center computer. The local police through INTERPOL, the international criminal police organization, can request that a search for the child be conducted in the country where the child may have been taken.

Second, the parent should report the abduction to the National Center for Missing and Exploited Children at (800) 843–5678. With the permission of the searching parent, the child's photograph and description may be circulated to the media in the country where the children may have been taken. Third, the child's name should be entered in the U.S. passport name check system and the State Department should be asked to conduct a welfare and whereabouts search.[117]

Once the child has been located, a possible solution to the abduction may be provided by the Hague Convention on the Civil Aspects of International Child Abduction. The convention is in force in nearly forty countries,[118] including the United States,[119] Mexico, Canada, and most of Europe. The countries that have signed the Hague Convention have agreed that a child who is habitually a resident in one country and who is removed to or retained in another country in breach of the left-behind parent's custody rights must be promptly returned to the country of the child's habitual residence.[120] The convention does not apply if the child has been abducted to a country that has not signed the convention or if the child is sixteen or older.

The left-behind parent should immediately contact the U.S. State Department's Office of Children's Issues in the Bureau of Consular Affairs to request assistance in securing the child's return. The Office of Children's Issues serves as the United States' Central Authority under the Hague Convention and is responsible for working with the foreign Central Authority to resolve the case.

Although there need not be a custody decree to invoke the convention, the left-behind parent must be able to prove that he or she was exercising a "right of custody"[121] at the time of the abduction and that he or she had not given permission for the child to be removed or to be retained in the foreign country beyond a specified, agreed-upon time. In the absence of a formal custody order, custodial rights are determined by state law.

It is important to act quickly. Under the Convention, the foreign country may refuse to return the child if the left-behind parent has waited more than one year after the abduction to initiate a proceeding, and the child, in the interim, has become settled in his or her new environment.[122] A foreign court may also refuse to order the return of a child (1) if there is a grave risk that the child would be exposed to physical or psychological harm or otherwise placed in an intolerable situation in his or her original country; (2) if the child objects to being returned, and the child has reached an age and a degree of maturity that justifies the court taking the child's views into account; or (3) if return would violate the fundamental principles of human rights and freedoms of the country where the child is being held.[123]

If the left-behind parent files an application for the child's return with the Office of Children's Issues, the State Department will forward it to the appropriate authorities in the foreign country and will work with those authorities to try to obtain the child's return. If the abducting parent does not voluntarily agree to the child's return, the left-behind parent may need to hire a lawyer in the foreign country to petition the courts there to order the child's return under the convention. In that case, the State Department can help the left-behind parent find a lawyer and can request a status report on the case six weeks after it is filed in the foreign court.[124]

It is important to remember that a Hague Convention proceeding is not a custody case. At a hearing under the Hague Convention, the judge's job is determine only *where* the custody hearing should take place, not *who* is entitled to custody of the child.[125] The goal of the Hague Convention is the child's swift return to his or her original country where the custody dispute can then be resolved, if necessary, in the courts of that country.

If an abduction has deprived the left-behind parent of visitation rights rather than custody, signatories of the Hague Convention have pledged to find a way for visitation to take place. Parents should be aware that most foreign courts are unlikely to return the child for visitation purposes and are more likely to order that the noncustodial parent be given access to the child in the new country.[126]

Resources

Children's Rights Council
220 I Street, N.E.
Suite 230
Washington, DC 20002
(800) 787-KIDS
(202) 547-6227

National Center on Women and Family Law
799 Broadway, Suite 402
New York, NY 10003
(212) 674-8200

National Center for Missing and Exploited Children
2101 Wilson Boulevard, Suite 550
Arlington, VA 22201
(800) 843-5678
(703) 235-3900

U.S. Department of State
Bureau of Consular Affairs
Overseas Citizens Services
Office of Children's Issues
2201 C Street, N.W., Room 4800
Washington, DC 20520-4818
(202) 736-7000
(202) 647-2688, (202) 647-2835 (fax)

Notes

1. U.S. Commission on Interstate Child Support, *Supporting Our Children: A Blueprint for Reform* 5 (1992).

2. Patricia H. Shiono & Linda S. Quinn, "Epidemiology of Divorce" in *Children and Divorce* at 15, 21 (David and Lucile Packard Foundation, Center for the Future of Children 1994)(cited hereafter as *Children and Divorce*). In addition, nearly 5 million children live with a never-married parent and 4.9 million children live with a separated or widowed parent. *Id.* at 21.

3. *Id.* at 18.

4. Sanford N. Katz, "Historical Perspective and Current Trends in the Legal Process of Divorce" in *Children and Divorce, supra* note 2, at 47.

5. *Mumma v. Mumma,* 380 Pa. Super. 18, 550 A.2d 1341 (1988).

6. Linda D. Elrod, *Child Custody Practice and Procedure* § 5:01, at 2 (Clark Boardman Callaghan 1993) (cited hereafter as *Child Custody*).

7. Linda D. Elrod & Timothy B. Walker, *Family Law in the Fifty States*, 28 Fam. L.Q. 515 at 568, 586–88 (Winter 1994)(cited hereafter as *Family Law in the Fifty States*). *See, e.g.,* Cal. Fam. Code § 3080 (West Supp. 1994); Ind. Code § 31-1-11.5-21(f)(West Supp. 1994). In an interesting variation on a familiar theme, Louisiana's new joint custody law requires the court to appoint a "domiciliary parent," with whom the child primarily resides and who has the authority to make all decisions affecting the child, subject to court review at the request of the nondomiciliary parent. *See* La. Rev. Stat. Ann. § 9:335(B)(3)(West Supp. 1993).

8. *See, e.g.,* Cal. Fam. Code §§ 3081, 3082 (West Supp. 1993); Iowa Code Ann. § 598.41(2)(West Supp. 1994).

9. *See* U.S. Census Bureau, Current Population Reports, Series P-60, No. 173, *Child Support and Alimony: 1989* at 6–7 (1991); Jessica Pearson & Nancy Thoennes, *Supporting Children after Divorce: The Influence of Custody on Support Levels and Payments*, 22 Fam. L.Q. 319, 335–36 (Fall 1988); Judith S. Wallerstein & Sandra Blakeslee, *Second Chances: Men, Women and Children a Decade After Divorce* at 271 (1989).

10. *Malone v. Malone*, 842 S.W. 2d 621 (Tenn. App. 1992). *See generally Second Chances, supra* note 9, at 256–73.

11. Janet R. Johnston, "High-Conflict Divorce" in *Children and Divorce, supra* note 2, at 179; Karen Czapanskiy, "Child Support, Visitation, Shared Custody and Split Custody" 45 *Child Support Guidelines: The Next Generation*, (Margaret Campbell Haynes ed., American Bar Association Center on Children and the Law 1994); Janet R. Johnston, Marsha Kline & Jeanne M. Tschann, *Ongoing Postdivorce Conflict: Effects on Children of Joint Custody and Frequent Access*, 59 Am. J. Orthopsychiatry 576 (1989); David L. Chambers, *Rethinking the Substantive Rules for Custody Disputes in Divorce* 83 Mich. L. Rev. 477, 566–67 (1984). *See also Squires v. Squires*, 854 S.W.2d 765 (Ky. 1993)(Leibson, J. dissenting).

12. Naomi R. Cahn, *Civil Images of Battered Women: The Impact of Domestic Violence on Child Custody Decisions*, 44 Vand. L. Rev. 1041, 1064 (1991); Carol H. Lefcourt (ed.), *Women and the Law*, § 6.03[3], at 6–18 (Clark Boardman Callaghan 1993)(cited hereafter as *Women and the Law*).

13. Marianne Takas, *Improving Child Support Guidelines: Can Simple Formulas Address Complex Families?*, 26 Fam. L.Q. 171, 185 (Fall 1992)(estimating that shared custody increases childrearing costs by as much as 50 percent). This same article suggests that over time, many couples who intend to share caretaking responsibilities revert to a traditional pattern of one primary caretaker with visitation by the other parent. *Id.* at 188.

14. Mary Ann Mason, *From Father's Property to Children's Rights: The History of Child Custody in the United States* at 6 (1994).

15. *Child Custody, supra* note 6, § 1.06, at 14.

16. *See, e.g., Sukin v. Sukin*, 842 P.2d 922 (Utah App. 1992); *Marriage of Clingingsworth*, 254 Mont. 399, 838 P.2d 417 (1992).

17. Wash. Rev. Code Ann. § 26.09.187(3)(West Supp. 1994).

18. Elliot D. Samuelson, *The Divorce Law Handbook: A Comprehensive Guide to Matrimonial Practice* at 72 (1988). In recent years, some states have added statutory criteria to require judges to consider spousal abuse or domestic violence. *Child Custody, supra* note 6, at iii—iv (Supp. 1994).

19. *See, e.g., Lewis v. Lewis,* 189 W. Va. 598, 433 S.E.2d 536 (1993); *In re Marriage of Kovacs,* 121 Wash. 2d 795, 854 P.2d 629 (1993).

20. *Garska v. McCoy,* 167 W. Va. 59, 278 S.E.2d 357 (1981).

21. *Bohnsack v. Bohnsack,* 185 A.D.2d 533, 586 N.Y.S.2d 369 (3d Dep't 1992); *Egelkamp v. Egelkamp,* 362 Pa. Super. 269, 524 A.2d 501 (1987).

22. Janet M. Bowermaster, *Sympathizing with Solomon: Choosing Between Parents in a Mobile Society,* 31 J. Fam. L. 791, 849–50 (1992–93).

23. Jeff Atkinson, 1 *Modern Child Custody Practice,* § 4.12, at 240–41 (1986).

24. *See, e.g., Gulley v. Gulley,* 852 S.W.2d 874 (Mo. App. 1993); *Synakowski v. Synakowski,* 191 A.D.2d 836, 594 N.Y.S.2d 852 (3d Dep't 1993); *In re Marriage of Fennell,* 485 N.W.2d 863 (Iowa App. 1992); *Thomas v. Thomas,* 608 So. 2d 755 (Ala. Civ. App. 1992).

25. *Child Custody, supra* note 6, § 4:08, at 11. *See, e.g., In re Marriage of Kovacs,* 121 Wash. 2d 795, 854 P.2d 629 (1993).

26. *Synakowski v. Synakowski, supra* note 24; *In re Marriage of Eastlund,* 344 N.W.2d 276 (Iowa App. 1983)

27. *See Linda R. v. Richard E.,* 162 A.D.2d 48, 561 N.Y.S.2d 29 (2d Dep't 1990); *Fullmer v. Fullmer,* 761 P.2d 942 (Utah App. 1988); *Burchard v. Garay,* 42 Cal. 3d 531, 724 P.2d 486 (1986), 229 Cal. Rptr. 800. *See generally* Edward L. Raymond, Jr., "Mother's Status as 'Working Mother' as Factor in Awarding Child Custody," 62 A.L.R. 4th 259 (1988). *See also Ireland v. Smith,* 214 Mich. App. 235, 542 N.W.2d 344 (1995)(reversing trial judge's decision to award custody to father when mother placed child in day care so she could attend college).

28. Martha Albertson Fineman, *The Illusion of Equality: The Rhetoric and Reality of Divorce Reform* 181–84 (1991); *Women and the Law, supra* note 12, § 6.09, at 6–33; Chambers, *supra* note 11, 83 Mich. L. Rev. at 561–64 (recommending primary caretaker rule for children five and under); Martin Guggenheim, "The Best Interests of the Child: Much Ado About Nothing?" in *Child, Parent, & State* at 33–34 (1994).

29. Ross A. Thompson, "The Role of Fathers After Divorce" in *Children and Divorce, supra* note 2, at 217, 221; Ronald K. Henry, *"Primary Caretaker": Is It a Ruse?,* 17 Family Advocate, 1, at 53 (Summer 1994).

30. *Child Custody, supra* note 6, § 6:02, at 3–4.

31. *See* Tex. Fam. Code Ann. § 14.033 (West Supp. 1994).

32. *See, e.g.,* Ariz. Rev. Stat. Ann. § 25-332(A)(6)(West Supp. 1994); Colo. Rev. Stat. § 14-10-124(1.5)(f)(1993); Pa. Cons. Stat. Ann. tit. 23, § 5303(a)(West 1991).

33. *See, e.g. In re Marriage of Shanklin,* 484 N.W.2d 618 (Iowa App. 1992); *Catherine D. v. Dennis B.,* 220 Cal. App. 3d 922, 269 Cal. Rptr. 547 (1st Dist. 1990). *But see Hakas v. Bergenthal,* 843 P.2d 642 (Alaska 1992)(custody cannot be taken away from mother solely as sanction for noncooperation without considering child's best interests).

34. *See* Joan Zorza, *"Friendly Parent" Provisions in Custody Determinations,* 26 Clearinghouse Rev. 921 (Dec. 1992); Naomi Cahn, *Civil Images of Battered Women: The Impact of Domestic Violence on Child Custody Determinations,* 44 Vand. L. Rev. 1041, 1065 & n.130, 1068 and 1091 (1991).

35. Ky. Rev. Stat. § 403.340(3)(c)(Michie Supp. 1992). *See Squires v. Squires, supra* note 11.

36. Jessica Pearson & Jean Anhalt, *Examining the Connection Between Child Access and Child Support,* 32 Fam. & Conciliation Cts. Rev. 93, 96 (Jan. 1994).

37. *Id. See generally*, Robert B. Strauss, *Supervised Visitation and Family Violence*, 29 Fam. L.Q. 229 (1995).

38. *Child Custody, supra* note 6, § 16.05, at 9. *See, e.g.*, Alaska Stat. § 25.24.060 (Michie 1991); Colo. Rev. Stat. § 13-22-305 (Supp. 1993); Minn. Stat. § 518.619 (West 1994).

39. *See, e.g.*, Alaska Stat. § 25.20.80 (Michie 1991); Cal. Fam. Code § 3170 (West Supp. 1993); Conn. Gen. Stat. § 46b-53a (West Supp. 1994); Colo. Rev. Stat. § 13-22-311 (1993); Iowa Code § 598.41(2)(West Supp. 1994); Me. Rev. Stat. Ann. tit. 19, § 752(4) (West Supp. 1993); Wis. Stat. § 767.11(5)(West 1993).

40. *Women and the Law, supra* note 12, § 7A.08[4], at 7A-19 & n. 68.

41. *Child Custody, supra* note 6, § 16.05, at 10.

42. Linda Silberman & Andrew Schepard, *Court-Ordered Mediation in Family Disputes: The New York Proposal*, 14 N.Y.U. Rev. L. Soc. Change 741 (1986).

43. Harriet N. Cohen, "Mediation in Divorce: Boon or Bane?" in 5 *The Women's Advocate* (Mar. 1984).

44. *See, e.g.*, Colo. Rev. Stat. § 13-22-311(1)(1993); Fla. Stat. ch. 44.102(2)(b)(West Supp. 1994); La. Rev. Stat. Ann. § 9:363 (West Supp. 1994); Minn. Stat. Ann. § 518.619, subd. 2 (West Supp. 1994).

45. *See, e.g., Hadick v. Hadick*, 90 Md. App. 740, 603 A.2d 915 (1992); *but see Daigle v. Daigle*, 609 A.2d 1153 (Me. 1992).

46. *See, e.g.*, N. H. Rev. Stat. Ann. § 458:17-a (Supp. 1993); N.J. Stat. Ann. section 9:2–4(a)(West 1993).

47. *Leary v. Leary*, 97 Md. App. 26, 627 A.2d 30 (1993); *Weiderholt v. Fischer*, 169 Wis. 2d 524, 485 N.W.2d 442 (Wis. App. 1992). For a fuller discussion, *see* Linda Elrod, *Counsel for the Child in Custody Disputes: The Time is Now*, 26 Fam. L.Q. 53 (Spring 1992).

48. *Child Custody, supra* note 6, §§ 12:08–12:09, at 14–18.

49. *Id.* § 12:13, at 22.

50. *See Family Law in the Fifty States, supra* note 7, at 568 (Winter 1994).

51. *See, e.g., Treutle v. Treutle*, 197 Mich. App. 690, 495 N.W.2d 836 (1992)(wishes of six-year-old not considered); *In re Marriage of Andersen*, 236 Ill. App. 3d 679, 603 N.E.2d 70, 177 Ill. Dec. 289 (2d Dist. 1992) (great weight given to fourteen-year-old's preference).

52. *In re Marriage of Ulland*, 251 Mont. 160, 823 P.2d 864 (1991); *Sellers v. Sellers*, 555 So. 2d 1117 (Ala. Civ. App. 1989). *See generally Child Custody, supra* note 6, § 4:11, at 15.

53. *In re Marriage of Plummer*, 709 P.2d 1388 (Colo. App. 1985); *Comm. ex rel. Stoyko v. Stoyko*, 267 Pa. Super. 24, 405 A.2d 1284 (1979).

54. *Family Law in the Fifty States, supra* note 7, at 502, 582–83 (Winter 1994). *See, e.g., In re Nolte* 241 Ill. App. 3d 320, 609 N.E.2d 381, 182 Ill. Dec. 78 (3d Dist. 1993).

55. *Morrow v. Morrow*, 591 So. 2d 829 (Miss. 1991); *cf. Carrico v. Blevins* 12 Va. App. 47, 402 S.E.2d 235 (1991)

56. *Child Custody, supra* note 6, § 4:25 at 38. *See, e.g., Van Hoesen v. Van Hoesen*, 186 A.D.2d 903, 590 N.Y.S.2d 139 (3d Dep't 1992).

57. *Child Custody, supra* note 6, § 4:26, at 40. *See generally* Robert A. Beargie, *Custody Determinations Involving the Homosexual Parent*, 22 Fam. L.Q. 71, 74–78 (Spring 1988).

58. *M.A.B. v. R.B.*, 134 Misc. 2d 317, 510 N.Y.S.2d 960 (Sup. 1986); *S.N.E. v. R.L.B.*, 699 P.2d 875 (Alaska 1985); *Doe v. Doe*, 16 Mass. App. Ct. 499, 452 N.E.2d 293 (1983).

59. *S.E.G. v. R.A.G.*, 735 S.W.2d 164 (Mo. App. 1987).

60. *See, e.g., Pennington v. Pennington,* 596 N.E.2d 305 (Ind. App. 1992); *Chicoine v. Chicoine,* 479 N.W. 2d 891 (S.D. 1992). *But see Blew v. Verta,* 420 Pa. Super. 528, 617 A.2d 31 (1992); *In re Marriage of Walsh,* 451 N.W.2d 492 (Iowa 1990).

61. La. Rev. Stat. Ann. § 9:361 (West Supp. 1994). For a full discussion of this issue, *see* The Family Violence Project of the National Council of Juvenile and Family Court Judges, *Family Violence in Child Custody Statutes: An Analysis of State Codes and Legal Practice,* 29 Fam. L.Q. 197 (1995).

62. La. Rev. Stat. Ann. § 9:364(A).

63. *Family Violence in Child Custordy Statutes, supra* note 61, 29 Fam. L.Q. 197, 199, 225–27. *See also* Joan Zorza, *Guide to Interstate Custody: A Manual for Domestic Violence Advocates,* National Center for Women and Family Law, app. F (1992).

64. Naomi R. Cahn, *Civil Images of Battered Women: The Impact of Domestic Violence on Child Custody Decisions,* 44 Vand. L. Rev. 1041, 1064–68 (1991). *See also Family Violence in Child Custody Statutes, supra* note 61.

65. Minn. Stat. Ann. § 518.17, subd. 1(12)(West Supp. 1994). *See also Knock v. Knock,* 224 Conn. 776, 621 A.2d 267 (1993). *But see In re Lutgen,* 177 Ill. App. 3d 954, 532 N.E.2d 976, 127 Ill. Dec. 147 (2d Dist. 1988), *appeal denied,* 125 Ill. 2d 565, 537 N.E.2d 811, 130 Ill. Dec. 482 (1989)(upholding child custody award to man who had choked his wife to death in front of their children, court ruled that domestic violence factor was only one of many factors to be considered in determining the children's best interests).

66. Colo. Rev. Stat. § 14-10-124(4)(1987); Ky. Rev. Stat. Ann. § 403.270(3)(Michie 1992).

67. *See e.g.,* Minn. Stat. Ann. § 518.619 subd. 2 (West Supp. 1994).

68. Joan Zorza, *Using the Law to Protect Battered Women and Their Children,* 27 Clearinghouse Rev. 1437, 1440 (April 1994). *See also Supervised Visitation and Family Violence, supra* note 37, 29 Fam. L.Q. 229.

69. 28 U.S.C. § 1738A (West 1994). Notwithstanding the reference to parental kidnapping in the law's name, the Parental Kidnapping Prevention Act applies to all interstate custody and visitation disputes arising from a divorce, not just kidnapping cases. It does *not* apply to child support proceedings.

70. 9 Uniform Laws Ann. (U.L.A), pt. 1, at 115 *et seq.* (West 1988).

71. 28 U.S.C. § 1738A(b)(4) & (c)(2)(A),(B)(West 1994).

72. For a clear and full description of this notoriously complex aspect of child custody law, *see* Jeff Atkinson, 1 *Modern Child Custody Practice,* ch. 3 (Kluwer 1986)(cited hereafter as *Modern Child Custody Practice*).

73. *Id.* § 3.12, at 129–30.

74. 28 U.S.C. § 1738A(c)(2)(B)(West 1994); UCCJA § 3(a)(2).

75. *Modern Child Custody Practice, supra* note 72, § 3.15, at 141.

76. 28 U.S.C. § 1738A(c)(2)(C); UCCJA § 3(a)(3).

77. *Guide to Interstate Custody, supra* note 63, at 36–37.

78. *See, e.g., Ward v. Ward,* 611 N.E.2d 167 (Ind. App. 1993); *Blotske v. Leidholm,* 487 N.W.2d 607 (N. D. 1992). *But see McMillen v. McMillen,* 529 Pa. 198, 602 A.2d 845 (Pa. 1992).

79. The UCCJA was written in the 1960s to protect children from child snatching, principally by their fathers. It was not foreseen that the UCCJA might become, as some battered women's advocates have argued, a weapon to be used against women fleeing domestic violence and child abuse. For a detailed account of the impact of the UCCJA on cases involving battered women, *see Guide to Interstate Custody, supra* note 63. *See also Women and the Law, supra* note 12, § 6A.01[3][a][iii].

80. 28 U.S.C. § 1738A(d)(West 1994). *See, e.g., Michalik v. Michalik*, 164 Wis. 2d 544, 476 N.W.2d 586 (Wis. App. 1991), *aff'd* 172 Wis. 2d 640, 494 N.W.2d 391 (1993).

81. *Modern Child Custody Practice, supra* note 72, § 3.21, at 155.

82. *Kumar v. Superior Court*, 32 Cal. 3d 689, 652 P.2d 1003, 186 Cal. Rptr. 772 (1982); *Curtis v. Curtis*, 574 So. 2d 24 (Miss. 1990).

83. UCCJA § 8(b).

84. *Modern Child Custody Practice, supra* note 72, § 3.22, at 158.

85. UCCJA § 8(b).

86. *See, e.g., In re Custody of Thorenson*, 46 Wash. App. 493, 730 P.2d 1380 (1987)(refusing to enforce Florida modifications after custodial mother left Florida to protect herself and her children from father's abuse). For a detailed discussion of the difficulties of predicting how any individual interstate case will be decided, *see* Anne B. Goldstein, *The Tragedy of the Interstate Child: A Critical Re-examination of the Uniform Child Custody Jurisdiction Act and the Parental Kidnapping Prevention Act*, 25 U.C. Davis L. Rev. 845, 923 (1992).

87. UCCJA § 16.

88. UCCJA §§ 6(b) & (c), 7(d).

89. UCCJA §§ 8(c) & 15(b).

90. 42 U.S.C. § 663 (West 1991). The federal Parent Locator Service is discussed in detail in chapter 2.

91. 18 U.S.C. § 1073, *Historical and Statutory Notes* (West Supp. 1994).

92. Joseph R. Hillebrand, *Parental Kidnapping and the Tort of Custodial Interference: Not in a Child's Best Interests*, 25 Ind. L. Rev. 893, at 902–6 (1992).

93. *Id.* at 907–8 & n. 115. *See, e.g., D & D Fuller CATV Construction, Inc. v. Pace*, 780 P.2d 520 (Colo. 1989); *Wood v. Wood*, 338 N.W.2d 123 (Iowa 1983).

94. *Larson v. Dunn*, 460 N.W.2d 39 (Minn. 1990).

95. *See, e.g.*, Tex. Penal Code Ann. § 25.03(a)(2)(West 1994).

96. Minn. Stat. Ann. § 609.26, subd. 4 (West 1994); Ind. Code § 35-42-3-4(e)(West Supp. 1994). *See Vanness v. State*, 605 N.E.2d 777 (Ind. App. 1992).

97. 18 U.S.C. § 1201(a)((West Supp. 1994).

98. 18 U.S.C. § 1204 (West Supp. 1994).

99. *Hamlin v. Hamlin*, 302 N.C. 478, 276 S.E.2d 381 (1981). *Cf. Roberts v. Fuhr*, 523 So. 2d 20 (Miss. 1987).

100. *See, e.g., Soltanieh v. King*, 826 P.2d 1076 (Utah App. 1992). *See also* Ind. Code §§ 31-1-11.5-20(d) & 31-6-6.1-11(j)(West Supp. 1994)(notice of passport application must be given to court issuing custody order).

101. *Modern Child Custody Practice, supra* note 72, § 7:01, at 390. A surprising number of these efforts meet with success. One study found that 37 percent of the noncustodial parents who sought to gain custody as a result of the planned move were successful. Thirty-

nine percent of noncustodial parents who sought to enjoin the move succeeded in imposing restrictions on the move. *Id.*

102. *See, e.g.,* Ill. Ann. Stat. ch. 40, § 609 (West Supp. 1992); Mass. Gen. Laws Ann. ch. 208, § 30 (West 1987); Minn. Stat. Ann. § 518.175(3)(West 1990); N.J. Stat. Ann. § 9:2–2 (West 1993); N.D. Cent. Code § 14–09–07 (1991).

103. *Bryan v. Bryan,* 99 A.D.2d 743, 471 N.Y.S.2d 650, 651 (2d Dep't 1984). *But see Tropea v. Tropea,* 1996 N.Y. LEXIS 300 (N.Y. March 26, 1996)(Court lists five factors to be considered in a relocation decision and notes that predominant emphasis is to be placed on what outcome is most likely to serve the best interests of the child).

104. Bowermaster, *supra* note 22, at 804–10. *See, e.g., Leslie v. Leslie,* 180 A.D.2d 620, 579 N.Y.S. 2d 164 (2d Dep't 1992)(ordering mother to return to live within 50 miles of the child's father or lose custody and dismissing her desire to pursue a doctoral degree at the University of Virginia as insufficient to deprive father of regular access to his son); *Elkus v. Elkus,* 182 A.2d 45, 588 N.Y.S.2d 138 (1st Dep't 1992). *But see Tropea v. Tropea, supra* note 103 and *Browner v. Kenward,* 1996 N.Y. LEXIS 300 (N.Y. March 26, 1996).

105. Bowermaster, *supra* note 22, at 829. *See, e.g., Ballard v. Wold,* 486 N.W.2d 161 (Minn. App. 1992); *In re Marriage of Smith,* 491 N.W.2d 538 (Iowa App. 1992).

106. *See, e.g., In re Marriage of Murphy,* 834 P.2d 1287 (Colo. App. 1992); *In re Marriage of Pfeiffer,* 237 Ill. App. 3d 510, 604 N.E.2d 1069, 178 Ill. Dec. 546 (Ill. App. 1992); *Gruber v. Gruber,* 400 Pa. Super. 174, 583 A.2d 434 (1990)

107. *See* Bowermaster, *supra* note 22, at 796. It has been suggested that draconian limits on the custodial parent's right to relocate have an especially adverse impact on women. Women constitute the majority of custodial parents, and in states that place a high priority on the visitation rights of noncustodial parents "mothers as caretakers are often expected to sacrifice their own interests [in career advancement, in better paying jobs, in proximity to their extended families] and limit their freedom to relocate in order to keep their children close to their noncustodial fathers. . . . Noncustodial fathers, on the other hand, are not asked to make sacrifices to be near their children." *Id.* at 848–49.

108. *Child Custody, supra* note 6, § 7:07 and app. 7A. *See, e.g.,* Cal. Fam. Code § 3101 (West Supp. 1993); Fla. Stat. Ann. §§ 61.13(2)(b)(2)(c)(Westlaw 1995); Md. Fam. Code section 9–102 (Michie 1993); N.Y. Dom. Rel. L. § 72 (West Supp. 1994). *But see Brooks v. Parkerson,* 454 S.E.2d 769, 265 Ga. 189(1995) (Georgia's grandparent visitation statute violated parents' constitutionally protected right to raise their children without undue state interference).

109. *Fairbanks v. McCarter,* 330 Md. 39, 622 A.2d 121 (1993).

110. *In re Marriage of Lindsey,* 158 Ill. App. 3d 769, 511 N.E.2d 198, 110 Ill. Dec. 363 (4th Dist. 1987). *See generally,* Annotation, "Grandparents' Visitation Rights" 90 A.L.R. 3d 222 (Supp. 1994).

111. *Strouse v. Olson,* 397 N.W.2d 651 (S.D. 1986).

112. *Drennen v. Drennen,* 52 Ohio App. 3d 121, 557 N.E.2d 149 (1988)(visitation denied to paternal grandmother whose son had raped mother in front of three-year-old child).

113. *See generally* David L. Chambers, "Stepparents, Biologic Parents and the Law's Perception of 'Family' After Divorce" in Stephen D. Sugarman & Herma Hill Kay, *Divorce Reform at the Crossroads* 103, 108 (1990). *See e.g., In re Marriage of Allen,* 28 Wash. App. 637,

626 P.2d 16 (1981)(using test more stringent than "best interests" but less stringent than "unfitness").

114. *See, e.g., Stockwell v. Stockwell,* 116 Idaho 297, 775 P.2d 611 (1989). *Cf. In re Dunn,* 79 Ohio App. 3d 268, 607 N.E.2d 8 (1992)(awarding custody to stepmother rather than to biological mother after biological father's death).

115. *Child Custody, supra* note 6, § 7:14, at 29.

116. *Id. See, e.g., Atkinson v. Atkinson,* 160 Mich. App. 601, 408 N.W.2d 516 (1987); *Bryan v. Bryan,* 132 Ariz. 353, 645 P.2d 1267 (Ariz. App. 1982); *Spells v. Spells,* 250 Pa. Super. 168, 378 A.2d 879 (1977).

117. The office to contact for the passport name check is the Bureau of Consular Affairs, Division of Passport Services, Office of Passport Policy and Advisory Services, U.S. Department of State, 1111 19th St., N.W., Washington, DC 20522-1705; telephone (202) 955-0377; fax (202) 955-0230. To request a welfare and whereabouts search, contact the State Department's Office of Children's Issues, Overseas Citizens Services, Bureau of Consular Affairs, 2201 C Street, N.W., Room 4800, Washington, DC 20520-4818; telephone (202) 736-7000 or (202) 647-2688; fax (202) 647-2835.

118. As of May 1995, the convention was in effect between the United States and Argentina, Australia, Austria, Bahamas, Belize, Bosnia-Herzegovina, Burkina Faso, Canada, Chile, Croatia, Cyprus, Denmark, Ecuador, Finland, France, Germany, Greece, Honduras, Hungary, Ireland, Israel, Italy, Luxembourg, Macedonia, Mauritius, Mexico, Monaco, Netherlands, New Zealand, Norway, Panama, Poland, Portugal, Romania, Slovenia, Spain, Sweden, Switzerland, and the United Kingdom. *See* Linda Silberman, *Hague International Child Abduction Convention: A Progress Report,* 57 Law and Contemp. Probs. (Summer 1994) and News Notes, *Child Abduction,* 21 Fam. L. Rep. (BNA)1268 (1995).

119. Congress passed the International Child Abduction Remedies Act in 1988 to implement the convention. *See* 42 U.S.C. 11601 et seq. (West 1994).

120. The term *habitual residence* is left undefined by the Hague Convention. Courts have struggled to define it. *See Friedrich v. Friedrich,* 983 F.2d 1396 (6th Cir. 1993); *Levesque v. Levesque,* 816 F. Supp. 662 (D. Kan. 1993).

121. The convention defines *right of custody* as including "rights relating to the care of the person of the child and, in particular, the right to determine the child's place of residence." *See* Hague Convention, art. 5(a), 19 I.L.M. 1501 (1980). A left-behind parent who does not have physical custody of the child may nonetheless have a custody right if there is an outstanding custody order requiring that parent to consent to a relocation of the child. *But see Viragh v. Foldes,* 415 Mass. 96, 612 N.E.2d 241 (1993)(visitation is not a right of custody).

122. Hague Convention, art. 12.

123. Hague Convention art. 13(b) & art. 20.

124. *See generally,* U.S. Department of State, Bureau of Consular Affairs, *International Parental Child Abduction* at 9 (1993).

125. *Tahan v. Duquette,* 259 N.J. Super. 328, 613 A.2d 486 (1992).

126. Linda Silberman, *Hague Convention on International Child Abduction: A Brief Overview and Case Law Analysis,* 28 Fam. L.Q. 31 (Spring 1994).

11

Child Support

Since the 1970s, the national debate over unpaid child support has grown as bitter as any divorce. Spurred by the escalating cost of federal welfare payments for children whose fathers were seen as shirking their support obligations, Congress stepped in to "federalize" an aspect of family law that up until twenty years ago had been the exclusive province of the states.

In quick succession, Congress passed the Social Services Amendments of 1974,[1] the Child Support Enforcement Amendments of 1984,[2] the Family Support Act of 1988,[3] and the Child Support Recovery Act of 1992.[4] Taking aim at child support awards that were too low and too unpredictable, federal law gave the states until October 1, 1989 to put in place mandatory numerical child support guidelines applicable to all child support cases.

Under federal law, child support guidelines are required to be uniform throughout each state, to take into account all of an absent parent's income and to provide, among other things, for the child's healthcare needs.[5] The mandatory guidelines are backed by federal laws requiring automatic withholding of support from parents' wages, authorizing the interception of income tax returns to collect overdue support, and mandating a host of other measures designed to make it easier to locate absent parents, establish paternity for nonmarital children, and obtain and enforce support orders.

In spite of this flurry of legislative activity, unpaid child support remains an urgent national problem.[6] Study after study has documented dramatic increases in child poverty and dramatic declines in children's standards of living after their parents separate.[7] Census data reveal that only half of the mothers who have child support orders actually collect the full amount they are owed. Twenty-five percent receive partial payments and another quarter receive no payments, at all.[8]

Many mothers do not even have child support orders in the first place. According to census data, only 72 percent of divorced mothers have support orders. Among never married mothers, the figure is far lower—only 24 percent have an award of support for their children.[9]

Custodial fathers, though far fewer in number, face similar child support collection problems. A Wisconsin study found that only 30 percent of custodial fathers had a child support award, and of those who did, 40 percent received no payment from the noncustodial mother.[10]

Fierce disagreement prevails as to why children do not receive the full support they deserve and what to do about it. Fathers' advocates have questioned the wisdom of child support collection efforts that focus predominantly on coercion of the absent parent. Citing studies that suggest that noncustodial parents who remain actively involved with their children are more likely to meet their support obligations,[11] they have sought ways to enlist both parents in their children's postdivorce lives.

Others argue forcefully that many of the states' child support guidelines are at fault. Pointing to research that has found that when parents live apart, the children's standard of living falls by an average of 26 percent while that of the noncustodial parent rises by 34 percent, advocates for custodial mothers and their children suggest that the guidelines need to be revised to achieve greater parity between the children's standard of living and that of the noncustodial parent.[12]

Still others doubt the viabiity of a state-based system for ordering and collecting child support and have urged the United States to adopt a national child support guideline and to follow the lead of other industrialized countries by implementing a national system of publicly funded child support benefits. Like the social security system, an assured child support benefit system would use the Internal Revenue Service to collect support payments from obligated parents and would guarantee a minimum amount of child support to those legally entitled to receive private support.[13]

The debate over these issues is expected to rage into the twenty-first century. In the meantime, this section offers an overview of where the law on child support stands today.

Who is entitled to receive child support?

When once-married or never-married parents no longer live together (whether or not they are formally separated or divorced), the parent who has custody of the children is generally entitled to child support from the non-custodial parent. This is true even if the custodial parent and child are receiving public assistance or if the custodial parent is working.

Who is obliged to pay child support?

Parents are obliged to pay child support whether or not they were ever married. Parents also have an obligation to support all of their children, not just the children they live with. Thus, even if the noncustodial parent is married to someone else or supporting other children, he or she has a continuing obligation to support the children of a previous marriage or relationship. The noncustodial parent who has the legal obligation to pay child support is known as the *obligor*.

Does divorce end the obligation of the noncustodial parent to pay child support?

No. All parents have a legal obligation to support their children after divorce, regardless of whether or not they have custody of the children.

Are mothers as well as fathers required to pay child support?

Yes. Child support statutes are gender-neutral and require the noncustodial parent to pay child support to the custodial parent. When the mother is the noncustodial parent, she is required to pay child support in the same manner as a father with the same income.

If the custodial parent's income is higher than that of the noncustodial parent, must the noncustodial parent still pay child support?

Yes. Children are entitled to support from *both* parents. The noncustodial parent must pay support even if the parent with whom the child resides has a higher income or more property.

Do child support laws apply to children born out of wedlock?

Yes. The Supreme Court of the United States has ruled that it is unconstitutional to discriminate against children because they were born out-of-wedlock.[14] Federal child support laws require states to apply their child support guidelines to the children of divorced, separated, and never-married parents.

Moreover, federal law requires states to have an effective and accessible mechanism to establish paternity for nonmarital children. States must permit paternity claims to be brought any time until the child's eighteenth birthday;[15] state law must require all parties to a contested paternity proceeding to submit to genetic testing;[16] and states must offer simplified procedures for men to acknowledge paternity in the hospital immediately before or after the child's birth.[17]

How is the amount of child support actually computed?

In simple terms, child support guidelines establish a mathematical relationship between a parent's income and the amount of child support. Although the precise formulas differ from state to state, there are two basic types of guidelines: those that set the support at a specific portion of the noncustodial parent's income and those that establish the total support necessary and prorate that amount according to the income of each parent.[18]

The *percentage-of-income formula*, which has been adopted by thirteen states, is the simplest.[19] It sets child support as a percentage of the noncustodial parent's income, with the percentage growing larger as the number of children to be supported increases. Wisconsin's percentage of income formula, for instance, sets child support at 17 percent of gross income for one child, 25 percent of gross income for two, 29 percent for three, 31 percent for four, and 34 percent for five or more children.[20]

Some states base their percentage-of-income formula on net income instead of gross income. Some use constant percentages, regardless of the parent's income, while others use different sets of percentages depending on the parent's income level. Minnesota, for example, requires a noncustodial parent with a net income of $600 a month to pay 19 percent of his or her net income for the support of two children, while a noncustodial parent with a monthly income over $1,000 would pay 30 percent of his or her net income to support the same number of children.[21]

An important theoretical advantage of the percentage-of-income formula is that it permits the automatic updating of support awards.[22] Otherwise, there is a tendency in many instances for the value of support orders to erode over time, as inflation eats into the support award. Most courts in percentage-of-income states, however, express support awards in fixed dollar terms instead of as a percentage of income and so do not take advantage of the model's built-in flexibility.[23]

The most widely used child support formula is the *income shares* model, which takes into account the combined incomes of both parents in establishing the presumptive child support amount.[24] The calculation of child support under this formula, some version of which has been adopted in thirty-two states,[25] involves several basic steps.

First, the income of the two parents is added together. Then a basic child support obligation is computed based on the parents' combined income. This amount is derived from economic data on the cost of raising children in an intact, two-parent household,[26] minus average amounts for health insurance, childcare, and extraordinary medical expenses. In states that use the income shares method, the basic child support obligation varies from 18 to 24 percent of the two parents' income for one child, 28 to 37 percent for two children, 35 to 46 percent for three children and up to 46 or 61 percent for six children.[27] Percentages decline as family income increases.

Next, a total child support obligation is computed by adding in actual expenditures for work-related childcare and for extraordinary medical care. Finally, the total support obligation is prorated in proportion to each parent's income. The custodial parent keeps her or his share to spend directly on the child. The noncustodial parent's share is payable as child support.[28]

A third model used for calculating child support is the *Melson formula*, named for Judge Elwood F. Melson of Delaware Family Court. The Melson formula has been adopted by Delaware, Hawaii, Montana, and West Virginia. For poorer parents, it seeks to ensure that neither parent falls below the poverty level in order to meet child support obligations. At the same time, it allows the children of a wealthy noncustodial parent to share in that parent's higher standard of living.

The Melson formula first subtracts from each parent's net income a self-support reserve, now $620 a month in Delaware. The *self-support reserve* is set at subsistence level and is designed, in theory, to ensure that each parent keeps enough income for his or her basic needs. The next step is to award to each child a *primary support amount* which, like the self-support reserve, is calculated at subsistence level: $275 per month for one child, $485 for two children, $660 for three children, and $132 for each additional child. This amount, plus actual work-related childcare expenses and extraordinary medical expenses, is then allocated between the two parents in proportion to their income.[29]

After deducting the self-support reserve and the pro rata share of the children's primary support needs, a percentage of the noncustodial parent's remaining income is allocated to additional child support as a standard of living adjustment: 17 percent for the first child, 26 percent for two children, 33 percent for three children, and 4 percent for each additional child. Total child support is determined by adding together the noncustodial parent's share of primary support and the standard of living allowance.[30]

In addition to the basic formulas, there are many other features of the child support guidelines that vary from state to state. Some states require payment for expenses such as medical care, childcare, and education in addition to the basic child support amount. Other states include some or all of those kinds of expenses in the basic support amount.[31] A small number of states also make adjustments for visitation-related transportation expenses.

May courts deviate from the mandatory guidelines?

Yes. To deviate from the child support award required by the formula set forth in each state's guidelines, the court must use criteria established by the state and make detailed findings in writing or on the record as to why the guideline amount would be unjust or inappropriate in a given case, taking into account the best interests of the child.[32]

Some states' guidelines provide that where parental income exceeds a certain figure, the courts have discretion in setting child support. In New York, for instance, if the parents' combined income exceeds $80,000, the court has broad discretion in awarding child support based on income above that figure, and may choose either to follow the guidelines' formula or to deviate from them.[33]

At the lowest end of the income scale, many states have created a self-support reserve designed to shelter a minimum, poverty level amount of income so that the obligor can cover his or her own subsistence needs and minimal work expenses. For these parents, most states have established a minimum support order, typically $50 per month.[34]

What counts as income for purposes of computing child support?

Federal regulations implementing the federal child support laws require state guidelines to take into consideration "all earnings and income of the absent parent."[35] Some states have very specific lists of items that count as income. Other state guidelines are more general and require the court to consider "all income."

Ordinarily, income includes such items as salary, overtime pay, commissions, bonuses, interest, dividends, rents, royalties, income derived from assets, a trust or an inheritance, income derived from a business or self-employment, retirement benefits and pensions, Social Security benefits, disability benefits, worker's compensation, and unemployment compensation.[36]

Some states will impute income if a parent has voluntarily reduced his or her income by quitting a job or deferring salary.[37] In those situations, the court may order child support based on the parent's "unexercised ability to earn"[38] even if the parent wants to go back to school[39] (which could lead to higher earnings) or stay home with small children from a second marriage.[40]

A majority of states base their child support computations on gross income. Others use adjusted gross income, with deductions permitted for prior support orders and some very limited expenses.[41] A significant minority of states base child support awards on net income, which is typically defined as gross income minus taxes and deductions that are mandated by the employer as a condition of employment.[42] Thus, deductions for a mandatory retirement plan are usually allowed but not voluntary retirement contributions.

Some states permit health insurance premiums for the benefit of the noncustodial parent's children or spouse to be subtracted from gross income.[43] In some states, alimony paid to one or more former spouses may be deducted from gross income before a child support award is computed.[44]

Can divorcing parents agree on the amount of child support to be paid?

Yes, but courts will review the agreement and are not required to approve it. Parents can agree on an appropriate child support arrangement, including allocation of basic support, payment for the costs of health insurance and medical expenses, educational expenses and childcare costs. However, such agreements must be reviewed by the court and will be approved only if the court finds that (1) the support agreement is consistent with the state's child support guidelines or (2) the support agreement deviates from the state's guidelines for valid reasons. In that case, the court must set forth in writing the reasons for approving a deviation from the guideline amounts.

Courts will almost never approve an agreement in which the custodial parent agrees to waive child support in exchange for the noncustodial parent's promise not to insist on visitation. Barring unusual circumstances, parents cannot contract away their children's rights to support.[45]

Is child support taxable income?

No. Unlike alimony or spousal support, child support is neither taxable income to the recipient parent nor deductible by the payor parent.

Who is entitled to claim the child's dependency exemption on income tax forms?

In 1984, Congress passed legislation that grants the exemption for a child to the custodial parent, unless the custodial parent signs a waiver form allowing the noncustodial parent to take the exemption.[46] The majority of state courts have since held that they are empowered to allocate the dependency exemption to the noncustodial parent by ordering the custodial parent to sign the waiver.[47]

The waiver (IRS Form 8332 or its equivalent) may be for the current tax year, for several specified years (i.e., alternate years), or for all future years. The noncustodial parent must attach the release form to the return for which the exemption is being claimed.[48]

How is a child covered for health insurance after divorce?

Health insurance coverage for the children of divorce is a pressing problem of national dimensions. A Census Bureau study found that healthcare benefits were included in only 40 percent of child support awards and that only two-thirds of the absent fathers ordered to provide healthcare benefits for their children actually did so.[49]

According to the federal regulations developed to implement the 1988 Family Support Act, states' child support guidelines must "provide for the child(ren)'s health care needs, through health insurance coverage or other means."[50] Judges who fail to provide for the child's medical support must explain why health insurance coverage is not in the child's best interests.[51]

Unfortunately, even when the child support order contains a requirement that the noncustodial parent obtain insurance coverage for the children, enforcement of that order is often very difficult. The U.S. Commission on Interstate Child Support, created by the 1988 Family Support Act, heard testimony from custodial parents who described obligors who failed to enroll their children as ordered or who, if they enrolled them, proceeded to pocket the insurance reimbursements instead of forwarding the money to the custodial parent who had incurred the out-of-pocket medical expenses. Witnesses also described insurance carriers who refused to provide coverage unless the child lives with the enrolled employee and who refused to accept claims filed by the custodial parent on behalf of the enrolled parent's children.[52]

Several states have sought to redress these inequities. Connecticut, for instance, passed a law prohibiting the obligor from interfering with the timely processing of claims and requiring the obligor to turn benefits over to the custodial parent promptly.[53]

A major obstacle to state efforts to enforce broad medical coverage for children in single-parent households has been the Employee Retirement Income Security Act of 1974 (ERISA). Although ERISA deals primarily with pension plans, it preempts state regulation of health insurance plans offered by employers who self-insure. The U.S. General Accounting Office has estimated that as of 1990, 56 percent of the country's workers were covered by self-insured ERISA plans and were thus exempt from state laws that seek to protect the healthcare coverage of children.[54]

To fill the regulatory void that ERISA created and to alleviate some of the problems detailed by the U.S. Commission on Interstate Child Support, Congress included in the 1993 Omnibus Budget Reconciliation Act a number of provisions dealing with medical care coverage for children.[55] The Act directs all states to pass laws requiring insurance companies and employers to assist in the enforcement of medical support orders.[56] An employer, even a self-insured employer covered by ERISA, must comply with the terms of the new state laws provided it has been served with a "qualified medical child support order" issued by a state court.[57]

Under the required state laws, insurers are prohibited from denying coverage to children whose parents are not married or to children who do not live in the enrolled parent's home or in the insurer's service area.[58] Employers served with a qualified medical child support order must allow the child to be enrolled on the parent's policy at any time, not just during periods of open enrollment, and must deduct the employee/noncustodial parent's share (if any) of health insurance premiums from the employee's salary.[59] Insurers and self-insured employers must provide the custodial parent with information about enrollment, process claims submitted by the custodial parent, and make payments to the custodial parent.[60]

For how long must a parent pay child support?

Parents must support their children until they reach the age of majority (which is now eighteen in all but a handful of states) unless the child is "emancipated" before then. A child may become emancipated by marriage, by becoming self-supporting, or by not residing with either parent. In states where the age of majority is still twenty-one, attending college is usually not considered an emancipating event.

Some states that set majority at eighteen have enacted special laws designed to help children finish high school or college by authorizing judges to continue to order child support up to age nineteen or higher if the child is enrolled in high school or other educational program.[61]

Many, but not all states, require parents to support disabled adult children beyond the age of majority if the disability occurred before the child reached majority.

Can a noncustodial parent be ordered to pay for college?

Yes. The child support statutes in some states expressly permit courts to order a noncustodial parent to pay for college costs or other educational expenses.[62] Even in states without express statutory authority, courts have exercised their discretion to order the payment of college expenses.

In considering this issue, courts take into account a number of factors, such as the cost of the education and the financial resources of both parents; the parents' own educational background; the child's academic talents; the child's financial resources; the child's ability to earn income during the year; the quality of the child's relationship to the noncustodial parent and the likelihood that the parent would have paid for the child's education if there had been no divorce.[63]

Some noncustodial fathers have argued that requiring them to pay for college places a burden on them that courts do not place on parents in intact families, who can bid a "fiscal farewell" to their children at age eighteen. Most courts have rejected the constitutional challenge to the court-ordered payment of college expenses.[64] They have noted that divorced parents are less likely to help their children get a college education than married parents and that their children are left professionally and financially handicapped vis-à-vis children from intact families. Courts have held that the state has a legitimate interest in minimizing the disruptive impact of divorce on children's lives.

Of course, parents may agree in writing that one or both of them will pay for college. Courts usually uphold such agreements and will require the parent who has promised to do so to pay the college expenses sought.

Can child support be withheld from the obligated parent's paycheck?

Yes. One of the most powerful provisions of the federal child support laws is the mandate that states establish procedures for withholding child support payments from the wages of parents who owe child support. As of January 1, 1994, the Family Support Act of 1988 requires that all new child support orders provide for automatically withholding child support payments from the obligated parent's paycheck, regardless of whether or not support payments are late.[65]

Federal law permits an exception to immediate withholding if the court finds good cause or if the parents both agree to another arrangement.[66] However, a parent who falls at least one month behind in support payments is subject to withholding even in these cases.[67]

Withholding may be used not only to collect current support but to recoup overdue payments (known as *arrearages*) as well. States have the option, under federal law, to apply withholding to income other than wages and to order withholding, for example, from bonuses, commissions, retirement benefits, rental or interest income, or unemployment compensation benefits.[68]

Withholding for child support payments is automatic and is treated like any other form of payroll deduction, such as income tax, social security, or union dues. An employer may not avoid the duty to withhold child support from an employee's paychecks by refusing to hire or by disciplining or firing an employee who owes child support. An employer who fails to comply with an order to withhold is liable for the full amount of the child support it should have withheld from the parent's wages.[69]

The amount that may be withheld from an employee's salary is governed by the Consumer Credit Protection Act. For a parent who has a second family, the maximum amount of withholding is 50 percent of the parent's disposable earnings. For a parent without a second family, the maximum withholding is 60 percent. Those limits are increased by 5 percent (to 55 percent and 65 percent respectively) if payments are in arrears for twelve weeks or more[70] and do not apply at all to income from sources other than wages.

Can child support be withheld from the obligated parent's income tax refund?

Yes. Another important tool made available by the 1984 Child Support Enforcement Amendments is the interception of the federal and state tax refunds of parents whose child support obligations are overdue.[71] The federal tax refund offset option is available to parents receiving AFDC if the amount owed by the custodial parent is at least $150; for non-AFDC recipients, the arrearage must be at least $500.[72] In AFDC cases, the parent who owes support must be at least three months behind in child support payments.[73]

The state, which alone has the authority to request a federal income tax intercept, must first notify the owing parent of its intention to request the intercept and explain the procedures for contesting it. If the intercepted refund involves a joint tax return, the other person on the return who is not the target of the intercept is entitled to his or her share of the refund before the rest is used to cover the overdue child support.[74]

How is a support order enforced against a self-employed parent?

Because a self-employed parent usually does not have wages from which child support can be automatically withheld, enforcement of child support against self-employed obligors is not easy. A judge can order the self-employed obligor to post a cash bond with the court clerk or with the local child support enforcement agency. If payments are missed, they can be subtracted from the bond money.[75]

If payment is in arrears, a court may also enter a judgment for the amount of the arrears. The judgment can be enforced by placing a lien on the owing parent's home, boat, car, or other property and selling it at a foreclosure sale. Or the judgment can be the basis for attaching the money in the recalcitrant parent's bank account, his or her Social Security benefits, or other income or assets in the obligor's name. These remedies, of course, are also available to enforce support if a wage earner is in arrears on his or her child support payments.

States such as Arizona, California, Illinois, and Vermont have laws that prohibit state occupational licensing departments from issuing or renewing an occupational, business, or professional license for any applicant who owes child support arrears.[76] The U.S. Commission on Interstate Child Support has recommended that states go further and empower their motor vehicle agencies to deny a driver's license or vehicle registration if the applicant has an outstanding warrant for failing to appear in a parentage or child support proceeding.[77]

In addition, all states are required by the federal child support laws to develop procedures for reporting parents who are $1,000 or more in arrears in their child support payments to consumer credit rating bureaus.[78]

May a child support order be modified?

Yes. All states permit a child support order to be modified upward or downward based on proof of a substantial change in the parents' financial circumstances or the child's needs. In addition, federal law requires that child support orders be reviewed every three years unless neither parent requests a review or, in AFDC cases, if the review would not be in the child's best interests.[79]

However, child support orders may only be modified prospectively. The 1986 Bradley amendment to the federal child support laws effectively bars retroactive modifications that would wipe out past-due support obligations.[80]

To avoid having to return to court for a modification of the support order, some parents who enter into a support agreement try to anticipate modifications in a variety of ways. They may make provision for automatic cost of living adjustments; use sliding scale formulas tied to the payor or the payee's income; exchange information such as W-2 and 1099 forms, tax returns, and pay stubs on a periodic basis and recalculate support under the applicable support guidelines in accordance with the updated information; or require notification of change of employment and change of residence.[81]

What if the custodial parent does not know where to find the noncustodial parent?

A custodial parent who needs to obtain or enforce a child support order but who cannot find the noncustodial parent may enlist the assistance of a child support enforcement agency run by the state or local government, known as a *IV-D agency.*[82] This assistance is available to all custodial parents, regardless of whether or not they receive public assistance.[83]

To initiate a search, the critical piece of information that the child support enforcement agency will need from the custodial parent is the absent parent's social security number. Social security numbers can be found on state and federal income tax returns, old insurance policies and hospital records, credit cards, bank accounts or, as a last resort, may be traced by the child support enforcement agency from the parent's name, place, and date of birth and the names of the absent parent's mother and father.

If it is unlikely that the missing parent has left the state, the state child enforcement agency will ask the state Parent Locator Service to conduct a search of state agency records (such as motor vehicle registrations, unemployment insurance records, state income tax, and correctional facilities). If the state child support enforcement agency finds that the missing parent has moved to another state, it can ask the other state to search and, at the same time, request a search by the federal Parent Locator Service. Some states share their data bases with each other so that the IV-D agency in the custodial parent's home state can simultaneously conduct a search in the computerized records of surrounding states.

Provided that it has the absent parent's name and social security number, the Federal Parent Locator Service can search for a current address in the records of the Internal Revenue Service, the Department of Defense, the National Personnel Records Center, the Social Security Administration, and the Veterans Administration.[84] Federal regulations require that searches for absent parents be completed within seventy-five days and, if unsuccessful at first, be repeated on a regular basis for at least three years.[85]

Neither the custodial parent nor his or her private attorney may directly ask the federal Parent Locator Service to conduct a search. Requests to use the locator service must come through the state child support enforcement agency.

There are, however, many steps that the custodial parent can lawfully take to conduct her or his own search for the absent parent. Child support advocates have suggested contacting occupational and professional licensing bureaus (for example, if the missing parent is a doctor, lawyer, nurse, pharmacist, stock broker, or insurance agent, the relevant licensing bureau may have the missing parent's place of employment), high school and college alumni offices, trade unions, fishing and hunting license bureaus, voter registration records, and the U.S. post office.[86]

If the absent parent is a member of the military, a useful search service is the Worldwide Military Locator Service which can provide the work address of active duty military members, based on the military member's full name and social security number.[87]

How is child support handled if the noncustodial parent lives in another state or moves to another state after a support order is issued?

Children whose divorced parents live in different states are the least likely to receive the child support to which they are entitled. Interstate child support cases represent approximately 30 percent of all child support cases, yet only 10 percent of all child support dollars are paid by out-of-state parents. According to one recent study, more than a third of custodial mothers in interstate cases reported that they received no child support whatsoever.[88]

To make it easier for a custodial parent or IV-D agency to obtain and to enforce a child support order in the interstate custody context, the National Conference of Commissioners on Uniform State Laws recently drafted a Uniform Interstate Family Support Act (UIFSA).[89] As of May 1996, UIFSA has been enacted in thirty states and the District of Columbia.[90] It has been introduced in many other states, and legislation is pending in Congress that would mandate its adoption by all states.

UIFSA is designed to improve upon and supercede the Uniform Reciprocal Enforcement of Support Act (URESA), some version of which had previously been adopted in all states.[91] UIFSA contains a very broad "long-arm" statute designed to give the state where the custodial parent and the children live the broadest possible authority to order support from an out-of-state noncustodial parent.[92] At the same time, UIFSA strives to be fair to the out-of-state parent by making it possible to participate meaningfully in the support case without having to travel. To this end, UIFSA allows an out-of-state parent and other out-of-state witnesses to testify by telephone or video conferencing and to submit documents to the court by fax.[93]

Once a support order has been issued, UIFSA seeks to simplify the process of enforcing it by allowing the custodial parent to bypass the courts and child support collection agencies in her or his own state and to mail the wage withholding order directly to the owing parent's out-of-state employer.[94] This triggers wage withholding without the necessity of a hearing unless the employee objects.

If the custodial parent needs the assistance of a court in the noncustodial parent's state to collect support, i.e. if the noncustodial parent has property or assets other than wages that are available to pay child support, UIFSA provides a mechanism for the child support order from the first state to be registered and enforced in the second state where the noncustodial parent lives.[95] The registration may be handled either by the custodial parent, a private attorney, or by an IV-D attorney. The court in the second state is then required by UIFSA to enforce the existing decree without modification.[96]

This principle of one-order-in-a-case-at-one-time is a significant departure from the procedure under URESA, which does not preclude the second state from modifying a support order prospectively in accordance with its own child support guidelines. Under UIFSA, if the noncustodial parent wishes to modify an existing support order, that modification petition must be presented in the state that issued the original support order, unless neither of the parents nor the child continues to live there[97] or both parents agree in writing that the second state should assume control of the case.

Are there other ways for a custodial parent to obtain or enforce an interstate child support order without having to travel to the state where the noncustodial parent lives?

Yes. In states that have not yet adopted the new UIFSA, some version of the Uniform Reciprocal Enforcement of Support Act (URESA) or Revised Uniform Reciprocal Enforcement of Support (RURESA) is still in place. With the addition of a few shortcuts made possible by UIFSA, the basic URESA procedures for establishing and enforcing a support order without the custodial parent having to travel to another state are expected to remain in place throughout the United States even after UIFSA is broadly enacted. It is therefore important for both custodial and noncustodial parents to understand the URESA process.

To obtain a support order using URESA, the custodial parent must file a verified petition in her or his home state (known as the *initiating state*) alleging that the noncustodial parent is chargeable with support of the child and is not located in that state.[98] To file the petition, the custodial parent may enlist the assistance of the local IV-D agency, hire a private or legal services attorney (if eligible), or handle the case alone. The petition will be sent by the initiating state court to the appropriate state court where the noncustodial parent lives (known as the *responding state*). Under UIFSA, the custodial parent has the further option of filing the case directly in the responding state, without first going through the judicial or administrative screening process in the initiating state.[99]

A child support hearing will then begin against the noncustodial parent in the responding state and child support will be set in accordance with the responding state's child support guidelines. The custodial parent need not travel to the responding state. In most states, a "petitioner's representative" associated with the IV-D agency in the responding state will appear as a surrogate attorney for the custodial parent who does not have a private attorney.

If the noncustodial parent appears and consents to an order, child support can be set immediately by the responding state's court. If the non-custodial parent contests responsibility for child support or contests the amount of child support, the petition may be returned to the initiating state to allow the custodial parent to present evidence.[100]

A written transcript of that evidence, together with any supporting documents the custodial parent may wish to submit, is then forwarded to the responding state, where the noncustodial parent may present a case and challenge the custodial parent's facts. After reviewing the entire record, the court in the responding state will enter a child support order in accordance with that state's guidelines. Payments under a URESA order are typically made to the court of the responding state and then forwarded to the initiating state.[101]

If the interstate problem is one of enforcing (rather than obtaining) a child support order against an out-of-state parent, the custodial parent can use URESA's procedures to register the support order in the state to which the noncustodial parent has moved.[102] Registration makes the order enforceable in the responding state as fully as in the initiating state.

In the vast majority of responding states that follow URESA, the court will allow the noncustodial parent the chance to present evidence of changed circumstances to justify a future modification of the child support order.[103] This practice has led to the proliferation of inconsistent support orders in a single case. It is this problem that UIFSA seeks to eliminate by requiring the second court to enforce the earlier support order without modification and by giving the first state continuing, exclusive jurisdiction to modify support orders.

Do courts take into account a noncustodial parent's other children in determining the amount of child support?

Yes, in some cases. At least half of all divorces involve at least one parent who has been married before and who may have children from a prior relationship. In addition, it is estimated that 75 percent of divorced persons remarry, and many of them have more children.[104] The problem of how to determine child support for the children of multiple families is a pressing one for which, as always, the solutions vary from state to state.

When a parent responsible for paying child support subsequently has other children, courts usually take a variety of approaches to determining child support for the earlier children. A few states, including Colorado, New Jersey, Oregon, and Wisconsin, give noncustodial parents credit for the support of subsequently born children which is deducted from that parent's income before it is plugged into the state's child support formula.[105] Other courts will compute the guideline amount without a credit, but will permit the noncustodial parent to argue that his or her support obligations for subsequent children warrant a downward deviation from the guideline amount.[106]

Usually, courts will not permit a downward deviation unless the noncustodial parent can show that his or her financial obligation to a second family has had an impact on his or her ability to support the children of the first marriage.[107] Some states preclude a parent from using subsequently born children as a "sword" to decrease support payments to the children of the divorce, but may permit a parent to use the new children as a "shield" if a former spouse seeks an upward modification.[108]

In some cases, however, a noncustodial parent's remarriage may be the basis for an increased support award. If a noncustodial parent's second spouse has income or other financial resources that offset the parent's obligations for a second family, some courts will take that fact into account in considering the income that is available to support children born of an earlier marriage or relationship.[109]

In awarding child support for children from a second marriage, a large majority of states take into account the fact that a noncustodial parent may have children to support from a prior marriage or relationship. In forty states, a noncustodial parent may deduct preexisting child support obligations from income in calculating child support.[110]

How is child support computed when the parents share physical custody?

Most child support formulas are based on the premise that one parent has sole or primary physical custody of the children and that the other parent plays a more limited caretaking role, which takes the form of periodic visitation.

Many states allow a discretionary adjustment (sometimes called a visitation abatement) to the child support allotment if visitation exceeds an amount that is considered to be typical visitation. In Maryland, a downward adjustment for shared physical custody is permitted if the child is expected to stay overnight at the noncustodial parent's home more than 35 percent of the time. In Hawaii, a downward adjustment of child support is permitted if the child spends more than one hundred days (27 percent of the year) with the secondary custodian.[111]

Other states, however, recognize that shared physical custody usually increases the cost of childrearing (sometimes by as much as 50 percent) and do not allow downward adjustments of child support based on custodial sharing.[112] States in this category recognize that shared physical custody commonly increases the noncustodial parent's expenses without substantially decreasing the custodial parent's fixed expenses for items such as housing, utilities, and clothing for the children.[113]

A few states such as Colorado, Idaho, Washington, and Wisconsin have developed formulas for computing child support in shared custody arrangements. The Wisconsin formula, for instance, gives the secondary custodial parent who cares for a child more than 30 percent of the time a proportional offset or credit for care that exceeds the 30 percent threshold.[114]

Are stepparents liable for child support after a divorce?

Generally, no. The biological link between the absent biological parent (usually the father) and the child is seen by most courts as more important than any other relationship. Consequently, the general rule is that when a child's custodial biological parent and stepparent divorce, the stepparent has no legal obligation to support his or her stepchildren.[115] The child is expected to fall back on support payments from the other, noncustodial biological parent, regardless of how long the stepparent may have lived with the child and regardless of the standard of living in the stepparent household.[116]

The basis for this general rule is articulated by courts in a variety of ways. Because the policy in many states is to encourage stepparents voluntarily to shoulder some of the burden of supporting stepchildren during the marriage, courts are reluctant to penalize stepparents who do so by extending the duty of support beyond marriage.[117] Other courts have suggested that to impose a postdivorce duty of support on stepparents would discourage stepparents from developing close relationships with their stepchildren for fear of incurring a permanent duty of support.[118]

Faced with the prospect of stepchildren left holding an empty bag after a second divorce, courts in some states have recognized several exceptions to the general rule and have held that a stepparent may incur a duty to pay child support if the stepparent has actively interfered with the child's ability to obtain support from the absent biological parent[119] or has induced the children to rely on him or her exclusively and abandon support claims against the other parent.[120] In addition, a stepparent who obtains custody or visitation with a stepchild may be expected to assume a duty of support.[121]

May a parent withhold child support if the other parent interferes with visitation?

No. The duty to pay child support and the right to visitation are legally distinct from one another. A noncustodial parent may not withhold child support in retaliation for the custodial parent's interference with his or her visitation with the child. Conversely, a custodial parent may not interfere with the child's visitation on the grounds that the noncustodial parent has failed to pay child support.[122] Both the Revised Uniform Reciprocal Enforcement of Support Act (RURESA) and the new Uniform Interstate Family Support Act (UIFSA) take a similar stance. Both make it clear that, in the interstate child support context, support payments may not be conditioned on compliance with visitation.[123]

However, fathers' advocates have argued that nonpayment of child support is often tied to fathers' lack of access to their children. Statistically speaking, fathers who do not visit their children—either because the mother has interfered with visitation or because the father lacks the commitment to visit his children regularly—are also less likely to pay child support.[124] To address these concerns, some states have developed innovative techniques to redress interference with the noncustodial parent's access to a child. For details, turn to chapter 1.

Are there criminal penalties for failure to pay child support?

Yes. A parent who willfully refuses to comply with a lawful order of child support, though able to do so, may be held in contempt of court and jailed or fined for a fixed period of time as punishment or for an indefinite period until the child support is paid.

In many states, a nonpaying parent may be also prosecuted for criminal nonsupport, which is a misdemeanor in some states and a felony in others. For many first-time offenders who plead guilty to nonsupport or who are found guilty of nonsupport after a trial, a typical sentence is probation, conditional on making regular child support payments as well as payments on any arrearage. Repeat offenders may be jailed or placed in a work release program so that they can continue to earn the money necessary to pay child support.[125]

As of October 1992, failure to pay child support in the interstate context has become a federal crime.[126] An out-of-state parent who has willfully failed to pay court-ordered child support for at least one year or who is at least $5,000 in arrears may be criminally prosecuted by the local United States attorney. For a first offense, the penalties include a fine and/or a prison sentence of up to six months in prison; for a second offense, the punishment is a fine and/or up to two years in jail.

Do adults have any obligation to support their parents?

Yes, at least to some extent. Twenty-eight states impose a statutory duty on an adult child to support elderly parents.[127]

Where is child support law heading?

A number of child advocates believe that state-based child support enforcement systems will never succeed in collecting the billions of dollars in unpaid child support that is owed to this nation's children. Several bills are now pending in Congress that would require the Internal Revenue Service to collect child support payments through a mandatory payroll deduction system similar to that used for the collection of federal income taxes. At the same time, some have suggested that before the IRS can take over the job of collecting child support, a uniform, national child support guideline will need to be put in place.

Others have recommended that Congress go further and enact a child support assurance program similar to ones that are in effect in Australia, Sweden, and other countries.[128] Under a child support assurance program, the federal government would collect all child support payments through a system of withholding from obligated parents and would then send a child support check each month to the custodial parent. Child support assurance would provide a minimum guaranteed amount of child support, even in those cases where the government was unable to collect payments from the owing parent or was able to collect only part of the amount owed.

Finally, the U.S. Commission on Child and Family Welfare has recently been created to consider a broad range of issues affecting the best interests of children. Its job will be to look closely at child support enforcement issues, as well as child custody, visitation, child abuse, and spousal abuse and to report back to the President and Congress.[129]

RESOURCES

ACES
Association for Children for Enforcement of Support
2260 Upton Ave.
Toledo, OH 43606
(800) 537-7072
(419) 472-6609

Center on Children and the Law
Child Support Project
American Bar Association
740 15th St. N.W.
9th floor
Washington, DC 20005
(202) 662-1720

Children's Rights Council
220 I Street, N.E., Suite 230
Washington, DC 20002-4362
(202) 547-6227
(800) 787-KIDS

National Center on Women and Family Law
799 Broadway, Room 402
New York, NY 10003
(212) 674-8200

National Child Support Enforcement Association
Hall of the States
400 North Capitol Street, N.W.
Suite 372
Washington, DC 20001-1512
(202) 624-8180

U.S. Department of Health and Human Services
Administration for Children and Families
Office of Child Support Enforcement
370 L'Enfant Promenade, S.W.
Washington, DC 20447
(202) 401-9370

Notes

1. Pub. L. No. 93–647, 88 Stat. 2337 (1974), *codified in part* as 42 U.S.C. §§ 651–669 (West 1991).

2. Pub. L. No. 98-378, 98 Stat. 1305 (1984).

3. Pub. L. No. 100-485, 102 Stat. 2343 (1988). *See also* 42 U.S.C. § 667(b)(2)(West 1991).

4. Pub. L. No. 102–521, 106 Stat. 3403 (1992), *codified* at 18 U.S.C. § 228 (West Supp. 1994).

5. Margaret Campbell Haynes, *Understanding the Guidelines and the Rules*, 16 Family Advocate, no. 2 at 14–15 (1993). *See generally* 45 C.F.R. § 302.56 (1993) and 56 Fed. Reg. 22335 *et seq.* (May 15, 1991).

6. Researchers have estimated that if paternity were established consistently and support orders were obtained and enforced based on reasonable standards for setting support, an additional $17 billion to $23 billion more than is currently being paid would be available to children in female-headed households. Paula G. Roberts, "Child Support Orders: Problems with Enforcement" in *Children and Divorce* 103 (David and Lucile Packard Foundation, Center for the Future of Children 1994).

7. G. Diane Dodson, "Children's Standards of Living Under Child Support Guidelines: Women's Legal Defense Fund Report Card on State Child Support Guidelines, Executive Summary," in *Child Support Guidelines: The Next Generation* 97 (Margaret Campbell Haynes ed., ABA Center on Children and the Law 1994). For a detailed analysis of the ongoing negative impact of divorce on women and children, *see* J. D. Teachman & K. M. Paasch, "Financial Impact of Divorce on Children and Their Families" in *Children and Divorce, supra* note 6, at 63.

8. Roberts, *supra* note 6, at 103 & n. 9, citing U.S. Bureau of the Census, *Child Support and Alimony: 1989*, Current Population Reports, Series P-60, No. 173, Washington DC: U.S. Government Printing Office, 1991. *See also* U.S. Department of Commerce, Bureau of the Census, Current Population Reports, Consumer Income, Series P-60, No. 187, *Child Support for Custodial Mothers and Fathers: 1991* at 2, 6 (1995). *But see* Sanford L. Braver et al., *Noncustodial Parents' Report of Child Support Payments*, 40 Family Relations 180 (April 1991).

9. U.S. Bureau of the Census, *Child Support and Alimony: 1989*, Current Population Reports, Series P-60, No. 173 (1991).

10. Roberts, *supra* note 6, at 103. *See also Child Support for Custodial Mothers and Fathers. supra* note 8, at 6.

11. *See, e.g.*, Sanford Braver et al., *A Longitudinal Study of Noncustodial Parents: Parents Without Children*, 7 J. Fam. Psych. 9 (1993); J. Pearson & N. Thoennes, *Supporting Children After Divorce: The Influence of Custody on Support Levels and Payments*, 22 Fam. L.Q. 319 (Fall 1988).

12. Dodson, *supra* note 7, at 98, 100. *See generally* Diane Dodson & Joan Entmacher, *Report Card on State Child Support Guidelines* at 71–77 (Women's Legal Defense Fund 1994).

13. Irwin Garfinkel, Maryfold S. Melli, John G. Robertson, "Child Support Orders: A Perspective on Reform," in *Children and Divorce, supra* note 6, at 95.

14. *See Pickett v. Brown*, 462 U.S. 1 (1983); *Trimble v. Gordon*, 430 U.S. 762 (1977).

15. 42 U.S.C. § 666(a)(5)(A)(West Supp. 1994).

16. 42 U.S.C. § 666(a)(5)(B)(West Supp. 1994).

17. 42 U.S.C. §§ 666(a)(5)(C) and 668 (West 1991 and Supp. 1994).

18. Victoria M. Ho, *Support for Second Families: Stretching Financial Resources to Cover Multiple Families*, 16 Family Advocate, no. 2 at 41 (1993).

19. Percentage-of-income guidelines are in use in Alaska, Arkansas, Georgia, Illinois, Minnesota, Mississippi, Nevada, North Dakota, Tennessee, Texas, and Wisconsin. New York and New Hampshire are also counted by some as percentage-of-income states because, although their worksheets appear to count custodial parent income, it has no mathematical effect on the support order calculation. *See* Robert G. Williams, "An Overview of Child Support Guidelines in the United States" in *Child Support Guidelines: The Next Generation, supra* note 7, at 6.

20. *Id.* at 5.

21. Minn. Stat. Ann. § 518.551(5)(West Supp. 1994).

22. Garfinkel, *supra* note 13, at 92, 96.

23. *Id.* at 92.

24. While the idea of including both parents' income seems fair on its face, it leads to the anomalous result of reducing the child support award as the custodial parent's earnings increase. In an intact, two-parent family, increased earnings of both parents would be available to the children and would not be offset against each other. *Children and Divorce, supra* note 6, at 87–88.

25. Alabama, Arizona, California, Colorado, Connecticut, Florida, Idaho, Indiana, Iowa, Kansas, Kentucky, Louisiana, Maine, Maryland, Michigan, Missouri, Nebraska, New Jersey, New Mexico, North Carolina, Ohio, Oklahoma, Oregon, Pennsylvania, Rhode Island, South Carolina, South Dakota, Utah, Vermont, Virginia, Washington, and Wyoming are income shares states. Massachusetts and the District of Columbia use a hybrid approach, based on a percentage of the obligor's gross income. However, custodial parent income above a certain threshold ($15,000 for one child in Massachusetts, $16,500 in the District of Columbia) is counted in the calculation and reduces the child support amount. *See* Williams, *supra* note 19, at 7.

26. Some commentators have suggested that this approach underestimates the cost of childrearing in a one-parent household where the custodial parent may incur additional expenses for chores such as home repairs, house cleaning, and car maintenance, "convenience" foods, and babysitting, functions which may be performed by the parents themselves in a two-parent household rather than paid for. *See* Nancy S. Erickson, *Child Support Manual for Legal Services* at 21–22, 247 & n.179 at 250 (Nat'l Center for Women and Family Law 1992)(cited hereafter as *Child Support Manual*).

27. Dodson, *supra* note 7, at 96.

28. *See* Williams, *supra* note 19, at 5–6.

29. Delaware Family Court, *Child Support Calculation*, Form 509 (1994).

30. *Id.*

31. *Child Support Manual, supra* note 26, at 221–22.

32. *See* 42 U.S.C. § 667(b)(2)(West 1991) and 45 C.F.R. § 302.56(g)(1993). *See generally* Linda D. Elrod & Timothy B. Walker, *Family Law in the Fifty States*, 27 Fam. L.Q. 515, 623–24 (Winter 1994)(cited hereafter as *Family Law in the Fifty States*).

33. N.Y. Dom. Rel. L. § 240(1-b)(c)(3)(Lawyers Coop 1990). *Cassano v. Cassano*, 85 N.Y.2d 649, 651 N.E.2d 878, 628 N.Y.S.2d 10 (1995) (court may apply statutory percentage to parental income over $80,000 threshold but should articulate reasons for doing so). *See also Earley v. Earley*, 484 N.W. 2d 125 (S.D.), *cert. denied*, 113 S. Ct. 272 (1992); *Voishan v. Palma*, 327 Md. 318, 609 A.2d 319 (1992).

34. Williams, *supra* note 19, at 3.

35. 45 C.F.R. § 302.56(c)(1)(1993) and 56 Fed. Reg. 22335, 22354 (May 15, 1991).

36. *See, e.g.*, Fla. Stat. Ann. § 61.30(2)(West Supp. 1994). *See generally* Lynne Gold-Bikin & Linda Ann Hammond, "Determination of Income" in *Child Support Guidelines: The Next Generation, supra* note 7, at 29–36; *Family Law in the Fifty States* at 616–22 (Winter 1994).

37. *See, e.g.*, N.Y. Dom. Rel. L. section 240(1-b)(b)(5)(v) (Lawyers Coop 1990).

38. *Olson v. Olson*, 189 Mich. App. 620, 473 N.W.2d 772 (1991), *aff'd*, 439 Mich. 986, 482 N.W.2d 711 (1992).

39. *In re Marriage of Mitteer*, 241 Ill. App. 3d 217, 608 N.E.2d 607, 181 Ill. Dec. 534 (4th Dist. 1993); *In re Marriage of Ilas*, 12 Cal. App. 4th 1630, 16 Cal. Rptr. 2d 345 (4th Dist. 1993).

40. *Brody v. Brody*, 16 Va. App. 647, 432 S.E.2d 20 (1993) (imputing income to mother who quit $54,000 a year job to have a baby with her second husband); *Roberts v. Roberts*, 173 Wis. 2d 406, 496 N.W.2d 210 (1992); *Bencivenga v. Bencivenga*, 254 N.J. Super. 328, 603 A.2d 531 (N.J. App. 1992).

41. Gold-Bikin, *supra* note 36, at 32.

42. *Id.*

43. *Id.*

44. *Child Support Manual, supra* note 26, at 289.

45. Jeff Atkinson, 2 *Modern Child Custody Practice*, § 10.10 at 501 (1986). *See Tanner v. Roland*, 598 So. 2d 783 (Miss. 1992).

46. 26 U.S.C. § 152(e)(West Supp. 1994).

47. Mary Johanna McCurley & Darrell Cook, *Releasing the Dependency Exemption*, 15 Family Advocate 20–21 (Fall 1992). *See, e.g., Monterey County v. Cornejo*, 53 Cal. 3d 1271, 812 P.2d 586, 283 Cal. Rptr. 405 (1991). *But see Blanchard v. Blanchard*, 261 Ga. 11, 401 S.E. 2d 714 (1991)(minority view that state court lacks authority to award dependency exemption to noncustodial parent).

48. Mark J. Miller, *Who Gets the Dependency Exemptions?* 15 Family Advocate at 17 (Fall 1992).

49. U.S. Bureau of the Census, Current Population Reports, Series P-60, no. 173, *Child Support and Alimony: 1989* at 1, 8–10 (1991).

50. 45 C.F.R. § 302.56(c)(3)(1993) and 56 Fed. Reg. 22354 (May 15, 1991). *See also* 42 U.S.C. § 662(b)(West 1991).

51. Paula Roberts, *Securing Medical Insurance Coverage for Children Through the Child Support System*, 25 Clearinghouse Rev. 1436, 1438 & n.15 (March 1992).

52. U.S. Commission on Interstate Family Support, *Supporting our Children: A Blueprint for Reform* at 136–39 (1992).

53. Conn. Gen. Stat. Ann. § 46b-84(c)(West Supp. 1994).

54. Margaret Campbell Haynes, *Supporting Our Children: A Blueprint for Reform*, 27 Fam. L.Q. 7, 21 (Spring 1993).

55. Pub.L. No. 103–66, § 13623; 107 Stat. 633 (1993). *See* 42 U.S.C. § 1396g-1 and 29 U.S.C. § 1169(a)(West Supp. 1994).

56. 42 U.S.C. § 1396g-1 (West Supp. 1994).

57. 29 U.S.C. § 1169(a)(2) & (a)(4)(West Supp. 1994). *See generally* Gary A. Shulman, *Qualified Medical Child Support Order Handbook* (1994).

58. 42 U.S.C. § 1396g-1(a)(1)(West Supp. 1994).

59. 42 U.S.C. § 1396g-1(a)(3)(A) & (D)(West Supp. 1994).

60. 42 U.S.C. § 1396g-1(a)(5)(West Supp. 1994). In addition, states are also required to develop procedures to garnish the noncustodial parent's wages or to withhold his or her state tax refund if the noncustodial parent pockets the insurance reimbursements instead of forwarding the money to the custodial parent who incurred the out-of-pocket medical expenses. 42 U.S.C. § 1396g-1(a)(6).

61. *Child Support Manual, supra* note 26, at 173–75 and n. 4 & 10. *See, e.g.*, Cal. Fam. Code § 3901 (West 1993).

62. Colo. Rev. Stat. 14-10-115(1.5)(1993); Mass. Gen. L. ch. 208, § 28 (West Supp. 1994); N.Y. Dom. Rel. Law § 240(1-b)(c)(7)(Lawyers Coop 1990); Pa. Cons. Stat. Ann. § 4327 (West Supp. 1995).

63. *See* Annotation, *Responsibility of Noncustodial Divorced Parent to Pay for, or Contribute to, Costs of Child's College Education*, 99 A.L.R. 3d 322 (Supp. 1994). *See also* Glen A. Smith, *Education Support Obligations of Noncustodial Parents*, 36 Rutgers L. Rev. 588 (1984).

64. *Childers v. Childers*, 89 Wash. 2d 592, 575 P.2d 201 (1978). *But see Curtis v. Kline*, 666 A. 2d 265 (Pa. 1995) and *Byrnes V. Caldwell*, 665 A. 2d 1160 (1995)(Pennsylvania's college tuition law violates the equal protection clause; court found no rational basis for treating some students who need college tuition assistance from their parents any differently than others are treated). *See generally* Alexandra Dylan Lowe, *Divorced Dads Challenge Tuition Law*, ABA Journal at 22–23 (Aug. 1995).

65. 42 U.S.C. § 666(a)(1) and 666(b)(West Supp. 1994) and 45 C.F.R. § 303.100 (1993). For a comprehensive survey of child support enforcement techniques, including withholding, *see* U.S. Department of Health and Human Services, Administration for Children and Families, Office of Child Support Enforcement, *Interstate Child Support Remedies* at 127–38 (1989)(cited hereafter as *Interstate Child Support Remedies). See also* U.S. Department of Health and Human Services, Administration for Children and Families, Office of Child Support Enforcement, *Wage Withholding for Child Support: An Employer's Guide* at 1,3 (June 1992).

66. Pub. L. No. 100–485, § 101(b), 102 Stat. 2345 (1988), *codified* at 42 U.S.C. § 666(a)(8)(B). *See also* 55 Fed. Reg. 33414 (Aug. 15, 1990) and 42 U.S.C. § 666(b)(3).

67. 42 U.S.C. § 666(b)(3)(B)(West Supp. 1994).

68. 42 U.S.C. § 666(b)(8)(West Supp. 1994)(giving states the option of extending withholding to income other than wages); 45 C.F.R. § 302.65 (1993)(withholding of unemployment compensation).

69. 42 U.S.C. § 666(b)(6)(C) & (D)(West Supp. 1994).

70. 15 U.S.C. § 1673 (West 1982). *See also Child Support Manual, supra* note 26, at 340–41.

71. 42 U.S.C. § 664 and 666(a)(3); 45 C.F.R. § 303.71 (1993)(IRS full collection services) and 303.72 (federal tax refund offset)(1993). *See generally* Elizabeth S. Beninger,

"Federal and State Income Tax Refund Intercepts" in *Interstate Child Support Remedies, supra* note 65, at 151–57.

72. 45 C.F.R. § 303.72(a)(1993).

73. 45 C.F.R. § 303.72(a)(2)(ii)(1993). *See generally,* U.S. Department of Health and Human Services, Administration for Children and Families, Office of Child Support Enforcement, *Federal Tax Refund Offset Program for Child Support Enforcement* (May 1993).

74. Jeff Atkinson, 2 *Modern Child Custody Practice,* § 10.39 at 550 (1986). *See also* Geraldine Jensen & Katina Z. Jones, *How to Collect Child Support* at 59 (Association for Children for Enforcement of Support 1991)(cited hereafter *How to Collect Child Support*).

75. *How to Collect Child Support, supra* note 74, at 49. *See* 42 U.S.C. § 666(a)(6)(mandating that states develop procedures to require the absent parent to give security, post bond, or give some other guarantee to secure payment of overdue support)(West Supp. 1994). California's Child Support Security Act, for example, requires obligors to establish a support security deposit in an interest-bearing account established exclusively for the payment of child support. If an obligor is more than ten days late in paying support, the court may order disbursement of the amount owed and order the obligor to replenish the account. *See* Timothy B. Walker & Linda D. Elrod, "Family Law in the Fifty States: An Overview", 26 Fam. L.Q. at 327 (Winter 1993).

76. *See* Ariz. Rev. Stat. Ann. § 25-320(I)(West Supp. 1993(permitting state licensing board to hold hearing and suspend license of obligor who is at least one month in arrears); Cal. Welf. & Inst. Code § 11350.6 (West Supp. 1994); Ill. Comp. Stat. Ann. ch. 5, § 100/10-65(c)(West's Smith-Hurd 1993); Vt. Stat. Ann. tit. 15, § 795 (1993)(applicants for business or professional license must certify that they are not in arrears in child support payments).

77. U.S. Commission on Interstate Child Support, *Supporting Our Children: A Blueprint for Reform* at 172–73 (1992). Legislation pending in the U.S. Congress would require states to develop procedures to suspend the driver's licenses, professional licenses, and recreational licenses of parents who fail to meet their child support obligations. *See* Robert Pear, *House Bill Links Licenses To Child-Support Payments,* N.Y. Times, A22 (March 24, 1995).

78. 42 U.S.C. § 666(a)(7)(West Supp. 1994) and 45 C.F.R. § 303.105(b)(1993). *See also* Pub. L. No. 102-537, 106 Stat. 3531 (1992)(amending Fair Credit Reporting Act to require reporting of overdue child support on consumer reports).

79. 42 U.S.C. § 666(a)(10)(B)(i) and (ii)(West Supp. 1994).

80. 42 U.S.C. § 666(a)(9)(West Supp. 1994).

81. Thomas P. Malone, *Negotiating a Support Agreement,* 16 Family Advocate, no. 2, at 46 (1993).

82. These state and local government agencies are known as *IV-D agencies* in reference to Title IV-D of the Social Security Act, which governs state enforcement of child support for the recipients of public assistance and which requires states to assist custodial parents in locating support obligors and in obtaining and enforcing support orders.

83. Custodial parents who receive AFDC or Medicaid can get this help for free. Others who want help may be asked to pay an application fee (which may not exceed $25) as well as a small additional charge if the state needs to use the Federal Parent Locator Service for help in finding the obligor. *See* 45 C.F.R. § 302.33 (1993)(availability of IV-D services to individuals not receiving AFDC).

84. *See generally* Margaret Campbell Haynes, "Locating Absent Parents and Their Assets," in *Interstate Child Support Remedies, supra* note 65, at 15–17.

85. 45 C.F.R. §§ 303.3(b)(3) & (5) and 303.11(b)(5)(1993).

86. *How to Collect Child Support, supra* note 74, at 31–32.

87. U.S. Department of Health and Human Services, Administration for Children and Families, Office of Child Support Enforcement, *Child Support Enforcement in the Military* at 4 (1991). *See also* President Clinton's Executive Order No. 12953 issued Feb. 27, 1995, reprinted in 21 Fam. L. Rep. (BNA) 2039(1995)(ordering federal agencies, including the military, to "cooperate fully in efforts to establish . . . and enforce the collection of child and medical support").

88. Haynes, *supra* note 54.

89. For the final text of the new Uniform Interstate Family Support Act with prefatory notes, Commissioners' comments and explanatory footnotes, *see* John J. Sampson, *Uniform Interstate Family Support Act (with Unofficial Annotations),* 27 Fam. L.Q. 93 *et seq.* (Spring 1993). The text and official comments also appear in 9 Uniform Laws Annotated (U.L.A.), Part I at 121 *et seq.* (West Supp. 1994).

90. UIFSA has been enacted in Alaska, Arizona, Arkansas, Colorado, Delaware, District of Columbia, Florida, Idaho, Illinois, Indiana, Kansas, Louisiana, Maine, Massachusetts, Minnesota, Montana, Nebraska, New Mexico, North Carolina, North Dakota, Oklahoma, Oregon, Pennsylvania, South Carolina, South Dakota, Texas, Utah, Virginia, Washington, Wisconsin, and Wyoming. *See* Linda D. Elrod & Robert G. Spector, *A Review of the Year in Family Law: Children's Issues Take Spotlight,* 29 Fam. L.Q. 741, at 772 (Table 3)(Winter 1996). *See also* John J. Sampson & Harry L. Tindall, *Texas Family Code Ann.,* ch. 159 (Aug. 1996).

91. The Uniform Reciprocal Enforcement of Support Act (URESA) and the Revised Uniform Reciprocal Enforcement of Support Act (RURESA) may be found in 9B Uniform Laws Annotated (U.L.A.) (West 1987). For a clear overview of the differences between the old RURESA and the new UIFSA, *see* Linda Ann Hammond, *A Summary of the Differences Between the Revised Uniform Reciprocal Enforcement of Support Act and the Uniform Interstate Family Support Act* (September 1993), available from the U.S. Department of Health and Human Services' Office of Child Support Enforcement.

92. Uniform Interstate Family Support Act, § 201.

93. Uniform Interstate Family Support Act, § 316(e) & (f).

94. Uniform Interstate Family Support Act, § 501. Three states (Maine, Montana, and South Dakota) have chosen not to enact UIFSA's direct interstate income withholding. *See Texas Family Code Ann., supra* note 90.

95. Uniform Interstate Family Support Act, §§ 601–608.

96. Uniform Interstate Family Support Act, §§ 205, 206, 603(c), and 609–612.

97. Uniform Interstate Family Support Act, § 205.

98. For a detailed description of URESA procedures, *see* Margaret Campbell Haynes, *The Uniform Reciprocal Enforcement Support Act* in *Interstate Child Support Remedies, supra* note 65, at 63–114.

99. Uniform Interstate Family Support Act, § 301(c).

100. Revised Uniform Reciprocal Enforcement of Support Act (RURESA), § 20. *See also Interstate Child Support Remedies, supra* note 65, at 80.

101. *Id.* at 94.

102. *Id.* at 100–4, 110.

103. *Id.* at 106–11.

104. Marianne Takas, *Improving Child Support Guidelines: Can Simple Formulas Address Complex Families?*, 26 Fam. L.Q. 171 (Fall 1992).

105. Marianne Takas, *Addressing Subsequent Families in Child Support Guidelines* in *Child Support Guidelines: The Next Generation, supra* note 7, at 40.

106. *See generally* Ho, *supra* note 18, at 41–42.

107. *See, e.g.*, N.Y. Dom. Rel. Law § 240 (1-b)(f)(8)(Lawyers Coop 1990).

108. *See Child Support Manual, supra* note 26, at 306. *See, e.g.*, Fla. Stat. Ann. § 61.30 (West Supp. 1994).

109. Ho, *supra* note 18, at 42. *See, e.g., Johnson v. Johnson*, 468 N.W. 2d 648 (S.D. 1991).

110. Garfinkel, *supra* note 13, at 90 & n.42.

111. Karen Czapanskiy, *Child Support, Visitation, Shared Custody and Split Custody* in *Child Support Guidelines: The Next Generation, supra* note 7, at 44.

112. *Id.* at 44–46. *See In re Marriage of Mrvicka*, 496 N.W.2d 259 (Iowa. App. 1992); *State ex rel. Lara v. Lara*, 495 N.W.2d 719 (Iowa 1993).

113. Czapanskiy, *supra* note 111, at 45–46.

114. Takas, *supra* note 104, at 185–87. *See also* Czapanskiy, *supra* note 111, at 46–48.

115. *DeNomme v. DeNomme*, 375 Pa. Super. 212, 544 A.2d 63 (1988); *Wiese v. Wiese*, 699 P.2d 700 (Utah 1985)(stepfather whose name was on child's birth certificate and who treated child as his own owed no support after his divorce from child's biological mother). For a thoughtful overview of this area of the law, *see* David L. Chambers, "Stepparents, Biologic Parents and the Law's Perception of 'Family' After Divorce," in Stephen D. Sugarman & Herman Hill Kay, *Divorce Reform at the Crossroads* at 108 (1990).

116. *Id.* at 115.

117. *DeNomme v. DeNomme, supra* note 115.

118. *In re Marriage of Holcomb*, 471 N.W.2d 76 (Iowa App. 1991).

119. *Miller v. Miller*, 97 N.J. 154, 478 A.2d 351 (1984).

120. *A.R. v. C.R.*, 411 Mass. 570, 583 N.E.2d 840 (1992).

121. Jeff Atkinson, 2 *Modern Child Custody Practice*, § 10:32 at 536 (1986).

122. *Id.*, § 10.08 at 498. *See also Interstate Child Support Remedies, supra* note 65, at 233–38.

123. RURESA § 23; UIFSA § 305(d).

124. R. A. Thompson, *The Role of the Father After Divorce* in *Children and Divorce, supra* note 6, at 224.

125. *How to Collect Child Support, supra* note 74, at 51–52.

126. Child Support Recovery Act of 1992, Pub. L. No. 102–521, 106 Stat. 3403 (1992), *codified* at 18 U.S.C. § 228 (West Supp. 1994).

127. *See* Ann Britton, *America's Best Kept Secret: An Adult Child's Duty to Support Aged Parents*, 26 Cal. W. L. Rev. 351 (1990).

128. Garfinkel, *supra* note 13, at 95–96. *See also* Maureen A. Pirog-Good, *Child Support Guidelines and the Economic Well-Being of Children in the United States*, Family Relations 453–62 (October 1993); Harry D. Krause, *Child Support Reassessed*, in Stephen D. Sugarman & Herma Hill Kay, *Divorce Reform at the Crossroads* 166 (1990).

129. Child Support Recovery Act of 1992, Pub. L. No. 102-521, § 5, 106 Stat. 3403, 3406–9 (1992), *codified* at 42 U.S.C. § 12301, *Historical and Statutory Note* (West Supp. 1994).

III

Property Division and Alimony

Property Division

What counts as property to be divided between the spouses when a marriage ends in divorce?

Marital property consists of the physical and financial possessions that have been acquired by the spouses after their marriage and before their divorce. It includes tangible assets like cars, houses, furnishings, jewelry, real estate, boats, and artwork. It also includes financial assets such as cash, bank accounts, stocks, bonds, mutual funds, and businesses or business interests as well as the couple's financial liabilities or debts. Increasingly, property has come to include the couple's intangible career assets: their pensions and other retirement benefits, employee stock options, group medical and life insurance, and, in some states, the value of a professional education or professional license.

The courts' recognition of this "new property" represents a major legal milestone because most couples have very few tangible or financial assets. Once divided between the spouses at divorce, the value of their traditional assets is rarely enough to cover the down payment on a house.[1] It is their career assets—their earning capacity and the benefits flowing from their employment—that account for the bulk of what little wealth most families can call their own.[2]

Who owns the property acquired during marriage?

Until the 1970s, two distinctly different sets of legal rules governed the property of married couples. In *community property* jurisdictions (Arizona, California, Idaho, Louisiana, Nevada, New Mexico, Puerto Rico, Texas, Washington, and, recently, Wisconsin), all property acquired by the spouses during the marriage is considered joint property. These states take the view that the assets of the marriage have been earned by the joint efforts of both spouses, regardless of who receives a paycheck or who raises the children. All property acquired during the marriage is viewed as belonging to the marital "community" and therefore, when the spouses divorce, the starting point for the division of property is an equal fifty-fifty split—half to the wife, half to the husband.

The remaining states used to follow a *title* or *common-law system* that recognized each spouse's individual ownership of the property to which he or she held legal title. If the husband alone signed the deed to the house, he owned it. If he held title to the family car, it was his. Ordinarily, divorce courts had no power to "invade" the husband's title and award "his" property to his wife.[3]

Over the course of the past twenty-five years, most common-law states have abolished their strict title rules for purposes of divorce. Instead, they have instituted *equitable distribution* rules that permit divorce courts to divide between the ex-spouses all of the property acquired during the marriage, regardless of who holds title to a particular asset.[4]

The prevailing legal doctrine in equitable distribution states is similar to that of community property states. Marriage is increasingly seen as an economic and social partnership of equals to which each partner makes a contribution of commensurate value, whether as a breadwinner or as a caretaker of the children and the home. When that partnership ends, courts in equitable distribution states have the power to divide up the couple's assets to avoid leaving either spouse destitute. In fact, equalizing the former spouses' standard of living is sometimes mentioned as a goal of equitable distribution. However, because the amount of marital property available for distribution is so small in most cases, some observers have urged courts to focus their efforts instead on awarding and enforcing spousal and child support awards.

After marriage, is all property owned by the spouses considered joint property?

No. The vast majority of both community property and common law states recognize a category of separate property that belongs to the individual spouse, and that need not be shared with an ex-spouse after a divorce. The underlying legal theory is that divisible marital property includes only property acquired as a result of the efforts of one or both spouses during the marriage. Property acquired prior to the marriage or property given as a gift to a spouse by a third party belongs to that spouse alone.[5] In most states, property inherited by the spouse during the marriage is also separate.[6]

A small minority of states follow a "kitchen sink" approach to the division of marital property. In these states, the court may divide *all* property owned by either spouse at the time of the divorce, regardless of how or when the property was acquired.[7] An even smaller number of states follow a hybrid approach. In those states, only property acquired during the marriage may be divided unless such a division would leave one of the spouses with too little. In that case, a hybrid state may permit separate property to be divided between the spouses.[8]

In most states, the appreciation in value of a separate asset is considered separate property, as long as the appreciation has not resulted from the efforts of either spouse.[9] And property that is bought or exchanged for separate property typically remains separate property.[10] However, if separate property is placed in both spouses' names, i.e., if a husband or wife's name is added to the other spouse's bank or brokerage account after the marriage, many states presume that the separate property has been transmuted into marital property.[11]

Finally, property acquired after the divorce is filed (or even, in some states, after the point of permanent separation) is usually considered separate property.[12]

If a couple lives together before marriage, how is the property acquired during the period of cohabitation treated?

As a general rule, property acquired while a couple lived together before marriage is separate property, since it was not acquired during the marriage and was not paid for with marital dollars. However, some courts have carved out an exception for a house if it was bought before marriage on the understanding that it would become the family home.[13] And in a few states, other property acquired when the parties were living together before marriage is treated as divisible property, provided the spouse claiming a share of the property made some contribution to acquiring or maintaining it.[14]

What general principles govern the distribution of marital property?

As in many areas of family law, the answer depends on where the divorcing couple lives. Most community property states and a small number of common-law states either mandate the equal division of marital property or create a presumption that marital property should be divided equally unless the court finds that an equal division would be inequitable.[15]

The majority of states apply a doctrine of equitable distribution. Equitable distribution laws do not mandate a fifty-fifty split of marital assets. Nor do they, in contrast with child support guidelines, contain precise mathematical formulas for valuing a homemaker-spouse's nonmonetary contributions to the marriage.

Instead, they permit judges to distribute marital property in accordance with their view of the parties' needs and the equity of the individual divorce case before them. Most equitable distribution states spell out a list of factors judges must take into account in deciding on a fair property division. Rhode Island, a typical equitable distribution state, enumerates twelve factors a court must consider:

1. The length of the marriage;
2. The conduct of the spouses during the marriage;
3. The contribution of each of the spouses during the marriage to the acquisition, preservation, or appreciation in value of their respective assets;
4. The contribution and services of either spouse as a homemaker;
5. The spouses' health and age;
6. The amount and sources of income of each of the spouses;
7. The occupation and employability of each of the spouses;
8. The opportunity of each spouse for future acquisition of capital assets and income;
9. The contribution of one spouse to the education, training, licensure, business, or increased earning power of the other;
10. The need of the custodial parent to occupy or own the marital residence and to use or own its household effects taking into account the best interests of the children of the marriage;
11. Either spouse's wasteful dissipation of assets or any transfer or encumbrance of assets made in contemplation of divorce without fair consideration;
12. Any factor which the court shall expressly find to be just and proper.[16]

A minority of states also allows judges to take into account the relative degree of marital misconduct or fault,[17] while thirty-two states and the District of Columbia take into account the spouses' economic fault, i.e., the squandering of marital assets.[18]

In a property settlement, is each marital asset split between the parties?

No. Typically, each of the couple's marital assets is assigned a value and then thrown into the "pot." In other words, all assets are added up to arrive at a figure for the total worth of the marital property. In most divorces, the property settlement is then privately negotiated either between the spouses directly or by their lawyers. One marital asset may be assigned to one spouse in exchange for another asset of comparable value assigned to the other.

In some cases, alimony and property may be traded off against each other as part of a negotiated package deal. One spouse, for instance, may agree to a smaller property settlement in exchange for larger alimony payments or, conversely, may agree to waive an alimony claim in exchange for a larger property settlement.

Even when a judge divides the property, courts consider assets to be fungible and do not try to divide each and every asset between the litigants. However, some assets—such as a pension or a house—may account for such a large proportion of the couple's assets that the parties or the court will have to divide their value between the two spouses.

If the couple owns a house, which spouse is entitled to keep it?

For most families, the family home is the couple's most valuable tangible asset. If the couple has children, the family's house also serves as the basis for the children's ties to neighbors, friends, and teachers. Under the old fault-based divorce rules, the family home was traditionally awarded to the wife, who was technically the "innocent" party in many cases and was therefore entitled to a larger share of the marital property. If she had custody of the children, it was generally assumed that she needed the house to provide a stable home environment for the children after the divorce.

In recent years, there has been a trend in some states in favor of ordering a sale of the family home as a way of dividing the value of the home equally between the spouses. In Connecticut, for instance, during the 1970s, 82 percent of women were awarded the family home outright. By the 1980s, that number had fallen to 37 percent.[19] In San Diego, the percent of wives awarded the family home fell from 66 percent in 1968 to 42 percent in 1976.[20] In New York, long-married wives suffered a 14 percent decline between 1978 and 1984 in the likelihood of receiving the family home after divorce.[21]

The presence of young children in the home is taken into consideration by many judges but is by no means an absolute bar to a forced sale. In California, 66 percent of the couples who were forced to sell their homes had minor children.[22] In those cases where the father is awarded custody of the children, courts in some states appear to be more likely to award the house to the custodial parent.[23]

One approach that is commonly used by courts to avoid the family home's sale at the time of divorce is to keep the home in joint ownership and to postpone the sale until the children reach their majority. The spouse who receives custody then gets the use of the marital home until the youngest child turns eighteen.[24] Indeed, a number of states have now passed laws that expressly permit judges to delay the sale of the family home to minimize the disruptive impact of the divorce on children.[25]

If one spouse has rights to a pension, is the other spouse entitled to a share of that pension?

Yes. Within the past fifteen years, the vast majority of states has come to recognize pensions as marital property to be divided upon divorce. This is true not only for vested pensions (i.e., pensions to which an employee has an absolute right and which cannot be lost if the employee quits or is fired before retirement age) but for nonvested pensions as well.[26] Courts have reasoned that retirement benefits are deferred compensation earned throughout the employee's career and are thus part of the pool of marital funds available for distribution.[27]

This area of divorce law has been heavily influenced by legal developments at the federal level. The Retirement Equity Act, passed by Congress in 1984, made a number of sweeping changes in the way state courts handle pensions at divorce. The Act requires private pension plans to comply with a court-ordered division of a pension and permits all or part of a worker's pension and survivor benefits to be paid directly by the pension plan administrator to a former spouse if the plan has been served with a special type of court order that meets the federal requirements for a Qualified Domestic Relations Order (QDRO).[28] For a former spouse to retain a widow or widower's pension protection, however, the former spouse's entitlement to the survivor benefit must be carefully spelled out in the QDRO.

The Retirement Equity Act also addresses the problem that can occur when a worker elects, unbeknownst to his or her spouse, to forego survivor's coverage in favor of higher benefits during his or her own lifetime. The Act now prevents a married worker from opting out of survivor's benefits without the written consent of his or her spouse.[29] If a divorced spouse (a wife, for example) has received a court-ordered division of the pension that specifies that she is entitled to survivor benefits, the Act protects her rights to those benefits.[30]

For military personnel, the key law is the Uniformed Services Former Spouses' Protection Act (USFSPA). The USFSPA permits state courts to treat military retirement pay as marital property and to order payment of up to 50 percent of the retirement pay directly to the former spouse if the spouses were married for at least ten years while the employee was in the military.[31]

Some courts have interpreted the USFSPA to mean that USFSPA only bars direct government payments to a former spouse whose marriage lasted fewer than ten years of military service but does not otherwise prevent a state court from dividing military retirement benefits as a marital asset.[32] Similarly, some courts have awarded a former spouse more than 50 percent of the value of the retirement benefits, noting that the USFSPA's 50 percent limit applies only to direct federal payments of military retirement pay to a service member's former spouse.[33]

The thorniest legal questions relating to pensions and divorce involve procedures for valuing and dividing the pension. There are two basic approaches. In the case of younger couples with other assets, some courts prefer the *buy-out* or *cash-out method*, which awards the nonemployee spouse either a lump-sum settlement or an equivalent marital asset at the time of the divorce based on an estimate of the pension's present value. In the case of older couples who have been married for a long time and who have few other significant assets, some courts favor the *future share method*, which defers the division of the pension until the pension benefits are actually payable.[34]

If the employee-spouse worked either before or after the marriage (as well as during the marriage), his or her pension rights will include a marital property component and a separate property component that will need to be segregated before the pension is divided.[35] Typically, the marital property component equals the ratio between the number of months the employee-spouse worked while married and the total number of months the employee-spouse worked before retirement.[36] However, because an employee's salary on which pension benefits are based is often highest during the last years of employment, some courts have further reduced a nonemployee-spouse's share of the pension to reflect their view that later, postdivorce years of employment are worth more than earlier years.[37]

The fact that a pension may be deemed property to be shared upon divorce does not necessarily mean that each spouse will automatically be awarded half of the value of the pension. A recent survey of property settlements in New York found that only 14 percent of wives received half or more of the husband's pension and that the wife's average share was 10 percent.[38]

Are other fringe benefits treated as marital property?

Yes. Most courts have held that employee stock options are property to be valued and divided at divorce.[39] Some courts have ruled that accumulated vacation or personal leave time earned during the marriage is also divisible marital property.[40] Most courts, however, treat severance benefits for a postdivorce layoff as separate property.[41]

How do courts treat life insurance policies?

The answer depends on what kind of life insurance policy is at stake. *Whole life insurance policies* (also known as *cash value life insurance*) are akin to savings accounts because they are assets against which the owner may borrow. They also have a cash surrender value that is refunded if the policy is canceled. Whole life policies are therefore a valuable asset and are usually treated either as separate or marital property depending on what funds were used to pay the life insurance premiums. If a whole life insurance policy was purchased during the marriage using marital funds, the cash surrender value of the policy is generally considered to be divisible marital property.[42]

Term life insurance, on the other hand, has no cash surrender value at the end of the term. There is therefore usually nothing for the divorce court to divide if the insured spouse is still living at the time of the divorce.[43] Term life policies are more significant as a form of security for the payment of spousal or child support in case the payor spouse dies.

If one spouse is named as the beneficiary of a third person's life insurance policy and collects benefits under that policy during the marriage, the insurance proceeds are usually considered to be nondivisible separate property, on the theory that they are either a gift or an inheritance.[44]

Insurance policies issued by the United States government to its military and civilian employees present yet another situation. The Supreme Court of the United States has ruled that a state court may not interfere with the right of military personnel under federal law to designate and to change the designation of a beneficiary of a military life insurance policy.[45] It is therefore generally the rule that state divorce courts cannot award an interest in a federal life insurance policy to an ex-spouse if that interest conflicts with the wishes of the employee spouse.[46]

Suppose a wife has worked to pay for her former husband's education. Does she have a right to be paid back for her investment in his career when she and her husband get divorced?

As always, the answer depends on what state she lives in. In the pivotal case of *O'Brien v. O'Brien*, New York's highest court concluded that a wife who worked and contributed all her income to put her husband through medical school was entitled to a share of the value of his medical degree when her husband filed for divorce two months after he obtained his license to practice surgery.[47] The court computed the value of the husband's medical degree by calculating the difference between the expected income of the average college graduate and the average income of a surgeon and awarded the former wife 40 percent of the resulting difference.

The New York court reasoned that "a marriage is, among other things, an economic partnership to which both parties contribute as spouse, parent, wage earner or homemaker" and went on to offer its justification for treating professional degrees as marital property to be divided upon divorce:

[F]ew undertakings during a marriage better qualify as the type of joint effort that the . . . economic partnership theory is intended to address than contributions toward one spouse's acquisition of a professional license. Working spouses are often required to contribute substantial income as wage earners, sacrifice their own educational or career goals and opportunities for child rearing, perform the bulk of household duties and responsibilities, and forego the acquisition of marital assets that could have been accumulated if the professional spouse had been employed rather than occupied with the study and training necessary to acquire a professional license.[48]

Although New York stands virtually alone in treating a professional degree or license as a form of divisible property,[49] a growing number of states have passed laws requiring courts to compensate one spouse for his or her financial contribution to the other's professional education or degree. Known as *reimbursement alimony* in some states, this approach seeks to reimburse the working spouse for the out-of-pocket expenses of the professional spouse's education, plus interest.[50]

Even in states where the legislature has not passed a law on this subject, most courts will search for a way to compensate the supporting spouse for the financial support he or she provided to further the other's education.[51] This legal doctrine, of course, applies to men as well as to women. A husband who has worked to put his wife through graduate school is entitled to compensation when the couple divorces.[52] However, some courts are reluctant to grant reimbursement alimony unless the divorce occurs shortly after graduation, on the theory that if the divorce takes place much later, the spouses will have already enjoyed the benefits of the degree-related increase in earning capacity.[53]

A small number of states have declined to include educational assets acquired during the marriage in the divorce settlement.[54] These states reason that the value of the degree is highly speculative and emphasize that the degree lacks the hallmarks of traditional property, since it cannot be sold or exchanged in an open market.

How is a family business treated in a property settlement?

If the business was started during the marriage using marital funds, the business is considered marital property, to be thrown into the pot of assets to be divided upon divorce as are all increases in that business's value.[55]

The more perplexing legal issues arise when a business was started before the marriage and increased in value during the marriage. In a small number of states, the increase in value of separate property during marriage is automatically considered divisible marital property.[56] Other states say the opposite—that an increase in value of separate property remains separate property and is not divisible at divorce.[57] Most states, however, look at why the business became more valuable. Increases in value that result from inflation or favorable market conditions are considered separate property, while increases in value that can be traced to the efforts of either spouse are usually treated as divisible marital property.[58]

A variety of complex formulas have been developed by the courts to assign a dollar amount to the marital share of the appreciation of a family business that was formed before the marriage. This is one of the most complex aspects of divorce litigation and usually calls for the testimony of accountants and other expert witnesses.

Studies of divorce outcomes have found that wives rarely receive an actual share of a family business.[59] Instead, they may receive another asset of comparable value in the property settlement.

May a court divide a personal injury award?

As usual, it depends. Some states take the view that the injury is personal to the injured spouse and that all of the recovery is the injured spouse's separate property.[60] California, on the other hand, gives judges discretion to share personal injury recoveries between the spouses, with the proviso that if they do so, at least half of the award must go to the injured spouse.[61]

Other states take heed of the marital partnership theory that underlies their marital property system and have ruled that the portion of the recovery that represents lost earnings during the marriage and medical expenses paid for with marital funds should be treated as compensation for marital funds that were either spent or lost.[62] On the other hand, compensation for lost earnings after divorce or for pain and suffering are usually not considered to be part of the marital estate.[63]

How do courts treat worker's compensation and other disability benefits?

Courts are split on whether worker's compensation and other disability benefits are marital or separate property. A very few states treat worker's compensation as personal to the injured spouse, others treat it as marital property, and the majority of states look carefully at the nature of the benefit and what it is intended to compensate.[64] Reimbursement for lost wages during the marriage and for medical expenses paid for with marital funds is treated as divisible property, while compensation for postdivorce medical expenses or postdivorce loss in earnings is treated as separate property.

Veterans' disability benefits administered by the Veterans Administration and disability benefits received in lieu of military retirement pay are generally not considered to be divisible at divorce.[65] However, some courts have ruled that these benefits may be taken into account in awarding alimony or child support or may be considered as a factor justifying the award of a disproportionately larger share of marital property to the nonmilitary spouse.[66]

Can a divorced spouse collect social security benefits based on the earnings of a former spouse?

Yes. A divorced spouse aged sixty-two or older (a wife, for example) is entitled to collect social security benefits based on the earnings of a former spouse if their marriage lasted more than ten years.[67] Her social security check will equal half of her ex-husband's benefit based on his earning record, unless she would be entitled to more based on her own earnings (in which case the former wife gets the larger of the two benefits, not the sum of both).[68]

Unlike the division of a private pension, however, the benefits paid to the divorced spouse of a living worker are not taken out of her former husband's social security check. He will receive his full entitlement while she gets a separate check equal to 50 percent of his.[69]

Even if the former husband chooses to delay his retirement and postpones applying for social security, a divorced wife aged sixty-two or older may still collect social security benefits, provided that her former husband is eligible for social security, she meets the ten years of marriage test, and she has been divorced for at least two years.[70]

If the eligible employee dies, his or her former spouse may be eligible for one of several kinds of survivor benefits:[71]

1. *A divorced widow or widower benefit*, which is payable to a former spouse aged sixty or older who was married for at least ten years;

2. *A disabled divorced widow or widower benefit*, which is payable to a disabled former spouse aged fifty or older who was married for at least ten years; or

3. *A surviving divorced mother or father benefit*, which is payable, regardless of length of marriage, to a parent caring for the deceased worker's child who is under sixteen or disabled and entitled to collect child's benefits.

If the divorced spouse is also eligible for a government pension, his or her social security benefits may be reduced or offset by a portion of the pension benefits to which he or she might otherwise be entitled.[72]

How are health insurance benefits handled when a couple gets divorced?

One of the most financially devastating losses occasioned by divorce is the loss of health and hospital insurance. In most marriages, where either only one spouse is employed or only one spouse's employer offers health insurance, family members receive their healthcare coverage from the employed spouse's employer. When the marriage ends, the other spouse (who is usually the wife) may find that she and the children are stranded without health insurance.

Several solutions to this crisis have been advanced, although none is wholly satisfactory. Many states have passed insurance conversion laws that permit a divorced woman (or man) who was formerly covered by a spouse's group insurance plan to convert to an individual plan without having to prove eligibility for coverage.[73] While this approach allows the divorced spouse to avoid stringent "preexisting condition" exclusions imposed by many insurers, conversion policies are often too expensive for many divorced spouses.

In 1986, Congress passed a group health insurance continuation law. Under the Comprehensive Omnibus Budget Reconciliation Act of 1986 (COBRA), employers must allow divorced spouses and children to remain members of the former spouse's group health insurance plan, provided that they pay their own premiums.[74] The drawback to this approach is that the divorced spouse may remain in the group plan for only three years.[75]

Alternatively, an alimony award or a child support order may require a former spouse to maintain health insurance coverage for a former spouse or the children. The issue of healthcare coverage for children is discussed in greater detail in chapter 2.

ALIMONY, MAINTENANCE, AND SPOUSAL SUPPORT

What is alimony?

Alimony is a periodic payment made by one former spouse to the other in order to provide financial support to the economically dependent spouse. It is based on a variety of legal theories. Historically, alimony was awarded on the premise that a husband's responsibility for his wife's support was a lifelong obligation.[76] At the same time, the courts saw a need to help a former economically dependent wife avoid destitution when her marriage came to an end.

More recently, alimony has been awarded with the recognition that the earning capacity of the spouse who remained at home attending to childcare and homemaking responsibilities has been impaired by the years spent outside of the paid labor force. Alimony is seen as compensation for this contribution to the marriage and to the compensated spouse's financial success. In shorter marriages, it may be designed to help the uncompensated spouse become self-supporting. In longer marriages, where that is no longer possible, alimony serves as a kind of marital pension.[77]

Contrary to public perception, alimony is awarded in only a small minority of divorces. The U.S Census Bureau has estimated that of the 20.6 million ever-divorced or currently separated women in 1990, only 15.5 percent were ever awarded alimony.[78] The incidence of alimony awards is low not only for young women who have had relatively short marriages but for women over forty, of whom only 19.9 percent had alimony ordered.[79]

Is spousal support the same as alimony?

In many states, the term *alimony* is used interchangeably with the terms *maintenance* or *spousal support* to refer to payments by one former spouse to the other after marriage. However, in a few states, spousal support refers specifically to payments owed by one spouse to the other during the marriage. In Pennsylvania, for instance, mathematical guidelines similar to those used to award child support are used to determine the spousal support to which a spouse who has been abandoned is entitled.[80] *Alimony pendente lite* is a temporary spousal support award designed to cover the recipient's reasonable and necessary living expenses while the divorce is pending.

In this chapter, the terms alimony and spousal support are used interchangeably.

Are men entitled to alimony?

Yes. The Supreme Court has held that husbands as well as wives have a right to seek alimony.[81] However, it is more often women than men who have foregone or delayed education, training, employment, or career opportunities during marriage and childrearing and who have thus reduced or lost their lifetime earning capacity. Women therefore continue to constitute the principal applicants for spousal support.

Who decides how much spousal support a former spouse is entitled to?

Spousal support may be jointly agreed to by the parties or ordered by the court except in Texas, which does not permit permanent court-ordered alimony.

How is alimony treated for tax purposes?

Alimony payments are taxable to the spouse who receives them and are deductible from the income of the spouse who makes them.[82]

For how long a period of time is spousal support awarded?

Historically, in those cases where alimony was awarded, it was awarded until the dependent spouse died or remarried.

Beginning in the 1970s, a number of states passed laws allowing courts to award *rehabilitative, transitional,* or *short-term alimony* as an alternative to permanent alimony. These laws assumed that the dependent spouse might need help for a few years after the divorce to further her education or to seek additional job training but that, after several years spent improving her marketability, she should be given an incentive to become self-sufficient.[83]

Some states have gone even further and imposed mandatory time limits on alimony awards except under special circumstances. Delaware, for instance, limits alimony to 50 percent of the length of the marriage unless the couple has been married for more than twenty years.[84] Indiana limits alimony to three years unless the dependent spouse or a child in the spouse's custody is physically or mentally incapacitated.[85] Kansas's alimony statute contains a limit of 121 months, subject to reinstatement.[86] By 1986, twenty-five states had either specifically limited alimony to a set time period or allowed a court to impose a time limit on alimony awards.[87]

Research on the economic consequences of divorce has shown that women's per capita income and standard of living often decline dramatically after divorce, while those of men tend to increase.[88] Studies conducted in the mid-1980s found that not only did the number of alimony awards decrease dramatically in the prior decade but an even more dramatic decrease occurred in the duration of alimony awards. For instance, in New York, where four out of five alimony awards were for permanent alimony in 1978, by 1984 the majority of alimony awards were for a limited duration of slightly less than five years.[89]

More recently, higher courts in a number of states have taken a second look at the impact of short-term alimony and have found that it has created severe hardships for divorced women, particularly older women in long marriages. They have sought to fashion longer-term alimony awards that compensate the economically weaker spouse for the earning capacity she sacrificed during the years when she devoted herself to caring for her husband and their children.[90]

States taking this approach have focused on the concept of marriage as an economic partnership, with contributions made by both spouses that are valuable regardless of whether those contributions are made in a financial or nonfinancial form. When such an economic partnership dissolves upon divorce, the inequity of allowing the husband to maintain or increase his standard of living while the former wife's standard declines precipitously has persuaded a number of states to amend their alimony laws to increase the availability of permanent alimony.[91]

What factors do courts take into account in deciding whether to award spousal support?

In simple terms, spousal support is often described as a function of two factors: the needs of the applicant spouse and the other spouse's ability to pay. Many state laws, however, contain a long list of factors to be considered by the courts in assessing the need for alimony, such as:

1. Length of the marriage;
2. Age, physical health, and mental health of the two spouses;
3. Distribution of property;
4. Education level of each spouse at the time of the marriage and at the time of the divorce;
5. Each spouse's homemaker services and contributions to the career or career potential of the other spouse;
6. Earning capacity of the spouse seeking alimony, including educational background, training, employment skills, work experience, length of absence from the job market, custodial responsibilities for children, and the time and expense necessary to acquire sufficient education or training to enable her or him to find appropriate employment;
7. The possibility that the spouse seeking alimony can become self-supporting at a standard of living reasonably comparable to that enjoyed during the marriage and, if so, the length of time necessary to achieve that goal;
8. Tax consequences for each spouse;
9. Any agreement reached by the spouses before or during the marriage;
10. The needs of the spouse seeking alimony and the ability of the other spouse to meet his or her own needs and financial obligations while meeting those of the spouse seeking alimony.[92]

As this list of factors suggests, the decision to award alimony is a highly subjective one. Even within a single state, decisions as to whether to award alimony and if so, the amount and the duration of the alimony award, may vary substantially from county to county and from judge to judge.[93] Mandatory numerical guidelines for alimony are rare.[94] Instead, some divorce courts and experienced matrimonial lawyers rely on informal rules of thumb (such as a percentage—25 percent to 40 percent in some cases—of the higher earner's income minus a percentage—such as 50 percent—of the lower earner's income) that are not widely publicized.[95]

Marital fault also continues to play a role in alimony awards in a substantial minority of states. Once a formal bar to alimony in virtually all states, marital fault has been excluded as a factor in over half the states but may still may be considered as a factor in another twenty-four states and the District of Columbia.[96]

What tools are available to help a former spouse collect overdue spousal support payments?

It is a little-known fact that state and local child support enforcement agencies can also enforce spousal support, provided that the ex-spouse who is behind on his or her alimony payments is also behind on child support payments.[97] Wage withholding and state and federal income tax refund intercepts may be used to collect overdue child and spousal support simultaneously.[98] For details on child support enforcement, see chapter 2.

For someone seeking alimony enforcement but not child support enforcement, there are a number of remedies. Once the overdue alimony has been reduced to a money judgment against the former spouse, the person owed the money may obtain a levy on the former spouse's assets, even an IRA account.[99] And a former spouse who is found in contempt of court for failing to pay court-ordered alimony may be punished with a fine and/or imprisonment.[100]

The new Uniform Interstate Family Support Act (UIFSA), which has been enacted in thirty states and the District of Columbia, also provides a number of tools for the col-lection of spousal support where the two former spouses live in different states.[101] If the spousal support order includes a provision authorizing the withholding of alimony payments from an ex-spouse's wages, the recipient spouse can mail the order directly to the obligor's employer to initiate wage withholding.[102] Unless the employee objects, the order will trigger wage withholding without the need to hold an additional hearing.[103] UIFSA also provides that the state that issued the spousal support order has continuing, exclusive jurisdiction to hear any future petitions to modify the order.[104]

Under what circumstances may an award of alimony be modified?

Unlike property awards, which are generally not modifiable, an award of alimony may be modified in many states upon a showing that a change of circumstances has occurred since the entry of the award. Usually, the change must be substantial, ongoing, and unforeseen at the time that the spousal support was initially awarded.

If the income of the person obliged to pay increases substantially and the recipient's needs remain unmet, the court may grant a request by the receiving spouse for an increase in alimony payments.[105] If, on the other hand, the paying spouse's income decreases, courts commonly consider the reason for the decrease and the effect on the recipient before modifying an outstanding alimony award. If the court concludes that the payor voluntarily decreased his income in order to evade his spousal support obligations, courts often refuse to decrease the outstanding alimony award.[106]

The paying spouse's remarriage and the assumption of responsibility for a second family are usually not considered to be a change of circumstances sufficient to warrant terminating or reducing support payments to the recipient spouse.[107] Nonetheless, a few courts have allowed modification where remarriage has imposed an extraordinary burden on the paying spouse.[108]

Does cohabitation after divorce end the recipient's right to receive spousal support?

Eleven states have laws that end or modify alimony based on the recipient spouse's cohabitation.[109] In some states, the mere fact of cohabitation is enough to modify or terminate alimony. In others, cohabitation gives rise to a rebuttable presumption that some sort of benefit has accrued to the recipient spouse, who then bears the burden of proving that cohabitation has produced no change in her or his need for support.

The more common approach is for the court to consider cohabitation as one factor and to look at the duration of the cohabitation, any contributions made by the cohabitant to the support or expenses of the dependent spouse, and any other economic consequences of the cohabitation. If the recipient spouse has experienced no economic gain from the cohabitation, spousal support will usually not be decreased.[110]

On the other hand, if the spouse who owes alimony is living with someone whose salary or assets help reduce his living expenses, a few courts may take that fact into consideration in evaluating his ability to pay alimony.[111]

Does alimony end if the recipient spouse remarries?

The general rule is that alimony ends when the recipient remarries. There are, however, several exceptions. If the spousal support payments are reimbursement alimony, designed to reimburse one ex-spouse for supporting the other while he or she obtained an education or a professional degree, then remarriage is irrelevant and alimony is treated as if it were part of a property settlement and will not terminate upon remarriage.

In addition, the parties are free to agree to continue alimony payments beyond remarriage, and courts will usually enforce those agreements, provided that the parties' intent to continue alimony after remarriage is clearly spelled out in a written agreement.[112]

Finally, a small number of courts have held that since the purpose of alimony is to allow the parties to maintain a standard of living that does not fall drastically below that of the marriage, remarriage of the recipient spouse does not automatically justify terminating alimony payments but may be grounds for reducing them.[113]

RESOURCES

National Center on Women and Family Law
799 Broadway, Room 402
New York, NY 10003
(212) 674-8200

Pension Rights Center
918 16th St., N.W.
Suite 704
Washington, DC 20006
(202) 296-3776

NOTES

1. Lenore J. Weitzman, *Marital Property: Its Transformation and Division in the United States*, in *Economic Consequences of Divorce: The International Perspective* at 85 (1991)(cited hereafter as *Marital Property*). The now classic (and still controversial) study of the economic

impact of divorce is Lenore J. Weitzman's *The Divorce Revolution: The Unexpected Social and Economic Consequences for Women and Children in America* (1985)(cited hereafter as *The Divorce Revolution*).

2. In less than a year, the average couple can earn more money than all their tangible assets are worth. *Marital Property*, *supra* note 1, at 97. *See also The Divorce Revolution*, *supra* note 1, ch. 5.

3. *Marital Property*, *supra* note 1, at 90.

4. *Id.*

5. *See, e.g.*, Ariz. Rev. Stat. Ann. § 25-213 (West 1991); D.C. Code Ann. § 16.910 (Michie 1989); N.Y. Dom. Rel. Law § 236B(1)(d)(Lawyers Coop. 1990); Tex. Fam. Code § 5.01 (West 1993); Va. Code Ann. § 20-107.3 (Michie 1994). For more details, *see* J. Thomas Oldham's comprehensive text on divorce and marital property, *Divorce, Separation and the Distribution of Property*, § 6.02, at 6-3 through 6-13 (1994) (hereinafter cited as *Distribution of Property*).

6. *Distribution of Property*, *supra* note 5, § 6.03, at 6-14 through 6-16.

7. *Id.* § 3.03[2], at 3-7 & n.3.

8. *Id.* § 3.03[4], at 3-11 & n.23.

9. *Id.* § 6.04, at 6-17 through 6-22.

10. *Id.* § 6.06[2], at 6-28 & 6-29.

11. *Id.* at § 11.01[2], at 11-4. *See, e.g.*, *In re Reich*, 208 Ill. App. 3d 301, 566 N.E.2d 826, 152 Ill. Dec. 949 (4th Dist. 1991). *But see Mink v. Mink*, 163 A.D.2d 748, 558 N.Y.S.2d 329 (3d Dep't 1990).

12. *See* Linda Elrod & Timothy Walker, *Family Law in the Fifty States*, 27 Fam. L.Q. 515, 714–16 (Winter 1994)(cited hereafter as *Family Law in the Fifty States*).

13. *See Winer v. Winer*, 241 N.J. Super. 510, 575 A.2d 518, 528 (1990); *Weiss v. Weiss*, 226 N.J. Super. 281, 543 A.2d 1062 (1988), *cert. denied*, 114 N.J. 287, 554 A.2d 844 (1988).

14. *See, e.g.*, *Walters v. Walters*, 812 P.2d 64 (Utah App. 1991); *In re Marriage of Lindsey*, 101 Wash. 2d 299, 678 P.2d 328 (1984).

15. Timothy Walker, *Family Law in the Fifty States: An Overview*, 25 Fam. L.Q. 417, at 445–46 (1992). *See, e.g.*, Cal. Fam. Code § 2550 (West Supp. 1994)(equal division of community property); Ind. Code Ann. § 31-1-11.5-11(c)(West Supp. 1993)(presumes equal division of marital property is just and reasonable); Tex. Fam. Code § 3.63 (equitable division of community estate)(West 1993).

16. R.I. Gen. Laws § 15-5 through 16.1 (Supp. 1993).

17. Timothy Walker & Linda Elrod, *Family Law in the Fifty States: An Overview*, 26 Fam. L.Q. 319, 360–61 (Winter 1993).

18. Linda D. Elrod & Robert G. Spector, *A Review of the Year in Family Law: Children's Issues Take Spotlight*, 29 Fam. L.Q. 741, at 774 (Table 5)(Winter 1996)(cited hereafter as *A Review of the Year in Family Law: 1996*).

19. *Marital Property*, *supra* note 1, at 101–2.

20. *Id.* at 101.

21. Marsha Garrison, *Good Intentions Gone Awry: The Impact of New York's Equitable Distribution Law on Divorce Outcomes*, 57 Brook. L. Rev. 621, at 682 (1991)(hereinafter cited as *Good Intentions Gone Awry*).

22. *Marital Property, supra* note 1, at 102. *See also The Divorce Revolution, supra* note 1, at 79.

23. *Marital Property, supra* note 1, at 102.

24. *Distribution of Property, supra* note 5, § 13.02[1][f], at 13-23 & n.57.

25. *See, e.g.,* Cal. Fam. Code §§ 3800–3810 (West Supp. 1993); Fla. Stat. Ann. § 61.075(1)(h)(West Supp. 1994); Ind. Code Ann. § 31-1-11.5-11(c)(3)(West Supp. 1994); R.I. Gen. Laws § 15-5-16.1.1 (Michie Supp. 1993).

26. *See, e.g.,* Fla. Stat. Ann. §§ 61.075(5)(A)(4) & 61.076 (West Supp. 1994); Mass. Gen. Laws Ann. ch. 208, § 34 (West Supp. 1994) *See generally, Distribution of Property, supra* note 5, § 7.10[4], at 7-48 & 7-49.

27. *See, e.g., In re Marriage of Sedbrook,* 16 Kan. App. 2d 668, 827 P.2d 1222 (1992). *See generally,* Charles C. Marvel, *Pension or Retirement Benefits as Subject to Award or Division by Court in Settlement of Property Rights Between Spouses,* 94 A.L.R. 3d 176 (Supp. 1994).

28. 29 U.S.C. § 1056(d)(3)(West Supp. 1994). For a clear explanation of the effect of a Qualified Domestic Relations Order on different kinds of pension plans and benefits, *see* Pension Rights Center, *Your Pension Rights At Divorce, Private Pensions Legal Packet,* at 5–16 & 23–27 (1994).

29. 29 U.S.C. § 1055(c)(2)(A).

30. 29 U.S.C. § 1056(d)(3)(F)(West Supp. 1994).

31. 10 U.S.C. § 1408(d) & (e)(West Supp. 1994).

32. *King v. King,* 78 Ohio App. 3d 599, 605 N.E.2d 970 (1992); *LeVine v. Spickelmier,* 109 Idaho 341, 707 P.2d 452 (1985).

33. *Forney v. Minard,* 849 P.2d 724 (Wyo. 1993). For a full discussion of these and other legal issues arising out of military retirement and disability pay, *see Distribution of Property, supra* note 5, § 12.03, at 12–13 through 12–25.

34. For a useful overview of this complex area of matrimonial law, *see Distribution of Property, supra* note 5, § 7.10[6], at 7-74 through 7-85 and *Your Pension Rights At Divorce, Private Pensions Legal Packet, supra* note 28. *See also Family Law in the Fifty States, supra* note 12, at 702–6.

35. *See, generally, Distribution of Property, supra* note 5, § 7.10[5], at 7-50.1 through 7-73.

36. *Id.* at 7-52.

37. *Id.* at 7-64 through 7-66. *See, e.g., Petschel v. Petschel,* 406 N.W.2d 604 (Minn. App. 1987).

38. *Good Intentions Gone Awry, supra* note 21, at 683.

39. *Distribution of Property, supra* note 5, § 7.11, at 7-92.5 through 7-97. *See, e.g., In re Marriage of Walker,* 216 Cal. App. 3d 644, 265 Cal. Rptr. 32 (4th Dist. 1989). *Cf. Everett v. Everett,* 195 Mich. App. 50, 489 N.W.2d 111 (1992)(methodology for valuing stock options in property settlement).

40. *See, e.g., Grund v. Grund,* 151 Misc. 2d 852, 573 N.Y.S.2d 840 (N.Y. Sup. 1991); *Schober v. Schober,* 692 P.2d 267 (Alaska 1984). *But see In re Marriage of Battles,* 564 N.E.2d 565 (Ind. App. 1991) (vacation benefits not divisible property).

41. *Distribution of Property, supra* note 5, § 7.12[2], at 7-101 & 7-102. *See, e.g., In re Marriage of Holmes,* 841 P.2d 388 (Colo. App. 1992).

42. *Distribution of Property, supra* note 5, § 7-08[2], at 7-39. *See, e.g., Neal v. Neal,* 776 S.W. 2d 861 (Mo. App. 1989).

43. *See generally, In re Marriage of Spengler,* 5 Cal. App. 4th 288, 6 Cal. Rptr. 2d 764 (3d Dist. 1992); *In re Marriage of Coyle,* 61 Wash. App. 653, 811 P.2d 244, *review denied,* 117 Wash. 2d 1017, 818 P.2d 1099 (1991).

44. *Distribution of Property, supra* note 5, § 7.08[3], at 7-40. *See, e.g., Weekes v. Weekes,* 101 Idaho 213, 611 P.2d 133 (1980).

45. *Ridgway v. Ridgway,* 454 U.S. 46 (1981).

46. *Distribution of Property, supra* note 5, § 12.02[1], at 12-5. *See, e.g., McDaniel v. McDaniel,* 16 Fam. L. Rep. (BNA) 1494, 1990 U.S. App. LEXIS 12826 (4th Cir. July 31, 1990).

47. 66 N.Y.2d 576, 489 N.E.2d 712, 498 N.Y.S.2d 743 (1985).

48. *Id.* at 585, 498 N.Y.S. 2d at 747, 489 N.E.2d at 716.

49. A trial court in Massachusetts held in *Reen v. Reen,* 8 Fam. L. Rep. 2193 (1982), that an orthodontist's license could be treated as a marital asset distributable as property. Higher courts in Iowa and Kentucky have also treated a professional license as property but subsequently decisions by those same courts have appeared to limit the earlier cases to their specific facts. For a full discussion of this issue, *see* Virginia S. Renick, *Spousal Contribution to a Professional Degree Upon Divorce: The State of the Law* in *Valuing Professional Practices and Licenses: A Guide for the Matrimonial Practitioner,* at 27–60 (Ronald L. Brown ed., 1987).

50. *Marital Property, supra* note 1, at 129–32. *See, e.g.,* Cal. Fam. Code § 2641 (West Supp. 1993); La. Civ. Code art. 121 (West 1993).

51. *Distribution of Property, supra* note 5, § 9.02 at 9-3 through 9-29. *See, e.g., Culver v. Culver,* 497 N.W.2d 431 (N.D. App. 1993); *Forristal v. Forristal,* 831 P.2d 1017 (Okla. App. 1992); *Mahoney v. Mahoney,* 91 N.J. 488, 453 A.2d 527 (1982).

52. *See, e.g., Beckett v. Beckett,* 186 Mich. App. 151, 463 N.W.2d 211 (1990).

53. *Distribution of Property, supra* note 5, § 9.02[4], at 9–23. *See, e.g., Sweeney v. Sweeney,* 534 A.2d 1290 (Me. 1987).

54. *See, e.g., Lowery v. Lowery,* 262 Ga. 20, 413 S.E.2d 731 (1992). *See also* N.C. Gen. Stat. § 50-20(b)(2)(Michie 1987).

55. *Distribution of Property, supra* note 5, § 10.01, at 10-2 & 10-3.

56. *See, e.g.,* Colo Rev. Stat. § 14-10-113 (Bradford 1987); 23 Pa. C.S.A. § 3501(a) (West 1991).

57. *Distribution of Property, supra* note 5, § 10.02[3], at 10-9 & n.21. *See, e.g.,* Ariz. Rev. Stat. § 25-213 (West 1991); D.C. Code Ann. § 16-910 (Michie 1989); Minn. Stat. Ann. § 518.54 (West Supp. 1994).

58. *Distribution of Property, supra* note 5, §§ 10.02[3] & 10.02[4], at 10-9 through 10-20.

59. *Good Intentions Gone Awry, supra* note 21, at 683–84 (wives received no share of a family business in 78 percent of the cases where a family business was available for equitable distribution in New York). *See also The Divorce Revolution, supra* note 1, at 97 (businesses awarded to the husband in 80 percent of the cases, offset by interest-bearing notes or other assets of comparable value awarded to the wife).

60. *Unkle v. Unkle*, 305 Md. 587, 505 A.2d 849 (1986). *See also* N.Y. Dom. Rel. Law § 236B(1)(d)(2)(Lawyers Coop. 1990).

61. Cal. Fam. Code § 2603(b)(West Supp. 1994).

62. *Distribution of Property, supra* note 5, § 8.01[1], at 8-6. *See, e.g.*, Tex. Fam. Code § 5.01. *See also Kirk v. Kirk*, 577 A.2d 976 (R.I. 1990).

63. *Distribution of Property, supra* note 5, § 8.01[1], at 8-7 & n. 12.1. *See, e.g., Bandow v. Bandow*, 794 P.2d 1346 (Alaska 1990).

64. *See generally Distribution of Property, supra* note 5, §§ 8.02 & 8.03, at 8-20 through 8-32. *See, e.g., Leisure v. Leisure*, 605 N.E.2d 755 (Ind. 1993); *Schmitz v. Schmitz*, 255 Mont. 159, 841 P.2d 496 (1992).

65. *Mansell v. Mansell*, 490 U.S. 581 (1989); *Wallace v. Fuller*, 832 S.W. 2d 714 (Tex. App. 1992). *See generally Distribution of Property, supra* note 5, § 12.02[4], at 12-8, 12-9 & § 12.03[2], at 12-20 through 12-22, & Note, Mansell v. Mansell: *How It Changed the Definition of Marital Property for the Military Spouse*, 30 J. Fam. L. 97 (1991).

66. *Note, supra* note 65, at 104–5. *See, e.g., In re Marriage of Kraft*, 119 Wash. 2d 438, 832 P.2d 871 (1992); *Lambert v. Lambert*, 10 Va. App. 623, 395 S.E.2d 207 (1990).

67. *Marital Property, supra* note 1, at 115. *See* 42 U.S.C. § 402(b)(West Supp. 1994); 20 C.F.R. § 404.331 (1993) and Pension Rights Center, *supra* note 28, at 3.

68. Pension Rights Center, *supra* note 28, at 3.

69. *See* Harriet Newman Cohen & Ralph Gardner, Jr., *The Divorce Book for Men and Women: A Step-by-Step Guide to Gaining Your Freedom Without Losing Everything Else* 146 (1994) & Pension Rights Center, *supra* note 28, at 3.

70. 42 U.S.C. § 402(b)(West Supp. 1994).

71. 42 U.S.C. § 402(e)–(g)(West Supp. 1994); 20 C.F.R. §§ 404.336 404.340 (1993). *See also* Pension Rights Center, *supra* note 28, at 4–5.

72. Pension Rights Center, *supra* note 28, at 9–14.

73. *Marital Property, supra* note 1, at 135.

74. 29 U.S.C. §§ 1161–1168 (West Supp. 1994).

75. 29 U.S.C. § 1162(2)(A)(iv)(West Supp. 1994).

76. *The Divorce Revolution, supra* note 1, at 145.

77. *Id.* at 150, 390.

78. U.S. Census Bureau, Current Population Reports, Series P-60, No. 173, *Child Support and Alimony: 1989* 12 (1991).

79. *Id.*

80. Pa. Civ. Pro. R. 1910.16-3. *See also* Conn. Gen. Stat. § 46b-37(c)(West Supp. 1994).

81. *Orr v. Orr*, 440 U.S. 268 (1979).

82. 26 U.S.C. §§ 71 & 215 (West 1988). *See generally* Carol H. Lefcourt (ed.), *Women and the Law* § 3B.08 at 3B-32 through 3B-38 (1993)(cited hereafter as *Women and the Law*).

83. *See generally Family Law in the Fifty States, supra* note 12, at 539–43 (Winter 1994) and Fam. L. Rep. (BNA) Ref. File, *State Divorce Statutes* 401:001–453:002 (1991). *See, e.g.*, S.C. Code § 20-3-130(B)(3)(Lawyers Coop 1993). For an interesting variation on the rehabilitative alimony theme, *see In re Marriage of Peterson*, 491 N.W.2d 535 (Iowa App. 1992) (awarding rehabilitative alimony over husband's objections to former wife who was employed full time so that she could pursue a master's degree and increase her earning potential); *In re*

Marriage of Jacobson, 251 Mont. 394, 825 P.2d 561 (1992) (ordering rehabilitative alimony over husband's objections so that former wife could pursue a degree in computer science and accounting).

84. Del. Code Ann. tit. 13, § 1512(d)(Michie 1993).

85. Ind. Code Ann. § 31-1-11.5-11(e)(West Supp. 1994).

86. Kan. Stat. Ann. § 60-1610(b)(2)(Supp. 1993).

87. *Good Intentions Gone Awry, supra* note 21, at 630–31 & n.31.

88. *Id.*, at 633–34 & n.42–43, 720–24 (women and children in their custody emerged from divorce with an average per capita income approximately two-thirds of what it had been prior to divorce while the husband's per capita income rose substantially after divorce). *See generally, The Divorce Revolution, supra* note 1, at 191–92, 337–40 (one year after divorce, men experience a 42 percent improvement in their standard of living while women experience a 73 percent decline) and J.D. Teachman & K.M. Paasch, "Financial Impact of Divorce on Children and Their Families", in *Children and Divorce* 63 *et seq.* (David and Lucile Packard Foundation, Center for the Future of Children 1994). *But see* Felicia R. Lee, "Influential Study on Divorce's Impact Said To Be Flawed," *New York Times*, C6 (May 9, 1996)(new analysis finds that after divorce a woman's standard of living declines by 27 percent, while a man's rises by 10 percent).

89. *Good Intentions Gone Awry, supra* note 21, at 697–98.

90. Joan M. Krauskopf, "Rehabilitative Alimony: Use and Abuses of Limited Duration Alimony," in *Alimony: New Strategies for Pursuit and Defense* 70–74 (American Bar Assoc. 1988)(cited hereafter as *Alimony*). *See Goldman v. Goldman*, 28 Mass. App. 603, 554 N.E.2d 860 (1990); *Walter v. Walter*, 464 So. 2d 538 (Fla. 1985).

91. *See, e.g.*, Minn. Stat. Ann. § 518.552(3)(West 1990); N.H. Rev. Stat. Ann. § 458.19; N.Y. Dom Rel. Law § 236[B](6)(c)(Lawyers Coop. 1990). *See also In re Vendredi*, 230 Ill. App. 3d 1061, 598 N.E.2d 961, 174 Ill. Dec. 329 (1st Dist. 1992) (awarding permanent alimony after dissolution of twenty-eight-year marriage); *Leitsch v. Leitsch*, 839 S.W.2d 287 (Ky. App. 1992)(awarding permanent alimony to disabled husband).

92. Doris J. Freed & Timothy B. Walker, *Family Law in the Fifty States: An Overview*, 21 Fam. L.Q. 417 at 474 (Winter 1988).

93. *Good Intentions Gone Awry, supra* note 21, at 709–10.

94. Robert G. Williams, "Should There Be Child Support and Alimony Guidelines?" in *Alimony, supra* note 90, at 172. *See also Women and the Law, supra* note 82, § 3B.05[2][a], at 3B-26, n. 119 (citing alimony guidelines in several counties in Santa Clara and Los Angeles counties in California and Maricopa County, Arizona); and *In re Marriage of Burlini*, 143 Cal. App. 3d 65, 191 Cal. Rptr. 541 (1st Dist. 1983).

95. George Norton, "The Future of Alimony: A Proposal for Guidelines," in *Alimony, supra* note 90, at 177 & n. 3.

96. *A Review of the Year in Family Law: 1996*, note 18, 29 Fam. L.Q. at 770 (Table 1). *See, e.g., Hammonds v. Hammonds*, 597 So. 2d 653 (Miss. 1992), *appeal after remand* 1994 Miss. LEXIS 385 (Miss. 1994); *Smith v. Smith*, 847 P.2d 827 (Okla. App. 1993).

97. *Women and the Law*, § 3B.07, at 3B-31, 3B-32. *See also* Diane Dodson, *The Relationship Between Child Support and Alimony* 4 J. Am. Acad. Matr. Lawyers 25, at 54–56 (1988).

98. *See* 42 U.S.C. §§ 651–666, especially § 654(4)(B) & (6)(B)(West Supp. 1994).

99. *See Mallory v. Mallory,* 179 N.J. Super. 556, 432 A.2d 950 (1981); *Martini v. Martini,* 20 Fam. L. Rep. (BNA) 1017 (N.Y. Sup. 1993).

100. *See, e.g., Dozier v. Dozier,* 252 Kan. 1035, 850 P.2d 789 (1993).

101. For a further discussion of the UIFSA, see chapter 2.

102. Uniform Interstate Family Support Act, § 501.

103. *Id.*

104. *Id.,* §§ 205 & 206.

105. *See, e.g., Foxley v. Foxley,* 801 P.2d 155 (Utah App. 1990).

106. *Deegan v. Deegan,* 254 N.J. Super. 350, 603 A.2d 542, 546 (1992); *In re Marriage of Van Doren,* 474 N.W.2d 583 (Iowa App. 1991). *But see In re Marriage of Meegan,* 11 Cal. App. 4th 156, 13 Cal. Rptr. 2d 799 (4th Dist. 1992)(husband who left well-paying job to enter a monastery and become a priest was entitled to a reduction in spousal support to zero).

107. *Wei v. Wei,* 248 N.J. Super. 572, 591 A.2d 982 (1991); *In re Marriage of Coyle, supra* note 43.

108. *Hanson v. Hanson,* 47 Wash. 2d 439, 287 P.2d 879 (1955). *See generally* Melvyn Frumkes, *The Impact of Remarriage on Alimony,* in *Alimony, supra* note 90, at 111.

109. *Family Law in the Fifty States, supra* note 15, 25 Fam. L.Q. at 462–63.

110. James B. Boskey, *Postmarital Cohabitation,* in *Alimony, supra* note 90, at 116 (1988). *See, e.g., McVay v. McVay,* 189 W. Va. 197, 429 S.E.2d 239 (1993)(reduction in alimony to $1 not warranted where cohabitation did not change former wife's financial condition); *Haag v. Haag,* 609 A.2d 1164 (Maine 1992).

111. *In re Marriage of Tapia,* 211 Cal. App. 3d 628, 259 Cal. Rptr. 459 (2d Dist. 1989).

112. Frumkes, *supra* note 108, at 110.

113. *In re Marriage of Smith,* 103 Or. App. 614, 798 P.2d 717 (1990). *See also In re Marriage of Gilliland,* 487 N.W.2d 363 (Iowa App. 1992)(rehabilitative alimony that is designed to make wife self-supporting does not automatically end upon remarriage).

PART 2

Protecting Children from Harm

IV

Constitutional Rights of Families

Do families have constitutional rights?

Yes. Even though the United States Constitution makes no mention whatsoever of either parents or families, the legal rights of parents to bear children, raise their offspring, and guide them according to their own beliefs have nonetheless been held to be protected by the Constitution. Correlatively, children have the right to be raised by their parents free from unjustified interference by state officials. These rights in combination are often called the *right of family integrity* and are regarded as part of the highest law of the land.

Since most children are too young to make binding decisions for themselves, an adult is usually required to make most important decisions on behalf of a child. Much of the law concerning family rights therefore involves determining who should have the authority to decide how to raise a child. As we shall see, American law has traditionally answered that question in favor of the child's biological parents. For this reason, much of the language regarding family rights is discussed in terms of parental rights. However, the term *parental rights* encompasses a far broader idea than merely the power of a parent over his or her child. Rather, the term is a substitute for the basic notion that childrearing and family life are primarily private matters of intimate association of family members.

In our system of government, the Supreme Court has the responsibility of deciding ultimately what the Constitution means and how its succinct statements of fundamental law are to be applied to ever-changing situations. For this reason, the meaning of the Constitution is subject to change because the members of the Court change over the years and because ideas or policies considered acceptable in one era (for instance, school segregation) are unacceptable in another time.

But one notion—the primacy of parental rights—has remained fairly constant since the Court first considered the issue more than seventy years ago. What this means is that the state's power to regulate the lawful prerogatives of parents over their children or to intrude into the realm of family life is severely limited by the Constitution.

In 1923, for example, the Supreme Court struck down a Nebraska law that prohibited the teaching of a foreign language in state-run schools because "the right of parents . . . to instruct their children" is protected by the due process clause of the Fourteenth Amendment to the Constitution.[1] In a 1944 opinion the Court wrote, "It is cardinal with us that the custody, care and nurture of the child reside first in the parents, whose primary function and freedom include preparation for obligations the state can neither supply nor hinder."[2] In 1972 the Court reaffirmed this notion by stating: "The history and culture of Western civilization reflect a strong tradition of parental concern for the nurture and upbringing of their children. This primary role of the parents in the upbringing of their children is now established beyond debate as an enduring American tradition."[3]

How important are family rights considered to be in the American legal system?

They are held in very high esteem. It might even be said that they command the highest respect of all personal rights protected by the Constitution. The Supreme Court has determined that the right of family integrity exists, despite no specific reference to it in the Constitution, among the penumbra of other rights protected by the Constitution.

Generally, the Bill of Rights protects a person's right to property and liberty. On several occasions, the Supreme Court has made clear that family rights are especially protected rights, superior even to other rights recognized by the Constitution. To cite only two of many illustrations, in 1953 the Supreme Court said that the custody rights of parents are "far more precious . . . than property rights,"[4] and in 1972 the Court stated, "It is plain that the interest of a parent in the companionship, care, custody, and management of his or her children 'come[s] to this Court with a momentum for respect lacking when appeal is made to liberties which derive merely from shifting economic arrangements.' "[5]

An essential element of the growth of the right of privacy has been the right of family privacy. In fact, the right of privacy was first secured in a 1965 case involving the marital relationship. In that case, the issue before the Supreme Court was the power of the state to prohibit the sale of birth-control devices. The Court declared unconstitutional a Connecticut law that banned their distribution. The Court held that a state may not interfere with marital privacy by prohibiting couples from using contraceptives. In a concurring opinion, Justice Goldberg wrote:

> Certainly the safeguarding of the home does not follow merely from the sanctity of property rights. The home derives its preeminence as the seat of family life. And the integrity of that life is something so fundamental that it has been found to draw to its protection the principles of more than one explicitly granted Constitutional right. . . . The entire fabric of the Constitution and the purposes that clearly underlie its specific guarantees demonstrate that the rights to marital privacy and to marry and raise a family are of similar order and magnitude as the fundamental rights specifically protected.[6]

Are these rights limited to parents?

No. As already stated, the Constitution does not mention the word *parent*. The Constitution protects privacy rights of all individuals. In an ever-changing society, our concepts of privacy and individual rights constantly evolve. Any individual is able to assert a privacy right against government encroachment.

Nonetheless, parents have rights to raise children and to make decisions about their upbringing that are superior to those of other adults who have cared for them. Although adults who act like parents, including extended family members and other significant adults in children's lives, have many rights recognized by the Constitution—at least when these adults are not competing against biological parents for the right to raise children—their rights are less firmly rooted in law and are more difficult to enforce.

What is a "family" within the meaning of the law?

The definition is growing all the time as society's cultural norms and practices change. However, law is commonly slow to react to social change. As a result, most of the important Supreme Court cases establishing the rights of families mentioned in this chapter involved biological families. The paramount conflict raised by those cases was a clash between state authority and parental authority over raising children. In each of those cases, the biological family was intact.

Today, there are a great number of people living in family relationships of all sizes and shapes. In addition to the biological, nuclear family, there are extended families, adoptive families, gay and lesbian families, stepfamilies, and foster families, among others. Many of these relationships are formed without any state involvement. Gradually, a number of these family relationships have obtained legal recognition, even resulting in constititutional protection. For example, extended families have been accorded constitituonal protection by the Supreme Court.[7] In addition, stepparents have been awarded custody and visitation with stepchildren over the objection of biological parents when courts have found that to be in children's best interests.[8] Several state courts have recognized gay and lesbian relationships as the equivalent to state-sanctioned marriages, at least for limited purposes such as being able to keep a lease after a domestic partner has died.[9]

Other family relationships are formed as a direct result of governmental involvement, such as foster families. Courts have been less willing to give these families the same rights as biological families. Sometimes, the effort to reunite children with biological parents (who may have harmed them or neglected them in the past and with whom they may no longer have any emotional bond) has resulted in breaking up a foster family that has formed strong emotional ties.[10] There is a growing interest among legal scholars and some courts in preserving and protecting a child's interest in the continuity of his or her ties to the people who have actually parented the child, as opposed to the child's ties to the persons who are his or her parents in name only.[11]

What are the practical effects of the rights of parents and the rights of family integrity?

They are much more than mere platitudes. They have meaning and value in almost every circumstance when the power of the government to "reach" into family life is called into question. The rights of parents and the rights of family integrity, in short, serve as a Constitutional barrier to protect family members from unreasonable or unnecessary intrusion by the state into family life.

For example, in the early 1970s, the city of East Cleveland, Ohio, enacted an ordinance that made it illegal for a house to contain residents who were not members of a single family. The city defined "family" in narrow terms that excluded cousins beyond a certain degree of relationship. Under this law, a woman was convicted of a crime because she lived with her son and two grandchildren who were cousins and had come to live with her after both of their mothers' deaths. The Supreme Court overturned the woman's conviction and declared East Cleveland's ordinance unconstitutional because it unreasonably invaded family life. The woman had a right to live with her grandchildren, the Court ruled, and the city had no power to interfere with that right.[12] "This Court has long recognized," the Court stated, "that freedom of personal choice in matters of marriage and family life is one of the liberties protected by the Due Process Clause of the Fourteenth Amendment."[13] Referring to a number of the same cases mentioned above, the Court added: "A host of cases . . . have consistently acknowledged a 'private realm of family life which the state cannot enter.' "[14] The Court concluded:

> Our decisions establish that the Constitution protects the sanctity of the family precisely because the institution of the family is deeply rooted in this Nation's history and tradition. It is through the family that we inculcate and pass down many of our most cherished values, moral and cultural. Ours is by no means a tradition limited to respect for the bonds uniting the members of the nuclear family. The tradition of uncles, aunts, cousins, and especially grandparents sharing a household along with parents and children has roots equally venerable and equally deserving of constitutional recognition. . . . [T]he Constitution prevents East Cleveland from standardizing its children and its adults by forcing all to live in certain narrowly defined family patterns.[15]

Do children have a constitutional right to the preservation of their emotional ties to the adults who have loved and care for them but who are not their biological parents?

The Supreme Court has recently declined to consider a number of cases in which this very issue was raised.[16] For now, the law usually presumes that children are best off being raised by their biological parents, all other things being equal. In many cases, however, children have lived with their biological parents for an insignificant amount of time or not at all when a custody dispute arises between the biological parents and the custodial parents. This question asks whether children who have lived with custodial parents for a long time have a constitutional right to remain with them when their biological parents are seeking custody.

These cases commonly arise in three different settings: (1) a dispute between preadoptive parents and the biological parents who do not consent to the adoption; (2) a dispute between foster parents and biological parents who were once unable to care for their children but presently are deemed by the state child welfare agency to be fit and able to do so; (3) a dispute between long-term caretakers and biological parents who for some reason asked the caretakers to raise the children and now want the children back. In the first two disputes, the law favors the biological parents and, upon a showing that the parents did not abandon their children, did not give proper consent to their adoption, and are currently fit and able to care for them, the biological parents often will win custody over the preadoptive or foster parents.[17] There is a growing number of scholars and advocates for children who criticize favoring the biological parent and who want to see cases decided strictly on the needs and best interests of the child.[18] In the third category of dispute—between long-term caretakers and biological parents— a weaker form of favoritism towards the biological parents exists. In these cases, the particular needs and interests of the children are taken into account more prominently. Courts often will award custody to the long-term caretakers even when they have found the biological parents to be fit and able to have custody because the bonding between the long-term caretakers and the children has become too firm to disrupt.[19]

NOTES

1. *Meyer v. Nebraska,* 262 U.S. 390, 400 (1923).

2. *Prince v. Massachusetts,* 321 U.S. 158, 166 (1944).

3. *Wisconsin v. Yoder,* 406 U.S. 205, 232 (1972).

4. *May v. Anderson,* 345 U.S. 528, 533 (1953).

5. *Stanley v. Illinois,* 405 U.S. 645, 651 (1972)(quoting *Kovacs v. Cooper,* 336 U.S. 77, 95 (1949) (Frankfurter, J. concurring)).

6. *Griswold v. Connecticut,* 381 U.S. 479, 495 (1965) (quoting *Poe v. Ullman,* 367 U.S. 497, 551–52 (1961) (Harlan, J. dissenting)).

7. *Moore v. City of East Cleveland,* 431 U.S. 494 (1977).

8. *See, e.g., Paquette v. Paquette,* 146 Vt. 83, 499 A.2d 23 (1985).

9. *Braschi v. Stahl Associates Company,* 74 N.Y.2d 201, 543 N.E.2d 49, 544 N.Y.S.2d 784 (1989).

10. *Procopio v. Johnson,* 994 F.2d 325 (7th Cir. 1993).

11. *See, e.g., In re Juvenile Severance Action No. S-114487,* 876 P.2d 1121 (Ariz. 1994); *In re Adoption/Guardianship No. A91-71A,* 334 Md. 538, 640 A.2d 1085 (1994); *In re Baby Boy C.,* 630 A.2d 670 (D.C. App. 1993), *cert. denied sub nom. H.R. v. E.O.,* 1994 U.S. LEXIS 5440 (1994). *See also* Suellyn Scarnecchia, *Who Is Jessica's Mother? Defining Motherhood Through Reality,* 3 Am. U.J. Gender & Law 1 (Fall 1994); Gilbert A. Holmes, *The Tie That Binds: The Constitutional Rights of Children to Maintain Relationships with Parent-like Individuals,* 53 Maryland L. Rev. 358 (1994).

12. *Moore v. City of East Cleveland, supra* note 7.

13. *Id.* at 499.

14. *Id.* (quoting Prince, *supra* note 2, at 166).

15. *Id.* at 503–4, 506.

16. *See, e.g., In re Doe*, 159 Ill. 2d 347, 638 N.E.2d 181, *cert. denied sub nom. Baby Richard v. Kirchner*, 63 U.S.L.W. 3366 (1994); *In re Clausen*, 442 Mich. 648, 502 N.W.2d 649 *stay denied sub nom. DeBoer v. Schmidt*, 114 S. Ct. 1, 14 (1993). *See generally*, Brief of Concerned Academics as Amici Curiae in Support of Application for Stay Filed on Behalf of Petitioner Jessica DeBoer in *DeBoer v. Schmidt*, No. A-64 (U.S. Supreme Court)(July 21, 1993).

17. For an example of the first line of cases, *see In the Interest of B.G.C.*, 496 N.W.2d 239 (Iowa 1992) (the "Baby Jessica" case); *In re Clausen, supra* note 16; *but see, e.g., In the Matter of Robert O.*, 80 N.Y.2d 254, 604 N.E.2d 99, 590 N.Y.S.2d 37 (1992). For an example of the second line of cases, *see Matter of Michael B.*, 80 N.Y.2d 299, 604 N.E.2d 122, 590 N.Y.S.2d 60 (1992). For an example of the third line of cases, *see Bennett v. Jeffries*, 40 N.Y.2d 543, 356 N.E.2d 277, 387 N.Y.S.2d 821 (1976).

18. *See e.g.*, Holmes, *supra* note 11; Barbara Bennett Woodhouse, *Hatching the Egg: A Child-Centered Perspective on Parents' Rights*, 14 Cardozo L. Rev. 1747 (1993); George Russ, *Through the Eyes of a Child, "Gregory K.": A Child's Right to be Heard*, 27 Fam. L.Q. 365 (1993); Barbara Bennett Woodhouse, *"Who Owns the Child?", Meyer and Pierce and the Child as Property*, 33 Wm. & Mary L. Rev. 995 at 1116–17 (1992); Charles Gill, *Essay on the Status of the American Child, 2000 A.D.: Chattel or Constitutionally Protected Child-Citizen*, 17 Ohio N.U.L. Rev. 543 (1991).

19. *Cf.* Carol A. Crocca, *Continuity of Residence As Factor in Contest Between Parent and Nonparent for Custody of Child Who Has Been Residing with Nonparent: Modern Status*, 15 A.L.R. 5th 692 (1993).

V

Child Abuse and Neglect

What are child protection laws? What is their principal purpose?

Child protection laws are the combination of child abuse and child neglect laws. These are defined in the following questions. The principal purpose of these laws is to protect children from future harm. This contrasts with the criminal law, the purpose of which is to punish wrongdoers for their past behavior.

A parent's past behavior is relevant in child protection only to the extent that it reflects on a parent's capacity to raise children adequately in the future. When courts declare a child to be in need of protection (that is, to have been abused or neglected), they are making a statement about the future likelihood of harm to the child. In criminal law, the court is concerned with determining guilt or innocence so that it may mete out the proper punishment to the guilty. In the child protection area, if the court is satisfied that a child is not at future risk of harm, the court will dismiss the case even if it finds that the parent has harmed the child in the past.

This important distinction between child protection and criminal law impacts on many procedural aspects of child protection proceedings. Because the purpose of child protection is nonpunitive, many of the constitutional rights of accused criminals are unavailable to parents in child protection cases. In addition, among some of the many differences between criminal and child protection proceedings, the laws defining child neglect are far more vague and broadly written than would be tolerated in criminal statutes; the quality of the evidence that may be relied upon to prove allegations of neglect is lower than permitted in criminal prosecutions; the amount of evidence needed to prove a case of neglect is less than would be necessary to convict in a criminal proceeding; and the standard of proof needed to adjudicate a parent unfit is lower than in criminal cases.

What is child abuse?

No two states have laws that define child abuse in exactly the same terms, but there are common aspects among all of them. Virtually every state law considers the infliction of serious physical injury or sexual abuse upon a child by a parent or custodian to be child abuse. Many state child abuse laws are defined broadly and permit child protection agencies to charge abuse when a parent creates a risk of serious physical injury or inflicts psychological abuse. Still others consider the infliction of any injury to be abusive, whether it is "serious" or not.

A typical definition of child abuse is found in the California law.

"[C]hild abuse" means a physical injury which is inflicted by other than accidental means on a child by another person. "Child abuse" also means the sexual abuse of a child or any act or omission . . . [of] (willful cruelty or unjustifiable punishment of a child) or . . . (unlawful corporal punishment or injury). "Child abuse" also means the neglect of a child or abuse in out-of-home care, as defined in this article.[1]

Can parents be found guilty of civil child abuse even if there is no direct evidence that their child's injuries were inflicted by them?

Yes. Many, perhaps most, acts of child abuse occur in the home with no witnesses other than the parents and the children themselves. Thus, most cases of child abuse hinge on circumstantial evidence, or evidence that proves guilt only by inference. To make it easier to protect children who have unexplained injuries, most states shift the burden to the parent to explain the child's injuries to the court's satisfaction. If the parent is unable to explain how a child was injured innocently in circumstances where it is reasonable to expect the parent to know the answer, in many states the court is permitted to conclude that the parent caused the injuries. Thus, if a child were injured at home when the parents were there and medical evidence indicates that the injury was not accidental, the parents will probably be found guilty of child abuse unless they are able to tell the judge how the child was injured (and the explanation also shows that the parents conduct did not fall below the minimum standard of care.)[2]

Can parents be found to have abused their children, even when the state does not claim the parents inflicted the injuries themselves?

Yes. It is sufficient to prove that parents have placed their children at serious risk to be found guilty of child abuse. If parents have permitted their children to be harmed or failed to take reasonable steps to avoid their harm, parents may be found guilty of abuse even when it is undisputed that the parent did not inflict the harm directly.[3] However, parents are not strictly liable for the injuries inflicted on their children. It is necessary to prove that the parents *deliberately* or at least *negligently* placed their children at risk before the parents will be found to have fallen below a minimum standard of care. Parents who have not themselves inflicted injuries on their children and who are accused of abuse will be able to successfully defend the charges if they can satisfy the court that they acted as reasonable parents would have acted in similiar circumstances. For example, if it is undisputed that a child was injured by a babysitter, the parents are guilty of the abuse only if they knew or had reason to know that it was dangerous to leave their child alone with the babysitter. However, if the parents did everything a reasonable parent could have done to avoid endangering their child, then the charges will not be sustained.

What is child neglect?

Neglect ordinarily refers to a lapse of care on the part of a parent, often involving some degree of willfulness. Generally, it covers situations in which parents do not do something that should be done, thereby placing the health and safety of their children in danger. Statutes may be quite detailed, enumerating specifics such as moral unfitness of a parent, mental or physical incapacity of a parent, and failure to send the child to school; or they may be couched entirely in broad phrases, such as lack of proper parental care, control, or guardianship. Even statutes that set out numerous specific grounds of neglect usually include a catch-all phrase to cover other situations.

Most states consider the failure of parents to supply their children with adequate food, shelter, clothing, and medical care to be child neglect. Leaving a child without adequate supervision for a certain length of time and abandonment are also considered acts of neglect in most states. Thus, if a child suffers from malnutrition because his or her parents do not feed him or her, or if the child does not get proper medical attention for a wound or injury (regardless of how it was caused) because the parents failed to take the child to a doctor, the parents may be charged with child neglect. Similarly, if parents leave their small children unattended overnight or longer and make no provisions for someone else to care for them, they may be accused of neglecting their children.

Many states include other categories of parental behavior as child neglect. In a number of states, the failure to ensure that one's child is receiving an education is considered neglect, as is a parent's "moral unfitness," use of drugs, or excessive use of alcohol. A parent's conviction of a serious crime may also be deemed neglect in some states. In Nebraska, leaving a child six years of age or younger in a motor vehicle unattended constitutes neglect.[4]

As stated at the beginning of this answer, child neglect is never defined as precisely as abuse. For example, some states define neglect as failure to provide a child with "proper" parental care or commission of an act that endangers a child's "morals." Naturally, these terms can mean a great number of things and they can sometimes result in arbitrary and irrational enforcement. Not surprisingly, some courts have relied upon these wide-ranging terms to find parents neglectful when they have exhibited only unusual behavior or actions with which a social agency or judge disagrees, without proof of actual harm or even impact on the "neglected" children. The constitutionality of laws containing vague definitions will be discussed below in this chapter.

Is the distinction between child abuse and child neglect a clear one?

Not always. The difference between abuse and neglect is often hazy. Some states make no legal distinction between the two and call them both "child maltreatment" or "child dependency." Sometimes, the distinction depends on the degree or severity of harm inflicted on the child. In many states, there is little difference between abuse and neglect in terms of the power of the court to remove children from the parents' home. However, in a number of states, courts may terminate parental rights sooner if there is a finding of abuse rather than neglect.[5]

Can children be removed from their parents without a showing of abuse or neglect merely because a court or agency concludes that removal is in the child's best interests?

No. The *best interests of the child standard* is a concept borrowed from divorce litigation. In that context, the best interests of a child are ascertained by weighing the positive and negative aspects of life with one parent against the positive and negative aspects of life with the other parent. Acting as arbiter between the two separating parents, a judge decides which one can provide the best environment for the child. The "best-interests" determination is justified because of the underlying assumption that both parents begin with an equal right to the child and that the balance is appropriately tipped to one side or the other by parsing the child's interests.

Abuse and neglect cases arise in a totally different setting. The state is not obliged to serve as arbiter between two parties, only one of whom can keep the child. Rather, the state is the moving party, the prosecutor, which is seeking to take the child away from his or her parent(s). The state and the parent do not begin with equal rights to the child.[6] To the contrary, if the parent "is a fit [parent]," the state has no legitimate interest at all in "needlessly separat[ing] him from his family."[7] Thus, although the best interests of the child standard is appropriate in a custody dispute between parents, courts have held that it is inappropriate when the state proposes to interfere with the relationship between the child and his or her own parents. As the Supreme Court has said, the due process clause would be offended "[i]f a State were to attempt to force the breakup of a natural family, over the objections of the parents and their children, without some showing of unfitness and for the sole reason that to do so was thought to be in the children's best interest."[8]

Up to what age of the child are parents liable for their abuse and neglect?

In the vast majority of states, the age to which children may be found neglected or abused is eighteen. In the other states the cutoff ranges from sixteen to twenty-one.

Can evidence of maltreatment of one child result in a finding of neglect or abuse of other children in the family, even if they were not specifically maltreated?

Yes. Evidence of parental neglect or abuse of one child may result in the automatic finding of abuse or neglect of other children in the same household even without any evidence of actual maltreatment of the other children.[9] The theory behind this rule is that evidence of abuse or neglect of one child may indicate that other children in the same family are in extreme danger of harm and that it is not necessary for parents to harm each child before a court will protect all of the children.

Does one have to be a parent to be charged with child abuse or neglect?

No. Most laws hold parents and persons acting in the role of a parent responsible for the abuse or neglect of children under their care. For example, New York's law extends responsibility to a parent "or other person legally responsible for a child's care,"[10] and in Maryland, the law encompasses any parent "or other person who has permanent or temporary care or custody or responsibility for supervision of a child."[11]

Even in states where statutes refer only to "parents," courts have construed this as a reference to any person having the care and control of a child.[12] This means that stepparents or a parent's boyfriend or girlfriend, or uncles and aunts who regularly care for their nieces and nephews, or even a babysitter or day-care worker may be liable for abusing or neglecting a child in his or her care.

Are child abuse and neglect crimes?

Intentionally caused injury to anyone is a crime, including injury to children. Child abuse, if it involves physical injury, is usually a criminal offense. Sexual abuse of one's own child is also a crime, whether or not it causes physical injury. Child neglect may or may not be a crime, depending on what type of behavior is considered. Since neglect encompasses a large scope of activity (and failure to act), some acts would constitute criminal conduct while others, especially those involving nonintentional inadequacies of parenting, might not.

This does not mean, however, that whenever an act of abuse could be prosecuted as a crime, it will be. Many factors go into the decision whether or not to treat child abuse as a crime. The most significant factor is the degree of harm suffered by the child. For example, when the abuse results in death, serious injury, disfigurement, or sexual molestation, criminal prosecutors commonly will exercise their discretion to prosecute. A second prominent factor is the relationship of the abuser to the child. Although the criminal law makes no distinction between parents and nonparents in determining whether an act of abuse is or is not a crime, when the person responsible for the abuse is the parent, prosecutors are more likely not to bring a criminal case and permit the case to be handled as a civil matter, in juvenile or family court. Because the purpose of child protection laws is to provide help and assistance to children and their parents rather than imprisoning the parents, parents are often not prosecuted in both the criminal and juvenile courts. Instead, these cases are prosecuted by welfare department lawyers in civil courts, not by district attorneys in criminal courts. When the abuser is someone other than a parent, however, there may be no purpose in handling the case in juvenile court, since the goal of preserving or restoring the family may not be applicable. In these cases, as when the abuser is a day-care worker or babysitter, commonly they are prosecuted as criminal matters or not at all.

How is abandonment defined?

Most state laws include abandonment as a condition of child neglect, but it is rarely defined. Most statutes simply state that children are deemed neglected if they are "abandoned" by their parents, guardians, or custodians. A few statutes are more specific. For example, in Arizona, abandonment is defined as "failure of the parent to provide reasonable support and to maintain regular contact with the child, including the providing of normal supervision, when such failure is accompanied by an intention on the part of the parent to permit such condition to continue for an indefinite period in the future. Failure to maintain a normal parental relationship with the child without just cause for a period of six months shall constitute prima facie evidence of abandonment."[13]

In all states, courts will decide whether the specific facts of each case constitute abandonment or not.

Can parents be charged with neglect for leaving their child with a friend for a short period of time?

Probably not, if the person with whom the child is left is responsible and able to meet the needs of the child.[14]

Obviously, leaving a child with a babysitter for an evening is not abandonment, provided the sitter is of suitable age and discretion. But if the child suffered some injury due to the babysitter's own unfitness, and the parents knew or should have known that the sitter was inadequate or had previously mistreated children, then the parents might be deemed neglectful.

In addition, the longer the amount of time parents leave their children with someone to care for them, the higher the responsibility courts will impose on the parents should something bad happen to the children. For example, if parents leave their child with a caretaker for a period of months, and the caretaker is not licensed as a foster parent, the parents will likely be held to a fairly strict standard of knowledge about the caretaker's ability to handle children.

The question of abandonment and leaving a child in the care of another person might best be answered by describing the facts of a particular case. In this case, child protection officials claimed that a child was neglected because she was living with her grandaunt, rather than with her parents. The child's mother was serving time in prison for armed robbery and the father worked full time. The juvenile court agreed with the protection officials and ruled that the child was "uncared-for." On appeal, however, the decision was reversed and the higher court ruled that the child was neither uncared-for nor abandoned. The court said that any other outcome would result in the "undesirable consequence of discouraging biological parents from even temporarily entrusting their children to someone who could give them better care."[15]

Do parents have the right to corporally punish their children?

Yes, as long as the punishment inflicted is reasonable and does not injure or harm the child. Thus, while parents have a right to spank their children, they may not do so in an excessive or abusive manner.[16]

Where is the line drawn between "reasonable" or "permissible" discipline and "excessive" or "abusive" punishment?

This is a difficult question to answer, since every case is determined by its own facts. Ultimately, it is up to a judge or a jury to decide if harsh discipline constitutes unreasonable or excessive force.

Historically, parents in the United States have had a great deal of latitude in punishing their children. The first known laws enacted by the colonists in 1654 permitted—in fact, required—corporal punishment of children who behaved "disrespectfully, disobediently, and disorderly."[17] Whipping was considered appropriate at that time.

Today, parents have considerably less authority over their children, at least with regard to the degree of force used upon them. This is largely attributable to the relatively recent societal recognition that children have rights independent of their parents and that the state must stand ready to protect children from harm inflicted upon them by parents. Thus, when a child's health or welfare is endangered or harmed, the state has the power to intervene in the otherwise private realm of family life and come to the aid of the child.

Corporal punishment and other forms of discipline are permitted, in the words of one court, as long it is "moderate [and] reasonable," in light of the age and condition of the child and other surrounding circumstances.[18] On the other hand, if punishment is inflicted with a "malicious desire to cause pain" or if it causes injury to the child, it will be deemed unreasonable, and the parent may be subject to penal or civil sanctions imposed by law.[19]

The age of the child is often a factor in determining reasonableness. For example, a spanking of moderate force might be reasonable if inflicted upon a four-year-old as punishment for running into a busy street. But a spanking with similar force upon a mere infant for any reason might be considered abusive—and therefore illegal—since an infant's threshold for injury is very low. Similarly, the nature of the penalty of the child may determine whether or not a particular punishment is reasonable. It might be reasonable to forbid a twelve-year-old to be out of the home past 7:00 P.M., but it would be unreasonable—and probably considered abusive—to lock the child in a closet to make sure he or she stays home.

The law considers parents sufficiently capable to distinguish between ordinary discipline and abuse. As stated by a Maryland court,

> Parents of ordinary intelligence are made aware that they do not subject themselves to the [child abuse] statute[s] by merely engaging in corporal discipline for the purpose of punishment or correction. Only when the line is crossed and physical injury is intentionally and maliciously or cruelly inflicted does criminal responsibility attach.[20]

Similarly, a New York court ruled that since there is no precise standard for the use of corporal punishment, courts must look at all circumstances of the case to see if parents exceeded the "balance of moderation" and were "cruel and merciless."[21] In the case it was deciding, the court found the father's conduct was "unreasonable, excessive and dangerous" to the child's physical, mental, and emotional well-being because he had beaten his thirteen-year-old daughter with a wooden shingle, leaving severe bruises on her buttocks and arms.

Therefore, if parental demands become unreasonable or parental discipline becomes abusive, the law imposes a limit on the rights of parents, and it will not hesitate—through its authorized agencies such as child-welfare departments or, when necessary, the court—to intervene in the otherwise protected area of the family for the purpose of protecting a child. When such intervention occurs, the law may require the parents to obtain some type of help for their problem, it may remove children from their custody (temporarily or, depending on the level of abuse, permanently), or it may hold the parent responsible for the commission of a crime.[22]

Can parents be charged with neglect for failure to provide adequate medical care for their children?

Yes. This can come about in a number of ways.

First, parents can be found neglectful for not providing or seeking proper medical care when their children need treatment for illness, injury, or serious physical disorder. Second, they can be charged with neglect for removing a child from a doctor's care or from a hospital before necessary treatment is completed. Third, if parents have been told by doctors or other health professionals that an operation or particular medical treatment is necessary, they might be found neglectful for refusing such treatment.

The most common case of parents refusing to consent to medical treatment occurs when religious beliefs conflict with the proposed treatment. Traditionally, courts have overridden a parent's religious objections only when the treatment was necessary to save the child from extreme physical harm or death. Parental refusal to consent to a blood transfusion that is required to save a child's life is commonly held to warrant intervention even though the refusal is based on sincere religious beliefs.[23] However, when the medical treatment is not necessary to save a child's life, courts are less willing to require the procedure over the parent's objection. In one case, for example, a neglect charge was brought against a parent who refused to permit plastic surgery to correct a child's massive harelip and cleft palate. In that case, the court found that the parent's and child's objections to the proposed surgery outweighed the potential benefits of the operation.[24]

However, it is not unusual today for courts to authorize medical care over parental objection even when treatment is not required to to save the child's life. In an Iowa case, for example,[25] the supreme court of that state approved the surgical removal of the tonsils and adenoids of children over the religious objections of the parents. It conceded that this medical procedure was not required to save the lives of the children but concluded, "Our paramount concern for the best interests and welfare of the children overrides the father's contention that absolute medical certitude of necessity and success should precede surgery."[26] A New York court went even further, ordering an operation that was not necessary to save the child's life and that exposed the child to substantial risk in order to correct a severe facial deformity.[27]

Child neglect proceedings are sometimes brought to ensure that children receive medical treatment prescribed by a doctor to which a parent is opposed.[28] For example in a well-known case in Massachusetts, parents of a child suffering from lymphocytic leukemia were unwilling to submit the child to chemotherapy, preferring the more controversial treatment of laetrile. The supreme court of that state considered the "primary right" of parents to raise children according to their own consciences but ruled that parents do not have the right to make life-and-death decisions about their children. The court ordered treatment over the parents' objections because evidence showed that the disease was fatal if untreated, that chemotherapy was the only medical treatment offering a hope of cure, and that the risks of the treatment were minimal compared with the consequences of allowing the disease to go untreated. The court pointed to the power of the state to protect children and distinguished its decision in this case, where treatment was necessary to save a child's life, from other cases in which medical treatment has been sought merely to briefly prolong life.[29]

However, this case should be contrasted with a second case decided in New York around the same time. In that case, parents of a child afflicted with Hodgkin's disease were charged with neglect when the child was treated only with nutritional and metabolic therapy and laetrile. However, because the child was under a licensed physician's care, New York's highest court ruled that the neglect case had to be dismissed.[30] The court ruled that parents are required only to make certain that their children are being cared for by a licensed physician; neglect laws are not designed to second-guess doctors or to punish parents for undertaking controversial but lawful treatments for their children.

If there is doubt whether the benefits of the proposed remedial treatment outweigh the potential risks involved, courts often will not override parental objection to the treatment.[31] Once a court has rejected medical necessity as the sole basis for overriding parents' wishes with respect to the medical care of their children, it must engage in complex balancing decisions, weighing parents' constitutional right to make all important child-rearing decisions concerning their children against the possible benefits of particular treatment to the child. Some courts have added to the factors for consideration the child's own desires, which may prove determinative. The Pennsylvania Supreme Court found it anomalous to consider children's wishes or opinions in other types of proceedings yet not allow them to express their views about undergoing a serious surgical procedure.[32] After considering the child's views, the court acquiesced in the child's desire not to have a spinal fusion.[33]

Even when intervention to protect children appears to be clear, parents may avoid being prosecuted criminally for failing to provide children with medical attention. In one recent case, for example, Minnesota's highest court refused to permit the prosecution for manslaughter of Christian Scientist parents who treated their diabetic child only with spitirual healing before he died. Minnesota law permits parents to select spiritual means or prayer to treat their children. Although the law also says that there is an exception in cases in which children are being neglected, the court ruled that the "statute does not go far enough to provide reasonable notice of the potentially serious consequences of actually relying on the alternative treatment methods the statute itself clearly permits." Because the parents could not know precisely when their conduct moved from being lawful to unlawful, it would violate basic notions of due process of law to prosecute them for their behavior. Accordingly, the indictment against them was dismissed.[34]

What is the appropriate court order in medical neglect cases?

In virtually all cases in which court intervention is sought solely to order a particular treatment to which the parents are opposed, the court's role is limited to issuing temporary custody orders not implying that the parent has failed in his or her duty to the child in any respect other than refusing to allow a particular kind of medical care. Thus, the court will transfer authority to consent to the authorized medical procedure to some person other than the parents—often the treating physician—but otherwise not interfere with any other parental perogatives.

Does a parent have the right to refuse medical treatment for a child when the treatment violates the parent's religious beliefs?

Generally, no. When parents have a religious objection, courts will weigh the interest of the state in protecting the child against the parent's right to religious freedom. Federal and state courts have unhesitatingly authorized medical treatment over a parent's religious objection when the treatment is relatively innocuous in comparison to the dangers of withholding medical care.[35] The right of a parent to practice religion does not include the liberty to expose the child to ill health or death.[36] Thus, even when the parent's decision to decline necessary treatment is based on constitutional grounds, such as religious beliefs, it must yield to the state's interests in protecting the health and welfare of the child.[37]

Generally, the courts' determination of whether to order treatment over parental religious objections involves an analysis of the probability of successful results as well as the nature of the treatment and its effect on the child.[38] Thus, courts have ordered treatment where the child had a better than 50 percent chance of surviving with a blood transfusion,[39] where the blood transfusion was 90 percent effective in treating the illness,[40] where chemotherapy treatment presented a 75 percent chance of short-term remission,[41] and where a blood transfusion was safe and necessary.[42] One court did not, however, order treatment where a radical form of chemotherapy had only a 40 percent chance of success.[43] Similarly, courts are reluctant to order medical care over parental religious objections when the child is not suffering from a potentially life-threatening illness. In non-life threatening situations, courts will attempt to accommodate parents' religious practices.[44] Recognizing the constitutional support for religious freedom, many neglect laws contain an exemption for religion-based grounds for making medical decisions.[45]

Under what circumstances can the parent refuse medical treatment for a child based on nonreligious objections?

Courts are sometimes required to determine the reasonableness of nonreligious parental objections to medical treatment in situations involving risky or unpleasant side effects. As with parental religious objections, courts will commonly analyze the probability of successful results as well as the nature of the treatments and their effect on the child. Factors generally considered by courts where parents have nonreligious objections to medical treatment include the seriousness of the condition, the likelihood of harm absent the treatment, the express wishes of the child, and the risks involved, as well as the likelihood of success of the treatment.

How is psychological harm defined?

Not all states include psychological harm as an aspect of abuse or neglect. Those that consider it part of the legal definition of child maltreatment do not define it very clearly. For example, New York includes in the definition of neglect a child whose mental or emotional condition has become impaired as a result of the parent's failure to exercise a minimum degree of care. The law defines "impairment of mental or emotional condition" in the following way:

"Impairment of mental or emotional condition" includes a state of substantially diminished psychological or intellectual functioning in relation to, but not limited to, such factors as failure to thrive, control of aggressive or self-destructive impulses, ability to think and reason, or acting out or misbehavior, including incorrigibility, ungovernability or habitual truancy.[46]

Wisconsin permits a court to assume jurisdiction over a child

[w]ho is suffering emotional damage for which the parent or guardian is unwilling to provide treatment, which is evidenced by one or more of the following characteristics, exhibited to a severe degree: anxiety, depression, withdrawal or outward aggressive behavior.[47]

The problem with extending traditional notions of abuse and neglect to include psychological harm is that it is very difficult to prove or, from the view of a parent who has been charged with psychological abuse and neglect, it is very difficult to disprove. In short, no one can really say what psychological harm means. Former Supreme Court Chief Justice Burger recognized this problem when he concurred in a case involving the rights of people diagnosed mentally ill. He said, "There can be little responsible debate regarding 'the uncertainty of diagnosis in this field and the tentativeness of professional judgment.' "[48]

In child-maltreatment cases, the problem becomes even more difficult, because a judge must weigh the possible consequences of ruling that psychological harm exists—that is, the trauma of removing the child from his or her parents—against the probability of harm if the child remains at home.

Can parents be charged with neglect for not sending their child to school?

Yes. More precisely, if parents do not assure that their children receive adequate educational instruction, they may be charged with neglecting the needs of their children. In certain cases, a parent's religious beliefs may protect them from a claim that they violated compulsory education requirements. In 1972 the Supreme Court held in *Wisconsin v. Yoder*[49] that a state could not compel Amish parents to send their children to school beyond the grammar school level. It is unclear how far this ruling may be extended. In *Yoder* the Court was satisfied that the education the children continued to receive outside of school by the Amish community adequately substituted for the education they would have received in school. Accordingly, *Yoder* may be seen simply as an application of the principle that parents may utilize alternative educational systems.

It has long been settled law that parents need not send their children to the established public schools to satisfy their obligation of providing education to the children.[50] In many jurisdictions, this freedom allows parents to select private schools or to teach their children at home.[51] If parents opt to instruct their children at home, they are held to an educational standard roughly equivalent to that of the local public schools.

Can parents be charged with neglect for failure to have their children immunized from disease?

Yes. Indeed, there is a relationship between immunization requirements and admission to public schools. Parental refusal to have a child immunized usually results in the child being denied admittance to public school. Courts have held that a neglect adjudication may be based either on the child's attending school in violation of health regulations or the parent's refusal of permission to vaccinate the child.[52]

May parents refuse to immunize their children on grounds of religious beliefs?

Perhaps. Although in the past the refusal to vaccinate a child was not excused on religious grounds, several states now provide by statute for religious exemptions from the compulsory vaccination law.[53] This may mean that parents who hold any conscientious religious belief inconsistent with vaccination, regardless of whether the belief is evidenced by formal church membership, will be exempted from the requirement that their children be immunized.[54]

Can parents be charged with child abuse or neglect for "moral unfitness" such as excessive drinking, drug use, or sexual promiscuity?

Yes, in some states. Even though the state's power to interfere with parental discretion is derived from its power to protect children from harm, many child neglect laws focus on parental behavior alone, whether or not such behavior endangers children. The term *moral unfitness* or *immoral parental behavior* is still found in a number of state neglect statutes. Naturally, these terms are not (and cannot be) interpreted in any consistent fashion. However, it is commonly required that the alleged immorality be linked in some measure to proof of a real or imminent danger to the welfare of the child. For example, excessive drinking may not be sufficient grounds for a finding of neglect unless the parent's alcoholism actually renders him or her unable to care adequately for the child.[55] In Rhode Island, a person is guilty of cruelty or neglect of a child, "who shall cause or permit the home of such child to be the resort of lewd, drunken, wanton or dissolute persons, or who by reason of neglect, cruelty, drunkenness or depravity, shall render the home of such child a place in which it is unfit for such child to live."[56]

Can parents be charged with neglect because their failure to provide adequate care is due to their financial inability to do so?

Technically, no. In every state, parents who need financial support to feed, clothe, and house their children are entitled to receive public assistance. A number of states expressly exclude indigency as a grounds for child neglect by requiring a showing that the parent has the financial means to correct the problems in the home.[57] In theory, public assistance benefits are adequate for parents to raise children in minimally acceptable circumstances. Unfortunately, it is common that parents who are very poor are charged with being neglectful for one reason or another and that reason often is connected to poverty. For example, as more parts of the United States suffer from an extreme shortage of adequate housing for people with low income, families become homeless, or they seek shelter in unsafe quarters. When child protection officials find children living in inadequate places, they charge parents with neglect.

Aren't some child abuse and neglect laws quite vague?

Yes. This is because legislatures wish to give child-protective agencies and courts a wide latitude in dealing with cases of child maltreatment, so a child who is being harmed or in severe danger of being harmed will not escape detection and help simply because the type of harm in a certain case was not specifically covered in a particular law. That is why definitions of maltreatment often include phrases like "without proper parental care" or "living under conditions injurious to a child's mental or physical health or welfare." One court explained that the term "neglect" has no fixed meaning but "acquires content from the specific circumstances of each individual case."[58]

The Supreme Court of the United States has emphasized three related but distinct dangers that make vague legislation intolerable in areas bordering on important constitutional rights. First, when state intervention is broadly authorized and inadequately channeled in these areas, there is a grave risk that the constitutional rights will be invaded frequently and that the invasions will be difficult to detect and remedy. Second, because vagueness of legislation is compounded by imprecise boundaries of constitutional protection, individuals are deprived of fair notice regarding the conduct that will subject them to state intervention; and the tendency to "steer clear" of the danger zone will inhibit constitutionally protected activity. Third, vague authorizations of state intervention lend themselves to arbitrary and discriminatory enforcement.[59]

One of the most serious vices of overly vague laws is that they permit implementers—social workers and juvenile court judges—to invoke state power in circumstances under which no legislative body ever contemplated or approved state action. Vague laws, in other words, allow arbitrary intrusions into the lives of families by failing to limit beforehand the discretion of social workers and childcare workers to remove children from their parents or to charge the parents with abuse or neglect and by allowing judges thereafter to rule against parents in situations in which the legislature made no determination that state intervention is appropriate.

Overly vague laws also offend basic notions of due process in that they fail to inform individuals of the conduct that they must observe or avoid in order to assure that they will not be subject to involuntary state intervention. One of the basic purposes of law is to publish rules of conduct to warn people what they may and may not do. Particularly in the area of childrearing, where the the law has historically favored keeping children with their biological parents if that can be done consistently with the state's interest in protecting children from gross harm, vague statutes have the fault of depriving parents of any fair warning that would enable them to conform their conduct to the law so as to guarantee that their children can continue to live with them.

These arguments, though persuasive in theory, rarely result in a declaration of the unconstitutionality of a child protection law. When courts have considered this question they have generally ruled that even criminal child-maltreatment laws are constitutional. For example, a Florida statute, which reads,

> Whoever, willfully or by culpable negligence, deprives a child of, or allows a child to be deprived of, necessary food, clothing, shelter, or medical treatment, or who, knowingly or by culpable negligence, permits physical or mental injury to the child, shall be guilty of a misdemeanor[60]

was upheld by the state supreme court against a claim that it was fatally vague.[61] And a Nebraska law that makes it a crime to engage in conduct that "endangers" the child or deprives the child of "necessary" food, clothing, shelter, or care was upheld by the state supreme court, which reasoned that the legislature's broad, protective purpose in protecting children justified the language in the statute.[62]

In fact, very few child abuse and neglect laws have been found unconstitutional for reasons of vagueness.[63] For example, West Virginia's highest court recently upheld a statute making conduct criminal which defined "neglect" as "the unreasonable failure by a parent . . . to exercise a minimum degree of care to assure [a] minor child's physical safety or health."[64] (There has been greater success challenging similarly worded laws permitting the termination of parental rights. For a discussion of this issue, see chapter 7.) However, not all neglect laws have been sustained when challenged on vagueness grounds. A Connecticut statute that prohibited "any act" that was "likely to impair the health or morals of [a] child" was held to be unconstitutionally vague by the Connecticut Supreme Court.[65]

Even if most child abuse and neglect laws are not unconstitutionally vague, do they violate the rights of parents to raise their children as they see fit?

No. Although the right to raise one's children free from state interference has been recognized by the Supreme Court to be one of the "basic civil rights of man" and "far more precious than property rights,"[66] it is not without limitation. The state, through a legal power known in Latin as *parens patriae*, has the power and duty to protect the health and welfare of children who are being harmed by their parents. Some aspects of child protection laws may unconstitutionally infringe on parents' rights (such as taking a child into protective custody without giving adequate due process rights to parents, as will be discussed later in this chapter), but the basic power of the state to insist that parents raise their children according to minimal standards is constitutional.[67]

Nevertheless, parents still enjoy the fundamental right to control the details of the upbringing of their children, and state interference with family life is justified only when there is a "compelling state interest."[68] When these principles are applied in real cases, there is an unclear line of demarcation between state laws designed to protect children from real or imminent harm and those that reach unnecessarily into realms of family life.

Seen in this light, child neglect laws that authorize state intervention into family life because of the parents' or "immorality or depravity,"[69] may well be subject to constitutional scrutiny. This is not necessarily because the phrases are vague. Rather, laws with definitions such as these suggest that the state is more concerned with regulating parental morality than with protecting children.

Do children have a constitutional right to a safe and nurturing home?

No, at least the Supreme Court of the United States has held that they do not. As already stated, all states have laws protecting children from harm imposed upon them by their parents or any other caretaker. As a result, children have the right to be raised free from serious harm. Beyond this, children have relatively few rights—whether these rights are asserted against the state or their parents.

Constitutional rights can be asserted only against the state, state officials, or persons acting under the authority of state law. Biological parents raising their children are not acting under authority of state law; for this reason, children can have no constitutional claims based on their parents' conduct towards them. Although children can assert constitutional rights against state officials, the Supreme Court has ruled that state officials are not responsible within the meaning of the Constitution for injuries inflicted on children by their parents, even when the state has become aware that the parent is dangerous to the child.[70] This decision also means that children cannot sue state officials when the conditions in their home are dangerous unless the danger is directly traceable to the actions of those officials.

However, there are groups advocating a constitutional amendment that would guarantee children, among other things, "the right to live in a home that is safe and healthy."[71]

REPORTING AND INVESTIGATING CHILD ABUSE AND NEGLECT

What happens when someone has reason to believe a child has been maltreated?

Every state has laws that create a mechanism for people to report their suspicions of child abuse and neglect. Some people are *required* by law to report their suspicions.

The theory behind reporting laws is that abused and neglected children are unable to ask for help. In addition, child abuse and neglect usually take place privately, in a home, with no witnesses other than the parents and children. Therefore, reporting laws are designed to bring cases of possible wrongdoing to the attention of public authorities who are in a position to help children and provide assistance to neglectful parents.

Who is required to report suspicions of child abuse or neglect?

In most states persons required to report include doctors, nurses, police officers, welfare workers, and teachers. Basically, most state laws require reporting from professionals who deal with children and are in a good position to detect certain telltale signs of child abuse and neglect. In New York, where the number of people required to report is among the greatest in the country, the list includes physicians, surgeons, medical examiners, coroners, dentists, dental hygienists, osteopaths, optometrists, chiropractors, podiatrists, residents, interns, psychologists, registered nurses, hospital personnel engaged in the admission, examination, care, or treatment of patients, Christian Science practitioners, schoolteachers and officials, social-service workers, day-care workers, foster-care workers, mental-health professionals, police officers, residential care facility volunteers, district attorneys and other law enforcement officers, and all other childcare workers.[72] In Alaska, even confessions to clergy may be reported as child abuse.[73]

In some states, hospital personnel are required to report all cases of newborns born with a physical drug dependency.[74]

What happens if a person required to report child abuse or neglect does not report?

Most state laws provide that persons required to report their suspicions of child abuse or neglect may be criminally prosecuted if they fail to do so. In other words, if a person has reason to believe that a child has been abused or neglected and is required by law to report but makes no report, that person has committed a crime (usually a misdemeanor).[75]

Criminal prosecutions for failure to report are extremely rare, however, and there are no reported convictions of persons who have failed to make such reports.[76] Nonetheless, asserted violations of mandatory reporting laws can lead to loss of one's job. In addition, in some states, statutes have been enacted that impose civil liability on individuals mandated to report suspicions of abuse who fail to do so when the failure is the proximate cause for subsequent injury to a child.[77] As a result of these possible consequences, mandatory reporting laws tend to make people report, even when there is doubt in their minds whether a child has been maltreated. The prospect for facing loss of income or, worse, for failure to report makes it almost certain that someone will err on the side of reporting rather than not reporting. This is especially so because making a mistaken report in "good faith" can never be the basis for liability.[78] In other words, whenever a mandated reporter has some reason to suspect maltreatment, that person may make a report and know that he or she is protected from being sued for invasion of privacy or some related violation of the parent's rights.[79] This does not mean reporters are free to disclose to anyone their suspicions of neglect or abuse. But as long as the communication was made in good faith, even when it is made to a relative or other person living in the home who is not suspected of abuse, the reporter will be immune from damages for any tort such as defamation or invasion of privacy.[80]

Other than those required to report cases of child abuse and neglect, can anyone else report?

Yes. Most states encourage all people—regardless of their professional standing—to report their suspicions of child abuse and neglect. Therefore, reports from neighbors, family members, and even strangers will be accepted, even though people making these reports are not required to report.[81]

To whom are such reports made?

Reports can be made to any official agency such as the police or the local department of welfare, but persons required to report are usually told to report to a specific office. Most states coordinate reports through civil agencies, such as a department of social welfare or a special child-protection unit of a social-service agency.

Are there centralized data banks containing reports of child abuse and neglect?

Yes. Virtually every state maintains a computerized statewide central register with files containing all reports of child abuse and neglect.[82] The amount of information kept in these registers varies from state to state but usually includes the name and address of the child, the nature of his or her alleged harm, the name and address of the parents or custodians, and the number of times, if any, previous reports involving the same child or parents were made. There is one national register of child abuse and neglect, but it is maintained for statistical purposes only, and names are not recorded.

In an important decision in 1994, a federal court ruled that the maintenance of child abuse and neglect records violates a person's constitutional rights when (1) the records may serve as a basis to deprive the individual of other rights and (2) the person does not have a reasonable opportunity to challenge the entry in the records.[83] In that case, the court ruled that persons whose names are maintained in New York's registry have a federal constitutional right to challenge the legality of keeping their names in the records because New York law requires all childcare employers to check the registry before hiring job applicants and permits employers to hire someone whose name appears in the registry only if the employer maintains a written record of the specific reasons why the person was determined to be appropriate.[84]

The court went on to hold that New York's procedures for maintaining its registry violate the federal constitution because there is too high a risk that a person's name will erroneously make its way into the registry. Under New York law, names will be placed in the registry whenever there is "some credible evidence" that the person is responsible for a child's maltreatment. The court held that this standard virtually ensures error, since it "does not require the factfinder to weigh conflicting evidence"; instead the state offical needs only to "present the bare minimum of material credible evidence to support the allegation." The "some credible evidence" standard, the court went on to observe,

is especially dubious in the context of determining whether an individual has abused or neglected a child. Such determinations are inherently inflammatory, and 'unusually open to the subjective values of' the factfinder. . . . They are especially open to such subjectivity when the factfinder is not required to weigh evidence and judge competing versions of events, and where one side has the greater ability to assemble its case.[85]

In holding New York's system unconstitutional, the court noted that far too many names are placed in the registry. According to the court, there were roughly 2,000,000 individuals on the rolls of the New York Central Register as of 1994. As the court noted, "We find it difficult to fathom how such a hugh percentage of New Yorkers could be included on a list of those suspected to child abuse and neglect, unless there has been a high rate of error in determinations."[86]

Is information contained in these reports considered confidential?

Yes, in most states. This includes reports communicated to and stored in central registers as discussed above. A 1974 regulation that guides the delivery of federal funds to states for child-abuse prevention and treatment programs requires states to pass laws making reports of child abuse and neglect confidential. These laws must make it a crime for any person to permit or encourage the dissemination of information on reports to anyone other than police and other agencies that investigate reports, courts, grand juries, state officials, researchers (if names are not released to them), persons authorized to take children into emergency protective custody, physicians who need to know if a child they are treating has been previously reported, the child in question, and the persons named in the report.[87]

The reason that there is great concern for the confidentiality of this information is that reports of abuse are just that—reports and nothing more. They are not conclusive determinations or judicial convictions. They are merely indications that someone is suspected of mistreating a child. The report may turn out to have been an honest mistake; it may have been made maliciously (by a jealous relative perhaps); or it may be accurate. But at the outset, it is just a report.

Does a parent have any legal recourse against a person who makes an inaccurate report?

There is usually no legal recourse available for the subject of a report to take against the person who first made the report, even if it turns out to be untrue or mistaken. This is because every state has a law that protects makers of reports from liability in any subsequent civil or criminal suit that arises out of the report. In practical terms, this means that neither the parent nor the child mentioned in a report can sue the maker of the report for libel, slander, invasion of privacy, or loss of reputation even if the "suspected" abuse or neglect turns out not to be abuse or neglect at all.

There is one qualification to all this: the reporter is granted immunity only if the report is made in "good faith." Thus, a parent or child may have the right to sue a reporter whose report was made maliciously or with no foundation in fact whatsoever or if the report was made for the sole purpose of harming the reputation of the parent or child reported.

What happens after a report of child abuse or neglect is made?

Most states have screening procedures for receiving a report. In these states, the person receiving the report makes a detemination of whether there is sufficient cause to undertake an investigation. This determination is based on many factors, including how the reporter obtained the information, the seriousness of the allegation, and the currency of the information. In only fifteen states must all reports be investigated without any preliminary determination of the appropriateness of an investigation.[88]

After a report is made and after the information is communicated to a central register (if one exists in that state), an investigation is started by one or two individuals from the local agency responsible for inquiring into such cases—usually the state or county department of welfare or social services.

Generally, the investigation must start within a very short period of time. In New York, for example, the investigation must begin within twenty-four hours of receipt of the report.[89] Investigators will go to the home or the place where the abuse or neglect allegedly occurred and speak with the parents or persons caring for the child. This will probably be the first time that the individual(s) will be aware that a report concerning them has been made.

If investigators come to a child's home to investigate allegations of child abuse, must the parent let them in?

No. The Fourth Amendment to the federal Constitution and parallel state constitutional guarantees against unreasonable searches and seizures apply to child protection investigations as well as to criminal investigations. The Supreme Court has held that home entries to enforce civil regulatory systems are governed by the Fourth Amendment and can ordinarily be made only with the parent's consent or under the authorization of a search warrant.[90]

The Fourth Amendment also applies to any seizure of the person,[91] and the courts have accordingly recognized that state authorities' removal of children suspected of being in need of protection must comply with the amendment's command of reasonableness. Courts have held that the removal of a child from his or her home without prior notice is not permissible unless exigent circumstances are shown.[92] They have also held that an ex parte removal (a judicially approved removal order obtained without the other side appearing) is not permissible unless it is necessary to ensure the child's safety against serious physical illness or injury or immediate physical danger.[93]

Do investigators have the right to examine children over the objection of their parents?

It depends. If the children are at home, the parents may refuse to permit entry to their home unless the investigators have a search warrant. Courts have ruled that all physical examinations of children in child protection investigations are considered searches under the Fourth Amendment.[94] However, searches are permitted even without a warrant using a balancing test of reasonableness. Once an investigator has reason to believe that a child has been harmed or is subject to a substantial risk of harm, courts are likely to conclude that a warrantless search of the child is reasonable.[95]

Do children have the right to speak with investigators over the parents' objections?

If the parents have a legal basis upon which to deny investigators access to their home, the parents probably can prevent their children from being interviewed by investigators. However, once an investigator is speaking with a child, the child has the right to cooperate fully with the investigator and answer all questions, even over the opposition of his or her parents. When children want the chance to speak with an investigator out of their parents' presence, the children are well advised to indicate this desire to the investigator. The child's reaction during an investigation can be grounds for an investigator to pursue the investigation over parental objection when there is probable cause to believe the child is in danger if the investigation were abandoned or delayed.

What remedies do families have for violations of their constitutional rights against unreasonable searches and seizures?

It is important to emphasize that, although the Fourth Amendment applies to civil cases, the most important remedy for enforcement of violations does not apply to these cases. The remedy of excluding evidence seized unlawfully is available only in criminal cases. The exclusionary rule in criminal cases has been justified by the Supreme Court as a necessary deterrent of official illegality. However, the cost excluding evidence of child abuse at trial because of constitutional violations is deemed by courts to be too high. Accordingly, courts will not refuse to admit proof of harm to children, regardless of the manner in which proof has been obtained.[96] For this reason, the Fourth and Fifth Amendments offer limited recourse to defendants in child protection cases.

Constitutional violations by child protection officials may, however, give rise to a cause of action for damages against those officials.[97]

If investigators come to the home of a child, do the adults have to talk with them?

No. A person has the right to refuse to talk to anyone, even if the person conducting the investigation is a police officer. Parents are not legally obligated to cooperate with these officials. The parent needs not answer questions asked of them.[98] Unless the investigators have a search warrant, the parent needs not admit them into his or her home.[99] Neither the refusal to answer questions nor the refusal to admit officials into the house may be used as evidence of the person's guilt or used to support the issuance of a warrant, as long as the manner of the refusal communicates no additional information that is suspicious.[100]

However, refusal to talk may be considered by the investigators as being uncooperative, causing them to assume that the parent has something to hide or cover up. If the parent's manner, together with the information that the investigating officials already have, does give them probable cause to conclude that the child has been abused or will be abused in the future, they may obtain a warrant; and if it also gives them reasonable grounds to believe that evidence of the abuse will be removed or destroyed, they may be able to enter the home without a warrant under a doctrine known as *exigent circumstances.*[101]

Persons who elect not to cooperate with a caseworker or police official investigating the possibility of child abuse should therefore not allow themselves to be drawn into conversation with the investigator; they should simply state that they have been advised that they are under no legal obligation to answer questions or to admit the investigator into their home, as the case may be, and should immediately terminate the conversation or close the door on the investigator. If they choose to admit the investigator into the house and if the investigator there observes any manifest evidence of child abuse or other criminal conduct, the investigator will ordinarily be able to take the child from the home without a warrant.

The legal picture is complicated considerably if the parent is receiving some form of public assistance conditioned upon consent to home visits by caseworkers or if the parent or another person in the household is on probation or parole. In these cases, investigators arguably have greater authority to require that parents admit them into their homes and answer their questions.[102]

If a parent or caregiver is asked questions by those conducting the investigation without being informed of the right to remain silent, can their answers be used against them in court?

Yes. A person under investigation for child abuse or neglect has fewer rights regarding self-incrimination than a suspect under investigation for committing a crime. They also have fewer rights than suspected criminals regarding unreasonable searches of their homes. In short, statements made by parents or caregivers to investigators or social-welfare workers under any circumstances can be used against them in subsequent court hearings.

Can their refusal to answer questions be used against them?

Yes, but only indirectly. A refusal to satisfy an investigator's inquiries during an investigation may lead the investigator to assume the worst about the suspect and could very well lead the investigator to exercise his or her considerable discretion and remove the child. Similarly, at trial, the judge may view the failure to cooperate with caseworkers as indicative of an unwillingness to correct unfavorable conditions in the home.

May children sue officials who fail to remove them from abusive parents once the officials learned that the children were at risk of harm?

Probably not. When state officials exercise their judgment and allow a child to remain in his or her parents' care or return them to the parents' custody, these officials are immune from suit for an error of professional judgment.[103] It is possible that children could sue officials if it could be shown that the officials acted deliberately in failing to protect the children.[104]

Do investigators have the right to speak with the child's doctor? Can a doctor testify in court against the parents?

The answer to both questions is yes. The doctor-patient "privilege," or confidentiality of communication, does not apply to parents of children who are suspected of being abused or neglected.[105]

May family members sue officials who investigate them as suspected child abusers?

Perhaps. The possibility of success depends on the facts of the case and the claimed wrong done. Lawsuits against officials who investigate allegations of child abuse may be brought in either federal or state court. In almost all cases, parents will not be able to sue officials for the *decision* to have removed a child from their custody.[106] All officials who investigate child abuse or neglect allegations are cloaked with some degree of immunity for their actions. If their immunity is said to be "absolute," then they cannot be sued or held liable for any wrongdoing under any circumstances relating to the actions that fall within the grant of immunity. However, if their immunity is said to be a "qualified, good faith" immunity, these officials are answerable in court for their conduct.

Certain acts engaged in by officials are cloaked with *absolute immunity*. Acts of officials that require the exercise of discretion—those that admittedly in hindsight may have been mistaken but required making choices at a particular moment—are most likely to be immune from attack.[107] Decisions to remove children from their parents fall into this category, unless the parent can show that the removal involved no real exercise in discretion, that under no circumstances could an investigator have concluded there was any basis to remove the children.

A second way of distinguishing among acts that are subject to challenge for damages is between acts that are *prosecutorial* in nature and those that are merely *investigative*. However, the line between these two acts is frequently blurred. For example, a federal court in 1989 failed to accord a social worker absolute immunity when she was sued for investigating a case and maintaining a name in the state's central registry even though the investigation was mandated by statute and the investigation could have led to prosecutorial action.[108] In contrast, a federal court in California in 1986, accorded absolute immunity to a caseworker in all facets of the investigation because an investigation is so intimately connected to the prosecutorial function.[109]

Other acts by officials may be subject to review in a lawsuit seeking damages. Challenges to the *manner* in which the investigation was conducted—as distinct from the decision itself to remove—fall into this category. Courts sometimes permit parents to sue officials for the way in which they conducted invesitgations.[110]

To win a lawsuit against officials who can claim *good faith immunity*, it is necessary to prove more than that their actions were misguided, negligent, or mistaken. It must be proven that they acted with actual malice or bad faith or at least that they acted recklessly in deliberate indifference to the rights of the people who are suing.

Do parents and children have the right to sue investigators who violate their rights during the investigation?

Yes. In one California case parents and their children were permitted to sue a school, a teacher, a nurse, a police officer, three caseworkers, and the county for worngfully detaining the children during an investigation of allegations of sexual abuse.[111] After a bus driver reported that he overheard a child make a remark of a sexual nature, the child and her sister were taken to a room at the school where the child was questioned repeatedly and where a vaginal examination of her was conducted. After this, the child was taken to a hospital and examined there. The examinations failed to reveal any clinical signs of molestation. Nevertheless, the child and her sister were held at the child protection offices for the next eleven hours.

During the course of the children's detention, a police officer told the mother incorrectly that her daughter had been the victim of sexual abuse and had a bloody vagina. When the mother demanded that the children be returned to her custody, she was permitted to take the children home only on condition that she sign an agreement not to allow the father to go near them. One week later, the matter was dropped entirely. No child protection proceeding was ever brought.[112]

In a second California case involving the circumstances under which an investigation was conducted, parents sued the county and police officers after the officers investigated a report of suspected child abuse.[113] In that case, the officers came to the house in full uniform, took the children into the bathroom without parental consent and required the children to disrobe. The officers searched the children's bodies for signs of abuse, including their genitals; the children were forced to disrobe and expose themselves to persons of different sex. Finding no signs of abuse, the officers told the parents the report was unfounded. The county claimed it was immune under the child-abuse reporting statute. However, the court held that the child-abuse reporting statute protects only the persons who made reports in good faith. The statute did not provide immunity to officials after the receipt of a report.[114]

In a second line of cases, Louisiana courts have permitted plaintiffs to seek damages at trial for harm arising out of investigation of abuse cases. In one case, parents and their son sued the Department of Health and Human Resources for removing the child from the parents' custody based on suspected child abuse, for breaking the child's arm while he was in the agency's custody, and for failing to return the child to his parents after learning that the child was not abused but instead suffered from Brittle Bone Disease.[115]

In that case, the child's mother brought him to a local hospital when he was five weeks old because he was crying excessively. A second visit revealed the child's right leg was fractured. After discovering the fracture, the mother was interviewed by hosptial personnel. In their opinion, the mother was unable to provide a satisfactory explanation for the fracture. An emergency order of removal was obtained from the juvenile court, and the child was placed in a local facility where his arm was broken a second time when an employee lifted him into his seat. Further hospitalization and tests revealed that the child had not been abused but suffered from osteogenesis imperfecta, more commonly known as Brittle Bone Disease. Despite the new diagnosis, the child was kept in the agency's care for more than three additional months.

The parents sued the agency for pain and suffering, loss of consortium, and embarrassment and humiliation. They specifically alleged, among other things, that the agency failed to properly train their employees. The appellate court ruled that the plaintiffs were entitled to have a jury determine whether the agency negligently discharged its duties in training employees, whether it was responsible for the child's broken arm after the child was in the agency's care, and whether its failure to recommend expedited return of the child after discovering the correct diagnosis was willful and reckless.

What happens after the investigation of a reported incident of child abuse is completed?

It depends entirely on what the investigation reveals. The investigators will determine whether the allegations contained in the initial report are true or false. The conclusion of the investigators is not necessarily based upon what would be considered evidence in a courtroom; it is based solely upon the results of the investigation, whether performed thoroughly or not.

In most states, the investigation will result in an agency report that a child's maltreatment was or was not discovered. However, the agency determination is not a legal decision. The conclusions of the investigators are purely administrative in nature; they cannot "convict" anyone of wrongdoing.

Of course, if the agency conducting the investigation thinks it is appropriate, it has the power to take the parents to court by filing a petition charging them with child abuse or neglect. The court will then decide if further action should be taken.

In many cases, even if the agency concludes that the report of abuse or neglect was true, it may decide not to go to court and to attempt to assist the family by offering services to them. These may include therapy or counseling for the parents and/or the child, medical services such as visiting nurses, day-care, or babysitting services, homemaker services, job training, new housing, or group counseling sessions with other parents. Sometimes the agency may suggest that the child be placed in temporary foster care. If the parents accept the offered assistance, the agency may conclude there is no need to take the case to court. Finally, the agency making the investigation may decide to do nothing further at all.

Are parents under any obligation to accept the services offered by the social-welfare agency?

No. Parents have an absolute right to refuse any offer of services they wish. This includes the right to resist offers of counseling and therapy for themselves or their children. It also includes the right to reject the suggestion that their child be placed in temporary foster care.

Sometimes, the agency may say to a parent, "You have the right to reject these services, but if you do, we will take you to court." However questionable it may be to make this threat in order to gain "voluntary" acceptance of their services, there is no question about the power of the agency to file a petition and ask a court to decide whether the parents have abused or neglected their children. If the court decides after a hearing that they did, then it has the power to order counseling or other services and even to remove the children from the parents' custody. Unlike services offered by the welfare agency, orders of the court cannot be rejected by the parents.

If, after investigating, the agency determines that the parents did abuse or neglect their child, can that decision be challenged?

Agency determinations can be challenged by the parents.[116] Parents have the right of access to information contained in the agency files so that they may challenge it if they wish. Usually, the only information withheld from the parents is the name of the person who made the report in the first place.

If the parents disagree with the agency's determination or any information in the report of the investigation, they have the right to an administrative hearing at which they may testify, produce witnesses on their own behalf, and cross-examine witnesses against them, for the purpose of having information they consider inaccurate either corrected or expunged.

If, after investigating, the agency negligently fails to protect the child from abusive parents, can that decision be challenged by the child or others on the child's behalf?

It depends. In many jurisdictions, the only persons authorized to petition the court are those who represent the agency responsible for investigating charges of abuse or neglect. In these jurisdictions, it may be that no one has standing to challenge the agency's determination not to proceed with a case against the parents. In other jurisdictions, judges will entertain requests by lawyers for children to review an agency's decision not to charge parents or will permit a child's lawyer to petition the court directly.

Removing a Child from Parental Custody in an Emergency

Is there any situation in which children may be taken from their parents without prior court approval?

Yes. Every state law authorizes police officers, doctors, or social-welfare agents to remove a child from his or her home (or, in the case of a doctor, to keep the child in a hospital) even if the parents object, if the person authorized by law believes that the child would die or be seriously injured if not removed. The theory behind these laws is that in emergency situations a child's life and safety are more important than parental rights or legal procedures.

State statutes vary regarding the circumstances under which a child may be summarily removed from the custody of his or her parents. The statutes commonly apply to situations in which there are grounds to believe that a child is in danger in the child's present surroundings and immediate removal is necessary for his or her protection. Some statutes are extremely vague, neither specifying the situations in which removal is warranted nor identifying who is to make the removal decision. For example, Oklahoma permits an immediate removal of a child "[i]f it appears that the child is in such condition or surroundings that his welfare requires that his custody be immediately assumed by the court."[117] By contrast, Texas allows "[a]n authorized representative of the Texas Department of Human Services, a law enforcement officer, or a juvenile probation officer" to remove a child without a court order when the removing official has "personal knowledge of facts which would lead a person of ordinary prudence and caution to believe that there is an immediate danger to the physical health or safety of the child and that there is no time to obtain a temporary restraining order or attachment."[118]

New York's law is also fairly typical. It permits a peace officer, an employee of a department of social services, or an agent of the Society for the Prevention of Cruelty to Children to take a child into protective custody without a court order and without parental permission, but only if the child is in such a condition that staying in the home would present an imminent danger to the child's life or health and only if there is not time to apply for an order of removal from a family court.[119] Physicians are also permitted to keep a child in their custody if they believe that returning the child to the family would create an imminent danger to the child's life and health.

Taking a child from his or her home without the consent of the parents and before a hearing is commenced is an extremely drastic step. It is taken rarely—only when the child is truly in danger. Most child abuse and neglect cases investigated by social-welfare agencies and most of those that reach the courts do not involve the emergency removal process described here.

If a child has been taken from his or her parents under an emergency removal law, may the parents contest this decision in court? If so, how soon after removal?

Emergency-removal statutes permit certain people to remove children believed to be in danger from their parents prior to a court hearing or a judicial termination. In all states, parents whose children were so removed are entitled to a court hearing shortly thereafter.

The time between the removal and the hearing varies from state to state, but all state laws require a hearing within a very short time. In New York, the hearing must be held "as soon as practicable" or no later than three days after the filing of an application by a parent or the child's lawyer for a hearing.[120] In North Carolina, the hearing must be held no later than five days after the authorities have assumed custody of the child,[121] and in Texas, the statute says a hearing should be held on the first working day after the child is taken into custody, but if the court is "unavailable," the hearing must be held no later than the third working day after the removal.[122]

Do parents have a right to be notified of and to be present at a postemergency removal hearing?

Yes. Due process of law requires that every effort be made to locate the parents of a child removed under emergency conditions. According to one federal court commenting on this point, the state is required to make "all reasonable efforts to serve upon (the parents) notice of this initial presentation to the court."[123] Once notified, parents have a right to be present at the postemergency removal hearing, to speak in their own defense, to present evidence and witnesses in their favor, and to cross-examine witnesses against them.

What must be proved at a hearing after an emergency removal?

Not all state laws are the same, but generally the agency must show that there was a valid reason for having removed the child in the first place and, if the agency still does not want the child returned, that continued protection outside the home is necessary. One federal court has ruled that the agency must show at least a "danger of immediate harm or threatened harm to the child" to justify an emergency removal.[124] If the agency does not meet its burden of proof, the child must be returned.

In addition, states are ineligible to receive federal matching funds to pay for the foster placement of a child unless "the removal from the home occurred pursuant to a voluntary placement agreement . . . or was the result of a judicial determination to the effect that continuation therein would be contrary to the welfare of such child."[125] As a further condition of receipt of federal money for foster care, it is required that a court specifically find that reasonable efforts have been made "(A) prior to the placement of a child in foster care, to prevent or eliminate the need for removal of the child from his home, and (B) to make it possible for the child to return to his home."[126] Although federal law does not prohibit the removal of a child without reasonable preventive or reunification efforts, it prohibits the agency from being paid out of federal funds for placements that are ordered without those efforts.

Many states require proof at the removal hearing that "reasonable preventive efforts" have been made. In these jurisdictions, the petitioning agency must prove either that preventive services have been used or that there are sufficient reasons to excuse the agency from using them in the particular case.[127] In cases of emergency, the failure to provide preventive services will usually be excused. Under the language of some state statutes, an emergency may be the only justification for the failure to use all available (or all possible) services that would allow the child to remain safely at home.[128]

What rights do parents and children have after a court approves the child's removal?

Parents and children retain a number of very important rights after the child has been removed from the home. Whenever an agency removes a child from the custody of his or her parent, it must develop an individualized case plan, which is required to provide for the child's placement "in the least restrictive (most family-like) setting available and in close proximity to the parents' home, consistent with the best interest and special needs of the child."[129] To implement these principles and reduce the dangers to children associated with a child's separation from loved ones, a foster care placement based upon extended family relationships is usually preferable to a placement outside the family. If necessary to assure the child's safety in a placement with relatives, the court can enter a protective order enjoining the parent from unsupervised visitation or other activities the court wishes to guard against.

Can one who removes a child under emergency circumstances be sued later by parents for having exercised bad judgment?

No, as long as the person who removed the child was one who was authorized by law to do so, and the removal was carried out in "good faith." Just as all states provide immunity from prosecution for making reports, immunity is also granted people who are authorized to remove children under emergency conditions.[130] However, the initial removal must have been undertaken in good faith that the removal was necessary at the time; no person who removes a child without reason or for malicious reasons will be immune from prosecution. Similarly, immunity will not shield someone who was not authorized by law to remove a child. Thus, if the law authorizes police officers and welfare employees only, anyone else who removes a child without parental permission will not be immune from prosecution.

Are all emergency removal statutes constitutional?

No. Some emergency removal laws contain overly broad or vague language. If a court determines that a statute's terms are too broad or vague, it may declare the law unconstitutional.

Laws are designed to be enforced evenhandedly. But if a statute authorizes people to take children into custody simply because their "welfare" or "best interest" requires it, too much discretion is given individuals—be they police officials, social workers, or judges—to decide who comes within the proper scope of the law. This, in turn, encourages arbitrary and discriminatory application.[131]

The problem of vagueness is considered more crucial in emergency-removal statutes than in definitions of neglect and abuse, because emergency-removal laws permit the swift removal of a child from his or her home—usually without a hearing—while determinations of neglect and abuse are made by judges after hearing evidence on all sides of the issue.

For this reason, a federal court once declared Alabama's statute authorizing emergency removal to be unconstitutionally vague. It permitted removal if the child was in "such a condition that its welfare requires that custody be immediately assumed." The court ruled that this statute violated parents' due process rights, because no precise definition of terms was given.[132] (On the other hand, a statute authorizing the removal of a child "to protect him from an immediate danger to his health or physical safety" was found constitutionally permissible as being precise enough to give warning to the parents and meaning to the authorities.)[133]

COURT PROCEDURES

What happens when parents are charged with neglect or abuse and taken to court?

If an abuse or neglect case comes to court, parents have a right to a hearing. Unless parents wish to admit that their child is abused or neglected, a child cannot be declared by a court to be abused or neglected without a hearing.[134] At this hearing, the agency would have to present evidence against the parents or custodians of the child in an attempt to prove that they mistreated their child, by showing that the child was harmed, deprived of adequate care, abandoned, or whatever the relevant definition of abuse or neglect in the state requires.

These hearings are usually held under civil rather than criminal laws and are held in family, juvenile, or children's courts rather than in criminal courts. Parents are usually referred to as *respondents* rather than *defendants*. The state prosecutes the case against the parents or on behalf of the child, but the state is usually represented by the attorney for the welfare or social-service agency rather than the district attorney. In most states, the hearing is closed to the public and is presided over by a judge, but in a few states judges may appoint referees, who make findings and recommendations.

How strong must the state's case be to prove abuse or neglect?

There is no overall rule regarding the standard of proof, or the strength with which the state must prove its case in all states.

A majority of states require the charges to be proven by a "preponderance of the evidence."[135] A number of states require proof by "clear and convincing evidence."[136] The *preponderance standard* means that a finding of neglect or abuse cannot be sustained unless more evidence than not—a "preponderance"—proves the case. The *clear and convincing standard* is higher: that is, it requires more definite proof by the state before neglect or abuse may be found. Both standards are less difficult for the state to meet than the burden required in criminal cases, namely, proof "beyond a reasonable doubt." But since child-maltreatment cases are civil, the criminal standard does not apply.

Do parents accused of neglecting or abusing their children have a right to a lawyer's help in defending themselves against charges?

Yes. In most states, this right is secured by statute.[137] In other states— where the legislatures have not granted to parents the right to counsel— most courts that have considered the question have held that due process requires the provision of free counsel to indigent parents in child-protective proceedings.[138] (Parents probably do not have a federally protected constitutional right to counsel in these proceedings. But they enjoy the right to counsel through state law.)[139]

Do children have a right to counsel in these cases?

Children, too, are granted free legal representation in most states, even though they may be too young to speak.[140] This representation may take the form of a lawyer or a guardian ad litem. The lawyer assigned to represent a child is never the same as the lawyer for the parent—the child's lawyer is independent and may assume a stance contrary to the interests of the parent. A typical hearing therefore, may involve three separate attorneys: one for the state, one for the parents, and one for the child.

At a hearing, may the court hear evidence or testimony by the child's doctor?

Yes. Normally, communications between a doctor and patient are confidential, and doctors may not testify about what was discussed or what a patient said during the course of treatment,[141] but this rule does not apply in child-protective proceedings for two reasons.

First, most states simply suspend the privilege in such proceedings as a matter of public policy in an effort to protect children.[142] Second, if a law has been broken—child abuse and neglect are both illegal—doctors are not required to honor the confidentiality of their communications.[143]

A few courts, however, have honored the privilege between a patient and a psychotherapist, if the patient is a parent seeking treatment according to a plan to help rectify the problem causing child maltreatment.[144]

At a hearing, may one parent be forced to testify against the other?

Generally, yes. This is so even in states that honor the *marital privilege*, which provides that one spouse may not be examined against the other, without the other's permission.[145] Just as in the case of doctor-patient communications, most states do not recognize the marital privilege in child protection cases.[146]

Do parents have the right to remain silent at trial?

Yes, if what they say may lead to their being prosecuted criminally. However, the court can treat a parent's failure to refute evidence of child abuse presented by the petitioner as evidence that what is being presented is true. The obligation of a party in a civil action is to contradict evidence against him or her in order to avoid an adverse judgment.[147] In addition, where state law places a burden of proof on the parent, his or her failure to meet that burden—for whatever reason—will result in a loss of the issue, the case, or both. Thus, although the parent's invocation of the Fifth Amendment privilege will allow them to avoid supplying evidence that can be used against them in a criminal prosecution, its practical effect may be to jeopardize the parent's chances of retaining custody of his or her child.[148]

Can the child's statements be admitted at the abuse or neglect trial without the child testifying in court?

Yes. In virtually every state, a child's statements made to a doctor or social worker will be admitted at the civil child abuse or neglect hearing simply by having the doctor or social worker repeat the words of the child without actually calling the child to the witness stand to testify in person. Even where it is necessary to have the child testify in person, some courts permit the judge to interrogate the child in chambers.[149]

In addition, even in criminal prosecutions for child abuse, where constitutional protections of the accused are greater and more forcefully protected, in recent years a number of states have liberalized the rules governing admissibility of out-of-court statements of child victims. Some states require that the child testify at trial as a prerequisite to the admission of his or her hearsay statements. In other states the statements are admissible whenever the child is unavailable to testify. There is a growing practice of allowing pretrial videotaping of the child's statements concerning abuse for use as evidence at trial. A number of states now provide for the admission into evidence of a videotaped deposition, and still others admit undeposed videotaped statements. Admission of a child abuse victim's videotaped, out-of-court testimony has been held not to violate an accused's constitutional rights.[150] Various forms of hearsay are admissible in several states when the out-of-court statement is the child victim's.[151]

However, there are limits to the admissibility of a child's testimony when the accused is unable to be present during the giving of the testimony. In *Coy v. Iowa*,[152] the Supreme Court held that the confrontation clause of the Sixth Amendment was violated by a statutorily authorized procedure under which a screen was placed between a criminal defendant and child complainants while they testified in a case involving sex crimes. The Court found that "the Confrontation Clause guarantees the defendant a face-to-face meeting with witnesses appearing before the trier of fact" and further ruled that the trial court must make individualized findings that a particular witness needed special protection before it would be permissible to deviate from the traditional rule that witnesses must testify in the presence of the accused.[153] Two years later, the Court approved of the use of one-way closed-circuit television and other procedures "necessary to protect a child witness from trauma that would be caused by testifying in the physical presence of the defendant, at least where such trauma would impair the child's ability to communicate," provided the defendant is given a full opportunity to cross-examine the witness and the court has made a "case-specific" finding that the procedure is necessary to prevent real trauma to the witness.[154]

What are "validators" and when may they be used in child abuse cases?

Validators are persons who interview a child victim (often using props such as anatomically correct dolls) and then offer to testify in court that, in their opinion, the child was abused or the child is being truthful in reporting that he or she was a victim of abuse. Validators are commonly used in child abuse, and particularly sexual abuse, cases to explain the conduct of the victim when that conduct may appear to a jury to be inexplicable or inconsistent with common sense. For example, the child may have waited a long time before reporting the abuse or the child, after making the charge of abuse, may have retracted the charge. Validators are used in these circumstances to explain how it is possible that the child was nonetheless abused.

However, validators have been used in a variety of circumstances. The admissibility of their testimony raises several distinct issues, on some of which the courts are divided. Sometimes validators are asked whether, in their opinion, the child whom they interviewed was a victim of sexual abuse. Sometimes they are asked whether, in their opinion, the child's statements that he or she was a victim of sexual abuse are true. There is strong support for the proposition that validators may not testify that in their opinion the child is telling the truth.[155] However, if the validator limits his or her testimony to describing the symptoms exhibited by the victim and the pattern of responses exhibited generally by child victims of sexual abuse, some courts have held that this testimony is admissible and may be used by a trier of fact to support a finding that the particular child was indeed sexually abused.[156]

Even this more limited use of validators to testify concerning patterns of behavior that constitute a syndrome is subject to objections on the ground that the testimony lacks sufficient scientific reliability to be admissible.[157] Many state courts follow the classic rule of *Frye v. United States*,[158] that evidence based on a new scientific method of proof can be admitted only upon a showing that the method has been generally accepted as reliable in the scientific community in which it was developed. Expert opinion regarding children's reactions to sexual experiences and to interviews using anatomically correct dolls has been held by a number of courts to be a new scientific method of proof that must meet the *Frye* requirement of demonstrated reliability as a condition of admissibility.[159]

Another form of expert testimony used in child abuse cases is based on the so-called child abuse profile. An expert may be called to testify that a particular case fits the profile and that, therefore, in the expert's opinion, the accused committed an act of child abuse. However, most courts routinely reject this evidence on the grounds of its unreliability and prejudicial impact.[160] Testimony concerning "profiles" is considered irrelevant to any disputed issue of fact unless it is being proffered to prove that the parent actually abused his or her child as alleged in the charge, and for that purpose it is inadmissible because the proponent of the evidence cannot meet the burden of establishing its scientific reliability.[161]

However, in 1993, the Supreme Court of the United States loosened the requirements for admitting expert testimony. In *Daubert v. Merrell Dow Pharmaceuticals, Inc.*,[162] the Court ruled that Rule 702 of the Federal Rules of Evidence, rather than *Frye*, should govern the admissibility of expert evidence. Under Rule 702, the proponent of evidence needs only demonstrate that the expert testimony "will assist the trier of fact to understand the evidence or to determine a fact in issue," not that the evidence is accepted by the scientific community. If this test is followed in child abuse cases, it will be easier for the proponent to be able to have admitted validator and other expert testimony.

If a court rules that a child is abused or neglected, do the parents and the child have a right to appeal the decision?

Yes. Although less than half of the states mention the right to appeal in their statutes, all states permit all parties (including parents and children) to appeal adverse neglect and abuse decisions to higher courts.[163]

If a court rules that a child is not abused or neglected, does the child have a right to appeal the decision?

Yes, at least if the child was represented by counsel in the trial court. When children are represented by counsel, they usually are considered "parties" for purposes of filing motions and appeals from decisions with which the child is in disagreement.

CONSEQUENCES

What can the state do if a court rules that the parents have abused or neglected their children?

If a court decides that a child is neglected or abused, it can order that the child be removed from the custody of the parents for a specified period of time. If, within that period of time, the parents do nothing to correct the problem that resulted in the finding of neglect or abuse, it is possible that the temporary separation will result in a permanent termination of parental rights. (See chapter 7.)

Courts are not required to remove the child from the custody of his or her parents, even if abuse or neglect is proven. A less drastic sanction may be imposed, such as placing parents on probation for a period of time and requiring them to engage in a specific rehabilitative or educational program while the child remains with them in their home. For example, a court might require the parent to engage in counseling, therapy, or parent-training programs, to accept periodic visits by homemakers, or to use day-care centers.

As often happens, the court may order the child to be removed from the home and placed in temporary foster care and order the parents to participate in a rehabilitation program that might include many of the services listed above. If, after a period of time, the parents make no use of court-ordered services or show no progress in their training or rehabilitation whatsoever, they may face court proceedings to terminate their parental rights.

While a few states have laws permitting a court to impose criminal sanctions after a ruling of abuse or neglect,[164] criminal penalties are not commonly imposed. Thus, as a result of having their children judged abused or neglected, parents will rarely be fined or imprisoned, but they do face the awesome risk of having their children temporarily or permanently removed from their home.

May a child sue a parent for money damages resulting from physical abuse?

It depends. Virtually every jursidiction today allows children to sue their parents for injuries they have sustained as a result of deliberate, intentional, or malicious wrongful behavior by parents towards children; examples of such behavior include sexual and physical abuse. In recent years, legislatures and courts have made it easier for victims of sexual or child abuse to sue their parents after the victims have themselves become adults.[165] However, what constitutes wrongful behavior is not always clear. For example, a child may recover damages caused by a parent who has physically abused the child, unless the injuries were inflicted from reasonable corporal punishment for disciplinary purposes.[166]

May parents be sued by their children for raising them less than adequately?

Probably not, at least when the claimed parental inadequacy does not rise to the level of physical or sexual abuse.[167]

RESOURCES

National Center on Child Abuse and Neglect
63 Inverness Drive East
Englewood, CO 80112-5117
(303) 792-9900

National Committee to Prevent Child Abuse
332 S. Michigan Ave., Suite 1600
Chicago, IL 60604
(312) 663-3520

National Association of Counsel for Children
205 Oneida St.
Denver, CO 80822
(303) 322-2260

NOTES

1. Cal. Penal Code § 11165.6 (West 1992).

2. *See, e.g.*, N.Y. Fam. Ct. § 1046(a)(ii) (McKinney 1983); *Matter of Philip M.*, 82 N.Y.2d 238, 624 N.E.2d 168, 604 N.Y.S.2d 40 (1993) (if parents cannot explain injuries sustained by children while in their care, court may presume parental responsibility); *In Interest of Weber*, 181 Ill. App. 3d 702, 537 N.E.2d 428, 130 Ill. Dec. 361 (5th Dist. 1989) (court properly entered finding of neglect when child suffered bruise of an unknown cause while in mother's exclusive care).

3. *State v. Williquett*, 129 Wis. 2d 239, 385 N.W.2d 145 (1986) (a person with a duty toward a child who exposes that child to a foreseeable risk of abuse can be charged under the criminal child abuse statute just as if he or she had directly inflicted the harm). *But see, State v. Rundle*, 176 Wis. 2d 985, 500 N.W.2d 916 (1993).

4. Neb. Rev. Stat. § 28-710(3)(d) (1989).

5. Tenn. Code Ann. § 37-1-147(d)(2) (1991) (severe child abuse allows immediate removal), Fla. Stat. Ann. § 39.464 (1)(d) (Westlaw West 1995) (egregious abuse).

6. *See Meyer v. Nebraska*, 262 U.S. 390 (1923).

7. *Stanley v. Illinois*, 405 U.S. 645, 652–53 (1972).

8. *Quilloin v. Walcott*, 434 U.S. 246, 255 (1978), quoting *Smith v. Organization of Foster Families*, 431 U.S. 816, 862–63 (1977) (Stewart, J. concurring). *See also Moore v. City of East Cleveland*, 431 U.S. 494 (1977) (plurality opinion).

9. *Custody of Michel*, 28 Mass. App. Ct. 260, 549 N.E.2d 440 (1990); *In the Matter of Appeal in Pima County Juvenile Dependency Action*, 162 Ariz. 601, 785 P.2d 121 (1990). *But see, J.H. v. Cabinet for Human Resources*, 767 S.W. 2d 330 (Ky. App. 1988) (adjudication of one child as being abused, neglected, and dependent cannot form the basis of similar adjudication of sibling in absence of other evidence relating directly to the second child).

10. N.Y. Fam. Ct. § 1012(a) (McKinney 1983). ('respondent' includes any parent or other person legally responsible for a child's care.")

11. Md. Code Ann., Fam. Law § 5-701(b)(i) (1991).

12. *See, e.g., State v. Smith*, 485 S.W.2d 461 (Mo. App. 1972).

13. Ariz. Rev. Stat. Ann. § 8-546(A)(1). *See also*, § 8–201(1).

14. *See, e.g., State v. Laemoa*, 20 Or. App. 516, 533 P.2d 370 (1975).

15. *Welfare Commissioner v. Anonymous*, 33 Conn. Sup. 100, 103, 364 A.2d 250, 252 (1976). *See also Diernfeld v. People*, 137 Colo. 238, 323 P.2d 628 (1958); *In re Valdez*, 29 Utah 2d 63, 504 P.2d 1372 (1973). *See also, Petition of D.S.S. to Dispense with Consent to Adoption*, 389 Mass. 793, 452 N.E.2d 497 (1983) (a presumption that leaving a child in the care of others for more than one year is abandonment is unconstitutional).

16. *D.S.S. v. Father & Mother*, 294 S.C. 518, 366 S.E.2d 40 (1988) (parents unsuccessfully claimed that abuse prosecution infringed upon their religious freedom to follow the Bible in disciplining their child).

17. Act of Colony of Massachusetts Bay of New England, 1654, Mass. Bay Records, vol. III (1644–1657) at 355, cited in *Commonwealth v. Brasher*, 359 Mass. 550, 552, 270 N.E.2d 389, 391 (1971).

18. *See, e.g., People v. Green*, 155 Mich. 524, 536, 119 N.W. 1087, 1089 (1909); *State v. Black*, 360 Mo. 261, 227 S.W.2d 1006 (1950).

19. *See, e.g., Hinkel v. State*, 127 Ind. 490, 26 N.E. 777 (1890); *Neal v. State*, 54 Ga. 281 (1875).

20. *Bowers v. State*, 283 Md. 115, 128, 389 A.2d 341, 349 (1978).

21. *In re Roy*, 71 A.D.2d 815, 418 N.Y.S.2d 913 (4th Dep't. 1979).

22. *E.g., State v. Hunt*, 2 Ariz. App. 6, 406 P.2d 208 (1965).

23. *See, e.g., In re Ivey*, 319 So. 2d 53 (Fla. App. 1975); *People ex rel. Wallace v. Labrenz*, 411 Ill. 618, 104 N.E.2d 769, *cert. denied*, 344 U.S. 824 (1952); *Raleigh Fitkin-Paul Morgan Memorial Hosp. v. Anderson*, 42 N.J. 421, 201 A.2d 537, *cert. denied*, 377 U.S. 985 (1964).

24. *In re Seiferth*, 309 N.Y. 80, 127 N.E.2d 820 (1955). *Accord, In re Frank*, 41 Wash. 2d 294, 248 P.2d 553 (1952).

25. *In re Karwath*, 199 N.W.2d 147 (Iowa 1972).

26. *Id.* at 150.

27. *In re Sampson*, 65 Misc. 2d 658, 317 N.Y.S.2d 641 (Fam. Ct. 1970), *aff'd*, 37 A.D.2d 668, 323 N.Y.S.2d 253 (3d Dep't 1971), *aff'd*, 29 N.Y.2d 900, 278 N.E.2d 918, 328 N.Y.S.2d 686 (1972) (per curiam).

28. *See, e.g., In re Welfare of Price*, 13 Wash. App. 437, 535 P.2d 475 (1975); *In re Seiferth, supra* note 24.

29. *Custody of a Minor*, 375 Mass. 733, 379 N.E.2d 1053 (1978).

30. *Matter of Hofbauer*, 47 N.Y.2d 648, 393 N.E.2d 1009, 419 N.Y.S.2d 936 (1979).

31. *See, In re Hudson*, 13 Wash. 2d 673, 126 P.2d 765 (1942) (en banc).

32. *In re Green*, 448 Pa. 338, 292 A.2d 387 (1972).

33. *In re Green*, 452 Pa. 373, 307 A.2d 279 (1973).

34. *State v. McKown*, 475 N.W.2d 63, 67 (Minn. 1991), *cert. denied*, 112 S. Ct. 882 (1992).

35. *Newmark v. Williams*, 588 A.2d 1108 (Del. Sup. Ct. 1991).

36. 52 A.L.R.3d 1118–19 (1973).

37. *Matter of Storar*, 52 N.Y.2d 363, 380, 420 N.E.2d 64, 73, 438 N.Y.S.2d 266, 275, *cert. denied*, 454 U.S. 858 (1981) *citing In re Sampson*, 29 N.Y.2d 900, 278 N.E.2d 918, 328 N.Y.S.2d 686 (1972).

38. *Custody of a Minor, supra* note 29.

39. *Application of President and Directors of Georgetown College, Inc.*, 331 F.2d 1000 (D.C. Cir.), *reh'g denied*, 331 F.2d 1010, *cert. denied*, 377 U.S. 978 (1964).

40. *In re Cabrera*, 381 Pa. Super. 100, 552 A.2d 1114 (1989).

41. *Application of L.I. Jewish Med. Ctr.*, 147 Misc. 2d 724, 557 N.Y.S.2d 239 (N.Y.Sup. 1990).

42. *Jehovah's Witnesses In State of Washington v. King Co. Hospital Unit No. 1*, 278 F. Supp. 488 (1967), *aff'd*, 390 U.S. 598 (1968).

43. *Newmark v. Williams, supra* note 35.

44. *Walker v. Superior Court*, 47 Cal. 3d 112, 763 P.2d 852, 253 Cal. Rptr. 1 (1988) (California's statutory scheme reflects a willingness to accommodate religious practice when children do not face serious physical harm).

45. *See, e.g.,* D.C. Stat. Ann. § 16-2301(9) (1966 & Supp. 1978); Fla. Stat. Ann. § 39.01(37) (West 1988); La. Child. Code § 1003(8), 10(B) (Westlaw West 1994).

46. N.Y. Fam. Ct. § 1012(h) (McKinney 1983).

47. Wis. Stat. Ann. § 48.13(11) (West 1987).

48. *O'Connor v. Donaldson*, 422 U.S. 563, 584 (1975) (*quoting Greenwood v. United States*, 350 U.S. 366, 375 (1956).

49. 406 U.S. 205 (1972).

50. *Pierce v. Society of Sisters*, 268 U.S. 510 (1925).

51. *People v. Levisen*, 404 Ill. 574, 90 N.E.2d 213 (1950); *In re Richards*, 166 Misc. 359, 2 N.Y.S.2d 608 (N.Y.Child.Ct.), *aff'd*, 255 A.D. 922, 7 N.Y.S.2d 722 (3d Dep't 1938).

52. *Mannis v. State ex rel. DeWitt School Dist. No. 1*, 240 Ark. 42, 398 S.W.2d 206, *cert. denied*, 384 U.S. 972 (1966); *In re Elwell*, 55 Misc. 2d 252, 284 N.Y.S.2d 924 (N.Y. Fam. Ct. 1967); *In re Marsh*, 140 Pa. Super. 472, 14 A.2d 368 (1940). *But cf. State v. Dunham*,

154 Ohio St. 63, 93 N.E.2d 286 (1950) (no neglect when there was no evidence that the parent had done anything to prevent the child's immunization).

53. *See, e.g.*, N.Y. Pub. Health Law § 2164 (9) (McKinney 1993).

54. *See, Maier v. Besser*, 73 Misc. 2d 241, 341 N.Y.S.2d 411 (N.Y. Sup. 1972).

55. *See, e.g.*, N.Y. Fam. Ct. § 1012(f)(i)(B) (McKinney 1983).

56. R.I. Gen. Laws § 11-9-5 (1981).

57. *See, e.g.*, N.Y. Fam. Ct. § 1012(f)(i)(A) (McKinney 1983); Fla. Stat. Ann. § 39.01 (37) (West 1988); La. Child. Code § 1003(10)(b) (Westlaw West 1990), Wis. Stat. Ann. § 48.981 (1)(d) (West 1987). *See also, Matter of D.C.*, 561 A.2d 477 (D.C. App. 1989) (agency bears burden of proof in neglect cases that neglect is not due to lack of financial means).

58. *In re Brooks*, 63 Ill. App. 3d 328, 337, 379 N.E.2d 872, 879 (1st Dist. 1978).

59. *See, e.g.*, *Thornhill v. Alabama*, 310 U.S. 88 (1940); *Smith v. Goguen*, 415 U.S. 566, 572–76 (1974); *Coates v. City of Cincinnati*, 402 U.S. 611, 614–16 (1971).

60. *State v. Riker*, 376 So. 2d 862 (Fla. 1979) (citing Fla. Stat. Ann. § 827.04(2)).

61. *Id.*

62. *State v. Crowdell*, 234 Neb. 469, 451 N.W.2d 695 (1990).

63. *See, e.g.*, *People v. Jackson*, 140 Mich. App. 283, 364 N.W.2d 310 (1985) (statute proscribing child cruelty, as "cruelly and unlawfully punishes," was not unconstitutionally vague); *State v. Cameron*, 485 So. 2d 599, 602 (La. App. 1986), (Statute prohibiting "entic[ing] . . . any child under the age of seventeen . . . to . . . [p]erform any sexually immoral act" held not vague); *People In Interest of J.A.*, 733 P.2d 1197 (Colo. 1987) (statute prohibiting sexual assault on a child and referring to "knowingly" touching the victim's intimate parts held not vague); *Teubner v. State*, 742 S.W.2d 57 (Tex. App. 1987), (conviction of parents for crime of "bodily injury to child" held not to be vague because penal code defines and limits behaviors that will be actionable).

64. *State v. DeBerry*, 185 W. Va. 512, 514, 408 S.E.2d 91, 93, *cert. denied*, 112 S. Ct. 592 (1991).

65. *State v. Schriver*, 207 Conn. 456, 457, 542 A.2d 686, 687 (1988). *See also, People v. Villacis*, 143 Misc. 2d 568. 569, 541 N.Y.S.2d 178, 179 (N.Y. Sup. 1989) (declaring unconstitutional a subdivision of New York's penal law declaring that one is guilty of endangering the welfare of a child if he or she "knowingly acts in a manner likely to be injurious to the . . . welfare of [the] child").

66. *Stanley v. Illinois, supra* note 7, at 651 (quoting *Skinner v. Oklahoma*, 316 U.S. 535, 541 (1942) (quoting *May v. Anderson*, 345 U.S. 528, 533 (1953)).

67. *See, e.g.*, *State v. McMaster*, 259 Or. 291, 486 P.2d 567 (1971).

68. *See, e.g.*, *Alsager v. District Court*, 406 F. Supp. 10 (S.D. Iowa 1975), *aff'd*, 545 F.2d 1137 (8th Cir. 1976); *Roe v. Conn*, 417 F. Supp. 769 (M.D. Ala. 1976).

69. *See, e.g.*, Tenn. Code Ann. § 37-1-102(b)(10)(B) (1991).

70. *DeShaney v. Winnebago County Department of Social Services*, 489 U.S. 189 (1989). For an interesting critique of the DeShaney decision, *see* Akhil Reed Amar and Daniel Widawsky, *Child Abuse as Slavery: A Thirteenth Amendment Response to DeShaney*, 105 Harv. L. Rev. 1359 (1992).

71. *See*, National Taskforce for Children's Constitutional Rights, P.O. Box 1620, Litchfield, Conn. 06759, (203) 567-KIDS.

72. N.Y. Soc. Serv. Law § 413(i) (McKinney 1992).

73. See *Walstad v. State*, 818 P.2d 695 (Alaska App. 1991).

74. *See, e.g.*, Fla. Stat. Ann. § 415.503(10)(A)(2) (Westlaw West 1995); Mass. Gen. Laws Ann. Ch. 119, § 51A (West 1993); Minn. Stat. Ann. § 626.5562(2) (West 1983 & Supp. 1994); Okla. Stat. Ann. tit. 21, § 846(A)(2) (West 1983 & Supp. 1995).

75. *See, e.g.*, N.Y. Soc. Serv. Law § 420(1) (McKinney 1992).

76. *See e.g.*, *People v. Dossinger*, 122 Misc. 2d 853, 472 N.Y.S. 2d 808, 812 (N.Y. Sup. 1983), *aff'd as modified*, 106 A.D.2d 661, 482 N.Y.S.2d 915 (2d Dep't 1984). *See also*, Douglas Besharov, The Vulnerable Social Worker, Liability For Serving Children and Families (1985).

77. *See, e.g.*, N.Y. Soc. Serv. Law § 420(2) (McKinney 1992).

78. *See, e.g.*, Fla. Stat. Ann. § 415.511(1)(a) (West 1993); Iowa Code Ann. § 232.73 (West 1994).

79. *See, e.g.*, *Maples v. Siddiqui*, 450 N.W.2d 529 (Iowa 1990), *Gross v. Haight*, 496 So. 2d 1225 (La. App. 1986); *Awkerman v. Tri-County Orthopedic Group*, 143 Mich. App. 722, 373 N.W.2d 204 (1985); *Gross v. Myers*, 229 Mont. 509, 748 P.2d 459 (1987); *Davis v. Durham City Schools*, 91 N.C. App. 520, 372 S.E.2d 318 (1988).

80. *See, e.g.*, *Satler v. Larsen*, 131 A.D.2d 125, 520 N.Y.S.2d 378 (1st Dep't 1987).

81. N.Y. Soc. Serv. Law § 414 (McKinney 1992).

82. *See, e.g.*, N.Y. Soc. Serv. Law § 422 (McKinney 1992).

83. *Valmonte v. Bane*, 18 F.3d 992 (2d Cir. 1994). *But see Hodge v. Jones*, 31 F.3d 157 (4th Cir.), *cert. denied*, 115 S. Ct. 581 (1994).

84. N.Y. Soc. Serv. Law § 424-a(2)(a) (McKinney 1992).

85. *Valmonte v. Bane, supra* note 83, at 1004 (quoting *Santosky v. Kramer*, 455 U.S. 745, 762 (1982).

86. *Id.*

87. 45 C.F.R. § 1340.14(i) (1991).

88. *See* 9 ABA Juv. & Child Welfare Reporter 112, 14 (1990).

89. N.Y. Soc. Serv. Law § 424(6) (McKinney 1992).

90. *Camara v. Municipal Court*, 387 U.S. 523 (1967); *cf. Marshall v. Barlow's Inc.*, 436 U.S. 307 (1978); *Welsh v. Wisconsin*, 466 U.S. 740 (1984); *but see Wyman v. James*, 400 U.S. 309 (1971) (home visits by caseworkers administering welfare programs in which aid is conditioned upon visitation do not require a warrant); *Griffin v. Wisconsin*, 483 U.S. 868 (1987) (home entries by probation officers under reasonable procedures for probationary supervision do not require a warrant).

91. *See, e.g.*, *Terry v. Ohio*, 392 U.S. 1 (1968); *Sibron v. New York*, 392 U.S. 40 (1968); *Davis v. Mississippi*, 394 U.S. 721 (1969); *Hayes v. Florida*, 470 U.S. 811 (1985).

92. *See, e.g.*, *Doe v. Staples*, 706 F.2d 985 (6th Cir. 1983), *cert. denied*, 465 U.S. 1033 (1984).

93. *In re Juvenile Appeal*, 189 Conn. 276, 455 A.2d 1313 (1983). *See also Roe v. Conn, supra* note 68 (removal without notice and hearing is not permissible except to prevent danger of immediate harm or threatened harm to the child; and, even, in these cases, a prompt postremoval hearing is required).

94. *Darryl H. v. Coler*, 801 F.2d 893, 901-2 n.8 (7th Cir. 1986).

95. *See, e.g.*, *White v. Pierce County*, 797 F.2d 812, 815–16 (9th Cir. 1986).

96. *See In the Matter of Diane P.*, 110 A.D.2d 354, 494 N.Y.S.2d 881 (2d Dep't 1985); *In re Christopher B.*, 82 Cal. App. 3d 608, 147 Cal. Rptr. 390 (3d Dist. 1978); *In the Matter of Robert P.*, 61 Cal. App. 3d 310, 132 Cal. Rptr. 5 (1st Dist. 1976), *appeal dismissed*, 431 U.S. 911 (1977). *Contra, In the Matter of Melinda I.*, 110 A.D.2d 991, 488 N.Y.S.2d 279 (3d Dep't 1985).

97. *See, e.g., Duchesne v. Sugarman*, 566 F.2d 817, 829 (2d Cir. 1977) (officials responsible for the retention of children without consent may be liable to parents for damages under the federal civil rights act); *Spurrell v. Bloch*, 40 Wash. App. 854, 701 P.2d 529 (1985) (police officer who removed children from their home upon a suspicion of neglect when the removal was not reasonably necessary to protect the children from imminent danger was subject to damages for false imprisonment). *See also supra* note 76.

98. *Cf. Kolender v. Lawson*, 461 U.S. 352, 360 n. 9 (1983).

99. *Cf. Camara v. Municipal Court, supra* note 90.

100. *Cf. Florida v. Royer*, 460 U.S. 491, 498 (1983) (plurality opinion) (a suspect's "refusal to listen or answer [when questioned by public officials] does not, without more, furnish . . . grounds [for detention of the suspect]"); *Brown v. Texas*, 443 U.S. 47 (1979).

101. *See White v. Pierce County, supra* note 95.

102. *See generally* Wyman v. James, *supra* note 90; *Griffin v. Wisconsin, supra* note 90.

103. *See, e.g., Salyer v. Patrick*, 874 F.2d 374 (6th Cir. 1989). *See also DeShaney v. Winnebago County Department of Social Services, supra* note 70.

104. *See generally Estelle v. Gamble*, 429 U.S. 97 (1976).

105. *See, e.g.*, N.Y. Fam. Ct. Act § 1046 (a)(vii) (McKinney 1983); Minn. Stat. Ann. § 626.556(8) (West 1983).

106. *See, e.g., Vosburg v. Department of Social Services*, 884 F.2d 133 (4th Cir. 1989).

107. *Salyer v. Patrick, supra* note 103.

108. *Achterhof v. Selvaggio*, 886 F.2d 826 (6th Cir. 1989). *See also Austin v. Borel*, 830 F.2d 1356 (5th Cir. 1987).

109. *Mazor v. Shelton*, 637 F. Supp. 330 (N.D. Cal. 1986). *See also Whelehan v. Monroe County*, 558 F. Supp. 1093 (W.D.N.Y. 1983); *Rosco v. County of Los Angeles*, 207 Cal. App. 3d 531, 254 Cal. Rptr. 894 (2d Dist.), *cert. denied*, 493 U.S. 917 (1989).

110. *Id. See also Meyers v. Contra Costa County Dep't of Social Services*, 812 F.2d 1154 (9th Cir.), *cert. denied*, 484 U.S. 829 (1987).

111. *Loeblich v. City of Davis*, 213 Cal. App. 3d 1272, 262 Cal. Rptr. 397 (3d Dist. 1989).

112. *But see Jenkins v. County of Orange*, 212 Cal. App. 3d 278, 260 Cal. Rptr. 645 (4th Dist. 1989) (absolute immunity for caseworker who removed child and sought her placement in temporary protective custody based on (false) report; caseworker is immune for investigating report and for taking child into custody even when case is dismissed by court after a hearing).

113. *Newton v. County of Napa*, 217 Cal. App. 3d 1551, 266 Cal. Rptr. 682 (1st Dist. 1990).

114. *Id.* at 1557–58, 266 Cal. Rptr. at 685.

115. *Hawkins v. State*, 543 So.2d 1052 (La. App. 1989).

116. *See, e.g.*, N.Y. Soc. Serv. Law § 422(7) (McKinney 1992). *See also Valmonte v. Bane, supra* note 83.

117. Okla. Stat. Ann. tit. 10, § 1104(d) (West 1987).

118. Tex. Fam. Code Ann. § 17.03 (West 1986).

119. N.Y. Fam. Ct. § 1024(a) (McKinney 1983).

120. N.Y. Fam. Ct. §§ 1027(a), 1028(a) (McKinney 1983); *Duchesne v. Sugarman,* *supra* note 97.

121. *See Newton v. Burgin,* 363 F. Supp. 782 (W.D.N.C. 1973), *aff'd,* 414 U.S. 1139 (1974).

122. Tex. Fam. Code Ann. § 17.03(c) (West 1986).

123. *Sims v. State Dep't of Public Welfare,* 438 F. Supp. 1179, 1193 (S.D. Tex. 1977), *rev'd on other grounds sub nom. Moore v. Sims,* 442 U.S. 415 (1979).

124. *Roe v. Conn, supra* note 68, at 778.

125. 42 U.S.C. § 672(a)(1) (1991).

126. 42 U.S.C. § 671(a)(15) (1991).

127. *See, e.g.,* Fla. Stat. Ann. § 39.408 (3)(a)(10) (West 1988 & Supp. 1994).

128. *See, e.g.,* Cal. Welf. & Inst. Code § 319(a) (West 1984); Va. Code Ann. § 16.1–252(E)(1) (Michie 1988).

129. 42 U.S.C. § 675(5)(A) (1991).

130. N.Y. Soc. Serv. Law § 419 (McKinney 1992) (general immunity for all reporters or removers).

131. *See, e.g., Herndon v. Lowry,* 301 U.S. 242 (1937); *Papachristou v. City of Jacksonville,* 405 U.S. 156 (1972).

132. *Roe v. Conn, supra* note 68.

133. *See Sims v. State Dep't of Public Welfare, supra* note 123, at 1192.

134. *In re Christina T.,* 590 P.2d 189 (Okla. 1979).

135. *See* N.Y. Fam. Ct. Act § 1046(b)(i) (McKinney 1983); *In re Tammie Z.,* 66 N.Y.2d 1, 484 N.E.2d 1038, 494 N.Y.S.2d 686 (1985) (preponderance of evidence standard in abuse and neglect proceedings does not violate due process); *In the Matter of A.S.,* 643 A.2d 345 (D.C. App. 1994 (same).

136. *See Hofmeister v. Bauer,* 110 Idaho 960, 719 P.2d 1220 (1986); *In re Jonathan,* 415 A.2d 1036 (R.I. 1980) (agency must show by clear and convincing evidence that the child has suffered or is likely to suffer harm).

137. *See, e.g.,* N.H. Rev. Stat. Ann. § 169-C:10 (1994).

138. *See, e.g., Cleaver v. Wilcox,* 499 F.2d 940 (9th Cir. 1974).

139. *See Lassiter v. Department of Social Services,* 452 U.S. (1981).

140. *See* 42 U.S.C. § 5106a(b)(6) (Supp. 1994) (in order to receive federal funds, state must provide a guardian ad litem to represent the child in all abuse or neglect proceedings.)

141. *See, e.g.,* Cal. Evid. Code §§ 917, 992 (West 1966); Ill. Ann. Stat., ch. 735, § 5/8-802 (Westlaw West 1994); N.Y. Civ. Prac. L. & R. § 4504(a) (McKinney 1992).

142. *See, e.g., In re Doe Children,* 93 Misc. 2d 479, 402 N.Y.S.2d 958 (N.Y. Fam. Ct. 1978); N.Y. Fam. Ct. § 1046(a)(vii) (McKinney 1983); Iowa Code Ann. § 232.96(5) (West 1994); Wash. Rev. Code § 5.60.060 (4)(a) (West 1963 & Supp. 1994).

143. *See, e.g.,* American Medical Association, Principles of Ethics, § 9.

144. *Matter of S.W.,* 79 Cal. App. 3d 719, 145 Cal. Rptr. 143 (2d Dist. 1978); *People*

v. Bowman, 812 P.2d 725 (Colo. App. 1991); *People v. Farrow,* 183 Mich. App. 436, 455 N.W.2d 325 (1990) (admission of child abuse made to counselor in employer-sponsored counseling that was expressly confidential is protected and not admissible).

145. *See, e.g.,* Iowa Code Ann. § 232.96(5) (West 1994); Wash. Rev. Code § 5.60.060(1) (West 1963).

146. *State v. Willette,* 421 N.W.2d 342 (Minn. App. 1988) (there exists a statutory exception in Minnesota to all privileges in child sexual abuse cases. Traditional justifications for recognizing the marital privilege were absent in cases where one spouse testifying against other on matters that were likely to have already destroyed marital harmony).

147. *See* 2 Wigmore, Evidence §§ 285, 289 (Chadbourn rev. 1979).

148. *See, e.g., Custody of Two Minors,* 396 Mass. 610, 487 N.E.2d 1358 (1986) (court may infer from parents' failure to testify in their own behalf that they lack the willingness or ability to care for their children's well-being); *In the Matter of the Welfare of J.W.,* 391 N.W.2d 791 (Minn. 1986), *cert. denied sub nom. Minor v. Bureau of Social Services,* 479 U.S. 1040 (1987) (court may deem a charge of child neglect to be admitted when the children's caretakers refuse to answer questions in a civil deposition on self-incrimination grounds during the pendency of a collateral criminal investigation).

149. *See, e.g., In re James A.,* 505 A.2d 1386 (R.I. 1986).

150. *State v. Daniels,* 484 So. 2d 941 (La. App. 1986).

151. *See, e.g., In Interest of K. L. M.,* 146 Ill. App. 3d 489, 496 N.E.2d 1262, 100 Ill. Dec. 197 (4th Dist. 1986) (statements made by a four-year-old to a caseworker regarding sexual abuse held admissible through the caseworker's testimony despite the defendant's objections based on the Sixth Amendment right to confrontation).

152. 487 U.S. 1012 (1988).

153. *Id.* at 1016.

154. *Maryland v. Craig,* 497 U.S. 836, 857 (1990).

155. *See, e.g., United States v. Azure,* 801 F.2d 336 (8th Cir. 1986); *State v. Lindsey,* 149 Ariz. 472, 720 P.2d 73 (1986); *Tevlin v. People,* 715 P.2d 338 (Colo. 1986); *State v. Holloway,* 82 N.C. App. 586, 347 S.E.2d 72 (1986).

156. *See, e.g., People v. Koon,* 724 P.2d 1367 (Colo. App. 1986).

157. *See generally* Note, *The Unreliability of Expert Testimony on the Typical Characteristics of Sexual Abuse Victims,* 74 Geo. L.J. 429 (1985).

158. 293 F. 1013 (D.C. Cir. 1923).

159. *See, e.g., In re Amber B.,* 191 Cal. App. 3d 682, 236 Cal. Rptr. 623 (1st Dist. 1987); *and see In re Sara M.,* 194 Cal. App.3d 585, 239 Cal. Rptr. 605 (1987) (evidence regarding the existence and symptomatology of a "child molestation syndrome" cannot be introduced to prove the fact that a child was abused because the evidence is lacking in established reliability).

160. *See, e.g., State v. Loebach,* 310 N.W.2d 58 (Minn. 1981).

161. *E.g., In re Sara M., supra* note 159.

162. 113 S. Ct. 2786 (1993).

163. *See, e.g., In Re Murray,* 52 Ohio St. 3d 155, 556 N.E.2d 1169 (1990).

164. *See, e.g.,* R.I. Gen. Laws § 11-9-5 (1981) (cruelty to or neglect of child can be a felony with punishment up to 3 years in jail, $1,000 fine, and counseling).

165. *See, e.g.*, Alaska Stat. § 25.23.180(i) (1992); Vt. Stat. Ann. tit. 12 § 522 (1973 & Supp. 1994).

166. *See, e.g., Foldi v. Jeffries*, 93 N.J. 533, 461 A.2d 1145 (1983); *Courtney v. Courtney*, 186 W. Va. 597, 413 S.E.2d 418 (1991).

167. *See, e.g., Burnette v. Wahl*, 284 Or. 705, 588 P.2d 1105 (1978); *Hansen v. Hansen*, 43 Colo. App. 525, 608 P.2d 364 (1979).

VI

Foster Care

Since the mid-1980s, there has been an explosion in the number of children living in foster care. As epidemics of AIDS, crack cocaine addiction, unemployment, and homelessness took their toll on families, the country's foster care population soared, from 262,000 children in 1982 to 442,000 in 1992, with the numbers rising by 45 percent from 1986 to 1990 alone.[1] With over 480,000 children in care in 1994, it is now estimated that the foster care population will surpass half a million in 1996.

Nearly half of the children in foster care enter the foster care system because they faced neglect or physical or sexual abuse at home.[2] An additional 22 percent enter care because of a parent's economic hardship, drug or alcohol abuse, homelessness, illness, or imprisonment.[3] An increasing number of foster children are infants,[4] some born to drug or alcohol-addicted mothers and abandoned at birth.[5]

The growth in foster care caseloads carries a heavy price tag. According to one estimate, taxpayers spent more than $11 billion on foster care for children in 1992.[6] Less easy to assess is the psychological price paid by children, an increasing number of whom experience multiple foster care placements,[7] who are caught in the limbo of foster care "drift."

Since the passage in 1980 of the Adoption Assistance and Child Welfare Act, the federal government has played an increasingly important role in setting national foster care policy. The most recent federal initiative in this area is the Family Preservation and Support Services Act of 1993 (Family Preservation Act).[8] Based, like the 1980 Act, on the twin premises that children in general do best when cared for by their birth parents and that parents who have abused or neglected their children can, with the right combination of services and support, learn to become capable parents,[9] the Family Preservation Act makes federal tax dollars available to the states for a variety of social-service programs designed to allow children at risk of foster care placement stay with their families.[10]

The family preservation effort remains the subject of national debate. Supporters of the family preservation approach include respected child advocacy organizations who see the family preservation initiative as a way of supporting poor and minority families who are overrepresented in the foster care population and who have been hard hit by cutbacks in other federal antipoverty programs as well as fiscal conservatives searching for ways to trim burgeoning foster care costs.[11]

Others, however, have sounded a cautionary note. Pointing to data on children killed or abused by their parents or caretakers after they have already come to the attention of child welfare agencies,[12] some argue that family preservation efforts need to be applied selectively so that children's safety is not jeopardized.[13] In addition, they question the wisdom, in some cases, of separating children from foster parents whom they know and love as their "real" parents, for the sake of reuniting them with birth parents who may be their parents in name only.[14]

What is foster care?

Foster care is a government-run system of providing 24-hour-a-day care for children who cannot live in their own homes, usually due to problems in the family. In some states, foster care is operated directly by the state government; in other states, a state agency provides some form of supervision, regulation, or standard setting, but local counties run the programs with varying degrees of autonomy.[15] In foster care, children live away from their parents in a variety of settings including individual foster homes and group facilities.

Is foster care meant to be temporary?

In most cases, yes. The foster parent-child relationship is viewed as a temporary one designed to provide the child with the benefits of living in a family setting (instead of institutionalized care) when residence outside of the child's original home is necessary.

What is foster care supposed to accomplish?

The theoretical goal of foster care is for the child to leave foster care within one or two years at most. While the child is in foster care, the state is required to provide a variety of social services to the child's parent(s). These services are intended to alleviate the problems that necessitated the child's entry into foster care in the first place, so that the child can eventually be returned to his or her biological family. These services may include parenting education, homemaker services, drug or alcohol rehabilitation programs, job training, or respite care.

When reunification of the child with his or her parents is not a realistic possibility because the parent is plainly unable to care for the child, an alternative goal is to find a new permanent family for the child through adoption. The adoptive parents may be the child's foster parents, members of the child's extended family, or other suitable adults.

Unfortunately, actual practice does not always conform to the theory. Many children spend years in foster care, unable to return to their biological families and yet still legally tied to them and thus unable to find a new permanent family through adoption.[16]

What are the age limits for children in foster care?

Children may enter foster care at birth up through eighteen years of age. Most states will not keep children in foster care after they reach eighteen, but many make exceptions and keep some children until they are twenty-one who are in college or are finishing up some kind of vocational training program.

Is foster care primarily a federal, state, or local concern?

Traditionally, protecting and caring for children was considered a matter of state rather than federal concern. However, faced with mounting evidence that children were being too readily placed in foster care and that, once placed, they were spending long periods of time in foster care limbo without moving either toward reunification with their family of origin or toward adoption, Congress concluded that there was a need for federal action to change local practices.

In the landmark Adoption Assistance and Child Welfare Act of 1980,[17] Congress sought to limit the amount of time children spent in foster care, first by requiring states to make "reasonable efforts"[18] to reunify the child with his or her biological family and then, if reunification was not a viable option, to find a new permanent family for the child through adoption. To enforce these mandates, Congress conditioned the receipt of federal foster care funds on compliance with the new federal foster care laws.

The Adoption Assistance and Child Welfare Act of 1980 requires states that receive federal foster care money to take steps to prevent the unnecessary separation of children from their parents, to assure a careful monitoring of children who are separated, and to provide an infusion of services into the family to facilitate the return of children to their parents (where appropriate). The Act also makes funds available to encourage the adoption of hard-to-place children for whom reunification with their original family is not possible.

The 1980 Act addresses all phases of the child protection process. First, it sets strict conditions for removal of children from their homes. In order to be eligible for federal money to subsidize foster care services under the Aid to Families with Dependent Children-Foster Care (AFDC-FC) program, a state must comply with the following requirements:

1. A child may be removed from his or her home only as a result of a judicial determination that continued residence in the home would be contrary to the welfare of the child.[19]

2. The state must remain responsible for the placement and care of the child.[20]

3. The child must be maintained in a foster home or child care institution.[21]

With regard to children who are in the state's care as a result of removal from their homes, the Act requires that the state do four things.

1. The state must make a determination in the case of each child whether the current foster placement is necessary and appropriate, whether the child can be or should be returned to his or her parents or freed for adoption, and what services are necessary to facilitate the return of the child or the placement of the child for adoption or legal guardianship.[22]

2. The state must develop a program of services designed to help children, where appropriate, return to families from which they have been removed or be placed for adoption or legal guardianship.[23]

3. The state must develop and maintain a case review system for each child receiving state supervised foster care which assures that (a) each child has a case plan designed to achieve placement in the least restrictive setting available and in close proximity to the parents' home, consistent with the best interests and special needs of the child;[24] (b) the status of each child is reviewed at least every six months by a court or an

administrative panel to determine (i) the need for and appropriateness of the placement and (ii) compliance with the case plan;[25] (c) each child in state supervised foster care has a dispositional hearing before a court or court-appointed body within eighteen months of placement and periodically thereafter to determine the future status of the child, including whether s/he should be returned home, continued in foster care for a specified period, placed for adoption, or, because of the child's special needs, continued in foster care on a permanent or long-term basis;[26] and (d) each child in state-supervised foster care is provided procedural safeguards with respect to termination of parental rights, changes in the child's placement and determinations affecting visitation privileges of parents.[27] The case plan, sometimes referred to as a service plan, may be challenged by the parents whenever they are dissatisfied with its provisions or the adequacy of the services provided. These challenges can be made in juvenile court itself or in a fair-hearing administrative review process.[28]

4. The state must develop a statewide information system from which the status, demographic characteristics, location and goals for placement of every child who is currently in foster care or who has been in foster care during the preceding twelve months can be determined.[29]

Although states are not obliged to obey these rules, a state's failure to implement them makes the state ineligible for any increase in federal foster care funds above the amount payable in 1979.[30] Many states have incorporated significant parts of the federal law into their own laws.

What are the circumstances that result in children entering foster care?

Most often, children enter foster care after their parents have been accused of neglect or abuse and a state agency has begun an investigation. Sometimes these children have been removed from their parents by court order declaring that the children cannot safely be cared for at home; in other instances, parents voluntarily request that the state take temporary custody of a child.[31]

Voluntary placement may be the result of a parent's temporary inability to care for a child resulting from the parent's incapacity or the child's special needs. Occasionally, parents who cannot afford to pay for a residential program they believe their children require will place them in foster care so that the state will pay for the placement. However, in theory children may not to be taken into foster care solely because of a parent's poverty or homelessness[32] or to obtain needed educational services.[33]

Are all children who have been abused or neglected placed in foster care?

No. Even when an investigator determines that a child is abused or neglected, federal law and many state laws require child welfare agencies to make "reasonable efforts" to keep children at home by providing services to families that address the problems causing the abuse or neglect, in order to avoid foster care.[34] This is based on the assumption that generally it is better for children to be raised by their biological parents if at all possible[35] and that parents who have abused or neglected their children can rehabilitate themselves and become capable parents if they are offered the right mix of services.

How are services provided to keep children out of foster care?

Most state and county child-welfare systems have some program of preventive services that are intended to prevent foster care placement for those children considered by the system to be at risk of foster care placement, usually because of conditions in the child's home.[36] These services are provided directly by caseworkers in the public system or under contract with private agencies.

Parents are not required to accept these services. However, when agency officials consider the problems in the home to be sufficiently serious, they will go to court and obtain an order forcing the parents to accept services or suffer the risk of having the court remove the child from their custody.

Preventive services include day care, emergency caretaker services, assistance in obtaining housing, mental health or substance abuse programs, job counseling, crisis counseling, assistance in budgeting and meal planning, and teaching of parenting skills.[37] Some preventive services are short term and intensive, focused on getting a family through a crisis and then establishing contacts for them with ongoing social-service programs. These programs are very expensive because workers work with only a few families at a time. However, proponents of preventive service programs argue that they result in significant cost savings when they can safely keep children out of foster care.[38]

May families sue to enforce their right to preventive services?

The answer to this question has been complicated by a recent decision of the Supreme Court of the United States. In 1992 the Court ruled that families cannot sue in federal court to enforce the federal requirement that states make reasonable efforts to avoid foster care placement before taking a child into custody because Congress did not intend to bestow on individuals the right to bring such a lawsuit.[39]

In many states, however, the *reasonable efforts standard* has been made part of state law. In these jurisdictions, it is possible that a lawsuit could be brought to enforce the relevant state statutes.[40] One court has even held that the right to preventive services is a federal constitutional right; as a constitutional right, it could be enforced in a state or federal court.[41]

Is there a right to a hearing with regard to a child's entry into foster care?

Yes. Even when the child's parent consents to the child's entry into foster care, a hearing must be held within 180 days of placement to determine whether the placement is in the child's best interests.[42] Unless a court finds the placement to be in the child's best interests, the court must reject the placement. If such a hearing is not held, federal law prohibits states from receiving reimbursement for a substantial portion of foster care costs.[43] When children enter foster care over parental objection, a prompt hearing must be held pursuant to the rules governing child abuse and neglect laws. (See discussion in chapter 5.)

Do parents have the right to a lawyer at such a hearing?

Generally, state law entitles parents who cannot afford to hire their own lawyers to a court-appointed lawyer when their children enter foster care. However, there is no federal constitutional right to counsel in such cases.[44]

Do children have a right to be represented at such a hearing?

Yes. Although the Supreme Court has never held that children have a constitutional right to be represented by counsel or a guardian ad litem when they are placed in foster care, most states require the appointment of counsel or a guardian for a child when a court case commences.[45] Commonly, children entering foster care are provided with free counsel or a court-appointed special advocate (known as a CASA) who is usually not a lawyer.

If parents voluntarily place their children in foster care, must the state later honor their request that the children be returned to them?

It depends. Some states provide that parents have the right to have their children returned on demand;[46] but when the child welfare department or foster care agency believes the child's interests would not be served by returning to the birth parents, it may file a petition in court alleging that the parents are unfit to care for the children. When this is done, the court will decide whether or not the child should be returned.

Is all foster care run by the government?

Not exactly. Most children who enter foster care are placed in the legal custody of the state or county social services agency. However, government foster care systems—state and county based—not only run their own foster care programs directly but also contract with private, nonprofit agencies to provide foster care services. These private agencies also offer preventive services.

Even when a child lives with foster parents supervised by a private foster care agency, the state or county agency that has arranged for the placement has legal custody of the child, is ultimately responsible for his or her care, and usually has final decision-making authority about the child's education, medical care, and discipline.[47]

What kind of private agencies provide foster care services?

There are a wide variety of private agencies providing foster care services. Many of these private agencies have religious affiliations and are either part of the local Catholic Charities organization, or a federation of Jewish philanthropies or are otherwise associated with a particular religious denomination. State or county foster care systems contract principally with private, nonprofit organizations; however, profit-making organizations may be used when children require special services, often related to the child's serious medical or emotional problems, that cannot otherwise be obtained.

Are private agencies allowed to discriminate among children in their care on the basis of race or religion?

No. When private agencies accept public money and perform governmental functions (as all of them do when they are used by local government as foster care providers), they are prohibited from discriminating against children on racial or religious grounds.[48] Moreover, private sectarian agencies must accommodate the religious needs of children in their care even when those needs conflict with the sectarian agencies' religious beliefs.[49]

Where do children live while they are in foster care?

The majority of children in foster care live in private homes with individuals who serve as foster parents. Nationally, 71.4 percent of children in foster care reside in foster family homes; the remainder live in group facilities and institutions.[50]

Under the federal law that governs state foster care systems, children are supposed to be placed in the "least restrictive, most family-like setting" that is appropriate for their needs.[51] Many states also have statutes that express a preference for children being placed first with extended family members, if possible,[52] or in foster families instead of group facilities.

Some children in foster care live with members of their extended family (such as grandparents, aunts, uncles, or cousins) who become licensed foster parents under at least nominal supervision by the government child welfare agency. Some states license relatives as foster parents and provide foster parent payments for these placements. This kind of foster care is sometimes called kinship foster care.[53] The Supreme Court has ruled that states may not discriminate against relative foster care providers who meet the requirements of the federal foster care program.[54] However, states may deny state-financed foster care payments to relatives so that limited funds can be used to purchase foster care for children who have no relatives to care for them.[55]

Many states have laws that either require or express a statutory preference for matching children with foster families of the same religious background as the child.[56] In interpreting one set of religious matching statutes, one court ruled that religious matching was permissible only if it was not mandatory, took each child's interests into account, and did not result in discrimination. Religion has been considered a relevant factor in matching children with foster parents because of the need to protect a child's religious heritage, as long as the use of this factor did not result in other constitutional violations.[57]

Many foster care systems also follow a practice of matching a child with a foster family of the same race as the child. The issue of race matching in foster care is the subject of considerable controversy. White or interracial couples who wish to care for black or biracial foster children have brought a number of lawsuits challenging the practice of race matching in foster care. In one case, for example, a child welfare agency in Pennsylvania decided to remove a black child from the home of his white foster parents who had cared for him for two years in order to place him with a black family. A federal court found the action unconstitutional and ruled that the local child welfare agency was required to return the child to the foster parents' care.[58] Others courts have concluded that race is a permissible factor to consider in placing a child in a foster home, as long as it is not the only factor considered.[59] For a further discussion of the law governing race matching in foster care and adoption, see chapter 8.

Are there any limits on the kinds of places a foster care system can send children to live?

Not many. Generally, a state or county foster care system only has the legal authority to place a child in a licensed foster family home or in a licensed facility. However, foster care officials may place children in institutions for the mentally ill or mentally retarded upon a showing that the child requires institutionalization. Similarly, a child may be placed in a foster care facility that restricts the child's activities and freedom, provided the program is necessary for the child's well-being.

Foster care officials also have the authority to send a child to a facility in another state, even if the child or the child's parents do not want the child to go, when these officials determine that the out-of-state facility is appropriate for the child. Although the practice of sending children to out-of-state facilities has been challenged in court, no court has prohibited it.[60] However, some limitations on a local official's discretion in determining where to send a child have been imposed by courts. One court, for example, found that sending foster children to abusive out-of-state facilities violates their constitutional rights.[61]

How are decisions made about what happens to a child in foster care?

Each child in foster care is assigned a caseworker, who is responsible for managing the child's case and, along with others, for making plans for the child's future. Federal law requires that a written *case plan* for each child be completed within sixty days of the child's entry into foster care,[62] and many states have specific time periods within which a written plan must be developed both for children in foster care and for children whose cases have been accepted for preventive services.[63]

Federal law and many state laws specify what must be included in the case plans. The case plans should identify the problems that created the need for foster care placement, the services to be provided to address the problems, the state's responsibility for providing the services, the parents' responsibilities, the specific placement most suited to meet the child's needs, a detailed visitation schedule, and the time frame within which the child is to be returned home, if that is the goal, or freed for adoption.[64] Perhaps the most important part of the case plan is the *permanent goal* (sometimes called the *permanency goal*) chosen for the child. This goal is the agency's ultimate plan for the child; the goal may include the return to parents or family members, adoption, guardianship, or discharge from foster care when the child reaches a certain age.[65]

Do courts play any role in deciding what happens to children in foster care?

Yes. Federal law requires that the plan for each child in foster care be reviewed every six months either by a local court or an administrative panel[66] and that each child in foster care receive a dispositional hearing no later than eighteen months after entry into foster care.[67] Many states have chosen to use the state courts, instead of the administrative review process, to conduct the six-month periodic reviews mandated by federal law. Whether conducted by courts or administrative agencies, the six-month reviews are designed to determine whether placement is still a necessity and whether the type of placement is still appropriate for the child. In addition, the review should evaluate the extent of compliance with the case plan and the progress made in ameliorating the conditions that led to the child's placement.

The dispositional review must be conducted by a court. At this hearing, a judge must decide whether the child should be returned to the parent, remain in foster care for a specified period (and if so what services should be provided), be placed for adoption, or remain in foster care on a long-term basis.[68] When the child is sixteen years old, the court must also consider whether services provided to the child will help the child make the transition to independent living.[69]

Are participants in these hearings entitled to lawyers?

Usually the child welfare agency responsible for the child has a lawyer to represent its position at these hearings, and any of the parties who have been able to either hire a lawyer or obtain the services of a lawyer through some kind of government-funded legal services program can be represented by a lawyer. If a party cannot otherwise obtain a lawyer, however, state law varies on whether a lawyer will be appointed to represent that party.[70]

There is no constitutional right to the appointment of lawyers at these periodic review hearings. The closest the Supreme Court has come to addressing this issue is in a case that raised the right to appointed counsel for parents in a proceeding to terminate parental rights. In that case, the Court noted that state law already provided for the appointment of free attorneys at an earlier stage, when the court was deciding whether children should be removed from their parents' custody as the result of abuse or neglect charges. The Court decided that there was no automatic right to counsel in proceedings at which the question of termination of parental rights would be decided and that the issue should be decided by the local courts on a case-by-case basis.[71]

Where do children go when they leave foster care?

It depends. They may return to their parents or other relatives; they may stay in their foster home and become adopted by their foster parents; they may be placed with other adoptive parents; they may be discharged to independent living; or they may move into another social services system such as the mental health system. Some children leave the foster care system and move into the juvenile justice or prison system if convicted of violating the criminal law. The most recent data on discharges from foster care show that of all children discharged in 1988, 61.9 percent (105,800) were reunited with their families and 8.4 percent (14,000) were adopted.[72] It has also been estimated that 10 to 38 percent of the homeless population are former wards of the foster care system.[73]

Do foster care officials have an obligation to prepare children to leave the system when they are old enough to live on their own?

Yes. Most state laws require foster care officials to provide programs and training to prepare children for what is called *independent living* as they approach eighteen, the age at which foster care ends for most children. At least one state court has found that this right is enforceable.[74] In that case, young men living in a city shelter system had been discharged from foster care without any assistance in living on their own or any preparation or training for adult life. The court ordered their discharge to be put off until the young men received the services to which they were entitled, such as career counseling and training in a marketable skill.

Federal law provides extra money for state foster care systems to provide independent living programs to train young people to cope with adult life once they leave foster care.[75] However, there are no reported lawsuits seeking to enforce this law against states that fail to provide the federally required services.

Can older teenagers leave the foster care system on their own, even if the state has not yet decided to discharge them?

Yes. As a practical matter, states have little legal recourse in trying to maintain control over older teenagers below the age of majority who want to leave foster care custody. The only way state officials can assert legal control over a child who runs away from foster care is by invoking the state's status offender or runaway laws. These laws allow juvenile courts to enter orders against young people that can result in their being placed in locked facilities against their will.

Many adolescents leave foster care earlier than the age of majority. Through a legal process called *emancipation*, an older adolescent may go to state court and seek a declaration that he or she is emancipated and is able to live on his or her own and to function as an adult.[76]

Finally, all older adolescents may leave foster care and government custody at their age of majority, unless the state has taken extraordinary steps to keep them under government control, such as initiating a proceeding to have them committed under the state's mental health laws.[77]

FOSTER PARENTS

How do people become foster parents?

Potential foster parents must be screened and approved before they can be licensed to receive and care for foster children. Although the process varies from state to state, generally individuals interested in becoming foster parents must apply either to a state or local child welfare agency or to a private childcare agency. Usually the screening process includes some sort of clearance with the police department to ensure that the applicant does not have a criminal record and a clearance through the state's child abuse registry to ensure that the applicant has not been found to have abused or

neglected other children.[78] In addition, routine screening procedures usually include checking on personal or professional references supplied by the
applicant.

What are the minimum qualifications to become a foster parent?
Both single individuals and married couples may apply to become foster parents. Although most states do not have maximum age requirements,
they commonly prefer individuals in good health with some experience with
children. Most states have rules about the available living accommodations,
such as separate bedrooms for boys and girls over a certain age, a certain
amount of square footage per child, and compliance with fire and safety
standards.

**Are there certain characteristics that disqualify a person from
becoming a foster parent?**
Generally, no. Foster care officials may not deny an application to become a foster parent based on the applicant's race, religion, or marital or
economic status. Many states also license lesbian women and gay men to be
foster parents, although New Hampshire has held that it is lawful to deny a
foster parent license based on the applicant's sexual preference.[79]

**If a foster parent applicant believes that he or she has been unfairly
denied a license, is there any recourse?**
Yes. Most states have administrative "fair hearing" procedures that an
applicant for a foster parent's license can use to challenge the agency's refusal
to grant a license. However, because the licensing decision is so discretionary, challenges are rarely successful. When an applicant believes that the application was rejected for improper reasons, such as the applicant's race or
religion, a challenge may be brought through administrative procedures or
in state or federal court based on state human rights laws or the state or federal Constitution.

**Do foster parents have the right to move with their foster children
out of state?**
Not unless the agency allows them to. Ordinarily, foster parents will not
be permitted to move out of the state. As long as the parents of the child
placed in foster care retain rights to their child, agencies will not permit an

out-of-state move. However, when the child's legal ties to his or her parents have been severed by a court, agencies may permit such moves if they are in the child's best interests.

Out-of-state placements are regulated by the Interstate Compact on the Placement of Children (ICPC or Compact).[80] The Compact requires that the sending agency receive approval from the higher levels of government before sending the child and that the receiving state provide some assurances that the facility is appropriately licensed and that supervision will be exercised over the child's care. Under the Compact, the receiving state must agree to exercise some minimal supervision of the foster home; however, the sending state retains legal custody of the child and the responsibility for making plans for the child's future.[81]

THE RIGHTS OF FOSTER CHILDREN, THEIR PARENTS, AND FOSTER PARENTS

Do either children or parents have a right to object to the children entering foster care?

Yes. Since taking a child into foster care custody is a substantial intervention into the traditionally private realm of the family, all states require that a hearing be available within a short time after the child is taken into foster care, usually within seventy-two hours. (See chapter 5.) Parents have the right to have an attorney appear on their behalf, and if they cannot afford to hire one themselves, most states provide for the appointment of a lawyer who will be paid for by the state.[82] Many states also provide children with either a court-appointed lawyer or a CASA (a court-appointed special advocate, who may not be an attorney) to represent their interests in such proceedings.

What role do the state courts play in overseeing what happens to children in foster care?

States must provide for court hearings every six months to review a child's placement in foster care and a full court review when a child has been in foster care for eighteen months.[83]

In addition, lawyers may initiate a court review hearing at any time during a child's stay in foster care to obtain necessary services or a particular placement for the child and to consider whether a child should be removed from a particular foster home, returned to his or her family, or whether proceedings should be initiated to free the child for adoption.[84]

What rights does a child have while in foster care?

In theory, foster children are entitled to a number of legal safeguards. Foster care officials must protect the welfare of the children in their care.[85] They must provide them with basic necessities—defined by one court as "minimally adequate food, clothing, shelter, medical care, safety [and] freedom from bodily restraint."[86] In addition, foster care officials must exercise "competent professional judgment" in the administration of the foster care system[87] and protect children from harm.[88]

In a recent court case challenging foster care conditions in the District of Columbia, a federal court ruled that foster children have a right to services and planning necessary to protect them from harm, including psychological harm caused by moving from one foster care placement to another without being settled in a permanent home.[89] Other courts have ruled that leaving children in foster homes over which the foster care authorities fail to provide proper supervision, despite warnings that the foster family may be abusive, is a sufficient violation of the child's rights to authorize the award of monetary damages to a child who has been harmed.[90]

State law commonly creates a series of other rights for foster care children. For example, most states require that a child be placed in the least restrictive setting, and many favor placement in the home of a suitable relative. Depending on state law, there may be an obligation for the state to provide "diligent efforts" to strengthen the relationship between parents and child to help in reunifying them[91] and if that does not work to seek a new permanent home for the child through adoption.[92] Most states, at least in theory, also have a policy against allowing children to be kept indefinitely in foster care,[93] and at least one state requires that parental rights be terminated after the parents have been given a reasonable time to correct problems that resulted in the child's placement.[94] Once parental rights have been terminated, many states require that the child welfare agency look for an adoptive family for the child.

In addition, a child in foster care also has the right to communicate freely through the mails with other people. However, this right can be restricted by the foster care agency if the mail is disturbing to the child, but then only for a limited period of time. Finally, as discussed earlier in this chapter, foster care officials must also make reasonable efforts to meet the religious needs of foster children.

Can children in foster care choose with whom they want to live?

No. Children only have a right to be placed in an adequate facility or home. In some states, foster children have a right to be placed with fit relatives. However, they do not have the right to be placed with particular foster parents or to choose the kind of facility in which to live. And, usually, they do not have the right to remain with a particular set of foster parents,[95] although there may be exceptions in unusual circumstances, as discussed in the answers to the next two questions.

If children have been living with foster parents for an extended period of time, do the children have a right to remain with them?

There is no simple answer to this question. If the choice is between the children remaining with foster parents and being moved to a new foster family, there is a greater chance of the children being permitted to remain with their foster parents provided the foster parents want them to stay. Even when the foster parents want the children to remain with them, however, agencies and the court may move children from one foster family to another when there are valid reasons to do so. If, for example, the long-term foster plan is adoption and the current foster family is not interested in adoption or is considered unsuitable as an adoptive family, children may be moved to a preadoptive foster family. For a discussion of whether it is permissible to remove children from their foster parents because the foster parents are of a different race than the child, see chapter 8.

When the choice is between being returned to the biological parent and staying in foster care, no jurisdiction recognizes a child's right to remain in foster care after a court has found the biological parent to be fit. However, as the following answer suggests, the law in this area is developing, and children have requested courts to allow them to become adopted by their foster parents even after a child welfare agency has concluded that the biological parents are ready to resume custody.

May a foster child initiate a proceeding to terminate his or her biological parents' rights in order to become eligible for adoption?

There is no clearcut answer to this question, which courts are just beginning to confront. In September 1992, a trial court judge in Orange County, Florida, made headlines when he granted an eleven-year-old foster child's petition to involuntarily terminate his biological parents' rights so that he could be adopted by his foster parents.[96] In what has since become famous as the *Gregory K.* case, Gregory, who had been in the foster care system for nearly three years, filed the petition to terminate in his own name, with his own privately retained legal counsel.[97] Gregory argued that his biological mother had abandoned him and that the state's child protective services agency had been remiss in not acting sooner to terminate her parental rights. The trial court agreed.

On appeal, the Florida appellate court upheld the decision to terminate Gregory K.'s mother's parental rights but found that the lower court had erred in letting Gregory file the action in his own name.[98] That error, however, was harmless, according to the appellate court, since separate petitions to terminate the biological mother's rights had also been filed on Gregory K.'s behalf by his foster father, his foster mother, his guardian ad litem and, belatedly, the state's child welfare agency.[99]

Although the precedential value of the *Gregory K.* case is unclear, the potential implications of the case are far-reaching. Questions have been raised in recent years about the wisdom of state and federal child welfare policies aimed at reuniting children with abusive or neglectful biological parents,[100] regardless of the psychological ties the children have formed to the foster parents or prospective adoptive parents who have cared for them, often for long periods of time. A number of observers have urged the courts to acknowledge that the existence of family bonds need not depend on the technicalities of blood ties and to protect children's emotional ties to those who have loved, nurtured, and sheltered them.[101]

How do children in foster care get adopted?

Many children who enter the foster care system cannot return to their parents, for a variety of reasons. Sometimes the parents' problems are too severe to be alleviated, even with services, sometimes the services are not provided or the parents refuse to accept them, and sometimes the parents have abandoned the children. When children cannot be reunited with their parents, and other family members are not available to raise them, the goal of foster care is to find a new, substitute family for them through adoption.

Children cannot be adopted without either (1) their parents' consent or (2) a legal proceeding that results in a court order severing their parents' rights so that the parents' consent to adoption is no longer legally necessary. Children enter the adoption process in a number of ways. Some parents may relinquish their children for adoption when the children enter the foster care system. In other instances, parents may decide to relinquish parental rights after their children have been in the foster care system for a while. In yet other instances, the child's caseworker may decide that adoption is the appropriate goal to pursue for the child, often because the parent does not seem likely to be able to resume custody within a reasonable period of time. In those instances, the caseworker first attempts to persuade the parent to surrender parental rights voluntarily. If the parent refuses and it appears that legal grounds exist, the worker will ask an attorney working for the foster care system to initiate proceedings to have the parents' rights severed.

In most foster care systems, the search for an adoptive home does not even begin until the child is legally free for adoption, either through a voluntary relinquishment of legal custody by the parents or because a court has ordered that their parental rights be terminated.

Do foster children have the right to be adopted?

Children do not have a constitutional "right to a permanent, stable adoptive home."[102] However, under federal guidelines and many state laws, a child is entitled to have the state social services agencies take reasonable steps to try to find an adoptive family for him or her.[103]

Can a foster care official seek to terminate parental rights and free a child for adoption as soon as a child enters a foster care system?

Not usually. Generally, state laws impose an obligation on the foster care system to first try to provide services to the child's biological family and to make an effort to restore the child to the family if at all possible. In New York, for example, parental rights cannot be terminated on the ground that a parent is unable to resume custody of the child without first proving that the agency responsible for the child has made "diligent efforts" to strengthen and encourage the parental relationship.[104] Other states have similar requirements.

Some state laws provide that parental rights may be terminated shortly after a child enters foster care in extreme circumstances, such as when a parent has been responsible for the death of a sibling or when a parent has subjected a child to severe abuse.[105] Because the parental relationship is considered a fundamental right, and the family relationship is accorded special protection,[106] courts are reluctant to bring a legal end to the relationship until they are sure that it cannot be salvaged.

Do children living in foster care have a right to contact with biological family members?

Yes, to a limited extent. Children have a right to associate with their brothers and sisters, which the state may not impair, even in its operation of the foster care system.[107] However, the state is not required to provide a certain minimum number of visits between a foster child and his or her siblings.[108]

Similarly, parents have the right to visit their children in foster care and children in foster care have the reciprocal right to visit their parents.[109] Visitation between parents and foster care children must be offered, and parents and children have a right to challenge the decision of the state to cut back or cut off visitation.[110] However, if state officials can show that children would be seriously harmed by such visits, courts will not require that the visits occur.

What rights do foster parents have?

It depends. In order to be allowed to take foster children into their home, foster parents enter into a contract with the foster care agency. Most of the foster parents' legal rights are set forth in these contracts. However, these contracts typically give foster parents very few rights. Instead, the contracts emphasize that the foster care agency retains the authority to make virtually all important childcare decisions, including the number of visits to be scheduled between the child and his or her parents and siblings, the length of time the child remains in foster care, and the ultimate decision whether to return the child to his or her family of origin or to place the child with an adoptive family. Agencies also retain the contractual authority to visit and inspect the foster home to monitor the well-being of the children.

A number of states give foster parents certain rights by statute. Still other rights may exist through constitutional protection. Statutory rights commonly include the right to intervene in various court or administrative proceedings, such as foster care review proceedings,[111] extension of placement proceedings, and termination of parental rights proceedings. These rights usually are given to foster parents only when they have cared for the same child for at least one year. State law may also provide foster parents with the right to a hearing to challenge the removal of foster children from their home[112] and may grant some foster parents priority in adopting children in their care if those children become legally available for adoption.

Foster parents have not fared well when invoking the Constitution to assert various rights. In an important case decided in 1977 by the Supreme Court of the United States, the Court held that a judicial hearing was not constitutionally required before removing children who had lived with foster parents for less than one year and was probably not even required when children had been in the same foster home for more than one year.[113]

However, other courts have found that foster parents may, as a matter of state law, be entitled to a hearing before the child can be removed from their custody.[114] In some states, if the foster parents are the child's biological relatives, they may have greater rights than foster parents who are not legally related to the children; at least one court has held that children may not be removed from the home of a foster parent who is biologically related to the children in her care without first affording her a hearing to determine whether there are sufficient reasons to change the children's placement.[115]

Foster parents have still other rights when their status of remaining foster parents is at stake. Thus, when the state attempts to revoke a foster parent's license or refuses to renew an expiring license, foster parents must be given an opportunity to be heard before the license may be withheld.[116]

May foster parents adopt foster children in their care?

Yes. However, only children whose parents' rights have been terminated are eligible to be adopted. Moreover, even when children are adoption-eligible, a court ultimately will determine who adopts the children. In many instances, foster parents will be the preferred and presumed adoptive parents. Indeed, most foster children who are adopted are adopted by their foster parents.

However, in some cases the agency considers the foster parents unacceptable as prospective adoptive parents and looks elsewhere to find an adoptive family. Depending on the reasons for rejecting the foster parents as adoptive parents, the state's actions may be subject to challenge. A 1994 federal law prohibits denying foster parents the right to adopt their foster child on the basis of the race, color, or national origin of the foster parents or the child.

If children have been living with foster parents for an extended period of time, do the foster parents have a right to continue to raise them?

They have the right to *attempt* to continue to care for their foster children and even to adopt them permanently. But there is no guarantee of success. In one recent case, foster parents had nursed a drug-addicted infant through chronic narcotic withdrawal and had cared for her for five years with the hope of eventually adopting her. When custody was returned to the child's biological mother (a former drug addict with a significant history of theft, child neglect, prostitution, forgery, and possession of stolen goods), a federal appeals court ruled that the foster parents had no basis under state or federal law to seek to maintain their long-term relationship with their foster child.[117]

Unless there are grounds to terminate the biological parents' rights, a child may not be adopted without parental consent. Moreover, if state law requires the return of the child to fit biological parents, the foster parents' rights are extremely limited. They often will have the right to be heard on the question of where the child should live, but they will not be able to prevent the child's return once a court finds that return is required under state law.

What are the rights of parents whose children are in foster care?

First, parents have the right to visit and maintain contact with their children, which may be interfered with only by showing that such visits would be harmful to the children. Under state and federal law, parents also have the right to services designed to alleviate the problems that led to their child's placement in foster care.[118] One state court has held that failure to provide these services constituted a violation of the parents'—and their children's—constitutional and state law rights.[119]

Parents have the additional right to seek the return of their children at any time during foster care. Moreover, parents retain some rights to consent to medical treatment, particularly nonemergency treatment. They may also have the right to influence their child's religious upbringing. For example, in some states, parents may determine the kind of religious training the child receives; but even in these states, a parent does not have an absolute right to insist that the child be placed with an agency or with foster parents of the child's own religion.[120]

Most importantly, parents have the right to the return of their children upon a showing that they are fit parents and can care for their children.[121]

How can the rights of parents, foster parents, and children be enforced?

They can be enforced in a variety of ways. The periodic court reviews described above provide an opportunity to raise the issue of whether specific rights are being violated, such as the parent's right to appropriate services or the child's right to contact with family members or to a permanent home. In addition, when the right is based on state law, the party whose rights have been violated—the child, the biological parent, or the foster parent—can ask for either an administrative hearing, if one is available, or bring a lawsuit directly in state court, seeking to have the rights vindicated.

In addition, federal courts will hear the claim if a constitutional right is being violated. A significant number of such actions have been brought by foster children, foster parents, and biological parents challenging various aspects of the operation of state foster care systems on constitutional grounds.[122]

RESOURCES

Children's Rights, Inc.
404 Park Avenue South, 11 Floor
New York, NY 10016
(212) 683-2210

Children's Defense Fund
25 E Street, N.W.
Washington, DC 20001
(202) 628-8787

Hear My Voice
P.O. Box 2064
2200 Fuller Road
Ann Arbor, MI 48106
(313) 747-9665

National Association of Counsel for Children
1205 Oneida Street
Denver, CO 80220
(303) 322-2260

National Foster Parent Association
226 Kilts Drive
Houston, TX 77024
(713) 467-1850

North American Council on Adoptable Children
970 Raymond Avenue, Suite 106
St. Paul, MN 55114-1149
(612) 644-3036

NOTES

1. Toshio Tatara, *U.S. Substitute Care Flow Data for FY92 and Current Trends in the State Child Substitute Care Populations*, VCIS *Research Notes* no. 9, at 3 (American Public Welfare Ass'n, Aug. 1993).

2. Toshio Tatara, *Child Substitute Care Population Trends FY82 through FY91—A Summary*, VCIS *Research Notes* no. 6, at 2 (American Public Welfare Ass'n, Aug. 1992).

3. *Id.*

4. *Id.* During the period from 1983 to 1988, the percentage of infants coming into care increased from 9.9 percent to 14.1 percent. *See also* Chapin Hall Center for Children at the University of Chicago, *Foster Care Dynamics 1989—92: A Report from the Foster Care Data Archive* at 24–25 (1994) (children under the age of one account for an increasing percentage of foster care admissions).

5. Jim Barden, *Hospitals Housing Healthy Infants*, N.Y. Times, July 26, 1992, at A20.

6. American Humane Society, Fact Sheet # 11 (Jan. 1994).

7. In fiscal year 1982, 19 percent of children in care were moved once and nearly 18 percent experienced two to four placements. By 1988, 25 percent of children experienced one placement change, and 22 percent of children changed their placement two to four times. Tatara, *Child Substitute Care, supra* note 2, at 4.

8. Pub. L. No. 103-66, 107 Stat. 649 *et seq*, 1993 U.S.C.C.A.N. 649, codified at 42 U.S.C. §§ 629–629e (West Supp. 1994).

9. Lucy Berliner, *Is Family Preservation in the Best Interests of Children?*, 8 J. Interpersonal Violence 556 (1993).

10. 42 U.S.C. § 629a(a)(1)(West Supp. 1994). Often overlooked in the national debate about "family preservation" is the fact that the Act's definition of family preservation services also includes "service programs designed to help children . . . be placed for adoption." *Id.* at § 629a(a)(1)(A)(ii).

11. *See, e.g.*, Children's Defense Fund, *The State of America's Children: 1991*, at 127–30; Peter Forsythe, *Homebuilders and Family Preservation*, 14 Child. Youth Serv. Rev. 37 (1992).

12. Richard J. Gelles, *Family Reunification/Family Preservation: Are Children Really Being Protected?*, 8 J. Interpersonal Violence 556, 560 (Dec. 1993) (cited hereafter as *Are*

Children Really Being Protected?) (suggesting that 30 percent to 50 percent of children killed by their relatives were known to child protective authorities beforehand). *See also* Karen McCurdy & Deborah Daro, *Current Trends in Child Abuse Reporting and Fatalities: The Results of the 1993 Annual Fifty State Survey*, at 14 (National Committee to Prevent Child Abuse, Apr. 1994).

13. For a comprehensive survey of research findings and a discussion of the difficulty of identifying families for whom family preservation services are effective, *see* John R. Schuerman et al., *Putting Families First: An Experiment in Family Preservation* (1994) and Kathleen Wells & David E. Biegel (ed.), *Family Preservation Services: Research and Evaluation* (1991).

14. *Are Children Really Being Protected? supra* note 12, at 560. *See also* Richard J. Gelles, *The Book of David: How Preserving Families Can Cost Children's Lives* (1996).

15. For example, California, Colorado, New York, and Pennsylvania, have foster care systems that are administered directly by the counties, under some state regulatory supervision. Cal. Welf. & Inst. Code § 16500 *et seq.* (West 1991); Colo. Rev. Stat. § 19-3-208 (Bradford 1994); N.Y. Soc. Serv. Law § 153 through 153-h (McKinney's 1992); 62 Pa. Stat. Ann. § 2171 *et seq.* Other states, such as Arkansas and Connecticut, have foster care systems that are administered directly by the state. Ark. Stat. Ann. § 9-28-201 *et seq.* (Michie 1993); Conn. Gen. Stat. Ann. § 17a-1 *et seq.* (West 1992).

16. Twenty-five percent of children spend nearly three years in foster care, and 10 percent spend more than five years in care. Toshio Tatara, *The Length of Time Children Spend in Substitute Care: A Review of the National Trends, VCIS Research Notes*, no. 8, at 3–5 (American Public Welfare Association, Mar. 1993). The evidence further suggests that if children are not discharged from substitute care within a relatively short time frame, they are likely to stay in care for a long period of time. *Id.* at 7.

17. Pub. L. No. 96–272 (1980), 94 Stat. 500, codified at 42 U.S.C. §§ 620–628, 670–679a (West 1991 and 1994 Supp.).

18. 42 U.S.C. §§ 671(a)(15) & 672(a)(1).

19. 42 U.S.C. § 672(a)(1).

20. 42 U.S.C. § 672(a)(2).

21. 42 U.S.C. § 672(a)(3).

22. 42 U.S.C. § 627(a)(1).

23. 42 U.S.C. § 627(a)(2)(C).

24. 42 U.S.C. § 675(5)(A).

25. 42 U.S.C. § 675(5)(B).

26. 42 U.S.C. § 675(5)(C).

27. *Id.*

28. 42 U.S.C. § 671(a)(12).

29. 42 U.S.C. § 627(a)(2)(A).

30. For a discussion of the details of the federal legislation and strategies to assure its implementation, *see* Mary Lee Allen et al., *A Guide to the Adoption Assistance and Child Welfare Act of 1980*, in *Foster Children in the Courts* at 575–611 (M. Hardin ed., 1983); Abigail English, *Litigating Under the Adoption Assistance and Child Welfare Act of 1980*, in *id.* at 612–44. *See also* Barbara L. Atwell, *A Lost Generation: The Battle for Private Enforcement of the*

Adoption Assistance Act of 1980, 60 U. Cin. Rev. 593 (1992). *But see Suter v. Artist M.* 112 S. Ct. 1360 (1992).

31. *See, e.g.,* N.Y. Soc. Serv. Law § 384-a (McKinney's 1992).

32. *Martin A. v. Gross,* 153 A.D.2d 812, 546 N.Y.S.2d 75 (1st Dep't 1989), *appeal dismissed sub nom., Cosentino v. Perales,* 75 N.Y.2d 808, 551 N.E.2d 603, 552 N.Y.S.2d 110 (1990).

33. *Christopher T. v. San Francisco Unified School District,* 553 F. Supp. 1107 (N.D. Cal. 1982).

34. 42 U.S.C. § 671(a)(15) & 672(a)(1). *See also, e.g.,* Cal. Welf. & Inst. Code §§ 16000, 16500.5, 16501 (West 1991 and 1994 Supp.); Colo. Rev. Stat. Ann. § 19-3-100.5 *et seq.* (Bradford 1994); N.Y. Soc. Serv. Law § 409, 409-(e)(1)(d) (McKinney's 1992).

35. Child Welfare League of America, *Standards for Services to Strengthen and Preserve Families with Children,* 1, 5 (1989); Child Welfare League of America, *Standards for Adoption Service,* 2 (1988). *But see* Elizabeth Bartholet, *Family Bonds: Adoption and the Politics of Parenting* (1993)(questioning conventional wisdom that blood ties are more significant than the ties of love and affection between parents and their nonbiological children); Gelles, *The Book of David, supra* note 14.

36. *See, e.g.,* N.Y. Soc. Serv. Law § 409-a (McKinney's 1992 and 1994 Supp.).

37. *See* 45 C.F.R. § 1357.15(e)(2)(1993).

38. Children's Defense Fund, *The State of America's Children: 1991* at 129; Marianne Berry, *An Evaluation of Family Preservation Services: Fitting Agency Needs to Family Needs,* 37 Social Work 320 (1992). *But see Putting Families First, supra* note 13; Peter H. Rossi, *Evaluating Family Preservation Programs: A Report to the Edna McConnell Clark Foundation* (University of Massachusetts Social and Demographic Research Institute, Aug. 1991).

39. *Suter v. Artist M., supra* note 30. Congress has acted to overturn *Suter* except to the extent that it upholds the unenforceability of 42 U.S.C. § 671(a)(15). *See* 42 U.S.C. § 1320a-2 (West Supp. 1995). *See also Jeanine B. ex rel. Blondis v. Thompson,* 877 F. Supp. 1268, 1281–85 (E.D. Wis. 1995).

40. *LaShawn A. v. Dixon,* 762 F. Supp. 959 (D.D.C. 1991), *aff'd in part, rev'd in part,* 990 F.2d 1319 (D.C. Cir. 1993), *cert. denied* 114 S. Ct. 691 (1994); *Martin A. v. Gross,* 138 Misc. 2d 212, 524 N.Y.S.2d 121 (N.Y. Sup. 1987), *aff'd,* 153 A.D.2d 812, 546 N.Y.S.2d 75 (1st Dep't 1989).

41. *Martin A. v. Gross, supra* note 40.

42. 42 U.S.C. § 672(e).

43. *Id.*

44. *Lassiter v. Department of Social Services,* 452 U.S. 18 (1981).

45. *See, e.g.,* Ariz. Rev. Stat. § 8-522 (West 1994); Cal. Welf. & Inst. Code § 679 (West 1984); Colo. Rev. Stat. § 19-3-203 (Bradford 1994); Minn. Stat. Ann. § 260.155(2)(West 1992); N.Y. Fam. Ct. Act, § 249 (McKinney 1992); Ohio Rev. Code Ann. § 2151.35.2 (1994). *See also Roe v. Conn,* 417 F. Supp. 769 (M.D. Ala. 1976).

46. *See, e.g.,* N.Y. Soc. Serv. Law § 384-a (McKinney's 1992).

47. For a full discussion of the responsibilities of the foster care agency and the foster parents, *see* Robert M. Horowitz & Howard A. Davidson, *The Legal Rights of Children* at 361–62 (1984).

48. *Wilder v. Bernstein,* 645 F. Supp. 1292 (S.D.N.Y. 1986), *aff'd,* 848 F.2d 1338 (2d Cir. 1988). *See also* 42 U.S.C. § 5115a (West Supp. 1995)(prohibiting the delay or denial of foster placement based solely on race, national origin, or color) and 60 Fed. Reg. 20272-75 (Apr. 25, 1995) (federal law prohibits foster care agencies from establishing orders of placement preference based on race, culture, or ethnicity). As this book was going to press, the House of Representatives voted to approve the Adoption Promotion and Stability Act of 1996, designed to further limit race discrimination in adoption. *See* H.R. 3286, 104th Cong., 2d Sess. (introduced April 23, 1996).

49. *Id.*

50. *Child Subsitute Care, supra* note 2, at 4.

51. 42 U.S.C. § 675(5)(A).

52. Cal. Welf. & Inst. Code § 16501.1(c)(West 1994); Colo. Rev. Stat. § 19-5-104(2) (1994); Mo. Rev. Stat. § 210.565(1) (West 1994).

53. *See* Karen Spar, *Kinship Foster Care: An Emerging Federal Issue,* CRS Report for Congress (Congr. Research Service, Sept. 27, 1993).

54. *Miller v. Youakim,* 440 U.S. 125 (1979).

55. *See* Karen Spar, *Kinship Foster Care, supra* note 53. *See also Lipscomb v. Simmons,* 962 F.2d 1374 (9th Cir. 1992); *King v. MacMahon,* 186 Cal. App. 3d 648, 230 Cal. Rptr. 911 (1st Dist. 1986). *But see Sockwell v. Maloney,* 431 F. Supp. 1006 (D. Conn. 1976), *aff'd,* 554 F.2d 1236 (2d Cir. 1977)(terminating foster care payments to children's aunt without notice or hearing violated due process); *Eugene F. v. Gross,* No. 1125/86 (N.Y. Sup.)(1986).

56. *See e.g.,* N.Y. Soc. Serv. Law § 373 (McKinney's 1992).

57. *Wilder v. Bernstein, supra* note 48.

58. *McLaughlin v. Pernsley,* 693 F. Supp. 318 (E.D. Pa. 1988), *aff'd,* 876 F.2d 308 (3d Cir. 1989). A 1994 federal law, the Multiethnic Placement Act, gives foster parents the right to challenge the denial of a foster care placement based solely on their race, color, or national origin or the race, color, or national origin of the foster child. *See* 42 U.S.C. § 5115a(b)(West Supp. 1995). *See also* H.R. 3286, *supra* note 48.

59. *In re Welfare of D.L.,* 486 N.W.2d 375 (Minn.), *cert. denied,* 113 S. Ct. 603 (1992); *DeWees v. Stevenson,* 779 F. Supp. 25 (E.D. Pa. 1991); *Petition of R.M.G.,* 454 A.2d 776 (D.C. App. 1982); *Drummond v. Fulton County Department of Family & Children's Services,* 563 F.2d 1200 (5th Cir. 1977), *cert. denied* 437 U.S. 910 (1978). *But see In re S.T.,* 497 N.W.2d 625 (Minn. App. 1993), *aff'd in part, rev'd in part* 512 N.W.2d 894 (Minn. 1994); *In re J.,* 19 Fam. L. Rep. (BNA) 1409 (N.Y. Fam. Ct. 1993); *Committee to End Racism in Michigan's Child Care System v. Mansour,* 12 Fam. L. Rep. (BNA) 1285 (1986).

60. *In re A.K.,* 153 Vt. 462, 571 A.2d 75 (1990); *Sinhogar v. Parry,* 53 N.Y.2d 424, 425 N.E.2d 826, 442 N.Y.S.2d 438 (1981).

61. *Gary W. v. Louisiana,* 437 F. Supp 1209 (E.D. La. 1976).

62. 42 U.S.C. § 675(1) & 45 C.F.R. § 1356.21(d)(2)(1993).

63. *See, e.g.,* Ariz. Rev. Stat. § 8-511, 8-515, 8-515.03 (West Supp. 1994); N.Y. Soc. Serv. Law § 409-e (McKinney's 1992).

64. 42 U.S.C. § 675(1) & 675(5)(B)(West 1991). *See also* Cal. Welf. & Inst. Code § 16501.1 (West Supp. 1994).

65. 42 U.S.C. § 675(1)(B) & 675(5)(B).

66. An administrative review is defined by federal law as "a review open to the partici-
pation of the parents of the child, conducted by a panel of appropriate persons at least one of
whom is not responsible for the case management of, or the delivery of services to, either the
child or the parents who are the subject of the review." 42 U.S.C. § 675(6).

67. 42 U.S.C. § 675(5)(B) & (C)(West 1991).

68. *See, e.g.,* Cal. Welf. & Inst. Code §§ 366.2, 366.21, 366.22 (West Supp. 1994).

69. 42 U.S.C. § 675(5)(C).

70. *See, e.g.,* Colo. Rev. Stat. § 19-3-202 (Bradford 1994); D.C. Rev. Stat § 16-
2312(c)(Michie 1989); Mass. Gen. Laws Ann. ch. 119, § 29 (West 1993).

71. *Lassiter v. Department of Social Services, supra* note 44.

72. *Child Substitute Care, supra* note 2, at 3. Since 1982, the percent of children who
left foster care to be reunited with their parents or relatives rose from 49.7 percent in 1982 to
61.9 percent in 1988. In contrast, the percent and number of foster children adopted declined over that same period, from 10.4 percent (17,900 children) in 1982 to 8.4 percent
(14,400 children) in 1988. *Id.*

73. Jim Barden, *When Foster Care Ends, Home Is Often the Street,* N.Y. Times, Jan. 6,
1991, at A1, col. 1.

74. *Palmer v. Cuomo,* 121 A.D.2d 194, 503 N.Y.S.2d 20 (lst Dep't 1986).

75. 42 U.S.C. § 677 (West 1991).

76. *See, e.g.,* Cal. Fam. Code § 7000 *et seq.* (West 1992); Conn. Gen. Stat. Ann. §
46b-150 (1986); Ill. Rev. Stat. ch. 40, para. 2201 *et seq.* (West 1980).

77. Until a child in foster care reaches the age of majority in the state, the state's child
welfare authorities can sign the child into a state mental hospital without the child's consent
and without any prior court proceeding, just as a parent can, according to the U.S. Supreme
Court's decision in *Parham v. J.R.,* 442 U.S. 584 (1979). However, the child is probably
entitled to some sort of a hearing on the continuing necessity for institutionalization, if one
is sought, according to the principles set out by the Court in that case. *See id.* at 619.

78. *See, e.g.,* Cal. Health & Safety Code §§ 1521.5, 1521.6 & 1522 (West Supp.
1994).

79. *Opinion of the Justices,* 129 N.H. 290, 530 A.2d 21 (1987).

80. *See, e.g.,* Cal. Fam. Code § 7901 *et seq.* (West 1994); N.Y. Soc. Serv. Law § 374-a
(McKinney 1992). The Interstate Compact on the Placement of Children is reprinted in
Joan H. Hollinger, ed., *Adoption Law and Practice,* § 3-A.15 (1993).

81. Interstate Compact on the Placement of Children, art. V(a).

82. *See, e.g.,* Colo. Rev. Stat. § 19-3-202 (1994).

83. 42 U.S.C. § 675(5)(B) & (C).

84. *In re Jamie "YY",* 176 A.D.2d 1004, 575 N.Y.S.2d 172 (3d Dep't 1991); *Little
Flower Children's Services v. Andrew C.,* 144 Misc. 2d 671, 545 N.Y.S.2d 444 (N.Y. Fam. Ct.
1989).

85. *Taylor v. Ledbetter,* 818 F.2d 791 (11th Cir. 1987), *cert. denied* 489 U.S. 1065
(1989); *L.J. v. Massinga,* 838 F.2d 118 (4th Cir. 1988), *cert. denied,* 488 U.S. 1018 (1989).

86. *Doe v. New York City Dep't of Social Servs.,* 670 F. Supp. 1145, 1172 (S.D.N.Y.
1987).

87. *LaShawn A. v. Dixon, supra* note 40. *Cf. Youngberg v. Romeo,* 457 U.S. 307 (1982).

88. *Taylor v. Ledbetter, supra* note 85, at 797 (court held that a child in foster care may

prevail against the state, under 42 U.S.C.A. § 1983, where it can be shown that "the state officials were deliberately indifferent to the welfare of the child"); *Doe v. New York City Dep't of Social Servs.*, 649 F.2d 134 (2d Cir. 1981), *appeal after remand*, 709 F.2d 782 (2d Cir.), *cert. denied* 464 U.S. 864 (1983). *See generally* Maureen S. Duggan, *Failure of State of Local Government Entity to Protect Child Abuse Victim As Violation of Federal Constitutional Right*, 79 A.L.R. Fed. 514 (Supp. 1994).

89. *LaShawn A. v. Dixon, supra* note 40, at 996. The federal court has since gone further and placed the District of Columbia's child welfare system into receivership. *See* Memorandum Opinion, *LaShawn A. v. Kelly*, Civ. No. 89-1754 (TFH) (D.D.C. May 22, 1995) (Hogan, J.).

90. *Taylor v. Ledbetter, supra* note 85; *Doe v. City of New York, supra* note 88.

91. *In re Anita "PP"*, 65 A.D.2d 18, 410 N.Y.S.2d 916 (3d Dep't 1978).

92. *Smith v. Lascaris*, 106 Misc. 2d 1044, 432 N.Y.S.2d 995 (N.Y. Fam. Ct. 1980). *Cf. In re Guardians of J.C.*, 129 N.J. 1, 608 A.2d 1312 (1991)(discussing standard for terminating parental rights based on potential harm to child caused by separation from a foster parent with whom the child has bonded).

93. *In re Interest of S.W.*, 220 Neb. 734, 371 N.W.2d 726 (1985).

94. *People in Interest of D.M.*, 367 N.W.2d 769 (S.D. 1985).

95. *Drummond v. Fulton County Department of Family & Children's Services., supra* note 59.

96. For a full discussion of the case and related legal issues, *see* George H. Russ, *Through the Eyes of a Child, "Gregory K.": A Child's Right to Be Heard*, 27 Fam. L.Q. 365 (Fall 1993)(cited hereafter as *Through the Eyes of a Child*). *See also* Gilbert A. Holmes, *The Tie That Binds: The Constitutional Right of Children to Maintain Relationships with Parent-like Individuals*, 53 Md. L. Rev. 358 (1994).

97. Under Florida law, a petition for termination of parental rights may be initiated either by an attorney for the state's child protective services agency or "by any other person who has knowledge of the facts alleged or is informed of them and believes that they are true." *Kingsley v. Kingsley*, 623 So. 2d 780 (Fla. App. 1993), *review denied*, 634 So. 2d 625 (1994).

98. *Id.*

99. *Id.* at 785. The state child welfare agency's decision to join in Gregory K.'s petition to terminate was a belated development in the case. In fact, it was the agency's earlier decision to attempt to reunite Gregory K. with his biological parents that triggered Gregory K.'s lawsuit. *Through the Eyes of A Child, supra* note 96, at 368.

100. *See, e.g.,* Gelles, *The Book of David, Biological Parents Aren't Better, supra* note 14; Don Terry, *When Children Kill Children: Boy, 11 Is Wanted in Chicago*, N.Y. Times, A1 Sept. 1, 1994; Celia W. Dugger, *Foster Child from Birth: Torn Between Two Families*, N.Y. Times, A1 July 26, 1994; Michele Ingrassia & John McCormick, *Why Leave Children with Bad Parents?*, Newsweek at 52 Apr. 25, 1994; Ahkil Reed Amar & Daniel Widawsky, *Child Abuse as Slavery: A Thirteenth Amendment Response to* DeShaney, 105 Harv. L. Rev. 1359 (1992).

101. *Through the Eyes of A Child, supra* note 96, at 386–89. *See generally* Suellyn Scarnecchia, *Who Is Jessica's Mother? Defining Motherhood Through Reality*, 3 Am. U. J. of Gender & the Law 1 (1994); Barbara Bennett Woodhouse, *Hatching the Egg, A Child-Centered Perspective on Parents' Rights*, 14 Cardozo L. Rev. 1747 (May 1993); Barbara Bennett

Woodhouse, *"Who Owns the Child?" Meyer and Pierce and the Child as Property*, 33 Wm. & Mary L. Rev. 995, at 1116 & n.658 (1992); Janet Leach Richards, *The Natural Parent Preference Versus Third Parties: Expanding the Definition of Parent*, 16 Nova. L. Rev. 733 (1992); Irv Leon, *What Is a Family?* (paper presented at the Sept. 30, 1994 annual conference of the DeBoer Committee for Children's Rights).

102. *Joseph A. v. New Mexico Dep't of Human Servs.*, 575 F. Supp. 346 (D.N.M. 1982); *Child v. Beame*, 412 F. Supp. 593 (S.D.N.Y. 1976).

103. *Joseph A. v. New Mexico Dep't of Human Servs.*, 575 F. Supp. 346 (D.N.M. 1983)

104. N.Y. Soc. Serv. Law § 384-b(7)(a)(McKinney's 1992).

105. *See, e.g.*, Colo. Rev. Stat. § 19-3-604(2)(d) & (g)(1994); Conn. Gen. Stat. Ann. § 17a-112(b) & (c) (West 1994).

106. *Stanley v. Illinois*, 405 U.S. 645 (1972); *Moore v. East Cleveland*, 431 U.S. 494 (1977); *Santosky v. Kramer*, 455 U.S. 745 (1982).

107. *Aristotle P. v. Johnson*, 721 F. Supp. 1002 (N.D. Ill. 1989).

108. *B. H. v. Johnson*, 715 F. Supp. 1387 (N.D. Ill. 1989).

109. *But see Winston v. Children and Youth Services of Delaware Cty.*, 748 F. Supp. 1128 (E.D. Pa. 1990), *aff'd*, 948 F.2d 1380 (3d Cir. 1991), *cert. denied*, 112 S. Ct. 2303 (1992) (no enforceable right of visitation under 1980 Adoption Assistance and Child Welfare Act).

110. 42 U.S.C. § 675(5)(C). *But see Fitzgerald v. Williamson*, 787 F.2d 403, 408 (8th Cir. 1986)(no hearing required before parents' visitation rights were reduced).

111. *See, e.g.*, Ariz. Rev. Stat. § 8-515(D)(West Supp. 1994).

112. *See, e.g.*, N.Y. Soc. Serv. Law § 400 (McKinney's 1992); N.J. Stat. Ann. § 30:4C-61(c)(5)(West Supp. 1994); Wis. Stat. Ann. § 48.64 (West Supp. 1994). *See also Brown v. County of San Joaquin*, 601 F. Supp. 653 (E.D. Cal. 1985); *In Interest of R.K.W.*, 689 S.W.2d 647 (Mo. App. 1985); *Katzoff v. Superior Court*, 54 Cal. App. 3d 1079; 127 Cal. Rptr. 178 (1st Dist. 1976). *But see Orsi v. Senatore*, 230 Conn. 459, 645 A.2d 986 (1994). If the child's removal is based on the race, color, or national origin of the child or the foster parents, a court challenge may be brought under a federal law. *See* 42 U.S.C. § 5115 a(b)(West Supp. 1995).

113. *Smith v. Organization of Foster Families for Equality and Reform*, 431 U.S. 816 (1977).

114. *Brown v. County of San Joaquin, supra* note 112. *But see Procopio v. Johnson*, 994 F.2d 325 (7th Cir. 1993).

115. *Rivera v. Marcus*, 696 F.2d 1016 (2d Cir. 1982).

116. *Timmy S. v. Stumbo*, 916 F.2d 312 (6th Cir. 1990).

117. *Procopio v. Johnson, supra* note 114.

118. 42 U.S.C.A. § 625(a)(1), 627(a)(2)(C), 671(a)(15), 675(1)(B)(West 1991).

119. *Martin A v. Gross, supra* note 40.

120. *Wilder v. Bernstein, supra* note 48.

121. *In re Michael B.*, 80 N.Y.2d 299, 604 N.E.2d 122, 590 N.Y.S.2d 60 (1992); *Wishinsky v. State Dep't of Human Resources*, 512 So. 2d 122 (Ala. Civ. App. 1987).

122. *Smith v. Organization of Foster Families, supra* note 113; *LaShawn A. v. Dixon, supra* note 40, at 996; *Taylor v. Ledbetter, supra* note 85; *Joseph A. v. New Mexico. Dep't of Human Servs., supra* note 102.

VII

Termination of Parental Rights

What is termination of parental rights?

Termination of parental rights is the permanent severance of the parent-child relationship. The effect of termination is that the parent is no longer legally related to the child and possesses neither rights to nor responsibilities for the child. The other effect of termination, and the principal purpose behind seeking termination, is that the child, who no longer has any legal parents, is legally free to be adopted into a new family.[1] Not all children whose parents' rights have been terminated are adopted; but once parental rights have been terminated, they may be adopted without their parent's permission, since they have no legal parents. Children whose parents' rights have been terminated but have not been adopted are wards of the state, and the state—usually through the local child protection agency—has the authority to consent to the child's adoption.

How are parental rights terminated?

There are two ways in which parental rights are terminated: voluntarily and involuntarily. The vast majority of the terminations are effected *voluntarily*. This is accomplished by the parents relinquishing the child to a licensed childcare agency or placing the child with an individual or couple chosen by the birth parents. (For a fuller discussion of adoption procedures, see chapter 8.)

Involuntary termination—the severance of the parent-child relationship without parental consent—is the primary focus of this chapter. Termination over the objection of the parents cannot be ordered except after a court conducts a hearing pursuant to state laws. These laws vary somewhat from state to state, but there are common threads among them, which will be discussed in the following questions and answers.

For what reasons may a state seek to terminate parental rights?

In most states, the law that sets forth the conditions permitting termination of parental rights usually requires proof of gross or long-standing neglect of parental obligations.

Every state law includes abandonment of children as a condition justifying termination, even though abandonment is defined differently by various state laws and courts. Most states also include repeated or unusually severe acts of neglect or abuse and parental incapacity or inability to care for children. Many states include mental illness,[2] conviction of a crime affecting the fitness of a parent,[3] and financial nonsupport[4] as conditions justifying termination. A few states even include parental "debauchery," "depravity," adultery, and fornication.[5]

May a state terminate parental rights without prior proof of wrongdoing?

Yes, at least in the sense that it is not necessary for a court to find that parents have abused or neglected their children before termination is pos- sible.

The power to terminate parental rights exists independent of the concept of parental wrongdoing. Termination commonly is sought when a child has not been living with his or her parents for a specified length of time (usually ranging between six months and several years) and when professionals responsible for the child's well-being conclude that the prospects of the child being reunited with his or her parents are remote. In these cases, the fault of the parent is immaterial. If there are grounds to terminate, it is no defense for a parent to prove that he or she has never harmed his or her child.

In New York, for example, the law of termination lists several conditions, all of which must be in existence for one continuous year before a court will order the termination of parental rights. These conditions are: the child must be in the care of a licensed childcare agency; the agency must make diligent efforts to encourage the parent-child relationship; the parents must have failed to maintain contact with or plan for the future of the child; and the best interests of the child must require termination of parental rights.[6] Unless all the conditions listed above exist for one year, parental rights may not be terminated. However, there is no requirement that the original placement of the child in the childcare agency was involuntary or the result of abuse or neglect.

Other states have similar requirements. In California, involuntary termination may be ordered when a child has been in care for one year and return to the parents would be detrimental to the child, or when neglect or chemical dependency has existed for one year.[7] Similarly, in Connecticut, the conditions permitting a finding of termination must prevail for one year or more. These include abandonment, failure of parental rehabilitation, continuing physical or mental disability of the parent, or absence of an ongoing parent-child relationship.[8]

But not all termination proceedings are started after a period of time of warning to the parents; some particularly grave or compelling circumstances allow action before requiring the matter to fall squarely into any of the enumerated statutory categories. Thus, in California, termination may result if parents have been convicted of a felony or a crime that proves their unfitness, or if they are deemed so severely developmentally disabled or mentally ill that they are unable to raise children.[9] And in Connecticut, in addition to the statutory grounds mentioned above, termination may be ordered if the "totality of circumstances" dictates immediate termination.[10]

Moreover, in a few states, fault may be an inherent part of the basis for seeking termination. For example, in some jurisdictions, parents who have severely or repeatedly abused their children may forfeit their parental rights.[11]

In still other cases, the grounds for the termination case are that the parent is unable to care for his or her child for reasons unrelated to "fault." For example, the reason for the termination case may be that the parent is mentally ill and thereby unable to have custody of children.[12] Or the parent may be imprisoned with a lengthy sentence.[13] In the latter circumstance, the parent may be at fault for the criminal wrongdoing that led to a prison sentence, but the parent may be faultless as a parent.

May parental rights be terminated merely because termination is found in a court to be in the child's best interests?

For most of this century, courts have refused to terminate parental rights without a clear showing of neglect, unfitness, harm, or abandonment.[14] The Supreme Court of Montana has interpreted its law to require a finding of parental unfitness before permitting termination of parental rights. The court reasoned:

The "best interests of the child" test is correctly used to determine custody rights between natural parents in divorce proceedings. . . . However, where third parties seek custody, it has long been the law in Montana that the right of the natural parent prevails until a showing of a forfeiture of this right. . . . This forfeiture can result only where the parent's conduct does not meet the minimum standards of the child abuse, neglect and dependency statutes.[15]

Similarly, the Massachusetts Supreme Judicial Court expressly overruled an earlier opinion authorizing the best interests standard for termination, declaring that the state may not break up a family without proof of parental unfitness.[16]

In 1979 the highest court in New York cleared up a possible misunderstanding resulting from an earlier case that was being quoted by many to mean that termination could be based on the best interests standard.[17] The court stated unequivocally:

A court may not terminate all parental rights by offering a child for adoption when there has been no parental consent, abandonment, neglect or proven unfitness, even though some might find adoption to be in the child's best interests.[18]

In the past two decades, however, a few courts have utilized the child's best interests as the legal standard in authorizing termination of the rights of parents, even though the parents have not been shown to be unfit,[19] and some states have enacted laws to this effect.[20] This means that the state does not have to prove any wrongdoing on the part of the parent or harm or injury to the child—it need only show that it would be in the child's best interests to be freed for adoption. This new trend runs counter to the traditional rule that a parent's right to custody may not be defeated simply because a child might be better served by having different parents.[21]

The Supreme Court of the United States has not handed down a clear opinion on whether termination for such reasons is constitutional and has, in fact, provided conflicting guidance in this area. In 1977 the Court unanimously ruled that the right of biological parents to the care and custody of their children is a "constitutionally recognized liberty interest that derives from blood relationship, state law sanction, and basic human right."[22] With this opinion, the Supreme Court reaffirmed the many cases decided in the past seventy years that gave constitutional protection to parental rights and legitimized the right of family integrity (see chapter 4).

Then, in 1977, the Supreme Court unanimously declared:

If a State were to attempt to force the breakup of a natural family, over the objections of the parents and their children, without some showing of unfitness and for the sole reason that to do so was thought to be in the children's best interest, [we] should have little doubt that the State would have intruded impermissibly on "the private realm of family life which the state cannot enter."[23]

Still another indication that parental rights may not be terminated without a showing of parental unfitness may be found by reference to the Supreme Court's decision in *Santosky v. Kramer*, where the Court said, "[a]ny *parens patriae* interest in terminating the natural parents' rights arises only at the dispositional phase, after the parents have been found unfit."[24]

However, in 1983, the Court announced that "the mere existence of a biological link" between a biological parent and his child was not entitled to constitutional protection in the absence of evidence that the parent had "grasp[ed] the opportunity" to "develop a relationship with his offspring" and to "accept[] some measure of responsibility for the child's future."[25] Where a parent has failed to assume any responsibility for a child's care and support, the Supreme Court has ruled that that parent's right to the child's custody may be terminated.

Are there any constitutional limits to the conditions for which parental rights may be terminated?

Yes. Because parents have a fundamental right to raise their children, states may not deprive them of the right except under compelling circumstances. Therefore, the grounds upon which a state may involuntarily terminate parental rights may not be minor ones, nor may they be defined in overly broad terms, such that the scope of potential termination could be interpreted in a way that sanctions termination for less-than-compelling reasons.

The best way to explain these principles is by example. The first major test of overly vague and broad termination statutes was made in 1973 when parents challenged an Iowa law that authorized termination for "refus[al] to give the child necessary parental care and protection." Another part of the same law permitted courts to order termination for parental conduct "likely to be detrimental to the physical or mental health or morals of the child."[26] Pursuant to this statute, the parents' parental rights to four of their five children had been terminated because their home was unkempt and their children were often dirty and unruly, even though there was no evidence or judicial finding that the children were harmed in any way. Nevertheless, a court terminated the parents' rights because, in the language of the statute, they failed to provide "necessary parental care," and their conduct was "likely to be detrimental" to the children. The parents appealed this decision, claiming that the law was so vague that it was unconstitutional. A federal court agreed, saying that Iowa's law (1) did not give "fair warning of what parental conduct is proscribed, (2) permit[ted] . . . arbitrary and discriminating termination, [and] (3) inhibited . . . the exercise of the fundamental right to family integrity."[27]

As a second example, an Arkansas law allowed termination if parents were found deficient in providing a child with "a proper home."[28] The Arkansas Supreme Court found this phrase unconstitutionally vague because it suggested a number of meanings. The court stated:

Using any of these meanings does little to make the words "a proper home," clearly understandable, so that it doesn't mean one thing to one judge, something else to another, and something yet different to still another. What is a proper home? A correct home? A suitable home? A fit home? An appropriate home? A home consistent with propriety? Is propriety to be determined ethically, socially or economically: Or on the basis of morality? Or prosperity? Is the standard a maximum, a minimum, a mean or an average?[29]

Thus, state laws setting forth grounds for termination that use language as vague or broad as the laws of Iowa and Arkansas are vulnerable to constitutional attack.

On the other hand, a number of state laws have survived similar legal challenges in state courts, even though their grounds for termination could be said to be almost as vague as those discussed above. A Pennsylvania law that permitted termination if a child was "without essential parental care, control or subsistence necessary for his physical or mental well-being" was not found to violate constitutional principles.[30] A New York statute that permitted termination for parents' "fail[ure] . . . [to] plan for the future of the child" was ruled not unconstitutionally vague.[31] Similarly, the Massachusetts standard of "best interest of the child" was found not to be vague,[32] nor was the Oklahoma standard that termination may result if a parent "fail[s] to give the child the parental care or protection necessary for his physical or mental health."[33] Also, a statute that authorized termination based on "emotional illness" withstood a constitutional challenge for vagueness in Colorado.[34]

Perhaps the reason many courts are willing to find rather imprecise language constitutional, when they might rule otherwise in reviewing similarly worded laws not concerned with children, is because, in the words of the Oregon Supreme Court, "[w]hat might be unconstitutional if only the parents' rights were involved, is constitutional if the statute adopts legitimate and necessary means to protect the child's interests."[35]

May a court terminate the parental rights of only one parent?

Yes. However, the purpose of the termination proceeding is to free the child for adoption. Unless all parental rights to a child have been terminated, the child is not freed for adoption. For this reason, it is not common for agencies to attempt to terminate the parental rights of only one parent. Nonetheless, there is no requirement that an agency seek termination of both parents' right or none at all.

More commonly, an agency seeks termination of both parents' rights, but the court rules that the agency has failed to prove its case against one of the parents. In these circumstances, the court may terminate the one parent's rights and not the other's.

Is there an upper age limit for the child in termination of parental rights proceedings?

Yes, in most states. As a general rule, termination proceedings may be brought only on behalf of children who are less than eighteen years of age. Although in most jurisdictions there is no upper age limit for a person to be adopted, agencies lose control over children in their custody when the children turn eighteen.

Is it required that the agency knows that the child will be adopted before termination will be permitted?

No. Depending on the jurisdiction and the agency responsible for planning for the child's future, the agency may or may not already have a definite adoptive parent in mind before seeking termination. In some cases, termination is sought because the child is believe to have bonded psychologically with the adult(s) with whom the child has been living, and the child's best interests are perceived to be advanced by terminating parental rights and thereby paving the way for the child's eventual adoption by his or her "psychological parent."[36] In other cases, termination is sought without regard to the actual prospects of the child's adoption as long as the agency has concluded that the prospects for reuniting with the parents are too remote. In these cases, termination is sought to eliminate an impediment to adoption even though an adoptive parent has not already been—and may never be—identified.

What must the state prove if parents are charged with abandonment?

As mentioned earlier, abandonment is defined differently in various states.[37] Generally, the variations revolve around the length of time parents must be absent from their children's lives before abandonment will be found to have occurred and whether a parent's intent to abandon should be considered.

For many years, most states required proof that the parents not only abandoned their children but *intended* to abandon them as well. This meant that mere absence from the home or from one's children was insufficient to support an order of termination; the state had to prove that the parents meant to abandon their children "forever" or that their conduct indicated a "settled purpose" of relinquishing all interests in their children.[38] This requirement was very difficult to meet, and, over the past twenty-five years, states have been permitting termination upon proof that the parents did not reside with their children for a certain length of time, whether they intended to return or not.[39]

But this change creates some problems of its own, such as how a court would interpret the facts in a situation where parents leave their child with a friend or relative so they can solve a specific problem without the demands of childraising, but have every intention of returning to resume caring for their child after the passage of an uncertain amount of time.

This situation was faced in Massachusetts by a parent who was injured and placed her child with a friend while she recuperated. When she returned to pick up her child, she found that the friend in turn had placed the child with the Department of Public Welfare. Upon seeking her child's return from the department, the mother was told that she could not resume custody because the child had been declared "abandoned," even though the mother had given custody to her friend less than two weeks before requesting return, and the Department of Public Welfare had had custody for only two days. The department claimed that they had reason to keep the child on authority of Massachusetts' definition of abandonment, which read:

Any child under fourteen years who is left in any place and who is seemingly without a parent or legal guardian available shall be immediately reported to the department, which shall proceed to arrange care for such child temporarily and shall forthwith cause search to be made for parent or guardian. If parent or guardian cannot be found or is unable or refuses to make suitable provisions for the child, the department shall make such lawful provision as seems for the best interests of such child.[40]

The mother took her case to court, claiming that the law was unconstitutional. The court did not agree that the Massachusetts definition of abandonment was unconstitutional, but it did rule that in this case it was applied in an unconstitutional manner because the mother was given no opportunity to contest the department's decision that she was unable to make "suitable provisions for [her] child."[41]

In many states, this problem is resolved by permitting parents to disprove a charge of abandonment if they can show that they maintained continuous, periodic contact with their children, by visiting them, writing, speaking on the telephone, and the like. Rare and infrequent instances of contact, however, usually fail to overcome a ruling of abandonment.[42]

Is placing a child in foster care "abandonment"?

No. Parents can be charged with abandoning their children *after* they have been placed in foster care if the parents have failed to keep in regular contact with their children and the agency responsible for their care; however, the decision to place a child in foster care can never be used against a parent as a factor to prove abandonment. To the contrary, every state's policy is to encourage parents to place their children in foster care when the parent is unable temporarily to care for his or her child.

Is imprisonment grounds for termination of parental rights?

Yes, in an increasing number of states. In some cases, imprisonment may be considered grounds for termination because it falls into the definition of abandonment. But in most states, courts have ruled that imprisonment, by itself, cannot support a finding of abandonment, since imprisonment does not establish a settled purpose to forego all parental duties.[43] These states follow the rule that one's "intention" to abandon must be proven, and, using it as a guide, incarceration cannot constitute abandonment, since being sentenced to prison cannot be equated with a desire to forever abandon one's children.

In all states, the fact that a parent is facing a lengthy term of imprisonment provides child protection agencies with the grounds to inquire into the plans the parent has made for his or her child. If the incarcerated parent is able to show both that he or she has made adequate childcare provisions for the child and that the incarcerated parent is maintaining contact (through letters, phone calls, or visits at the prison), in many cases the parent will be able to defeat an attempt to terminate parental rights. However, if an incarcerated parent simply leaves his or her child in foster care for a long time with no long-term plan other than foster care, a court may conclude that the parent has not made an adequate plan for the child.[44]

Finally, as mentioned previously, in some states, conviction of a crime, if the crime is a serious one (murder, armed robbery, and the like), provides evidence of abuse or neglect and it may be grounds for termination of parental rights.[45]

What rights do incarcerated parents have in termination cases?

Incarcerated parents, like all parents, have a right to notice of any proceeding against them and the right to be present in court. The court must provide incarcerated parents with transportation to court if the parent requests the opportunity to appear in person. Once in court, the parent (usually) has a right to court-assigned free legal representation. If an incarcerated parent fails to appear in court, the court will assume that all of the allegations against the parent are true and the most probable outcome of the case will be an order terminating parental rights.

May parental rights be terminated because of low intelligence or mental illness?

Perhaps, if the low intelligence or mental illness is so extreme that it makes parents incapable or caring for their children.

In light of the constitutional interests of biological parents in raising their children (see chapter 4), several federal courts have held that parents may not be involuntarily deprived of their children without a sufficient showing of harm to the child to justify termination.[46] A difficult problem arises, then, when a court must decide if parental rights should be terminated because evidence shows that certain parents are incapable of caring for their children due to their mental incapacity, even though there is no evidence of any past harm to the children or that the children have suffered under the care of their parents.

Some courts have found low or impaired intelligence alone—without any showing of harm to children—enough to justify termination.[47] But a number of states do not permit termination merely because parents are thought to be incapable of caring for a child, without some proof that they are in fact incapable. For example, the Missouri statute authorizes termination when a child has been abused, neglected, or in foster care for over one year, and the parent has

> [a] mental condition which is shown by competent evidence either to be permanent or such that there is no reasonable likelihood that the condition can be reversed and which renders the parent unable to knowingly provide the child the necessary care, custody and control.[48]

And an Oregon court ruled that proof of a mother's "antisocial personality" and that she was more likely than the average person to abuse her child "some day," was insufficient to terminate her parental rights. The court required some showing of a present failure to perform her parental role or evidence of substantial certainty that she would not be able to perform with minimal adequacy.[49] A middle ground is taken in Nebraska, where the law authorizes termination if "parents are unable to discharge parental responsibilities because of mental illness or mental deficiency, and there are reasonable grounds to believe that such condition will continue for a prolonged or indeterminate period."[50]

After a finding of abuse or neglect, what can a parent do to prevent termination of parental rights?

To prevent termination, it is crucial that parents follow the plan developed by the agency. As already explained in chapter 5, a plan for the care of the child must be developed for every child placed in foster care. The plan will include the actions the parents are expected to perform, such as enrolling in a treatment or vocational program. Parents should speak regularly with the caseworker assigned to assist them and should try to do the things the caseworker has suggested.

Another way to answer this question is to look at the grounds for termination in the jurisdiction and be certain not to engage in conduct that could lead a court to find that termination is appropriate. In general terms, this means a parent should stay in regular contact with the child and the agency and should take whatever steps are necessary to obtain return of the child's custody as quickly as possible.

Do children living apart from their parents have a right to be be freed for adoption by others?

Not exactly. However, the principle that children have the right to establish and remain in a stable parent-child relationship is recognized in federal law. The Adoption Assistance and Child Welfare Act and implementing regulations requires that timetables be adhered to when children enter foster care. If parents are unable to achieve progress toward reuniting with their children within eighteen months of a child's placement, agencies and courts must consider filing proceedings to terminate parental rights. In this sense, a child's right to a permanent and stable homelife is recognized by law. However, children do not have the right to prevent their return to their parents when courts conclude either that law requires their return because their parents have not forfeited parental rights or because such a return is in the child's best interests.

Do children have a right to file a termination proceeding against their parents?

Yes, in some jurisdictions. But it is important that this answer not be misunderstood. In some states, the agency, a foster parent who has cared for the child for a signficant period of time, or the child directly through court-appointed counsel may file a termination petition that would trigger the process by which a court ultimately decides whether to terminate parental rights. However, there must be grounds under state law for the termination proceeding to succeed. Unless the petition alleges that there are grounds under law to terminate parental rights, the petition will be dismissed. (For a further discussion of this issue, *see* the description of the *Gregory K.* case in chapter 6.)

Do children have a right to court review of an agency decision not to file a termination proceeding?

Yes, in most jurisdictions. Even in states where only the agency is authorized to file a termination proceeding, children and their counsel are not powerless to challenge the agency's refusal to file a petition. In many jurisdictions, there are a variety of devices available to representatives of children (counsel or guardians ad litem) to seek judicial review of the agency's decision. These devices include filing a motion for that purpose or requesting the court during a dispositional hearing or case planning review to direct the agency to file a termination proceeding.

Does the state have a duty to provide supportive services to parents before parental rights may be terminated?

Usually. As mentioned previously, in most states parental rights may be terminated only after a child has been involuntarily removed from the home or has been a ward of the state for a certain length of time. Once children are in foster care, the Adoption Assistance and Child Welfare Act of 1980 conditions the expenditure of federal matching funds for foster care upon the state's compliance with certain rules, including rules requiring the provision of rehabilitative and reunification services to the family. The Act itself does not compel a state to hold that its agents' failure to comply with these rules bars the termination of parental rights in a particular case. But that is the law in a number of states, including California, Connecticut, New York, Rhode Island, and Wisconsin.[51]

In some jurisdictions, for example, Delaware, state courts have ruled that agencies must comply with all federal rules before a termination of parental rights may be effected.[52] Without reliance on federal law, many states, including California, Kansas, New York, and Oregon, have passed laws that require proof that agencies have done everything in their power to assist the family before termination is permitted.[53] Still other states, including Florida and West Virginia, require that an agency offer a parent a performance agreement specifying the services the agency must take and the responsibilities of the parents before termination may be sought.[54] These supportive or rehabilitative services include counseling, homemaker assistance, parent training, employment training, individual or group therapy, and visits with the children. Missouri requires the court to consider "[t]he success or failure of the efforts of the juvenile officer, the division or other agency to aid the parent on a continuing basis in adjusting his circumstances or conduct to provide a proper home for the child."[55]

When the state is obligated to deliver these services and fails to do so, many courts will not permit a termination ruling to be made. Thus, to cite one of many examples, the Utah Supreme Court overturned a finding of termination because the mother was never informed of her alleged inadequacies or how to remedy them; neither was she provided with any training or rehabilitation.[56] Many other states require proof that efforts were undertaken to reunify the family before termination proceedings may be brought.[57]

There are two exceptions to the rule that states must assist parents in reuniting the family. First as noted earlier, in a few states parental rights may be terminated upon the immediate conclusion of a neglect or abuse hearing; under such circumstances, obviously, there would be no duty to provide services, since there is no time to do so. Second, even in states that require providing rehabilitative services before termination, the requirement is suspended if there is no possibility that the child's welfare will be improved as a result of such services. Thus, in New York, the law requires the agency to demonstrate that it put forth "diligent efforts to encourage and strengthen the parental relationship," but only "when such efforts will not be detrimental to the best interests of the child."[58] Following this exception, some courts have ruled that when there is clearly no possibility of rehabilitation, parental rights may be terminated notwithstanding the lack of supportive services, because the welfare of the child would not be served by futilely trying to reunite a family.[59]

Do parents have a right to be notified of the proceedings when the state seeks to terminate their rights?

Yes. Fundamental aspects of due process of law require that people be notified prior to proceedings in which their interests are at stake. Clearly, parents have a fundamental interest in the care and custody of their children (see chapter 4). Therefore, they have a right to receive prior, written notice of termination proceedings, including written notice of specific allegations against them so that they know what they are accused of doing (or not doing) and to have a reasonable opportunity to prepare their defense.[60] Also, if the parent seeks a voluntary termination, the child and state have the right to be notified.[61]

This does not mean, however, that parents will always know about termination proceedings against them before their cases are decided by a court. In many cases, efforts to serve parents with court papers are unsuccessful because the petitioning agency does not know the parents' location and is unable to serve them court documents. Courts will allow *substituted service* when a petitioning agency has demonstrated that, despite diligent efforts, it is unable to serve the parent personally. Substituted service usually takes the form of publication in a limited circulation newspaper in the parents' last known geographical community. Parents rarely receive actual notice when substituted service is used. Once the termination case in completed and the parent learns that his or her rights were terminated, it is possible to file papers in court seeking to reopen the proceedings. However, courts rarely will reopen these cases if significant time has elapsed since the termination order. Moreover, courts will never reopen these proceedings unless the parent can show—in addition to having a good reason for not knowing about the proceeding—there is a probability that the parent would win the case if it were retried.

Do parents have a right to be heard at termination proceedings?

Yes. For the same reason that parents have a right to prior notice of termination proceedings, they have a right to be present and state their case at the hearing.[62] This also includes the right to present witnesses on their behalf and to cross-examine witnesses against them.

If parents are not permitted to be present and to be heard at a termination hearing, it is probable that any decision made to terminate their rights could be attacked for constitutional irregularity.[63]

May parents be represented by an attorney in termination proceedings?

Yes. The state may not prevent parents from having their own lawyer represent them. When the Supreme Court established the right of accused criminals to be represented in court by an attorney, it commented on the importance of legal representation in court:

> The right to be heard would be, in many cases, of little avail if it did not comprehend the right to be heard by counsel. . . . Without it, [the accused], though he be not guilty, faces the danger of conviction because he does not know how to establish his innocence.[64]

In termination proceedings, do parents who cannot afford a lawyer have the right to have one free of charge?

Yes. Remarkably, however, the right to counsel in termination proceedings was created by state law (either the enactment of a statute or case decisional law.) The Supreme Court of the United States refused to require that indigent parents be given free counsel in every termination proceeding.[65] Instead, the Court ruled that whether parents have a federally protected constitutional right to free counsel in termination cases depends on the particular circumstances of each case.

Nonetheless, states are permitted to require counsel for parents even when the federal constitution does not require that result. Many states have relied on their state constitution in finding that parents must be provided with counsel in termination cases. The Oregon Supreme Court, for example, which mandated assigned counsel three years before the legislature required it, wrote:

> The permanent termination of parental rights is one of the most drastic actions the state can take against its inhabitants. It would be unconscionable for the state forever to terminate the parental rights of the poor without allowing such parents to be assisted by counsel. . . . If the parents are too poor to employ counsel, the cost thereof must be born by the public.[66]

The New York Court of Appeals, which also paved the way for that state's legislature requiring appointed counsel, concluded:

> The parent's interest in the liberty of the child, in his care and in his control, has long been recognized as a fundamental interest. . . . Such an interest may not be curtailed by the state without a meaningful opportunity to be heard, which in these circumstances includes the assistance of counsel.[67]

Since the Supreme Court held in 1981 that the federal Constitution does not require counsel for parents in every case, the few states that did not already provide parents with court-assigned counsel in termination proceedings changed their laws and now every state will assign counsel in such cases.[68]

However, because the right to counsel in every case is not required by the federal Constitution, some courts have held that parents do not have a right to *effective* representation of counsel.[69] This means that an appellate court may refuse to reverse an order terminating parental rights in some jurisdictions when the only claim the parent makes on appeal is that the parent's lawyer failed to provide a minimum level of professional competence.

In termination proceedings, is a lawyer provided to represent a child?

Not necessarily. Many states require courts to appoint a lawyer to represent the child in proceedings to terminate parental rights, even if the child is an infant.[70] Even if state law does not require that a lawyer be appointed, many courts will do so on their own accord.[71] When a lawyer is appointed, it means that he or she is paid by the court; neither the child nor the parents are required to pay for this representation.

Children are frequently represented by lawyers in termination proceedings because of the importance of the proceedings to the child. Indeed, few proceedings are of greater importance to the child. At one extreme, the outcome of the case subjects the child to being permanently separated from his or her parents and becoming a state ward. At the other extreme, the outcome may subject them to a return to biological parents who once endangered them and may cause them future harm. Lawyers are also provided children because of the danger that neither the state (which has charged the parents with abandonment or wrongdoing) nor the parents necessarily represent the interests of the children.

When children are not given lawyers to represent them, they usually will be assigned a guardian ad litem or a Court Assigned Special Advocate (CASA). Such assignments are different from providing children with lawyers. The guardian's or CASA's responsibilities are to ensure that the proceedings are conducted properly and that the child's interests are considered. In many cases, the guardian will tell the judge his or her personal opinion concerning the proper outcome of the case. Lawyers, on the other hand, usually are prohibited from expressing a personal opinion about the case and are expected to advocate the position the child wants.

The reason children are not invariably given a lawyer in these proceedings is that the Supreme Court of the United States has never ruled that a lawyer must be appointed to represent the child in termination proceedings. In 1967 the Court required the appointment of counsel in all juvenile delinquency hearings; it reasoned that since children accused of wrongdoing faced the possible deprivation of their liberty by commitment to a reform school or training school, they were entitled to the same constitutional right of legal counsel as adults facing criminal charges.[72] Most states have taken this to mean that they have a duty to appoint a lawyer to represent children in other hearings involving children as well, or at least in proceedings wherein the state seeks to intervene in a child's family life and make a decision affecting his or her future care and custody.

The Supreme Court's 1981 ruling in *Lassiter v. Department of Social Services*[73] that parents do not have an automatic right to counsel in termination proceedings almost certainly means that children do not have a federally protected right to counsel in every case.

If a lawyer is appointed to represent the child in termination proceedings, must he or she reflect the wishes of the child's parents?

No. The point of having a lawyer appointed for children is to have someone available to represent their wishes and their interests alone. The theory is that the court needs the input and assistance of someone who represents neither the state (which seeks termination) nor the parents (who may resist it), but the very subject of the proceeding, the child.

However, children who are the subjects of termination proceedings are often too young to speak for themselves, or, if they are old enough to speak, they may be unable to articulate or even identify their own interests. Thus, in a great many cases, lawyers representing children are unable to do what lawyers in most other proceedings do as a matter of routine: counsel clients and follow the instructions given by the clients. Lawyers for children are free to oppose the parents' position; they are free to side with the parents; and they usually are free to argue the position that they personally think is best for the child. Their discretion is very broad.

Do parents have a right to a trial by jury in a termination proceeding?

No, in most states.[74] In a majority of states, the hearing to determine whether parental rights are to be terminated is held by a judge only, who will make all final determinations of fact and law. There is a right to jury trials in a number of states including Oklahoma, Wisconsin, and Wyoming.[75]

How strongly must the state prove its case against parents?

At termination proceedings, the state has the burden of proving that parental rights should be terminated; parents do not have to prove their rights should not be terminated. If the state does not prove its case, parental rights will not be terminated.

The question then becomes, how *strongly* does the state have to prove its case; that is, what standard of proof does a court use in making its decision? In a criminal trial, the state must prove the defendant's guilt "beyond a reasonable doubt," the highest standard of proof used in American courts. In an ordinary civil trial, one party will win a case if it establishes proof by a "preponderance" of evidence, which translates numerically to 51 percent. In 1982 the Supreme Court ruled that the federal constitution requires proof in termination cases be no less than "clear and convincing" evidence.[76] This standard is somewhere in between a preponderance of the evidence and beyond a reasonable doubt and has the effect of making it more difficult for the state to prove its case. In other words, unless states prove their case in a "convincing" manner, parental rights will remain intact. States are permitted to use the even higher "beyond a reasonable doubt" standard of proof, as is used in New Hampshire and Louisiana.[77] Similarly, proof beyond a reasonable doubt is required when a state seeks to terminate the parental rights of Native Americans.[78]

Are termination orders always entered upon a court's finding that there are grounds for termination?

No. In most states, a separate dispositional hearing will be held after the trial phase of the case is completed and the court has made a finding that grounds to terminate parental rights exist. This separate dispositional hearing presents the court with the opportunity to decide whether termination is the most appropriate order to enter or whether, even though there is power to terminate, some other alternative would best serve the child's interests.

Do parents and children have a right to be present and to provide evidence at the dispositional hearing?

Yes. In those jurisdictions in which there are dispositional hearings, all parties have the right to attend and present evidence at the hearing.[79] However, it is common that children do not appear in court. Many people believe that children are better off being kept away from the court proceedings. If an older child wishes to attend the proceedings, however, it would probably violate his or her rights if the court barred the child from attending. In all events, the child's lawyer or guardian ad litem would attend the hearing.

What are the issues to be determined at the dispositional hearing?

The major difference between the inquiry at the trial and the dispositional hearings is that the only inquiry at the dispositional hearing will be the best interests of the child. At the trial phase, the court must determine whether the statutory grounds for termination exist. As already indicated earlier in this chapter, most courts will not terminate parental rights merely because doing so is in a child's best interests. At the disposition hearing, however, courts will look carefully at the plan for the child and determine whether termination will meet the child's best interests. Courts that conduct dispositional hearings usually will want to know whether an adoption is planned and how realistic the plan is. They will also want to consider the strength of ties between the child and his or her biological family.

What rights do relatives of children have in termination proceedings?

As a general rule, relatives, such as grandparents and aunts and uncles, have few rights to be heard at the trial phase of a termination proceeding. At that phase of the case, the principal inquiry for the court is whether the parents have failed to keep in contact or plan for their children or the severity of abuse the parents inflicted on the child. On these issues, relatives usually are given little to say. However, at the dispositional phase of a termination case, where the court will decide the future of the child, including whether to make the momentous decision to terminate parental rights, relatives frequently have a great deal to say about the child's best interests. For this reason, relatives usually are permitted to intervene at the dispositional phase of a case.

Relatives may or may not be given a free, court-assigned counsel, depending on the jurisdiction. Thus, it may be necessary for a relative to retain counsel in order to particpate effectively in the dispositional phase of the case.

What rights do foster parents have in termination proceedings?

Foster parents may enjoy more rights than the child's relatives. Depending on the jurisdiction, foster parents may be authorized to commence the termination proceeding when the child has been in their care for a specified period of time (usually at least one year), and no progress has been made to return the child to his or her parents.[80] Even in jurisidctions where foster parents have no right to file the termination petition or to participate at the trial stage of the case, they frequently will be permitted to intervene at the dispositional phase in order to be heard on the question of what final court order is in the child's best interests.

Are there any alternatives to termination?

Depending on the jurisdiction, there may be. In some cases, courts may consider arranging for permanent foster care or guardianship with parental visitation. This may be the most appropriate outcome when the parent and child have a meaningful relationship that the court is reluctant to completely sever.[81]

Are children invariably adopted after parental rights have been ordered?

No. It is common in many states that as many as 40 to 60 percent of children freed for adoption are not adopted after two years of the termination order.[82] In these cases, termination orders yield the worst of all results for children: a permanent severence of ties to the biological family and a permanent status of wardship in which the children are legally related to no one.[83]

Do parents and children have a right to appeal a court decision to terminate their rights?

In most states, yes.[84] This would include a right to counsel to prepare the appeal in those states where counsel is provided for the original hearing.[85]

NOTES

1. *See, e.g.*, Ill. Ann. Stat. ch. 750, para. 50/1 (Smith-Hurd 1993).

2. Ill. Ann. Stat. ch. 750, para. 50/1, § 1(D)(p) (Smith-Hurd 1993); Mo. Ann. Stat. §§ 211.447 (2)(2)(a), (2)(3)(c) (Vernon 1983 & Supp. 1994).

3. Cal. Fam. Code § 7825 (West 1994); *In re Arthur C.* 176 Cal. App. 3d 442, 222 Cal. Rptr. 388 (4th Dist. 1985); *Adoption of D.S.C.*, 93 Cal. App. 3d 14, 155 Cal. Rptr. 406 (4th Dist. 1979).

4. Mo. Ann. Stat. § 211.447(3)(3) (Vernon 1983 & Supp. 1994).

5. *See, e.g.*, Ill. Ann. Stat. ch. 750, para. 50/1, § 1(D)(i),(j),(k) (Smith-Hurd 1993) (depravity, adultery, fornication, habitual drunkenness); Neb. Rev. Stat. § 43-292(4) (debauchery, lewd and lascivious behavior) (1993).

6. N.Y. Fam. Ct. ACT § 614 (McKinney 1983); N.Y. Soc. Serv. Law § 384-b(7)(a) (McKinney 1992).

7. Cal. Fam. Code § 7828 (West 1994).

8. Conn. Gen. Stat. § 17a 112(c) (West 1992 & Supp. 1994).

9. Cal. Fam. Code § 7825, 7826, 7827 (West 1994).

10. Conn. Gen. Stat. § 17a 112(c) (West 1992 & Supp. 1994).

11. Tenn. Code Ann. § 37-1-147(d)(2) (severe child abuse) (1991); Fla. Stat. Ann. § 39.464(1)(a)(2)(d) (egregious abuse) (Westlaw West 1995).

12. Cal. Fam. Code § 7826 (West 1994).

13. *In re A.M.K.*, 105 Wis. 2d 91, 312 N.W.2d 840 (Wis. App. 1982) (court can terminate parental rights for inability to care for child due to long imprisonment).

14. *See, e.g., People ex rel. Portney v. Strasser,* 303 N.Y. 539, 104 N.E.2d 895 (1952); *Appeal of Renker,* 180 Pa. Super. 143, 117 A.2d 780 (Pa. 1955); *In re Clark's Adoption,* 38 Ariz. 481 1 P.2d 112 (1931).

15. *In re Fish,* 174 Mont. 201, 206, 569 P.2d 924, 927–28 (1977).

16. *Custody of a Minor,* 377 Mass. 876, 389 N.E.2d 68 (1979), expressly overruling *Petition of New England Home for Little Wanderers,* 367 Mass. 631, 328 N.E.2d 854 (1975).

17. *Bennett v. Jeffreys,* 40 N.Y.2d 543, 356 N.E.2d 277, 387 N.Y.S.2d 821 (1976).

18. *In re Sanjivini K.,* 47 N.Y.2d 374, 382, 391 N.E.2d 1316, 1320–1321, 418 N.Y.S.2d 339, 349 (1979); *see also Corey L. v. Martin L.,* 45 N.Y.2d 383, 380 N.E.2d 266, 408 N.Y.S.2d 439 (1978).

19. *See, e.g., In re Adoption of J.S.R.,* 374 A.2d 860 (D.C. App. 1977); *Petition of New England Home for Little Wanderers, supra* note 16; *In re William L.,* 477 Pa. 322, 383 A.2d 1228 (1978), *cert. denied sub nom. Lehman v. Lycoming County Children's Services,* 439 U.S. 880 (1978).

20. *See, e.g.,* D.C. Code Ann. § 16–304(e) (1966); Mass. Gen Laws Ann. ch. 210, § 3(a)(ii) (West 1987); Wash. Rev. Code Ann. § 26.33.010 (West 1986).

21. *See, e.g., Berrien v. Greene County Dept. of Pub. Welfare,* 216 Va. 241, 217 S.E.2d 854 (1975); *Bennett v. Jeffreys, supra* note 17.

22. *Smith v. Organization of Foster Families,* 431 U.S. 816, 846 (1977).

23. *Id.* at 862–63 (quoting *Prince v. Massachusetts,* 321 U.S. 158, 166 (1944)). *See also Quilloin v. Walcott,* 434 U.S. 246, 255 (1978).

24. *Santosky v. Kramer,* 455 U.S. 745, 767 n.17 (1982).

25. *Lehr v. Robertson,* 463 U.S. 248, 261–62 (1983).

26. *Alsager v. District Court,* 406 F. Supp. 10,14 (S.D. Iowa 1975), *aff'd,* 545 F.2d 1137 (8th Cir. 1976) (describing Iowa Code §§ 232.41(2)(b),(d).

27. *Id.,* at 21.

28. *Davis v. Smith,* 266 Ark. 112, 116, 583 S.W.2d 37, 40 (1979).

29. *Id.* at 121, 583 S.W.2d at 43.

30. *In re William L., supra* note 19, at 329 n.2, 383 A.2d at 1231 n.2 construing Pa. Adoption Act of 1970 § 311(2).

31. *In re Anthony L. 'CC',* 48 A.D.2d 415, 417, 370 N.Y.S.2d 219, 221 (3d Dep't 1975).

32. *New England Home for Little Wanderers, supra* note 16, construing Mass. Gen. Laws Ann., ch 210, § 3.

33. *Matter of Keyes,* 574 P.2d 1026, 1028 (Okla. 1977), *appeal dismissed* 439 U.S. 804 (1978).

34. *People in Interest of S.J.C.,* 776 P.2d 1103 (Colo. 1989) (en banc).

35. *State v. McMaster,* 259 Or. 291, 296, 486 P.2d 567, 569 (1971).

36. *See* Joseph Goldstein, Anna Freud, Albert Solnit, *Beyond the Best Interests of the Child* (1973).

37. *See, e.g.,* Cal. Fam. Code § 7822 (West 1994); N.Y. Soc. Serv. Law § 384-b(5) (McKinney 1992).

38. *See, e.g., In re Estate of Barazzi,* 265 Cal. App. 2d 282, 71 Cal. Rptr. 249 (2d Dist. 1968); *In re Adoption of Smith,* 38 Ill. App. 3d 217, 347 N.E.2d 292 (4th Dist. 1976), *cert.*

denied 431 U.S. 939 (1977). *Drury v. Lang*, 105 Nev. 430, 776 P.2d 843 (1989) (interpreting Nev. Rev. Stat. §§ 128.105, 128.012(1) as precluding a finding of "settled purpose" to abandon merely because parent failed to communicate for six months).

39. *See, e.g., In re B.J.*, 530 P.2d 747 (Alaska 1975); *Matter of I.R.*, 153 A.D.2d 559, 544 N.Y.S.2d 216 (2d Dep't 1989) (interpreting N.Y. Soc. Serv. Law § 384-b(5) as authorizing a legal determination of an intention to abandon based on proof of failure to visit or communicate for one year).

40. *White v. Minter*, 330 F. Supp. 1194, 1196 (D. Mass. 1971) (quoting Mass. Gen. Laws Ann. ch. 119, § 23(e)).

41. *Id.*

42. *See, e.g.*, Mo. Ann. Stat. § 211.447(4) (Vernon 1983 & Supp. 1994); *Matter of Adoption of B.C.S.*, 245 Kan. 182, 777 P.2d 776 (1989), *In re Shannon S.*, 41 Conn. Supp. 145, 562 A.2d 79 (Conn. Super. 1989).

43. *See, e.g., In the Interest of E.J.F.*, 161 Ill. App. 3d 325, 514 N.E.2d 544, 112 Ill. Dec. 881 (4th Dist. 1987) (Incarcarated mother's rights terminated only because she made no effort to fulfill plan for her child, which she could have done while incarcerated); *Murphy v. Vanderver*, 169 Ind. App. 528, 349 N.E.2d 202 (Ind. App. 1976); *In re Adoption of Maynor*, 38 N.C. App. 724, 248 S.E.2d 875 (1978); *In re Adoption of Jameson*, 20 Utah 2d 53, 432 P.2d 881 (1967).

44. *In the Matter of Gregory B.*, 74 N.Y.2d 77, 542 N.E.2d 1052, 544 N.Y.S.2d 535 (1989) (Imprisonment for a long time results in "permanent neglect" in New York because parent cannot plan for child—leaving child in foster care for a long period of time does not constitute a plan).

45. Cal. Fam. Code § 7825 (West 1994); *Adoption of D.S.C., supra* note 3.

46. *See, e.g., Alsager v. District Court, supra* note 26; *Roe v. Conn*, 417 F. Supp 769 (M.D. Ala. 1976).

47. *See, e.g., In re Interest of C.W.*, 226 Neb. 719, 414 N.W.2d 277 (1987); *In Interest of D.R.*, 463 N.W.2d 918 (N.D. 1990); *In Interest of McDonald*, 201 N.W.2d 447 (Iowa 1972); *In re William L., supra* note 19.

48. Mo. Ann. Stat. §§ 211.447 (2)(2)(a), (2)(3)(c) (Vernon 1983 & Supp. 1994).

49. *In re Wyatt*, 34 Or. App. 793, 579 P.2d 889 (1978).

50. Neb. Rev. Stat. § 43-292(5) (1993); *In re Interest of D.L.S.*, 230 Neb. 435, 432 N.W.2d 31 (1988).

51. *See, e.g.*, Cal. Fam. Code § 7828 (West 1994); Conn. Gen. Stat. Ann. § 45a-717 (West 1993); N.Y. Soc. Serv. Law §§ 384-b(7)(a), (8)(a)(ii), (8)(b)(ii) (McKinney 1992); R.I. Gen. Laws § 15-7-7; Wis. Stat. Ann. § 48.415(2)(b) (West 1987).

52. *E.g., Matter of Burns*, 519 A.2d 638 (Del. 1986).

53. Cal. Fam. Code § 7828 (West 1994); Kan. Stat. Ann. § 38–1583(b)(7) (1993); N.Y. Soc. Serv. Law § 384-b(7)(f) (McKinney 1992). *See also In the Matter of Sheila G.*, 61 N.Y.2d 368, 462 N.E.2d 1139, 474 N.Y.S.2d 421 (1984); *In re William, Susan, and Joseph*, 448 A.2d 1250 (R.I. 1982).

54. *See, e.g., Williams v. Department of Health and Rehabilitative Services*, 482 So. 2d 1371 (Fla. 1986); *State ex rel. Department of Human Services v. Cheryl M.*, 177 W. Va. 688, 356 S.E.2d 181 (1987).

55. Mo. Ann. Stat. § 211.447 (2)(3)(b) (Vernon 1983 & Supp. 1994).

56. *State in Interest of Walter B.*, 577 P.2d 119 (Utah 1978).

57. *See, e.g., Burk v. Department of Health and Rehabilitative Services*, 476 So. 2d 1275 (Fla. 1985) (before termination of parental rights may be ordered, the agency must first offer the abusing parent a performance agreement that allows him or her an opportunity to eliminate the conditions that caused the abuse); Williams v. Department of Health and Rehabilitative Services, *supra* note 54 (a performance agreement is the precondition to initiation of termination proceedings); *State ex rel. Department of Human Services v. Cheryl M.*, *supra* note 54 (when the parent requests a delay of the termination proceedings to allow an "improvement period," the court should grant this request; the agency is obliged to develop and present a case plan for court approval); *In Interest of D.L.D.*, 701 S.W.2d 152 (Mo. App. 1985) (termination cannot be ordered on the basis of parents' failure to follow service agreements not approved by the court). *But see S.E.S. v. Grant County Dep't of Welfare*, 594 N.E.2d 447 (Ind. 1992) (no longer required that reasonable services be provided to assist a parent in fulfilling parental obligations).

58. N.Y. Soc. Serv. Law § 384-b(7)(a) (McKinnney 1992). (New York law also excepts the diligent efforts requirement when the parent fails to keep the agency apprised of location for six months, or when incarcerated parent fails to cooperate with agency § 384-b(7)(e) (McKinney 1992).

59. *See, e.g., Matter of Appeal in Yuma County*, 172 Ariz. 50, 833 P.2d 721 (Ct. App. 1992) (services need not be provided when efforts to reunify the family would be futile); *In re J.D.M.*, 808 P.2d 1122 (Utah App. 1991) (state has no duty to provide rehabilitative treatment and assistance prior to termination of parental rights on grounds of abandonment; this duty exists only when parents are available and cooperate with the agency); *People in the Interest of M.K.*, 466 N.W.2d 177 (S.D. 1991) (state not required to provide all possible forms of parenting assistance for mentally impaired parents).

60. *See, e.g.*, Mass. Gen. Laws Ann. ch. 210, § 4 (West 1987).

61. *See, e.g., In the Matter of M.S.M.*, 781 P.2d 332 (Okla. App. 1989).

62. *See, e.g.*, Conn. Gen. Stat. § 45a-717(1) (West 1993).

63. *See, e.g., Rodriguez v. Koschny*, 57 Ill. App. 3d 355, 373 N.E.2d 47, 14 Ill. Dec. 916 (2d Dist. 1978).

64. *Powell v. Alabama*, 287 U.S. 45, 68–69 (1932).

65. *Lassiter v. Department of Social Services*, 452 U.S. 18 (1981).

66. *State v. Jamison*, 251 Or. 114, 117, 444 P.2d 15, 17 (1968).

67. *In re B.*, 30 N.Y.2d 352, 357, 285 N.E.2d 288, 290, 334 N.Y.S.2d 133, 136 (1972) (quoting *Cleaver v. Wilcox*, 40 USLW 2658).

68. *See, e.g.*, N.C. Gen. Stat. § 7A-289.23 (1981).

69. *See, e.g., Posner v. Dallas County Child Welfare*, 784 S.W.2d 585 (Tex. App. 1990). *But see In Interest of M.D.(S)*, 168 Wis. 2d 996, 485 N.W.2d 52 (1992).

70. *See, e.g.*, N.D. Cent. Code § 27-20-26 (1991); N.Y. Fam. Ct. Act § 241 (McKinney 1983).

71. *See, e.g., Wagstaff v. Superior Court*, 535 P.2d 1220 (Alaska 1975); *In re Orlando F.*, 40 N.Y.2d 103, 351 N.E.2d 711, 386 N.Y.S.2d 64 (1976); *Stapleton v. Dauphin County Child Care Service*, 228 Pa. Super. 371, 324 A.2d 562 (1974).

72. *In re Gault,* 387 U.S. 1 (1967).

73. *Supra* note 65.

74. *See, e.g., In re Shane T.,* 544 A.2d 1295 (Me. 1988).

75. *A.E. v. State,* 743 P.2d 1041 (Okla. 1987); Wis. Stat. Ann. § 48.422(4) (West 1987); Wyo. Stat. § 14-2-312 (1994).

76. *Santosky v. Kramer, supra* note 24.

77. *State v. Robert H.,* 118 N.H. 713, 716, 393 A.2d 1387 (1978); La. Rev. Stat. Ann. § 13:1603(A) (West 1983).

78. *Indian Child Welfare Act,* 25 U.S.C. § 1912 (f) (1979).

79. *See, e.g., In re Render,* 145 Mich. App. 344, 377 N.W.2d 421 (1985); *Matter of Welfare of N. W.,* 405 N.W.2d 512 (Minn. App. 1987). *But see In re Vasquez,* 199 Mich. App. 44, 501 N.W.2d 231 (1993)(incarcerated father not denied due process or equal protection when not at termination hearing).

80. *See, e.g.,* N.Y. Soc. Serv. Law § 392 (6)(c) (McKinney 1992).

81. *See* Garrison, *Why Terminate Parental Rights?,* 35 Stan. L. Rev. 423 (1983).

82. *See generally,* Martin Guggenheim, *The Effects of Recent Trends to Accelerate the Termination of Parental Rights of Children in Foster Care—An Empirical Analysis in Two States* 29 Fam. L.Q. 121 (1995).

83. *See Santosky v. Kramer, supra* note 24, at 766 n.15.

84. *See, e.g.,* N.Y. Fam. Ct. Act, § 1112(a) (McKinney 1992); *In Interest of Workman,* 56 Ill. App. 3d 1007, 373 N.E.2d 39, 14 Ill. Dec. 908 (3d Dist. 1978), *aff'd,* 76 Ill. 2d 256, 390 N.E.2d 900, 28 Ill. Dec. 541, *cert. denied* 444 U.S. 992 (1979).

85. *In Interest of Brehm,* 3 Kan. App. 325, 594 P.2d 269 (1979); *see also In re Ward,* 351 So. 2d 571 (Ala. Civ. App. 1977) (right to a free transcript on appeal); *In re Curtis S.,* 25 Cal. App. 4th 687, 30 Cal. Rptr. 2d 739 (5th Dist. 1994).

PART 3
Becoming a Family

VIII

Adoptive Families

Adoption is as old as Moses, found among the rushes by Pharoah's daughter who made him her son. It is as new as an infant abandoned on the steps of a police station halfway around the world and brought home by an American couple last month to become their daughter.

Adoption, in some form, has existed since the beginning of recorded time.[1] Yet it is only in the modern era that adoption has evolved from a means of providing a legal heir to families without male offspring to a legally sanctioned way of providing permanent families for children whose biological parents cannot or will not raise them.

For much of the twentieth century, the adoption process was used to create the illusion that the adopted child was the parents' biological child. Adoption agencies carefully matched children with adoptive parents in as many respects as possible—blond, blue-eyed babies born to Protestant birth parents were assigned to blond, blue-eyed Protestant adoptive parents— and the facts of the adoption itself were scrupulously hidden from public view. Birth parents and adoptive parents never met or knew each other's names. The facts surrounding the adoption were often concealed even from the adopted child, who might learn of them only by overhearing a whispered conversation among adults. The entire adoption process was designed to shield the birth mother from the stigma of having given birth to a child out-of-wedlock and to mask the adoptive parents' inability to conceive a child.

Today, many of the fundamental assumptions that have governed adoptions for much of this century are being called into question. Adoptive parents, for instance, are now routinely advised to tell their children at an early age about their adoption. Indeed, the very idea of concealing the fact of an adoption is unimaginable in many cases, as parents adopt infants (often from other countries) who look nothing like them or expand their family by adopting older children.

What was once unthinkable—that the birth parents and the adoptive parents should meet at the time of the adoption—has now become common, if not routine. For adopted children whose adoptions were completed many years ago and who now wish to make contact with their birth parents or biological siblings, an active search movement has emerged.

In many respects, however, the legal system still reflects the traditional view of adoption as a shameful secret and an option of last resort. Hearings on adoption petitions remain closed to the public. In most states, the child's original birth certificate is still sealed, and a new certificate is issued listing the adoptive mother and father in place of the parents who conceived the child. And in many instances, children's needs for permanence and emotional stability take second place to the competing claims of the adults involved.

Yet, like other aspects of family law, adoption law today is in a state of flux. In August 1994, the National Conference of Commissioners of Uniform State Laws approved a new Uniform Adoption Act, which has been forwarded to all fifty states with a recommendation that it be enacted by their legislature.[2] This model law seeks to promote the interest of children in being raised by parents who are committed to, and capable of, caring for them. It takes pains to ensure that the birth parents' decision to voluntarily relinquish a child for adoption has been fully and carefully thought through;[3] at the same time, the model law guarantees that once an adoption is granted, it cannot be overturned except during a strictly limited period of time.[4] The new Uniform Adoption Act departs from the historical practice of categorically excluding whole classes of prospective adoptive parents—whether on the basis of race, marital status, age, or other arbitrary factor—and seeks to protect children's ties to the people who have actually cared for and nurtured them.[5] It mandates disclosure and preservation of as much nonidentifying information about the child's medical and family history as possible while leaving it to the birth parents, the adoptive parents, and the adopted child to decide for themselves whether they wish to learn each other's identities or whether to maintain some kind of contact after the adoption is final.[6]

For the time being, however, adoption remains a crazy quilt of international treaties, federal statutes and regulations, state laws, and child welfare procedures that vary not only from state to state but from county to county and even judge to judge. This chapter looks both at some of the themes that are common to adoption law in the fifty states as well as some of the striking inconsistencies in how different states approach the formation of adoptive families.

What is adoption?

Adoption is the legal process by which a parent-child relationship is formed between a child and an adult who is not the child's biological parent. Following an adoption, the adoptive parent assumes all of the biological parent's responsibilities and rights. Except for stepparent adoptions, a judicial adoption decree ends the legal relationship between a child and the members of his or her biological family. The adopted child becomes in all respects the child of the adoptive parents.

Adoptions may be ordered only by the courts. A prospective adoptive parent must seek the court's permission to adopt; the judge will decide whether to approve the adoption based on what is in the child's best interests. To assist the judge in determining whether the adoption is in the child's best interests, state adoption laws require the prospective adoptive parents to undergo an independent evaluation (commonly known as a *homestudy*) to assess their suitability as parents.

How common is adoption?

Although uniform statistics on adoption are no longer routinely gathered, it is estimated that one million children in the United States live with adoptive parents and between 2 percent and 4 percent of American families include an adopted child.[7] It is estimated that nearly 120,000 adoptions were granted in 1990.[8]

How are children placed for adoption?

A child may be placed for adoption in one of several ways. Approximately half of all adoptions involve the adoption of a child by a relative, i.e., by a stepparent, a grandparent, an aunt, an uncle, a cousin, or some other member of the child's extended family.[9] These adoptions tend to confirm preexisting, informal custodial arrangements and often do not involve an adoption agency. Stepparent adoptions account for the bulk of relative adoptions.

Approximately 20 percent of adoptions involve children living in foster care who are placed with an adoptive family by an adoption agency charged with finding permanent homes for foster children who cannot return to their biological families.[10] These adoptions typically involve toddlers and older children, some of whom may have serious physical or psychological disabilities requiring medical treatment and devoted parental attention.

Most infants are placed for adoption with nonrelatives either by privately run, state-licensed adoption agencies or by private placement. In a *private-placement adoption*, the birth parent (usually the birth mother) selects the adoptive parent with or without the assistance of an intermediary. Infant adoptions account for about 25 percent of domestic adoptions.[11]

Approximately seven to ten thousand children born in other countries are adopted each year by American parents. The majority of these children are adopted through adoption agencies in the United States, although a significant minority are adopted by American parents who make direct contact with orphanages or other intermediaries in the foreign country.

How does an agency adoption work?

Prospective parents who want to adopt through an agency must file an application for adoption with that agency and pay an application fee. The parents are then interviewed and investigated by the agency, which typically requires prospective adoptive parents to conform to a strict (and sometimes arbitrary) set of requirements before they are considered eligible to adopt.[12]

The criteria used by adoption agencies to screen prospective parents vary widely, but often include age, marital status, income, race, health, and religion. Some agencies require that the prospective adoptive parents provide medical proof of infertility. If approved, the prospective adoptive parents are placed on the agency's waiting list until a child whom the agency's social workers consider suitable for that particular family becomes available for adoption.

The agency usually offers some form of counseling both to the prospective adoptive parents as well as to the birth mother (and birth father, if he is involved in the adoption decision). Counseling for the prospective adoptive parents is intended, at least in theory, to help them decide if adoption is the right choice for them and to explore some of the issues involved in parenting an adopted child.

Agency counseling for the birth mother is designed to help her decide whether to keep her child or to place the child for adoption. If the birth mother chooses adoption, she typically relinquishes her child directly to the agency rather than to the adoptive parents. The agency is responsible for obtaining her consent to the adoption if that is her plan for the child. If there is a known birth father whose consent is required, the agency must get his consent too.

The agency then selects an adoptive home for the child from among those it has placed on its waiting list. Agencies typically match children with prospective adoptive parents based on a variety of factors, including age, physical characteristics, intelligence, interests, race, religion, cultural background, socioeconomic background, and the parties' expressed preferences.[13]

Traditionally, adoption agencies placed a high premium on keeping the identities of both the birth parents and the adoptive parents confidential. Birth parents were told neither the names nor the addresses of the adoptive parents. Conversely, the adoptive parents were given no identifying information about the birth parents. An unbreachable wall of secrecy surrounded the adoption.

Responding to birth mothers' desire to play a greater role in selecting their child's adoptive parents, many agencies have recently modified their procedures to allow the birth mother to select the adoptive parents from among families that have been prescreened by the agency. In some cases, the selection remains anonymous: the birth parent is offered descriptions of the prospective adoptive parents with no identifying information.

In many instances, however, adoption agencies have agreed to serve as intermediaries between parties whose identities have been disclosed to each other.

What is a private-placement adoption?

A *private-placement adoption* (also known as an independent or direct adoption) gives the birth mother far greater control of the adoption process than a traditional agency adoption. In a private-placement adoption, the birth mother selects the adoptive parents. A birth mother may learn of the prospective adoptive parents' interest in adoption through an intermediary (such as a doctor, a minister, a lawyer, or a friend), through word of mouth, or by advertisements placed in local newspapers inviting the birth mother to call a toll-free number to reach the prospective adoptive parents.[14]

Private adoptions are permitted in all but a handful of states[15] and account for one-third of all unrelated domestic adoptions. An increasing number of states have now instituted a system of preadoption certification, which requires the prospective adoptive parents to undergo a background investigation before a child may be placed in their home.[16] The new Uniform Adoption Act permits a birth parent to place a child only with prospective adoptive parents who have received a favorable preplacement evaluation.[17]

Independent adoptions tend to proceed much more quickly than agency adoptions. Typically, the birth mother selects the prospective adoptive parents while she is still pregnant, and the child is placed with the adoptive parents immediately after the birth. Indeed, it is becoming common for the prospective adoptive parents to be present in the hospital delivery room when the birth mother gives birth.

Private placement adoptions are not without risks to the prospective adoptive parents, however. One of these risks is that the birth mother may change her mind and decide not to proceed with the adoption after the child is born. As discussed more fully below, a birth mother who intends before the birth to place her child with an adoptive family has the right to change her mind at any time before her consent is formalized in writing after the birth.

What is an open adoption?

An *open adoption* stands in contrast to traditional adoptions, which involved the total substitution of one family for another and the fiction that the adoptive family not only is but always was the child's only family.[18] Open adoptions reject this tradition and try to find some (usually small) role for the birth family after the adoption. In open adoptions, the adoptive parents and the child's birth family are far more likely to have met personally before the adoption is completed. In addition, the adoptive and birth parents will usually seek to maintain some form of ongoing contact over the years as the child grows older. That contact may take the form of periodic letters and the exchange of photographs or it may involve visitation with the birth parents, the child's biological siblings, or other biological relatives.

Contact with members of the adopted child's biological family may be especially significant in the adoption of some older children, who may have close emotional ties to siblings and other members of their biological family.[19] It may also be important in cases of stepparent adoptions, where the child may have an established relationship with the noncustodial parent (usually the child's biological father) and his relatives. On the other hand, open adoption (particularly in the case of newborns) is seen by some as weakening the role of the adoptive parents and unduly restricting their right to decide independently what is best for their children.[20]

Washington is one of the few states that expressly authorizes open-adoption agreements if the court finds that they are in the child's best interests.[21] Most state laws are silent on the issue of open adoption and lack provisions expressly authorizing it. Even so, unless the state expressly prohibits it, the parties may draft an open adoption agreement spelling out what kinds of contact the two families will maintain over time.

Most courts, however, are reluctant to force the adoptive parents to allow continued contact with the child's biological family and will not set aside an adoption or a consent to an adoption if the adoptive parents' fail to do so.[22] A few courts, on the other hand, have enforced open-adoption agreements over the objections of the adoptive parents, as long as the contact is in the child's best interests,[23] while other judges have denied an adoption petition or vacated an adoption decree based on what they perceive as an inconsistency between a birth parent's purported relinquishment of all parental rights and the retention of the right to visit the child.[24] Very occasionally, a court will use its equitable powers to facilitate a settlement of a contested adoption case that gives the birth parents some form of visitation.

How does a child become free for adoption?

There are two ways a child is freed for adoption: the child's birth parents may consent to the adoption and voluntarily relinquish their parental rights, or their parental rights may be involuntarily terminated by a court order. The involuntary termination of parental rights is explored in detail in chapter 7.

Who must consent to the adoption?

Unless the child's biological parents' parental rights have been involuntarily terminated by a court, the child's parents must consent to the adoption. If the child was born to married parents, the consent of both the child's mother and the child's father is required, even if the parents have since become separated or divorced.

When the child is born out of wedlock, the consent of the child's birth mother is always required. Whether or not the child's birth father's consent is required depends on a variety of factors that are discussed later in this chapter.

What is the procedure for parents to consent to the child's adoption?

Consents must be in writing and, in the case of the adoption of a newborn, are not valid or final until at least some period of time after the child is born.[25] Many states provide that a valid consent may not be signed until at least seventy-two hours after the child's birth.[26]

To ensure that a birth parent's consent is voluntary and informed, some states require that the consent be signed in the presence of a neutral individual, such as a judge, who is charged with explaining to the parent the consequences of executing the consent. Other states merely require that the consent be signed in front of a notary or other witnesses. Such informally executed consents are more susceptible to a subsequent challenge by a birth parent who has second thoughts about the adoption.

The new Uniform Adoption Act requires that consents be signed or confirmed in the presence of a someone with no stake in the outcome of the proceeding, such as a judge or a lawyer who is not representing the adoptive parents.[27] The safeguards for birth parents that are built into the Uniform Adoption Act's procedures for consenting to an adoption are designed to ensure that consents are knowingly and freely given. At the same time, these safeguards are likely to reduce the number of successful challenges to the validity of the adoption after the consent was signed, since a birth parent to whom the consequences of giving a consent have been carefully explained may find it harder to persuade a judge that her consent was coerced or not knowingly given.[28]

May a minor consent to the adoption of his or her child?

Yes. In most states, the fact that either or both birth parent(s) are themselves not adults does not affect their ability to consent to their child's adoption, although a small number of states require the consent of the parent or legal guardian of an unmarried parent who is under eighteen.[29] However, to safeguard the minor parent's rights, some states require that the minor parent must have the advice of independent legal counsel before the consent is executed,[30] and others permit or require the court to appoint a guardian ad litem for the minor parent.[31]

May the child's birth parents change their mind after they have consented to the child's adoption?

Most states provide that a consent or relinquishment is revocable for at least some period of time after being executed. Some states allow for the withdrawal of the consent at any time prior to the entry of the court's final decree of adoption if the court finds that the withdrawal of consent is in the best interests of the child whose adoption is being sought.[32] Other states provide a right to withdraw the consent within a prescribed time period, such as forty-five days in New York,[33] ten days in Alaska and Georgia, or five days in California.[34]

In some states, if a parent revokes his or her consent, the prospective adoptive parents have standing to protest the removal of the child from their home and may seek an involuntary termination of the birth parent's rights.[35] In New Jersey, a birth mother who seeks to revoke her consent before the adoption becomes final does not have an absolute right to change her mind. The prospective adoptive parents may argue that her parental rights should be terminated on grounds of "intentional abandonment" for failing to support or care for the child if the child has been in the prospective adoptive parents' care for six months or more.[36]

The Uniform Adoption Act provides that a parent who consents to the adoption of a newborn may revoke his or her consent within 192 hours after the child's birth.[37] If the birth parent consents to the adoption sometime beyond the eight-day period immediately after the birth when consent may be automatically revoked, the consent may not be revoked under the Act unless she or he establishes by clear and convincing evidence, presented before an adoption decree is issued, that the consent was obtained by "fraud" or "duress."[38]

What constitutes "duress"?

As a general proposition, courts prefer not to undo an adoption or to make it too easy for a birth parent to change his or her mind after formally signing a consent for adoption on which others have relied by taking a child into their home. Accordingly, courts have set a high standard for proving "duress." Duress means more than that the parent was subjected to financial strain or emotional stress at the time she or he made the decision to relinquish a child for adoption.[39] When a birth mother is able to prove only that her decision was difficult, or even that she was depressed and weakened by the baby's delivery, it is unlikely that a court will find duress.[40] Instead, duress requires a demonstration that a third party (the adoptive parent, the adoptive parent's lawyer, an employee of the adoption agency, or even the birth parent's own lawyer) put undue pressure on the birth parent and coerced her or him to sign the consent form.

The focus of the inquiry is first on the conduct of others (to determine whether it was improper) and second on the voluntariness of the parent's decision (to determine whether the parent's decision was improperly influenced by the wrongful conduct of others).[41] Thus, courts have permitted a birth mother to revoke her consent based on duress where her consent was given in response to threats from a spouse, undue parental pressure (in the case of an unwed teenage mother), or harassment by the staff of an adoption agency.[42] In a few states, however, a consent cannot be retracted on grounds of duress unless the undue pressure was placed on the parent by the prospective adoptive parents or persons acting on their behalf.[43]

Is the consent of the child's birth father required if he is not married to the child's birth mother?

Not in all cases. The Supreme Court of the United States has recognized that not all unwed fathers are alike and therefore they should not all be treated alike. Basically, the Court has recognized two categories of unwed fathers: (1) those who manifest "parenting behavior" during the mother's pregnancy or after the birth of the child and who have therefore earned the right to withhold consent from a proposed adoption of their child and (2) those who fail to perform the duties of a parent and may therefore be denied the right to veto a proposed adoption.[44]

The Court has made clear that "the mere existence of a biological link" between the unwed father and a child is not entitled to constitutional protection.[45] Instead, the biological connection is significant only to the extent that the birth father "grasps [the] opportunity" the biological connection provides to "develop a relationship with his offspring" and to "accept some measure of responsibility for the child's future."[46] An unwed birth father who has turned his back financially and emotionally on the birth mother during the pregnancy and who has failed to assume any responsibility for the child's support and care has no constitutional right to withhold his consent to an adoption. Thus, a number of courts have held that an unwed father has no right to veto an adoption when he knew or reasonably should have known of the pregnancy but failed to provide financial or emotional support to the birth mother during the pregnancy or to help pay for her birth-related expenses.[47]

The more difficult cases usually involve an unwed birth mother who wants nothing further to do with the birth father for any number of reasons (perhaps because the birth father has become physically violent, perhaps because their relationship was not a long-term one). In these cases, courts in some states have held that when the birth father offered some form of financial or emotional support (even if they were rejected by the mother), the father has done enough to establish his rights to the child and will be permitted to prevent the child's adoption over his objection.[48]

What if the unwed father does not learn about the pregnancy or the birth mother's adoption plans until after the child has been placed with the adoptive parents?

In recent years, several highly publicized adoption cases have involved birth fathers contesting the adoption of a child who was placed with an adoptive family by the birth mother without his knowledge. These "thwarted father" cases are relatively rare and courts have not been consistent in resolving them.

Ruling in favor of the biological father, courts in Illinois and Michigan have stressed the primacy of the biological connection and have ordered that children as old as four years who have lived since infancy with their adoptive families be removed from the only home they have ever known and transferred to the biological father who is, practically speaking, a stranger to the child.[49] Rejecting the claims of other thwarted fathers, courts in California, New York, and Arizona have stressed the child's need for a prompt determination of the finality of the adoptive placement and have imposed on the biological father the burden of showing why he did not come forward sooner to act like a responsible parent.[50]

Isn't it unfair to force a child to be uprooted from a secure home and placed with a biological parent who, for all practical purposes, is a stranger to the child?

As a general rule, courts presume that a child's best interests are served by being cared for by a biological parent. Unless the parent is unfit or gave up rights to the child, courts commonly award custody to the biological parent when the custody dispute is between a biological parent and another adult who has loved and cared for the child. However, in recent years, several states have begun to recognize that *exceptional circumstances* may justify denying the biologicial parent custody when a change of custody would be harmful to the child. Several courts have approved adoptions on this basis.[51] "Exceptional circumstances" may include the length of time the child has been with the adoptive parents; the strength of the attachment between the child and the prospective adoptive parents; how promptly after the child was placed for adoption the birth parent came forward to claim the child; the sincerity of the biological parent's desire to rear the child; the age of the child when placed for adoption; the possible emotional effects on the child of a change of custody; and the stability of the child's placement with the adoptive family.[52]

The new Uniform Adoption Act attempts to balance the interests of the child and the parents. It provides that a birth father's efforts to veto an adoption should be rejected when a court finds by clear and convincing evidence that placing the child in his custody would pose a substantial risk of harm to the child's physical or psychological well-being or would otherwise be detrimental to the child.[53] In assessing harm to the child, the Act expressly permits the court to consider, among other things, the child's age, the duration and suitability of the child's present placement, and the effect on the child of a change in custody.[54]

Where the birth mother has concealed the pregnancy or the adoption from the child's genetic father, it has been suggested that a damages action for fraud is the appropriate remedy for a birth father injured by the birth mother's actions.[55] A *specific performance remedy*, which disrupts an adoptive placement in order to rectify a wrong to the "thwarted" birth father, is troubling to those who are concerned about the emotional well-being of a child who has become profoundedly attached to her adoptive family.[56]

For this reason, even if an adoption proceeding must be dismissed or an adoption decree set aside for failure to obtain the birth father's consent, some states permit a hearing to be held to consider the question of the child's legal and physical custody in light of the child's best interests.[57] This is also the approach of the Uniform Adoption Act.[58]

Under what circumstances is an unwed father entitled to be notified that adoption proceedings are pending?

An unwed father who does not have the right to veto an adoption may still be entitled to notice of the adoption proceeding. Several states determine which unwed birth fathers are entitled to notice through the use of putative father registries. An unwed father wishing to be notified of an adoption proceeding must inform the registry within a certain period of time before or after the child's birth that he intends to claim paternity of the child.[59] Alternately, an unmarried birth father may qualify for notice of pending adoption proceedings if he has been identified by the birth mother as the child's father in a sworn written statement; was listed as the father on the child's birth certificate; has been adjudicated by a court to be the child's father; or was living openly with the child and the child's mother and holding himself out to be the child's father.[60]

Even when the birth father does not have the right to withhold his consent to the adoption, he may be permitted the opportunity to testify as to whether the proposed adoption is in the child's best interests.

Must the birth mother reveal the birth father's identity?

Because some women have good reason to fear violence, abuse, or humiliation if they identify the birth father, courts in several states have ruled that the birth mother's refusal to identify the birth father is not grounds for denying the adoption petition.[61] However, an "unknown" father, whose identity the birth mother declines to reveal, is at least entitled to an inquiry into whether his identity and whereabouts can be ascertained by other means in order to give him notice of the adoption proceedings.[62]

An adoption proceeding may be subject to challenge if a possible father is not identified and given notice, as discussed above. In addition, if the birth father is in the armed services, the Soldiers and Sailors Relief Act allows an order (such as an order terminating his parental rights) to be vacated if, during the father's period of service or within sixty days thereafter, it appears that he was prejudiced by reason of military service in presenting a defense.[63] Failure to name the child's birth father also deprives the adopted child of the opportunity to later gain access to his or her medical and genetic history.

If an adoption petition is denied because an adoption agency failed to obtain the birth father's consent, may the agency be held responsible?

Courts in several states have considered the contention that adoption agencies should be liable for failing to investigate the child's paternity and to take steps to ensure that the birth father's consent, if necessary, has been obtained.[64] For the most part, prospective adoptive parents' claims of social work malpractice, reckless infliction of emotional distress, and violation of the prospective parents' constitutional rights have been rejected, although at least one court has suggested that an adoption agency that fails to adequately investigate a child's paternity may have breached an implied duty of good faith and reasonable care.[65]

What kinds of payments may lawfully be made to a birth mother in connection with an adoption?

State laws differ widely concerning the type and amount of payments that may be made to a birth mother. Although payments made or offered for the purpose of inducing a parent to consent to a child's adoption are illegal, many states provide that the prospective adoptive parents may lawfully reimburse the birth mother for her medical expenses, attorney's fees and court costs, counseling, or other related expenses.[66] Some states go further and permit the prospective adoptive parents to also pay for the birth mother's living expenses.[67] Others do not define the amount or type of compensation a birth mother may receive and allow a birth mother to recover only those amounts and types that a court reviewing the adoption petition subsequently determines are reasonable.[68]

The disparity among states in terms of permissible reimbursable expenses has generated widespread confusion and raises the specter of birth parents or adoptive parents inadvertently subjecting themselves to criminal sanctions for violating state laws prohibiting baby-buying. To end this uncertainty, the new Uniform Adoption Act clearly spells out the kinds of costs and expenses prospective adoptive parents may pay for.[69]

As a deterrent to illegal child trafficking, prospective adoptive parents in virtually all states must provide a detailed accounting to the court of all payments they have made in connection with the adoption.[70] Most adoption laws, however, exempt relative adoptions from their financial disclosure requirements.

Must birth parents reimburse the prospective adoptive parents for money they spent in connection with the adoption if the birth parents change their mind and decide not to go forward with an adoption?

Usually, in the absence of fraudulent conduct on the part of the birth parent, the possibility that a birth parent may change his or her mind and decide not to proceed with an adoption is a risk that the prospective adoptive parents are expected to bear. A New Jersey court, for instance, held that the birth parents did not have to reimburse the adoptive parents for out-of-pocket expenses they incurred as a result of caring for a preadoptive child when the birth parents changed their mind and regained custody of the child.[71] The court reasoned that requiring reimbursement would have a detrimental effect on the birth parents' exercise of their right to develop their parent-child relationship.

As an alternative to a lawsuit against the birth parents, some states permit the sale of adoption termination insurance. Adoption termination insurance is designed to indemnify prospective adoptive parents involved in a private adoption for certain expenses when a birthparent elects not to go forward with an adoptive placement.

May the prospective adoptive parents' attorney also represent the birth parent(s) in an adoption?

Some states consider it a conflict of interest for the adoptive parents' attorney to also advise the birth parent(s). New York, for instance, expressly prohibits dual representation.[72] California strongly discourages dual representation but allows it, if written consent to the arrangement is given in advance by both sets of parents, and there is no reason to believe that the adoption will be contested.[73]

Is the child's consent to the adoption ever required?

Yes. Most states require the consent of a child who has attained a certain minimum age or maturity (typically ten, twelve, or fourteen, depending on the state).[74] The child's consent is usually in addition to and not a substitute for the consent of the birth parent(s) and may be dispensed with by the court in some states if the judge finds that the child's consent has been given or withheld contrary to the child's best interests.

Is a child entitled to separate representation in a contested adoption?

Yes, in many states. In an action to set aside a consent to an adoption or to invalidate a termination of parental rights, many states provide that the child is entitled to separate representation. In some states, however, the appointment of a guardian ad litem or an attorney for the child is left to the discretion of the court, while others require the appointment of a guardian ad litem or independent counsel for the child whenever an adoption is challenged.[75]

An attorney representing the child in a contested adoption may prepare fully for trial by making an independent investigation of the facts, undertaking pretrial discovery, and selecting and preparing expert witnesses. At the same time, it is often the job of the child's attorney to take whatever steps are necessary to prevent any of the other parties from abusing the pretrial discovery process to delay resolution of the case.[76] At trial, the child's attorney may challenge the reliability of evidence presented by the other parties and may choose to call and question expert witnesses.

What qualifications must prospective adoptive parents have in order to adopt a child?

Before an adoption petition may be granted, the prospective adoptive parent must undergo a background investigation (known as a *homestudy*) to assess his or her suitability as an adoptive parent.[77] A homestudy is usually conducted by a trained social worker and involves one or more personal interviews and a visit to the home of the prospective adoptive parent(s).

The interviews are designed to elicit information about the prospective parent(s), their personal history, marital status and family history, educational background and employment history, physical and mental health, financial circumstances, and reasons for wanting to adopt. Adoptive parents are typically required to provide proof of their income and assets in order to demonstrate that they are capable of supporting the child and to supply character references who can corroborate their suitability as prospective parents.

Many states require the prospective adoptive parents to be fingerprinted so that a background criminal check can be run. Some states also require a check of the state's child abuse registry.

How is an adoption finalized?

For nonrelative adoptions, virtually all states impose a fixed waiting period before the final adoption decree may be entered by the court. During the waiting period, the child lives with the prospective adoptive parents, who have temporary custody of the child.

The waiting period is designed to make sure that the prospective adoptive parents and the child are adjusting well to one another and to allow a social worker to assess the success of the placement. Typically, the waiting period is six months, although it is as long as one year in some states and as short as sixty days in others. Some states allow the waiting period to be shortened by the judge for good cause.

The waiting period begins in some states when the adoption petition is filed in court. More commonly, it begins when the child is placed in the adoptive parents' home or when an interim order is entered by the court giving the prospective adoptive parents temporary custody of the child.

Once the final adoption decree is entered, there is usually a limited period of time during which the adoption order can be appealed. Because of the need to ensure the stability of the child's placement, many states provide that a final decree of adoption may not be challenged for any reason after a certain period of time, usually one or two years but longer in some states.

What kind of information are adoptive parents entitled to receive about a prospective adoptive child's background and medical history?

Traditionally, adoptive parents were told very little about the medical or social background of the child they were adopting. The veil of secrecy that enveloped the entire adoption process shrouded the child's medical and family history as well. Adoption agencies typically took the stance that the parents "were better off not knowing," and so agencies neither made detailed inquiries nor revealed what little they knew.

Within the last twenty-five years, there has been a growing recognition of the usefulness of background information about the child and his or her biological family. Adoptive families and their physicians are better able to diagnose and to treat physical or emotional problems that may emerge after the adoptive placement if they are aware of the child's medical and social history. Access to accurate medical and genetic history gives adult adoptees the information they need to make their own informed childbearing plans.

In response to the growing awareness among physicians, adoption professionals, and adoptive families of the value of health-related information, states have passed laws permitting greater disclosure of background information to adoptive parents.[78] As might be expected, disclosure laws vary widely from state to state. In most states, disclosure is mandatory, but a minority of states let adoption agencies decide what should be disclosed.[79]

Some states require disclosure of the parents' medical history while others focus on the medical history of the child.[80] Only a few states require the disclosure of the medical and genetic history of biological relatives other than the birth parents,[81] and fewer still prescribe the efforts that should be undertaken by an adoption agency or other intermediary to collect the necessary information and transmit it accurately to the adoptive parents.[82] Some disclosure laws do not apply to independent adoptions, while others exempt stepparent and relative adoptions and still others appear to apply only to adoptions that follow a voluntary relinquishment rather than an involuntary termination of parental rights.[83]

The Uniform Adoption Act seeks to bring consistency and clarity to this issue. It clearly prescribes the kinds of medical and social information that must be collected and disclosed to the adoptive parents and provides a method for ensuring that the information is transmitted.[84]

Can an adoption agency be held responsible for misleading the adoptive parents about the child's medical or family history?

Yes. In 1986, the Ohio Supreme Court became the first appellate court in the United Stated to give adoptive parents the right to recover damages from an adoption agency that gave false information to the parents about the child's medical history. In *Burr v. Board of County Commissioners*,[85] the adoption agency invented a story about the child's birth parents, concealing from the adoptive parents the fact that the child's birth mother was a mildly retarded patient at a state mental hospital who suffered psychotic reactions. The adoptive parents sued the agency to recover the cost of medical care for their son who was diagnosed as having Huntington's chorea, an inherited neurological disorder for which round-the-clock nursing care was required.

Adoption agency liability is not limited to cases where the agency misrepresents facts about the child's history. Agencies may also be held liable for intentionally withholding adverse medical or psychological information from the adoptive family.[86] And several states have gone even further and allow an action against an adoption agency for negligently failing to disclose available information.[87]

The purpose of holding agencies accountable for failing to disclose pertinent medical and psychological information is not to guarantee that every child placed in an adoptive family will be perfectly healthy.[88] Rather, disclosure is needed to allow prospective adoptive parents to make an informed choice about the serious responsibility they are undertaking and to better prepare themselves financially and emotionally for the difficult parenting tasks they may face if they elect to adopt a child with medical or psychological disabilities.

Disclosure also serves to protect the adopted child, so that medical or psychological intervention can be sought before it is too late to be effective. This is especially important where the child has been exposed to alcohol or drugs during the pregnancy, has suffered sexual or physical abuse, or has a family history of schizophrenia, manic-depression, or other mental disorders. Awareness of the child's history can greatly aid diagnosis and treatment.[89]

Do prospective adoptive parents have the right to a hearing when an adoption agency decides to remove a child from their home for placement with another family before the adoption is finalized?

Yes, in some states. Depending on the state, prospective adoptive parents may be entitled to a court hearing to challenge the agency's decision to remove the child.[90] When an adoption agency unreasonably withholds consent to the adoption, courts sometimes dispense with the agency's consent and approve the adoption if it is in the child's best interests.[91]

May foster parents adopt their foster child?

As explained in chapter 6, a foster parent's principal function is to care for a child temporarily until the biological parent is able to resume child-rearing responsibilities. Consequently, for many years foster parents were precluded by the terms of their foster care contract from seeking to adopt foster children placed with them.[92] Indeed, foster care agencies have been known to move foster children from one foster home to another because the first set of foster parents had become too attached to the children in their care.[93]

However, important changes have occurred in the past decade. As epidemics of AIDS, crack cocaine addiction, and unemployment have taken their toll on families, the number of children in foster care is now approaching half a million. Increasingly, foster parents are being seen as excellent adoptive parents for children who cannot be reunited with their biological families. Today, a number of states give foster parents priority in the adoption of foster children.[94] Others give foster parents standing to file their own petition to terminate parental rights[95] or their own adoption petition.[96] In still other states, a foster parent is permitted to intervene if a petition is pending for the adoption of their foster child by another family.[97]

In considering a foster parent's petition for adoption, courts commonly look at the length and depth of the foster parent-child relationship.[98] When the contest is between a long-term foster parent and the child's biological relative (such as an aunt, an uncle, or a grandparent) who has had little or no contact with the child, courts sometimes will prefer the foster parent as an adoptive parent.[99]

Are subsidies available to help pay for raising an adopted child?

Yes. The Adoption Assistance and Child Welfare Act of 1980[100] tried to encourage the adoption of "hard-to-place" children by providing a financial subsidy that is paid to adoptive parents after the adoption is completed and that continues until the child reaches adulthood. The subsidy is available for children with "special needs" who might otherwise spend the rest of their lives in foster care. The subsidy is similar to preadoptive foster care payments; adoptive parents receive monthly checks to help defray the costs of raising the child.

The subsidy is particularly important when the adoptive parent was the foster parent. Without the subsidy, foster parents who were interested in adopting their foster child had to choose between forgoing adoption (and thereby ensuring their continued eligibility for foster care payments) or adopting the child and losing an important source of additional income to help pay for raising the child. A number of states supplement the federal subsidy and provide money even for adoptive children who do not meet the federal eligibility criteria.

For a child to be eligible for an adoption subsidy under the federal program, the state must determine that:[101]

1. The child cannot or should not be returned to his or her biological parents;

2. Because of the child's ethnic background, age, minority status, the presence of siblings who should not be separated, the child's medical condition, or the child's physical, mental, or emotional handicaps, he or she cannot be placed in an adoptive home without offering a subsidy or medical assistance to the prospective adoptive parents; and

3. Reasonable but unsuccessful efforts have been made to place the child with adoptive parents without a subsidy. This requirement may be waived in the case of foster parents who wish to adopt a foster child with whom they have developed significant emotional ties.

The federal subsidy program gives states wide latitude to define which children have "special needs." According to one survey of state subsidy programs, in Florida, children eight years or older meet the special needs test but in Wisconsin, children must be at least ten years old to qualify. In Indiana, minority children are eligible when they are at least two years old, but nonminority children must be at least six years of age.[102]

Available benefits include monthly cash payments up to the amount of foster care payments that would have been made if the child had remained in foster care. In addition, various social benefits, such as specialized day care, in-home support services, respite care, and counseling are available. Even more important, children are eligible for medical coverage through Medicaid. Finally, parents who adopt special needs children are eligible to be reimbursed for certain nonrecurring costs of the adoption itself, such as attorney's fees, court costs, adoption homestudy fees, transportation and reasonable costs of food and lodging directly related to the adoption process.

Eligibility for the federal subsidy depends on the child's financial circumstances, not those of the adoptive parents. The parents' income may not be taken into account in determining the child's eligibility for an adoption subsidy, although family income may be considered in deciding how much of a subsidy to award.

In order to receive adoption assistance benefits, the adoptive parents must enter into a written agreement with the state or agency providings to the adopted child. In most states, the agreement must be signed before the adoption is finalized.[103] The agreement sets out the amount of payments ands the child will receive and also addresses certain contingencies, such as what would happen were the family to move to another state. Ordinarily, when a family moves to a new state, the original state will be responsible for the cash subsidy, and the new state will be responsible for Medicaid coverage and the provision of various socials.[104] However, if a needed is not available in the new state, the original state may be financially responsible for providing the specified.[105]

Adoptive parents have a right to appeal a decision to deny adoption assistance as well as an agency's failure to adhere to the terms of the subsidy agreement. Most states require parents to start their appeal by using the state's designated fair hearing and appeals process at the local child welfare or adoption agency.

May parents of one race adopt a child of another?

Yes. However, in the vast majority of states, there has been an unwritten rule that transracial adoption—or at least the placement of African-American or biracial foster children with white parents or interracial couples—should be avoided at all costs.[106]

The de facto ban on transracial adoptions has been a legacy of the 1970s, although earlier laws prohibiting transracial adoptive placements date from this country's Jim Crow era of racial segregation. For a brief period of time in the 1960s, transracial adoptions were, if not common, at least viewed as a way of furthering the country's integrationist goals and of serving the needs of minority children trapped in the foster care system. By 1971, transracial placements had reached a peak of 2,574.[107]

In 1972, the National Association of Black Social Workers adopted a position paper opposing transracial adoption. Calling transracial adoption a "form of genocide,"[108] the position paper insisted that "black children should be placed only with Black families whether in foster care or for adoption."[109] Others joined with the NABSW in arguing that transracial adoption harmed black children by denying them their black heritage and the skills needed to survive in a racist society.[110]

Since the 1970s, several states have written same-race preferences into laws governing the placement of children in adoptive families.[111] California not only mandates same-race preference but prohibits the placement of children across racial or ethnic lines for a period of ninety days after a child has been relinquished or freed for adoption.[112] Even after the ninety-day period, California law prohibits transracial placement unless the adoption agency has documented that it has conducted a diligent search for a same-race family.[113] In other states, the preference for same-race placements is found in state regulations or state child-welfare-department policy manuals.[114]

Partly as a result of these race-conscious policies and partly as a result of inadequate efforts to recruit African American adoptive parents, thousands of African American and biracial children remain in foster care for disproportionately long periods of time after they are or could be free for adoption. Critics of the de facto ban on transracial adoption note that black children wait up to twice as long as white children for permanent adoptive placement and are much less likely than white children to be adopted.[115] They argue that restrictions on transracial adoption discriminate against black children by delaying or denying them access to permanent adoptive homes.

Some white foster parents who have not been permitted to adopt their minority foster children have challenged the constitutionality of agency policies against transracial adoption. Their efforts have met with mixed success in state and lower federal courts. Challenges to same-race preferences have been most successful where state laws flatly prohibit transracial adoption.[116] However, where race was only one of several factors considered in placing the child with a black adoptive family[117] or where the state child-welfare agency removed the child from a white foster home in order to allow for his or her adoption by a grandparent or other relative,[118] same-race placements have been upheld as constitutional.

The Supreme Court of the United States has yet to address the constitutionality of same-race placement preferences in adoption, although it has considered the issue of race in the related contexts of both marriage and divorce. In 1967 the Court struck down Virginia's ban on interracial marriage.[119] And in 1984 the Court unanimously ruled that it was unconstitutional to use race as the basis for deciding which of two biological parents should have custody of a child after their divorce.[120]

In the absence of guidance from the Supreme Court, Congress sought to strike a balance among the competing viewpoints on transracial adoption with the passage in October 1994 of the Multiethnic Placement Act. Like the new Uniform Adoption Act, the Multiethnic Placement Act provides that an agency receiving federal funds may not deny or delay a foster care or adoptive placement "solely on the basis of the race, color or national origin of the adoptive or foster parent, or the child, involved"[121] and permits any individual who has been harmed by an alleged violation of the Act to sue in federal district court for injunctive relief.[122]

At the same time, the Act permits state child welfare agencies to take into account the child's cultural, ethnic or racial background and the capacity of the prospective adoptive or foster parents to meet the needs of a child of that background.[123] To increase the pool of prospective minority adoptive parents, the Act also requires federally funded agencies to recruit potential foster and adoptive families that reflect the ethnic and racial diversity of children for whom foster and adoptive homes are needed.[124]

It is worth noting that the restrictions on transracial adoption described in this section apply principally to the adoption of foster children. Many couples and single parents adopt children of other races through private placement or through international adoptions.

Are there special rules for the adoption of a Native American child?

Yes. The adoption of Native American children is governed by a special federal law, the Indian Child Welfare Act of 1978 (ICWA).[125] The ICWA applies to any person under 18 who is either a member of an Indian tribe or who is eligible for membership in an Indian tribe and is the biological child of a tribe member.[126]

Most courts have held that the Act applies even if the child has never been part of an existing Native American family unit and has never lived within a Native American community or been exposed to Native American culture.[127] Indeed, the ICWA has been applied to preclude an unmarried, non–Native American mother from relinquishing her child for adoption by a non–Native American family of her choice, even though the birth father (an enrolled member of a tribe) had no contact with the mother during her pregnancy or after the child's birth and had no intention of raising the child himself.[128]

The ICWA gives tribal courts exclusive jurisdiction over child custody proceedings, including adoption, that involve a Native American child who resides or is domiciled within a tribe's reservation.[129] In interpreting the Act, the Supreme Court held that a pregnant Native American mother who wanted to place her infant twins for adoption outside the reservation and who left the reservation temporarily to give birth remained a domiciliary of the tribal reservation so that the tribe had exclusive jurisdiction over the placement of her children.[130]

If the child is neither a domiciliary nor a resident of any reservation, a state court must give notice of a termination of parental rights proceeding to the child's parent or Native American custodian and to the child's tribe[131] and must transfer custody of any case involving the termination of parental rights to the appropriate tribal court at the request of either parent, the custodian, or the tribe unless there is "good cause" to do otherwise or one parent objects.[132] In addition, the Act gives a Native American child's tribe and the child's Native American custodian the right to intervene in any state court adoption proceeding.[133]

Under the ICWA, a mandatory set of priorities governs the adoptive placement of Native American children. As a matter of federal law, preference for the placement of a Native American child is given first to members of the child's extended family, then to other members of the child's tribe and then to other Native American families.[134]

The ICWA's statutory placement preferences must be followed regardless of the wishes of the child's birth parents, unless good cause to the contrary is established.[135] Indeed, although the Act provides that "where appropriate" the preferences of the parent or child may be taken into account,[136] in practice many courts reject the parent's desire to place a child with non–Native American adoptive parents and overrule the parent's plans for his or her child's future.[137]

The ICWA also includes several special rules governing the adoption process for Native American children. Under the ICWA, no consent to a child's adoption is valid if given prior to the child's birth or within ten days thereafter.[138] The consent must be recorded before a judge and may be withdrawn for any reason at any time prior to the entry of a final adoption decree.[139] In addition, consent may be revoked within two years after the entry of a final adoption decree, based on fraud or duress.[140]

The standard under the ICWA for the involuntary termination of parental rights is stricter than that required in non–Native American cases.[141] Instead of requiring proof of parental unfitness by clear and convincing evidence, the ICWA provides that no termination of parental rights may occur unless there has been proof beyond a reasonable doubt, based on expert testimony, that continued custody by the parent or Native American custodian is likely to result in serious emotional or physical damage to the child.[142]

Like the issue of same-race placements for African American children, the ICWA remains controversial. Critics of the Act have argued that the ICWA stands for the proposition that Native American children are tribal resources; that Native American tribes, not parents, have the power to decide the fate of children who are subject to the Act; and that the Act subordinates the best interests of the child to that of the tribe.[143] Proponents, on the other hand, assert that the Act seeks to protect the unique social and cultural heritage of Native American communities and prevents the unwarranted placement of Native American children in non–Native American homes.

May a stepparent adopt the child of his or her spouse over the objections of the child's other biological parent?

Yes, although state laws on stepparent adoptions vary considerably from state to state. As a general rule, the absence of a genuine parent-child relationship between the child and his or her noncustodial biological parent may be grounds to terminate the parent's rights and to allow a stepparent adoption to proceed without the biological parent's consent.[144]

Some states permit adoption by a stepparent without the noncustodial parent's consent if that parent has failed to communicate with the child or provide for the child's support for at least one year.[145] Other states require a period during which the noncustodial parent has failed both to communicate with the child and pay support.[146] A few states have less stringent requirements and permit a stepparent adoption to take place over the noncustodial parent's objections if consent to the adoption has been "unreasonably withheld contrary to the best interests of the child."[147]

Although stepparent adoptions account for nearly half of all adoptions, these adoptions occur in only a small percentage of the households in which stepchildren reside. It is believed that stepparent adoptions are not more prevalent because many families are dissatisfied with the legal implications of stepparent adoptions: the child loses all her legal ties to her noncustodial parent and to that parent's extended family. In families where the child has a close emotional bond with a noncustodial father and the paternal grandparents, this may be a serious loss.

The new Uniform Adoption Act takes an approach to stepparent adoptions that is different from the traditional all or nothing approach. By allowing postadoption visitation by the noncustodial former parent, grandparents, or siblings when a court finds such contact to be in the child's best interests, stepchildren can have the advantage of living in a household with two legal parents (the custodial biological parent and adoptive stepparent), without losing access to their noncustodial parent's family.[148] By this arrangement, children can gain access to health insurance and other benefits through their adoptive stepparent and still benefit from contact with their noncustodial biological parent.

May single parents adopt?

Yes. In the very recent past, unmarried persons were either ineligible to adopt or, though technically not barred from adopting, found it practically impossible to adopt. Today, however, virtually all states allow unmarried persons to adopt. Nonetheless, some adoption agencies strongly prefer married couples over unmarried persons as adoptive parents. Such agencies regard single people as adoptive parents of last resort and tend to assign hard-to-place older, minority, or handicapped children to single parents.

Unmarried persons, like prospective adoptive couples, also have the option of independent, private-placement adoption or an intercountry adoption, if the child's country of origin is one that permits single-parent adoptions. Many single people who are unable to adopt through an agency are able to adopt independently.

May homosexuals adopt?

Yes, in many states. However, the specific answer depends on the setting in which the application to adopt is made. First, a gay or lesbian adult may seek to adopt a child as a single parent. As acceptance of single-adoptive parents has grown in recent years, there has been a slow but steady realization in many states that homosexuals should not be categorically excluded from consideration as prospective adoptive parents.[149] Only Florida and New Hampshire have statutes prohibiting homosexuals from adopting children.[150]

A more complex question is whether the gay or lesbian partner of a biological or adoptive parent may adopt the partner's child and become the child's second legal parent. This issue commonly arises among lesbian couples when one partner is the biological mother (either as a result of a prior heterosexual relationship or of a donor insemination). The partner seeks, as as in a stepparent adoption, to adopt the child with the mother's consent without severing the biological mother's parental rights. A small but growing number of states have permitted such adoptions in recent years.[151]

Courts that have permitted such adoptions generally conclude that children are best served by having two legal parents rather than one legal parent and one de facto parent. A child with two legal parents has two sources of support and inheritance rights, as well as access to an array of benefits, ranging from health insurance and social security to other benefits provided by the parents' employers. If the adults' relationship later ends, their status as the child's legal parents gives both of them standing to seek custody or visitation with the child.

Finally, there is the question whether a gay or lesbian couple may jointly adopt a nonbiologically related child. Adoption laws, for the most part, are silent on the question whether two unmarried adults may jointly adopt a child. Most adoption statutes speak in terms of adoptions by "an adult unmarried person" or "adult married persons."

Although courts in California have permitted lesbian couples to adopt a child they are raising even though neither woman is the child's biological mother,[152] other courts have denied joint applications to adopt filed by unmarried persons, regardless of sexual orientation.[153]

Are there special rules governing interstate adoptions?

Yes. If the birth mother lives in one state and the adoptive parents live in another, the adoption is considered an interstate adoption and must comply with the provisions of the Interstate Compact on the Placement of Children (ICPC), which has been enacted in all states.[154] The ICPC prohibits the interstate movement of children for the purpose of adoption unless the appropriate public child-welfare agency in the state where the child is to be received first approves of the arrangements.

Before an interstate adoption can occur, the *sending agency*[155] or person must send notice to the receiving state. The sending agency must identify the child, the child's parents, and the person or agency with whom the child will be placed, and must provide reasons for the transfer and evidence that the transfer has been properly authorized.[156] The designated compact administrator in the receiving state may request additional information regarding the placement.[157] The child may not be sent to the receiving state until the Compact administrator in that state notifies the sending state that the proposed placement appears to be in the child's best interest.[158] Unfortunately, Compact administrators in some states are slow to approve placements and add to the delay involved in adoptions.[159]

Penalties for violating the Interstate Compact vary from state to state. In most states, violation of the Compact is a misdemeanor punishable by a fine or a prison term of up to one year. States are further split on whether Compact violations also invalidate the adoption. Some courts have held that even though an independent adoptive placement had been made in violation of the Compact, the child's best interests may require that the adoption be allowed.[160] However, in one reported case a court ruled that failure to comply with the Compact required the child's return to the birth mother, even though she had initially consented to the adoption.[161] In order to deter Compact violations, at least one court has refused to approve the full amount of attorney's fees requested when the ICPC had not been adhered to.[162]

The Interstate Compact does not apply to all interstate adoptions, however. When a child is adopted by a relative (i.e. a stepparent, grandparent, uncle, aunt) from another relative, the ICPC does not apply.[163] However, the ICPC does apply to foster care and adoptive placements made by an agency that places the child with relatives in another state.[164] The ICPC also appears to apply to intercountry adoptions when the adoption is handled by an agency located in one state that places a child with adoptive parents living in a different state.

May grandparents adopt their grandchild?

Yes, although states differ on whether or not grandparents or other relatives are entitled to a special preference in adoption or even to notice of a pending adoption proceeding initiated by someone else. In some states, grandparents and other biological relatives such as aunts and uncles do not have a greater right to adopt than a nonrelative, while other states have passed laws that prefer adoptions by grandparents or other relatives over nonrelatives.[165]

When a grandparent petitions to adopt, he or she may be entitled to certain special privileges, such as an exemption from the state's preadoption certification requirements.[166] Even if a grandparent is not permitted to adopt because the child's birth parent objects, in certain cases it is possible for a grandparent who has raised a child since birth to obtain permanent custody of a child who has been all but legally abandoned by the birth parent.[167]

In addition, a grandparent who has custody of a child or who has been granted visitation rights is entitled under the Uniform Child Custody Jurisdiction Act to be notified of a pending adoption proceeding in another state and has the right to present evidence regarding the child's best interests.[168] Whether grandparents with no prior custody or visitation rights are entitled to intervene in a pending adoption proceeding depends on state law and varies from state to state.[169]

Do an adopted child's biological grandparents have the right to visit their grandchild after the adoption?

In most states, the answer depends on what kind of adoption is involved. The current trend is to allow grandparent visitation in stepparent adoptions provided that such visitation is in the child's best interests.[170]

However, when the child has been adopted by someone other than the child's stepparent or relative, many courts have been reluctant to order grandparental visitation over the adoptive parents' objections.[171] The theory is that the child is now a part of an entirely new family which is entitled to decide on its own who may or may not spend time with the child.

What laws govern the adoption of children from other countries?

Since the 1970s, the legalization of abortion, the growing social acceptance of single mothers, and the de facto ban on transracial adoptions have made it more difficult to adopt an infant in the United States. As a result, a growing number of persons who want to adopt a baby have chosen to adopt infants born in other countries. Other families, moved by the plight of children living in orphanages or on the street, have chosen to bring older children into their families through intercountry adoption.

Intercountry adoption is a more paperwork-intensive process than domestic adoption because the prospective adoptive parents must comply with at least three sets of laws: the adoption laws of the state in which they live, the immigration laws of the United States, and the adoption laws of the child's place of birth.

Most foreign adoptions are handled through adoption agencies in the United States that have established intercountry adoption programs. One advantage of an intercountry agency adoption is that the agency staff are available to guide prospective parents through the maze of red tape that can, at times, seem daunting. Where permitted by foreign law, however, some Americans prefer to contact directly an orphanage or an intermediary in the foreign country to initiate the adoption. This approach is commonly preferred by prospective adoptive parents who do not meet the sometimes arbitrary age or other eligibility criteria set by adoption agencies.

To bring a child into the United States for purposes of adoption, the prospective adoptive parents need to apply to the Immigration and Naturalization (INS) for an orphan visa for the child. An Orphan Petition (INS Form I-600) may be filed by any U.S. citizen and spouse, or by an unmarried U.S. citizen who is at least twenty-five years old.[172] If the Orphan Petition is approved, the child is considered an immediate relative of a U.S. citizen and will be issued an immigrant visa without having to join the long waiting lists of other visa applicants. However, the child must (like any other foreigner) still meet the other requirements for an immigrant visa and may be denied entry to the United States if he or she has a contagious disease.[173] Only children who meet the restrictive "orphan" definition set by the INS are eligible for an orphan visa to enter the United States. Under the Immigration and Naturalization Act, a prospective adoptive child is an orphan only if (1) the child's parents have died or disappeared; (2) the child has been abandoned or deserted by both parents; (3) the child has become separated from both parents; or (4) the child's sole or surviving parent is incapable of providing proper care for the child and has irrevocably released the child for emigration and adoption.[174]

The Immigration and Naturalizations's rules are significantly more restrictive than domestic adoption laws. Pursuant to the INS's interpretation of federal law, for instance, two living parents may not relinquish parental rights by a direct placement of the child with an adoptive parent. Unless they have abandoned their child to an institution (or worse, to the streets), the child is not an "orphan" under federal immigration law.[175] In addition, even when there is only a sole or surviving parent, the child may not enter the United States unless the parent proves that he or she cannot support the child by the standard of the child's country.[176] No such preconditions are imposed on birth parents in the United States when they desire to place their children for adoption.

Before issuing an orphan visa, the INS also requires that the prospective parents submit a homestudy performed in accordance with a recently developed set of detailed requirements.[177] As part of the homestudy, the homestudy preparer must assess the physical, mental, and emotional capacity and propensity for abuse and violence of the prospective adoptive parents and any adult member of their household, as well as the prospective adoptive parents' financial resources.

In 1993, sixty-six countries negotiated the Hague Convention on Protection of Children and Cooperation in Respect of Intercountry Adoption (known as the 1993 Hague Convention, for short).[178] If the 1993 Hague Convention is ratified by the United States, it would alter many of the current rules on intercountry adoptions.

It is difficult to predict for certain whether the Hague Convention will facilitate or impede intercountry adoptions. Much depends on how it is implemented in the United States (if the U.S. ratifies it) and around the world. On one hand, if the convention is ratified by the major sending countries, it may become easier to bring adopted children into the U.S., since, under the convention, the INS should be precluded from applying its stringent orphan definition to block or delay the entry of adopted children into the United States.[179] In addition, by requiring the receiving country to recognize the child's foreign adoption decree, the convention should also eliminate the need to readopt the child in the United States when there is already a valid foreign adoption decree.[180]

On the other hand, if the convention becomes a vehicle for curtailing independent intercountry adoptions or severely restricting the number of adoption agencies permitted to work in the field of intercountry adoption, more children around the world may spend their childhood in orphanages.

Must the adoptive parents travel to the child's country of origin in order to adopt the foreign-born child?

Yes, in most cases. Most countries require the prospective adoptive parents to travel to meet the child in the child's country of origin, to be screened by their child welfare department, and to participate in the court proceedings for the child's adoption. When the parents return to the United States, they then bring with them an adoption decree issued by the foreign court.

However, a small number of countries (notably India and South Korea) do not require prospective adoptive parents to travel to the child's country.

Rather, the screening process is handled by adoption agencies in the United States and the child's country of origin. The child is escorted to the United States by a volunteer and is met at the airport by his or her prospective adoptive parents. The child's adoption is then finalized in an American court in accordance with state law.

Does a child adopted from another country automatically become a U.S. citizen?

No. Advocates for adoptive parents have long argued that citizenship for foreign-born adopted children should be made automatic, based on the paperwork submitted to the INS for the orphan petition. However, at present, naturalization of foreign-born children is not automatic. Parents of a child adopted from another country must apply to have their child naturalized. It is recommended that they do so immediately upon their return to the United States with the child. To naturalize their child, the adoptive parents must fill out INS form N-643 (Application for a Certificate of Citizenship in Behalf of an Adopted Child) and bring their child (even an infant) to an in-person interview with an INS official.

Once the child has become a naturalized U.S. citizen, consular affairs officials at the U.S. State Department recommend that parents also apply for a U.S. passport for their child. A passport is a useful document to prove the child's identity and age for school purposes. Once a passport has been obtained, parents who misplace their child's certificate of citizenship can always call the State Department, where the child's certificate number can be traced from the passport application.

At what point is an adopted child covered by the adoptive parents' health insurance?

New federal legislation requires all employer group health plans that provide coverage for dependent children to cover adopted children from the time they are placed with the adoptive family.[181] Insurers may not delay coverage until the adoption decree becomes final, nor may they deny coverage to an adopted child on the basis of a medical condition that predated the child's adoptive placement.

The new law, which represents a significant step for adoptive families toward achieving parity with biological families, does contain a number of significant loopholes. Employers who are exempt from the Employee Retirement Income Security Act of 1974 (ERISA)—such as federal, state, and local governments, the U.S. military, and church groups—are not bound by the law's new protections for preadoptive children. Efforts are under way, however, to extend the new protections to children in adoptive families insured by CHAMPUS, the U.S. military insurance program.

Under what circumstances may an adopted child gain access to his or her original birth certificate and other information about his or her biological parents?

Over the past twenty-five years, a number of adult adoptees and birth parents have expressed an interest in meeting each other.[182] For some adult adoptees, "the search" is motivated by a number of factors, ranging from curiosity about their birth parents to the need (which may, in some cases, be urgent) for family medical and genetic history. For some birth parents, the search fills an emotional void represented by the relinquishment of a child many years earlier.

Only a small handful of states currently give adult adoptees access to their original birth certificates upon request.[183] In most states, adult adoptees need a court order to see their original birth certificates and must first convince a judge that they have a "compelling need" (such as a medical necessity) or other "good cause" for requesting access to that information.[184] In a large minority of states, the law authorizes adoptees and their birth parents to make use of confidential intermediaries.[185] In those states, an adult adoptee may pay for the services of a state-approved confidential intermediary to attempt to locate the birth parent and ascertain his or her willingness to meet or otherwise communicate with the adoptee.

In other states, there are mutual consent registries that exchange identifying information if both the adoptee and the birth parent submit their names to the registry.[186] If one or both parties have moved since the adoption was finalized, however, state registries are of limited utility. More helpful in such cases are some of the private national mutual consent registries maintained by organizations such as the Adoptees Liberty Movement Association or International Soundex Reunion Registry.

Some adoption practitioners recommend that, regardless of the availability of mutual consent registries and intermediary programs, it is good practice at the time of the adoption to give birth parents the option of signing a waiver of confidentiality which is designed to allow the child to obtain identifying information about the birth parents when the child reaches the age of majority.[187] The new Uniform Adoption Act has incorporated this suggestion and gives the birth parents the option, at the time of the adoption, of signing a release form giving the adult adoptee access to what otherwise would be confidential information about his or her family of origin.[188]

Is adoption limited to children?

No. An adult (that is, a person who has reached the age of majority, which is eighteen in most states) may be adopted by another adult. Adult adoptions occur for a variety of reasons. The adoption may formalize a de facto relationship that has existed for many years, as when a stepparent adopts an adult stepchild after the death of a noncustodial parent who had refused to consent to the adoption. The adoption of an adult may, alternatively, serve to provide the adoptive parent with a legal heir to inherit the adoptive parent's estate or to take a share of a testimentary gift from another member of the adoptive parent's family.

Virtually the only issue in an adult adoption proceeding is whether the adults involved intend to create a parent-child relationship between themselves. If so, the adoption will usually be granted. If, however, the court perceives that the adoption is designed to confer legal status on an adult relationship between sexual partners, the adoption will almost certainly be disapproved.[189]

For an adult adoption, the consent of the adoptee and the prospective adoptive parent are required. Under the new Uniform Adoption Act, the consent of the prospective adoptive parent's spouse may also be necessary, unless he or she is withholding consent contrary to the best interests of the adoptee or unless the spouses are separated.[190] Rarely is there any requirement that the adult adoptee's spouse or parents consent.[191]

RESOURCES

Adoptive Families of America
3333 Highway 100 North
Minneapolis, MN 55422
(800) 372-3300
(612) 535-4829

Adoptive Parents Committee
P.O. Box 3525
Church Street Station
New York, NY 10008-3525
(212) 304-8479
(516) 326-8621
http://www.wp.com/apc

Hear My Voice
P.O. Box 2064
2200 Fuller Road
Ann Arbor, MI 48106
(800) 95-VOICE
(313) 747-9665

Institute for Black Parenting
9920 La Cienega Blvd, Suite 806
Inglewood, CA 90301
(310) 348-1400

International Concerns Committee for Children
911 Cypress Drive
Boulder, CO 80303
(303) 494-8333

National Adoption Information Clearinghouse
5640 Nicholson Lane
Suite 300
Rockville, MD 20852
(301) 231-6512

North American Council on Adoptable Children
970 Raymond Avenue, Suite 106
St. Paul, MN 55114-1149
(800) 470-6665
(612) 644-3036

NOTES

1. For an overview of the history of adoption, from Moses to the present day, *see* Joan H. Hollinger, ed., *Adoption Law and Practice*, § 1.02 (1993), and Burton Z. Sokoloff, *Antecedents of American Adoption* in *Adoption* at 17 (David and Lucile Packard Foundation, Center for the Future of Children) (1993).

2. The 1994 Uniform Adoption Act, which supercedes the less comprehensive Uniform Adoption Act of 1969, is reprinted in volume 9 of the Uniform Laws Annotated. Copies may also be obtained from the National Conference of Commissioners on Uniform State Laws, 676 North St. Clair Street, Suite 1700, Chicago, IL 60611, (312) 915-0195. References throughout this chapter to the Uniform Adoption Act are to the 1994 version of the Act.

3. Uniform Adoption Act, §§ 2-404, 2-405, 2-406.

4. *Id.* § 3-707.

5. *Id.* §§ 1-102, 2-104.

6. *Id.* §§ 2-106, 2-404(e), 6-104.

7. Kathy S. Stolley, *Statistics on Adoption in the United States*, in *Adoption, supra* note 1, at 26.

8. *Id.* at 29 and Box 1.

9. *Id.*

10. *Id.*

11. *Id.*

12. For a critical look at agency adoptions, *see* Cynthia Martin, *Beating the Adoption Game* (1990); *see also* Mark T. McDermott, *The Case for Independent Adoptions* in *Adoption, supra* note 1, at 146. *But see* L. Jean Emery, *The Case for Agency Adoptions* in *Adoption, supra* note 1, at 139.

13. Ann M. Haralambie, *Handling Child Custody, Abuse and Adoption Cases*, vol. 2, § 14.17, at 92 (McGraw-Hill 1993) (cited hereafter as *Handling Adoption Cases*).

14. Although such advertisements are legal in some states, they are illegal in a considerable number of others. *See, e.g.*, Ala. Code § 26-10A-34; Cal. Family Code § 8609(a)(West 1994); Fla. Stat. Ann. § 63.212(a)(h)(West 1994); Ga. Code Ann. § 19-8-24 (1990); Ky. Rev. Stat. Ann. § 199.590(1)(Michie 1991); Mass. Ann. Laws ch. 210, § 11A.

15. Colorado, Connecticut, Delaware, and Massachusetts do not permit direct parental placement.

16. *See, e.g.*, Ariz. Rev. Stat. Ann. § 8–105 (West 1993); N.Y. Dom. Rel. Law § 115-d (McKinney 1994).

17. Uniform Adoption Act, §§ 2-102(a) and 2-201(a).

18. For a general overview of the historical notion of parenthood as an exclusive status, *see* Katherine Bartlett, *Rethinking Parenthood As an Exclusive Status: The Need for Legal Alternatives When the Premise of the Nuclear Family Has Failed*, 70 Va. L. Rev. 879 (1984).

19. *Petition of Dep't of Social Serv. To Dispense with Consent to Adoption*, 392 Mass. 696, 467 N.E.2d 861 (1984); *Matter of Adoption of Anthony*, 113 Misc. 2d 26, 448 N.Y.S.2d 377 (N.Y. Fam. Ct. 1982); *Matter of Dana Marie E.*, 128 Misc. 2d 1018, 492 N.Y.S.2d 340 (N.Y. Fam. Ct. 1985). *See generally* Judy E. Nathan, *Visitation After Adoption: In the Best Interests of*

the Child, 59 N.Y.U.L. Rev. 633 (1984) and Danny R. Veilleux, *Open Adoptions,* 78 A.L.R. 4th 218 (1990).

20. *In re M.M.,* 156 Ill.2d 53, 619 N.E.2d 702, 189 Ill. (Dec. 1, 1993). *Cf. Hatch on Behalf of Angela J. v. Cortland County Dept. of Social Serv.,* 199 A.D.2d 765, 605 N.Y.S.2d 428 (3d Dep't 1993).

21. Wash. Rev. Code Ann. § 26.33.295 (West Supp. 1993). *See also* N.M. Stat. Ann. § 32A-5-35 (1994); Ind. Code Ann. § 31-3-1-13 (1994). Minnesota's new adoption law will also permit postadoption agreements for visitation or communication that may be enforced in certain circumstances approved by the court. *See* Joan H. Hollinger, ed., *Adoption Law and Practice,* § 13.02 (Supp. 1994). This two-volume, comprehensive survey of adoption law is cited hereafter as *Adoption Law and Practice.*

22. *See, e.g., In re D.M.H.,* 135 N.J. 473, 641 A.2d 235 (1994); *In re Adoption of J.H.G.,* 254 Kan. 780; 869 P.2d 640 (1994); *In re M.M.,* 156 Ill. 2d 53, 189 Ill. Dec. 1, 619 N.E.2d 702 (1993); *Petition of S.O.,* 795 P.2d 254 (Colo. 1990); *In re Gregory B.,* 74 N.Y.2d 77, 542 N.E.2d 1052, 544 N.Y.S.2d 535 (1989). *See also* Uniform Adoption Act, § 3-707(c).

23. *Loftin v. Smith,* 590 So. 2d 323 (Ala. Civ. App. 1991), *Michaud v. Wawruck,* 209 Conn. 407, 551 A.2d 738 (1988).

24. *In re Adoption of C.R. Topel,* 571 N.E.2d 1295 (Ind. App. 1991); *Matter of Adoption of Jennifer,* 142 Misc. 2d 912, 538 N.Y.S.2d 915 (N.Y. Fam. Ct. 1989).

25. *See* Wash. Rev. Code Ann. § 26.33.160(d)(West Supp. 1994)(consent to an adoption may not be presented to the court for approval until forty-eight hours after it is signed or forty-eight hours after the birth, whichever occurs later).

26. *See, e.g.,* Ill. Comp. Stat. Ann. ch. 750, § 50/9 (West 1994); N.J. Stat. Ann. § 9:3-41(e)(West Supp. 1994); 23 Pa. Cons. Stat. Ann. § 2711(c)(West Supp. 1994). *See generally H. Joseph Gitlin, Adoptions: An Attorney's Guide to Helping Adoptive Parents* at 38–39 (1987).

27. Uniform Adoption Act, § 2-405(a).

28. The new Act also requires, for instance, that before signing a consent, the birth parent must be informed of the meaning and consequences of the adoption, the availability of personal and legal counseling, the procedure for releasing background health information, and the availability of procedures for the consensual release of the parent's identity to an adoptee, an adoptee's direct descendant, or an adoptive parent. Uniform Adoption Act, §§ 2-404(e) & 2-406(d).

29. Minn. Stat. Ann. § 259-24(2)(West Supp. 1992); N.H. Rev. Stat. Ann. § 170-B:5 (1994).

30. Kan. Stat. Ann. § 59-2115 (West 1994). *See also* Uniform Adoption Act, § 2-405(c)(parent who is a minor must have had the advice of a lawyer who is not representing an adoptive parent or adoption agency).

31. Wash. Rev. Code. Ann. § 26.33.070 (West 1994)(court must appoint guardian ad litem).

32. *See, e.g.,* Haw. Rev. Stat. § 578-2(f)(1985); N.D. Cent. Code § 14-15-08 (Michie 1991); 23 Pa. Cons. Stat. Ann. § 2711(c)(West Supp. 1994); S.C. Code Ann. § 20-7-1720 (1993). *See also Stubbs v. Weatherby,* 126 Or. App. 596, 869 P.2d 893 (1994), *review granted* 319 Or. 406 (1994). *See generally Adoption Law and Practice, supra* note 21, § 8.02[1][a].

33. N.Y. Dom. Rel. Law § 115-b(3)(a)(Lawyers Coop 1993). The forty-five day rule applies to out-of-court consents and does not give the birth parent an automatic right to regain custody of the child. *See id.* § 115-b(3)(b) & (4)(a)(iv). Under New York law, a consent that is executed before a judge may not be revoked. *Id.* § 115-b(2)(a).

34. Alaska Stat. § 25.23.070 (1991); Ga. Code Ann. § 19-8-9(b)(Michie Supp. 1990); Cal. Fam. Code § 8814.5 (West 1994). For a state-by-state summary of revocation periods and other key features of the state adoption laws of the fifty states, *see Adoption Law and Practice, supra* note 21, App. 1-A.

35. *In re Baby Boy S.*, 420 Pa. Super. 37, 615 A.2d 1355 (1992).

36. N.J. Stat. Ann. §§ 9:3-46 and 9:3-48 (West 1994). *See generally In re D.M.H.*, 135 N.J. 473, 641 A.2d 235 (1994).

37. Uniform Adoption Act §§ 2-404(a), 2-408(a)(1).

38. *Id.* § 2-408(b)(1).

39. *Hensman v. Parsons*, 235 Neb. 872, 458 N.W.2d 199 (1990); *In re Appeal in Navajo County Juvenile Action No. JA-691*, 171 Ariz. 369, 831 P.2d 368 (Ariz. App. 1991); *Wooten v. Wallace*, 177 W. Va. 159, 351 S.E.2d 72 (1986).

40. *Handling Adoption Cases, supra* note 13, at 86. *See, e.g., Anonymous v. Anonymous*, 23 Ariz. App. 50, 530 P.2d 896 (1975).

41. *Henriquez v. Adoption Centre, Inc.*, 641 So. 2d 84 (Fla. App. 1993), *aff'd on rehearing*, 641 So. 2d at 88 (1994).

42. *In the Matter of Kira M.*, 116 N.M. 514, 864 P.2d 803 (N.M. App. 1993)(threats by a spouse); *In re Sims*, 30 Ill. App. 3d 406, 332 N.E.2d 36 (4th Dist. 1975)(threats by teenager's parents); *Methodist Mission Home v. N.A.B.*, 451 S.W.2d 539 (Tex. Civ. App. 1970) (adoption agency pressure); *Sorentino v. Family & Children Society*, 72 N.J. 127, 367 A.2d 1168 (1976)(adoption agency pressure). *See generally Adoption Law and Practice, supra* note 21, § 8.02[1][b]; Gary D. Spivey, *What Constitutes Duress in Obtaining Parent's Consent to Adoption of Child or Surrender of Child to Adoption Agency*, 74 A.L.R.3d 527 (1976 and 1994 Supp.)

43. Ill. Rev. Stat. ch. 40, para. 1513.

44. *See* Comments, Uniform Adoption Act, § 2-401. *Compare Lehr v. Robertson*, 463 U.S. 248 (1983) and *Quilloin v. Walcott*, 434 U.S. 246 (1978) with *Caban v. Mohammed*, 441 U.S. 380 (1979) and *Stanley v. Illinois*, 405 U.S. 645 (1972). For an overview sympathetic to the position of the unwed father, *see* Deborah L. Forman, *Unwed Fathers and Adoption: A Theoretical Analysis in Context*, 72 Tex. L. Rev. 967 (1994)(cited hereafter as *Unwed Fathers and Adoption*).

45. *Lehr v. Robertson, supra* note 44, at 261–62 & n.18.

46. *Id.* at 262.

47. *See, e.g.*, Fla. Stat. Ann. § 63.032(14)(West 1994) and *In re Adoption of Baby E.A.W.*, 658 So. 2d 961 (Fla. 1995); *Matter of Adoption of Baby Boy S.*, 16 Kan. App. 2d 311, 822 P.2d 76 (1991); *In re Adoption of Doe*, 543 So. 2d 741 (Fla.), *cert. denied* 493 U.S. 964 (1989); *In re Baby Girl K.*, 113 Wis. 2d 429, 335 N.W.2d 846 (1983), *appeal dismissed*, 465 U.S. 1016 (1984).

48. *In re Adoption of Baby Boy B.*, 254 Kan. 454, 866 P.2d 1029 (1994); *Abernathy v. Baby Boy*, 437 S.E.2d 25 (S.C. 1993). *See also In re Kelsey S.*, 1 Cal. 4th 816, 823 P.2d 1216, 4 Cal. Rptr. 2d 615 (1992). On the issue of the birth mother's autonomy in making an

adoptive placement decision, *see* Mary L. Shanley, *Unwed Fathers' Rights, Adoption, and Sex Equality: Gender-Neutrality and the Perpetuation of Patriarchy*, 95 Colum. L. Rev. 60 (1995); Karen Czapanskiy, *Volunteers and Draftees: The Struggle for Parental Equality*, 38 U.C.L.A. Law Rev. 1415, 1418–22 (1991) and Katherine T. Bartlett, *Re-Expressing Parenthood*, 98 Yale L.J. 293, 321–26 (1988).

49. *See, e.g., Petition of Kirchner*, 164 Ill. 2d 468, 649 N.E. 2d 324, 208 Ill. Dec. 268 (1995), *cert. denied sub. nom. Doe v. Kirchner*, 132 L. Ed. 2d 846, 115 S. Ct. 2599, 2600 (1995); *Petition of Doe*, 159 Ill.2d 347, 638 N.E.2d 181, 202 Ill.Dec. 535, *cert. denied sub. nom. Baby Richard v. Kirchner*, 115 S. Ct. 499, 130 L. Ed. 2d 408 (1994); *In re Clausen*, 442 Mich. 648, 502 N.W.2d 649 (1993), *stay denied sub nom. DeBoer v. DeBoer*, 114 S. Ct. 1 (1993). Ironically, among courts that favor the biological father, the term "stranger" is used to refer to the adoptive parents with whom the child has lived for all of his or her life, while the biological parent whom the child has never met is dubbed the "real" parent. *See, e.g., Petition of Doe*, 159 Ill. 2d 347, 638 N.E.2d at 182, 188 & 190 (1994).

50. *Adoption of Michael H.*, 10 Cal. 4th 1043, 898 P. 2d 891, 43 Cal. Rptr. 2d 445 (1995); *Appeal in Pima County Juvenile Severance Action No. S-114487*, 179 Ariz. 86, 876 P.2d 1121 (1994); *Robert O. v. Russell K.*, 80 N.Y.2d 254, 604 N.E.2d 99, 590 N.Y.S.2d 37 (1992). *But see In the Matter of Raquel Marie X.*, 76 N.Y.2d 387, 559 N.E.2d 418, 559 N.Y.S.2d 855 (1990).

51.* *See In re Jasmon O.*, 8 Cal. 4th 398, 33 Cal. Rptr. 2d 85, 878 P. 2d 1297 (1994), *reh'g denied*, 1994 Cal. LEXIS 5765 (1994). *In re Adoption No. A91–71A*, 334 Md. 538, 640 A. 2d 1085 (1994); *In re Baby Boy C.*, 630 A.2d 670, 683 (D.C. App. 1993), *cert. denied sub nom. H.R. v. E.O.*, 115 S. Ct. 58 (1994). *See also* D.C. Code § 16–2353 (1989); Mich. Comp. Law Ann. § 710.39 (West 1993). *Cf. Bennett v. Jeffreys*, 40 N.Y.2d 543, 356 N.E.2d 277, 387 N.Y.S.2d 821 (1976).

52. *In re Adoption No. A91-71A, supra* note 51, 640 A.2d at 1097.

53. Uniform Adoption Act, § 3-504(d)(3) & (4). *See also* Cal. Fam. Code § 3041(West 1994)(standard for judging custody in contest between biological and nonbiological parent is "detriment" to the child). For a detailed discussion of the implications of the Uniform Adoption Act for contested adoption cases, *see* Joan H. Hollinger, *Adoption and Aspiration: The Uniform Adoption Act, the DeBoer-Schmidt Case, and the American Quest for an Ideal Family*, 2 Duke J. of Gender Law & Policy 15 (1995).

54. *Id.* at § 3-504(e). For a fascinating look at some contested adoption cases from the child's perspective, *see* Barbara Bennett Woodhouse, *"Hatching the Egg": A Child-Centered Perspective on Parents' Rights*, 14 Cardozo Law Review 1747 (1993).

55. Martin Guggenheim, *Why Should A Perjurer Win Custody?*, New York Newsday, Aug. 17, 1994.

56. *See, e.g., Petition of Kirchner, supra* note 49, 649 N.E. 2d at 343–64 (McMorrow, J., dissenting); *In re Petition of Doe*, 254 Ill. App. 3d 405, 627 N.E.2d 648, 651–52, 194 Ill. Dec. 311 (1st Dist. 1993), *rev'd*, 159 Ill. 2d 347, 638 N.E.2d 181 (1994); *In re Clausen, supra* note 49, 502 N.W.2d at 668–89 (1993)(Levin, J., dissenting). The significance to the child of her attachment to her "psychological" parents is explored in the classic work by Joseph Goldstein, Anna Freud & Albert J. Solnit, *Beyond the Best Interests of the Child* (1973). *See generally*, Brief of Concerned Academics As *Amici Curiae* In Support of Application for Stay Filed on Behalf of Petitioner Jessica DeBoer, *DeBoer v. Schmidt*, No. A-64 (U.S. Supreme

Court) (July 21, 1993). *Cf.* Carol A. Crocca, *Continuity of Residence As Factor in Contest Between Parent and Nonparent for Custody of Child Who Has Been Residing with Nonparent: Modern Status*, 15 A.L.R. 5th 692 (1993).

57. *See* 750 Ill. Con. Stat. (ILCS) § 50/20 (amended July 3, 1994); *Matter of Adoption of J.J.B.*, 894 P. 2d 994, 1007–11 (N.M. 1995) (a finding that parental rights were improperly terminated does not mechanically result in the award of custody to the biological parent); *In re C.C.R.S.*, 892 P. 2d 246 (Colo. 1995); *Lemley v. Barr*, 176 W. Va. 378, 343 S.E.2d 101 (1986); *E.E.B. v. D.A.*, 89 N.J. 595, 446 A.2d 871 (1982), *cert. denied sub nom. Angle v. Bowen*, 459 U.S. 1210 (1983); *Sorentino v. Family and Children's Society of Elizabeth*, 74 N.J. 313, 378 A.2d 18 (1977). *See generally* Homer H. Clark, Jr., *The Law of Domestic Relations in the United States*, vol. 2 at 532–35 (2d ed. 1987); *In re Bridget R.*, 41 Cal. App. 4th 1483, 1996 Cal. App. LEXIS 37, 49 Cal. Rptr. 2d 507 (1996), *review denied* (children have substantive as well as due process right to be protected against precipitous removal from prospective adoptive parents' home and are entitled to a hearing on their custody).

58. Uniform Adoption Act, §§ 2-408(f), 2-409(f), 3-506(a), 3-704.

59. *See, e.g.*, Ariz. Rev. Stat. Ann. § 8-106.01 (1994)(filing may be made with the registry before the child's birth or within 30 days thereafter); Ind. Code Ann. section 31-3-1.5-1 through 31-3-1.5-20 (West 1994)(filing may be made within 30 days after the child's birth or by the date the adoption petition is filed, whichever is later, or before the child's birth); N.Y. Soc. Serv. Law § 372-c. For a full discussion of these and other state laws that require the unwed father to take some specific legal action before he is entitled to notice of the adoption, *see Unwed Fathers and Adoption, supra* note 44, 72 Tex. L. Rev. at 1001-7.

60. N.Y. Dom. Rel. Law § 111-a(2)(Lawyers Coop 1994).

61. *See, e.g., Evans v. South Carolina Dep't of Social Serv.*, 303 S.C. 108, 399 S.E.2d 156 (1990); *In re Karen A.B.*, 513 A.2d 770 (Del. Supr. 1986); *In re Adoption of Christopher L.*, 113 Misc. 2d 904, 450 N.Y.S.2d 269 (N.Y. Sur. 1982). *But see* 45 C.F.R. §§ 302.70 (a)(5) & 303.5 (g)(1995), reprinted in 59 Fed. Reg. 66204, 66249-50 (Dec. 23, 1994)(requiring states to develop procedures to encourage more birth fathers to informally acknowledge paternity at birth, in the hospital).

62. *See, e.g.*, Del. Code Ann., tit. 13, § 1105(a)(9)(Michie 1993); *Augusta Co. Dep't of Social Serv. v. Unnamed Mother*, 3 Va. App. 40, 348 S.E.2d 26 (1986). *See also* Uniform Adoption Act, § 3-404.

63. 50 App. U.S.C. §§ 501 *et seq.*, especially 50 App. U.S.C. § 523 (West 1990).

64. *Engstrom v. State*, 461 N.W.2d 309 (Iowa 1990); *Petrowsky v. Family Serv. of Decatur, Inc.*, 165 Ill. App. 3d 32, 518 N.E.2d 664, 116 Ill. Dec. 42 (4th Dist. 1987), *appeal denied*, 119 Ill. 2d 574, 522 N.E.2d 1256, 119 Ill. Dec. 397 (1988).

65. *Petrowsky v. Family Serv. of Decatur, Inc.*, *supra* note 64.

66. *See, e.g.*, Ariz. Rev. Stat. Ann. § 8-114 (West 1993); N.Y. Soc. Serv. Law § 374(6); N.Y. Dom Rel. Law § 115(8)(Lawyers Coop 1994).

67. Fla. Stat. Ann. § 63.212(1)(d)(West Supp. 1994); Tenn. Code Ann. § 36-1-135 (Michie Supp. 1993); Utah Code Ann. § 76-7-203 (Michie Supp. 1994).

68. *See e.g.*, Colo. Rev. Stat. Ann. § 19-5-213 (Supp. 1994).

69. Uniform Adoption Act, § 7-103.

70. *See, e.g.*, Cal. Fam. Code § 8610 (West 1994); N.Y. Dom. Rel. Law § 115(8).

71. *A.L. v. P.A.*, 213 N.J. Super. 391, 517 A.2d 494 (1986), *cert. denied*, 107 N.J. 110, 526 A.2d 181 (1987). *But see Gorden v. Cutler*, 324 Pa. Super. 35, 471 A.2d 449

(1983)(birth parents who changed their mind required to reimburse prospective adoptive parents for their expenditures for birth mother's prenatal care and delivery).

72. N.Y. Soc. Serv. Law § 374 (McKinney's 1994). *See also In re Anonymous*, 131 Misc. 2d 666, 501 N.Y.S.2d 240 (N.Y. Sur. 1986).

73. Cal. Fam. Code § 8800 (West 1994).

74. Fla. Stat. Ann. § 63.062(1)(c)(West Supp. 1994)(age 12, but court may waive need for child's consent); 750 Ill. Comp. Stat. 50/12 (Smith Hurd 1993)(age 14); Mass. Ann. Laws ch. 210, § 2 (West 1987)(age 12); N.J. Stat. Ann. § 9:3-49 (West 1993)(age 10); N.Y. Dom. Rel. Law § 111(a)(age 14, unless the court dispenses with the requirement of consent).

75. *Compare* N.Y. Family Court Act, § 249(a)(requiring appointment of law guardian where prospective adoptive parents oppose birth parent's revocation of consent) and Tex. Fam. Code Ann. § 11.10 (West 1986) with Colo. Rev. Stat. § 19-4-110 (1994)(appointment of guardian ad litem for the child is discretionary) and Wash. Rev. Code Ann. § 26.33.070 (West 1986). *See generally Adoption Law and Practice, supra* note 21, §§ 6.01[6][b] & 8.03[3]. The Uniform Adoption Act, § 3-201(b), requires the appointment of a guardian ad litem for the child in a contested proceeding. For a full discussion of the difference between a guardian ad litem and independent counsel for the child, *see* chapter 1 on child custody.

76. *Adoption Law and Practice, supra* note 21, § 8.07[3][a][iii].

77. *See, e.g.*, Wash. Rev. Code Ann. § 26.33.190 (West Supp. 1994).

78. For a comprehensive survey of all aspects of the law relating to the disclosure of the adopted child's medical and social history, *see* D. Marianne Brower Blair, *Getting the Whole Truth and Nothing But the Truth: The Limits of Liability for Wrongful Adoption*, 67 Notre Dame L. Rev. 851 (1992)(cited hereafter as *Wrongful Adoption*).

79. *Compare, e.g.*, N.Y. Soc. Serv. Law § 373-a (McKinney Supp. 1994) and Tex. Fam. Code Ann. § 16.032 (West Supp. 1994)(mandating disclosure) with S.C. Code Ann. § 20-7-1780(D)(1993)(agency discretion).

80. *Wrongful Adoption, supra* note 78, at 867 and nn. 78 & 79.

81. *Id.* at n. 80. *See, e.g.*, Iowa Code Ann. § 600.8 (West Supp 1994); Ky. Rev. Stat. Ann. § 199.520(4)(a)(Michie 1991).

82. *Wrongful Adoption, supra* note 78, at 868. *Compare, e.g.*, Ohio Rev. Code Ann. § 3107.12 (1989)(detailing steps that must be taken to obtain child's medical and social history) with Haw. Rev. Stat. § 578-14.5(b)(Supp. 1992)(requiring adoption agencies to make "reasonable efforts" to collect medical history).

83. *Wrongful Adoption, supra* note 78, at 867 & n.77.

84. Uniform Adoption Act §§ 2-106, 6-103, 7-105.

85. 23 Ohio St. 3d 69, 491 N.E.2d 1101 (1986).

86. *Michael J. v. County of Los Angeles, Dep't of Adoptions*, 201 Cal. App. 3d 859, 247 Cal. Rptr. 504 (2d Dist. 1988). *See also Snyder v. Mouser*, 149 Ind. App. 334, 272 N.E.2d 627 (1971)(state agency had a duty to warn foster parents of child's psychiatric problems and homicidal propensities). *But see Collier v. Krane*, 763 F. Supp. 473 (D. Colo. 1991).

87. *M.H. v. Caritas Family Serv.*, 488 N.W.2d 282 (Minn. 1992); *Roe v. Catholic Charities*, 225 Ill. App. 3d 519, 588 N.E.2d 354, 167 Ill. Dec. 713 (5th Dist. 1992), *appeal denied*, 146 Ill.2d 651, 602 N.E.2d 475, 176 Ill. Dec. 821 (1992); *Wallerstein v. Hospital Corp. of America*, 573 So. 2d 9 (Fla. App. 1990), *review denied*, 584 So. 2d 997 (Fla. 1991); *Meracle v. Children's Serv. Society*, 149 Wis. 2d 19, 437 N.W.2d 532 (1989). *But see Richard P. v. Vista Del Mar Child Care Serv.*, 106 Cal. App. 3d 860, 165 Cal. Rptr. 370 (2d Dist. 1980); *Foster*

v. Bass, 575 So. 2d 967 (Miss. 1990); *Griffith v. Johnston*, 899 F.2d 1427 (5th Cir. 1990), *cert. denied* 498 U.S. 1040 (1991).

88. Contrary to popular myth that holds that all adoptive parents are looking to adopt the "Gerber baby," there are in fact waiting lists of prospective adoptive parents for children with spina bifida or with Down's syndrome. *Wrongful Adoption, supra* note 78, at 863–64 & n.58.

89. *Id.* at 879–80.

90. *Mitch v. Bucks Co. Children & Youth Soc. Serv. Agency*, 383 Pa. Super. 42, 556 A.2d 419 (1989); *In re Joseph*, 420 A.2d 85 (R.I.1980). A 1994 federal law, the Multiethnic Placement Act, gives adoptive parents the right to challenge the denial of an adoptive placement based on their race, color, or national origin or the race, color, or national origin of the child. *See* 42 U.S.C. 5115a(b)(West Supp. 1995).

91. *See, e.g.*, Cal. Fam. Code § 8820(West 1994); Mass. Gen. Laws Ann. ch. 210, § 2A (West 1987); N.J. Stat. Ann. § 9:3-47(a)(West 1994); Tex. Fam. Code Ann. § 16.05). *See also In re Petition to Adopt S.T.*, 497 N.W.2d 625 (Minn. App. 1993), *aff'd in part, rev'd in part* 512 N.W.2d 894 (Minn. 1994); *Ex parte R.C.*, 592 So. 2d 589 (Ala. 1991); *In re Haun*, 31 Ohio App. 2d 63, 286 N.E.2d 478 (1972).

92. *Adoption Law and Practice, supra* note 21, § 3.02[2] at 3–14. *But see In re Adoption of McDonald*, 43 Cal. 2d 447, 274 P.2d 860 (1954).

93. *Smith v. Organization of Foster Families for Equality and Reform*, 431 U.S. 816, 818 at n.1 (1977).

94. *See, e.g.*, Cal. Fam. Code § 8704(c) & (d)(West 1994); Ill. Comp. Stat. Ann., title 750, ch. 50/15.1 (Smith-Hurd 1994); N.Y. Soc. Serv. Law § 383(3)(Lawyers Coop 1994).

95. N.Y. Soc. Serv. Law § 392(6)(c)(1994).

96. *Patterson v. Robbins*, 295 Ark. 511, 749 S.W.2d 330 (1988). *But see In re Adoption of S.C.P.*, 364 Pa. Super. 257, 527 A.2d 1052 (1987).

97. *In re B.C.*, 749 P.2d 542 (Okla. 1988); *Berhow v. Crow*, 423 So.2d 371 (Fla. App. 1982). *But see Lewis v. Catholic Social Services*, 253 Mont. 369, 833 P.2d 1023 (1992); *Johnson v. Burnett*, 182 Ill. App. 3d 574, 538 N.E.2d 892, 131 Ill. Dec. 517 (3d Dist. 1989).

98. *Berhow v. Crow, supra* note 97.

99. *In re Petition to Adopt S.T., supra* note 91; *Petition of Department of Social Services to Dispense with Consent to Adoption*, 22 Mass. App. Ct. 62, 491 N.E.2d 270, *review denied*, 397 Mass. 1104, 494 N.E.2d 388 (1986).

100. Pub. L. No. 96-272, 94 Stat. 500, *codified in pertinent part* at 42 U.S.C. § 673. Readers should be aware that as this book was going to press, Congress was considering legislation that might impact the federal adoption subsidy program. Organizations listed in this chapter's "Resource" section can provide updates on legislative developments in this area.

101. 42 U.S.C. § 673(c). For a detailed discussion of adoption subsidies, *see Adoption Law and Practice, supra* note 21, ch. 9.

102. *Adoption Law and Practice, supra* note 21, § 9.03[1][b]. *See also* North American Council on Adoptable Children, *Adoption Subsidies* at 3.

103. *See, e.g.*, Minn. Stat. Ann. § 259.40(2)(West Supp. 1994). *See also* National Adoption Information Clearinghouse, *Subsidized Adoption: A Source of Help for Children with Special Needs and Their Families* at 4.

104. *See generally Adoption Law and Practice, supra* note 21, § 9.06[1] and the *Interstate*

Compact on Adoption and Medical Assistance, reprinted in *Adoption Law and Practice,* app. 9-A, § 9-A.04.

105. *Adoption Law and Practice, supra* note 21, § 9.06[1], at 9-44, and § 9.06[2], at 9-45.

106. For a comprehensive survey of the law in this area, *see* Elizabeth Bartholet, *Where Do Black Children Belong? The Politics of Race Matching in Adoption,* 139 U. Pa. L. Rev. 1163 at 1183–1200 (May 1991)(cited hereafter as *Where Do Black Children Belong?*). Professor Bartholet also covers some of this same ground in chapter 6 of her book, *Family Bonds: Adoption and the Politics of Parenting* (1993).

107. *Where Do Black Children Belong?, supra* note 106, at 1178.

108. From the position paper developed at the National Association of Black Social Workers' Conference in Nashville, Tenn., Apr. 4–9, 1972, reprinted in Rita Simon & Howard Alstein, *Transracial Adoption* 50–52 (1977).

109. *Id.* at 50. *See also* Valerie Phillips Hermann, *Transracial Adoption: "Child-Saving" or "Child-Snatching",* 13 Nat'l Black L.J. 147 at 149 (1993); Joyce Ladner, *Mixed Families* 74–77 (1977).

110. Contrary to these assertions, the empirical studies of transracial adoption reveal that children involved in transracial placements have done well in terms of achievement, adjustment, self-esteem, and racial identity. *Where Do Black Children Belong?, supra* note 106, at 1207–26. *See generally,* A. R. Silverman, *Outcomes of Transracial Adoptions,* in *Adoption, supra* note 1, at 104–17 (1993); Rita Simon & Howard Alstein, *Adoption, Race and Identity Crisis* (1992); Rita Simon & Howard Alstein, *Transracial Adoptees and their Families: A Study of Identity and Commitment* (1987).

111. *See* Minn. Stat. Ann. §§ 259.255 & 259.28(2) (West Supp. 1994); Ark. Stat. Ann. § 9-9-102 (Michie 1993). *But see* Conn. Gen. Stat. Ann. § 45a-727(c); Ky. Rev. Stat. Ann. §§ 199.471 & 199.473 (Michie 1991); Tex. Code Ann. § 16.081 (West 1994)(barring discrimination against children or prospective adoptive parents on the basis of race or ethnicity).

112. Cal. Fam. Code § 8708 (West 1994).

113. *Id.* § 8709(c).

114. *Where Do Black Children Belong?, supra* note 106, at 1189, n. 68 (citing, among other things, a South Carolina Department of Social Service manual that provides a same-race placement preference and permits a search for a same-race family to occur for a maximum of twelve months after a child has been freed for adoption).

115. *Id.* at 1201–2. For a detailed overview of the psychological costs of same-race preference policies, *see* Kim Forde-Mazrui, *Black Identity and Child Placement: The Best Interests of Black and Biracial Children,* 92 Mich. L. Rev. 925 (1994).

116. *McLaughlin v. Pernsley,* 693 F. Supp. 318 (E.D. Pa. 1988), *aff'd* 876 F.2d 308 (3d Cir. 1989); *Committee to End Racism in Michigan's Child Care System v. Mansour,* 12 Fam. L. Rep. (BNA) 1285 (1986); *Compos v. McKeithen,* 341 F. Supp. 264 (E.D. La. 1972); *In re Adoption of Gomez,* 424 S.W.2d 656 (Tex. Civ. App. 1967).

117. *DeWees v. Stevenson,* 779 F. Supp. 25 (E.D. Pa. 1991); *Petition of R.M.G.,* 454 A.2d 776 (D.C. App. 1982); *Drummond v. Fulton County Department of Family & Children's Serv.,* 563 F.2d 1200 (5th Cir. 1977), *cert. denied* 437 U.S. 910 (1978). *But see In re Petition to Adopt S.T., supra* note 91; *In re J.,* 19 Fam. L. Rep. (BNA) 1409 (N.Y. Fam. Ct. 1993).

118. *In re Welfare of D.L.*, 486 N.W.2d 375 (Minn. 1992), *cert. denied*, 113 S. Ct. 603 (1992); *Petition of D.I.S.*, 494 A.2d 1316 (D.C. App. 1985). For a general overview of the constitutional and other legal issues at stake in transracial adoptions, *see* Timothy P. Glynn, *The Role of Race in Adoption Proceedings: A Constitutional Critique of the Minnesota Preference Statute*, 77 Minn. L. Rev. 925 (1993).

119. *Loving v. Virginia*, 388 U.S. 1 (1967).

120. *Palmore v. Sidoti*, 466 U.S. 429 (1984).

121. 42 U.S.C. § 5115a(a)(1)(West Supp. 1995). *See also* Uniform Adoption Act, §§ 2–104(c).

122. 42 U.S.C. § 5115a(b)(West Supp. 1995).

123. 42 U.S.C. § 5115a(a)(2)(West Supp. 1995). *But see* U.S. Department of Health & Human Services, Office of Civil Rights, Administration for Children & Families, *Policy Guidance on the Use of Race, Color, or National Origin as Considerations in Adoption & Foster Care Placements*, 60 Fed. Reg. 20272, 20274 (Apr. 25, 1995)(consideration of race permissible only on an individualized basis that focuses on the needs of a particular child and the capacities of particular prospective parents). As this book was going to press, Congress was considering the Adoption Promotion and Stability Act of 1996, designed to further limit race discrimination in adoption. *See* H.R. 3286, 104th Cong., 2d Sess. (introduced April 23, 1996).

124. *See Policy Guidance, supra* note 123.

125. 25 U.S.C. §§ 1901–1963 (West 1983).

126. 25 U.S.C. § 1903(4). One expert on the ICWA has noted that the Act exalts a child's Indian heritage above any other, so that a child who is fifteen-sixteenths Hispanic and one-sixteenth Native American may be subject to the Act. *Handling Adoption Cases, supra* note 13, at 132.

127. *In the Matter of Baby Boy Doe*, 123 Idaho 464, 849 P.2d 925, *cert. denied sub nom.*, *Swenson v. Oglala Sioux Tribe*, 114 S. Ct. 173 (1993); *In re Adoption of Lindsay C.*, 229 Cal. App. 3d 404, 280 Cal. Rptr. 194 (1st Dist. 1991)(applying ICWA to bar stepparent adoption); *In re Adoption of Baade*, 462 N.W.2d 485 (S.D. 1990). *But see In re Adoption of Crews*, 118 Wash. 2d 561, 825 P.2d 305 (1992); *In re Hampton*, 1995 La. App. LEXIS 1877 (July 6, 1995); *In re Bridget R.*, 41 Cal. App. 4th 1483, 1996 Cal. App. LEXIS 37, 49 Cal. Rptr. 2d 507 (1996), *review denied* (ICWA applies only where the birth parents maintain a significant social, cultural, or political relationship with their tribe). Legislation to add an "existing Indian family" exception to the Indian Child Welfare Act was being considered in Congress as this book went to press. *See* H.R. 3286, 104th Cong., 2d Sess. (introduced April 23, 1996).

128. *In the Matter of Baby Boy Doe, supra* note 127.

129. 25 U.S.C. § 1911(a).

130. *Mississippi Board of Choctaw Indians v. Holyfield*, 490 U.S. 30 (1989).

131. 25 U.S.C. § 1912(a). An *Indian custodian* is an Indian who has legal custody of an Indian child under tribal law or custom or state law, or to whom the parent has transferred temporary physical care, custody, or control. 25 U.S.C. § 1903(6).

132. 25 U.S.C. § 1911(b).

133. 25 U.S.C. § 1911(c).

134. 25 U.S.C. § 1915(a).

135. *Id.* Compare *In re Adoption of M.T.S.*, 489 N.W.2d 285 (Minn. App. 1992) with *In re Interest of C.W.*, 239 Neb. 817, 479 N.W.2d 105 (1992).

136. 25 U.S.C. § 1915(c).

137. *Handling Adoption Cases, supra* note 13, § 15.14, at 131.

138. 25 U.S.C. § 1913(a).

139. *Id.* at § 1913(c).

140. 25 U.S.C. § 1913(d).

141. *Santosky v. Kramer*, 455 U.S. 745 (1982).

142. 25 U.S.C. § 1912(f).

143. *Adoption Law and Practice, supra* note 21, § 4.02[8], at 4-74. *See generally* Joan H. Hollinger, *Beyond the Best Interests of the Tribe: The Indian Child Welfare Act and the Adoption of Indian Children*, 66 U. Det. L. Rev. 451 (1989).

144. *Adoption Law and Practice, supra* note 21, § 2.10[3][c].

145. *Id.* at 2–98. *See, e.g.*, N.J. Stat. Ann. § 9:3-46 (West Supp. 1994).

146. *See, e.g.*, Cal. Fam. Code § 8604 (1994). For a thought-provoking discussion of this issue, *see* David L. Chambers, *Stepparents, Biologic Parents and the Law's Perception of "Family" After Divorce* in Stephen D. Sugarman & Herma Hill Kay, *Divorce Reform at the Crossroads* 118–21 (1990).

147. Ariz. Rev. Stat. Ann. § 8-106(c)(West Supp. 1993); Wash. Rev. Code Ann. § 26.33.120 (West 1994).

148. Uniform Adoption Act, §§ 4-102 & 4-112.

149. *In re Adoption of Charles B*, 50 Ohio St. 3d 88, 552 N.E.2d 884 (1990)(homosexuals should not be categorically excluded from adopting).

150. Fla. Stat. Ann. § 63.042(3)(West 1985); N.H. Rev. Stat. Ann. § 170-B:4 (1994). The constitutionality of the New Hampshire law has been upheld by the New Hampshire Supreme Court. *Opinion of the Justices*, 129 N.H. 290, 530 A.2d 21 (1987). The constitutionality of the Florida law is still being litigated. *See Cox v. Fla. Dep't of Health and Rehab Serv.*, 656 So. 2d 902 (Fla. 1995).

151. *See In re Dana*, 86 N.Y. 2d 651, 660 N.E.2d 397, 636 N.Y.S. 2d 716 (1995); *In re Adoption of Minor Child*, 21 Fam. L. Rep. (BNA) 1332 (D.C. Super. Ct. Fam. Div.)(1995); *Adoption of B.L.V.B.*, 160 Vt. 368, 628 A.2d 1271 (1993); *Adoption of Tammy*, 416 Mass. 205, 619 N.E.2d 315 (1993); *In re Adoption of Evan*, 153 Misc. 2d 844, 583 N.Y.S.2d 997 (N.Y. Sur. 1992); *In re Adoption Petition of L.S. & V.L.*, 17 Fam. L. Rep. (BNA) 1523 (D.C. Super. Ct. Fam. Div. 1991). *But see In re Angel Lace M.*, 184 Wis. 2d 492, 516 N.W.2d 678 (1994).

152. *See In re M.M.D.*, 1995 D.C. App. LEXIS 141 (June 30, 1995) and cases cited in *In re Adoption of Evan, supra* note 151, at 1002.

153. *Matter of Adoption of Hope*, 150 Misc. 2d 319, 571 N.Y.S. 2d 182 (N.Y. Fam. Ct. 1991) (rejecting unmarried heterosexual couple's joint petition to adopt woman's biological children). *But see In re Jacob*, 86 N.Y. 2d 651, N.E. 2d 397, 636 N.Y.S. 2d 716 (1995)(permitting unmarried man to adopt girlfriend's son).

154. *See, e.g.*, Cal. Fam. Code § 7901 *et seq.* (West 1994); N.Y. Soc. Serv. Law § 374-a (McKinney 1992). The ICPC is reprinted in *Adoption Law and Practice, supra* note 21, § 3-A.15.

155. "Sending agency" is defined by the Interstate Compact on the Placement of Chil-

dren (ICPC) as anyone, including a private person, state, or municipal official, or charitable agency, who sends, brings, or causes to be sent or brought any child to another state for placement. ICPC, art. II(b).

156. ICPC, art. III(b).

157. ICPC, art. III(c).

158. ICPC, art. III(d).

159. *In re Jennifer M.*, 7 Cal. App. 4th 728, 9 Cal. Rptr. 2d 428 (4th Dist. 1992).

160. *In re Adoption No. 10087*, 324 Md. 394, 597 A.2d 456 (1991); *In re Adoption of Baby "E"*, 104 Misc. 2d 185, 427 N.Y.S.2d 705 (N.Y. Fam. Ct. 1980).

161. *In re Adoption of T.M.M.*, 186 Mont. 460, 608 P.2d 130 (1980).

162. *Matter of Adoption of Calynn M.G.*, 137 Misc. 2d 1005, 523 N.Y.S.2d 729 (N.Y.Sur. 1987).

163. ICPC, Art. VIII(a).

164. *Id.*

165. *Compare In re B.B.M.*, 514 N.W.2d 425 (Iowa 1994) and *In re R.P.*, 12 Kan. App. 2d 503, 749 P.2d 49 (1988) with *In re Welfare of D.L.*, *supra* note 118 (upholding preference for adoption by relatives in Minnesota's Minority Adoption Act).

166. Ariz. Rev. Stat. Ann. § 8-105(P)(Supp. 1992).

167. *In Interest of D.G.*, 246 N.W.2d 892 (N.D. 1976). *Cf. In Interest of Brandon L.E.*, 183 W. Va. 113, 394 S.E.2d 515 (1990). *See generally* Carol A. Crocca, *Continuity of Residence as Factor in Contest Between Parent and Nonparent for Custody of Child Who Has Been Residing with Nonparent—Modern Status*, 15 A.L.R. 5th 692 (1993).

168. *In re Interest of Brandon*, 179 Wis. 2d 114, 507 N.W.2d 94 (1993); *In re Steven C*, 169 Wis. 2d 727, 486 N.W.2d 572 (Wis. App. 1992).

169. *Adoption Law and Practice*, *supra* note 21, § 13.03[4], at 13-97 & nn. 68–69 & Supp. at 135.

170. *In re Groleau*, 585 N.E.2d 726 (Ind. App. 1992);*Lingwall v. Hoener*, 108 Ill. 2d 206, 483 N.E.2d 512, 91 Ill. Dec. 166 (1985); *Mimkon v. Ford*, 66 N.J. 426, 332 A.2d 199 (1975). *See generally* Peter A. Zablotsky, *To Grandmother's House We Go: Grandparent Visitation after Stepparent Adoption*, 32 Wayne L. Rev. 1 (Fall 1985) and *Adoption Law and Practice*, *supra* note 21, § 13.03[3].

171. *Suster v. Dep't of Human Serv.*, *314 Ark. 92, 858 S.W.2d 122 (1993); In re Martin*, 68 Ohio St. 3d 250, 626 N.E.2d 82 (1994). *See generally*, Linda D. Elrod, *Child Custody Practice and Procedure*, § 7:09 (Clark Boardman Callaghan 1994) and *Adoption Law and Practice*, *supra* note 21, § 13.03[4].

172. 8 U.S.C. § 1101(b)(1)(F)(West Supp. 1994). If the prospective adoptive parents intend to adopt a child from another country but have not yet identified a specific child, they can get a headstart on the immigration paperwork by using the INS I-600A form, "Application for Advance Processing of Orphan Petition."

173. H. Joseph Gitlin, *Adoptions: An Attorney's Guide to Helping Adoptive Parents* 101 (1990).

174. 8 U.S.C. § 1101(b)(1)(F)(West Supp. 1994).

175. 8 C.F.R. § 204.3(b), published in vol. 59 of the Federal Register at 38881 (Aug. 1, 1994). *See generally* Stephanie Sue Padilla, *Adoption of Alien Orphan Children: How United States Immigration Law Defines Family*, 7 Geo. Immigr. L.J. 817 (Dec. 1993).

176. 8 C.F.R. § 204.3(b). New INS regulations also appear to make it more difficult

to adopt a child born out of wedlock and relinquished by the birth mother as the child's sole parent in countries where all children are deemed legitimate from birth. *Id.*

177. 8 C.F.R. § 204.3(e), 59 Fed. Reg. 38876 *et seq.* (Aug. 1, 1994).

178. 32 I.L.M. 1134 (Summer 1993).

179. Hague Convention, art. 18 & 23.

180. Hague Convention, art. 23–27. *See generally* Peter H. Pfund, *Intercountry Adoption: The 1993 Hague Convention: Its Purpose, Implementation and Promise,* 28 Fam. L.Q. 53 (Spring 1994). Adoption proceedings in the United States will still be necessary for children who are adopted from countries, such as India or Korea, that do not permit the adoption to occur in the child's country of origin but that allow the child to be escorted to the U.S. for the purpose of adoption there.

181. 29 U.S.C. § 1169(c)(West 1994).

182. The now classic and still controversial book about "the search" is Arthur Sorosky, Annette Baran & Reuben Pannor's *The Adoption Triangle* (Anchor Books 1984).

183. Alaska Stat. § 18.50.500 (1991); Kan Stat. Ann. § 65-2423 (1993); Tenn. Code Ann. § 36-1-141 (birth certificate available unless birth parents object); Wash. Rev. Code Ann. 26.33.345 (for adoptions finalized after Oct. 1, 1993, adult adoptee may obtain non-certified copy of original birth certificate unless birth parent has filed nondisclosure request). New Jersey may soon join these ranks. *See* Joseph F. Sullivan, *Bill Would Let Adoptees See Birth Records,* N.Y. Times Dec. 6, 1994.

184. For a detailed account of what constitutes "good cause" for unsealing confidential adoption records, *see Adoption Law and Practice, supra* note 21, § 13.01[3].

185. *Adoption Law and Practice, supra* note 21, § 13.01[3][c] and App. 13-A.

186. *See, e.g.,* Cal. Fam. Code §§ 9203-04 (West 1994); Conn. Gen. Stat. Ann. §§ 45a-755, 45a-756 (West 1993); N.H. Rev. Stat. Ann., tit. 170-B:19 (1994); N.Y. Pub. Health Law §§ 4138-c through 4138-d (McKinney 1992); Tex. Hum. Res. Code Ann. §§ 49.001 et seq (West 1990).

187. *Handling Adoption Cases, supra* note 13, at 108.

188. Uniform Adoption Act sections 2-404(e), 6-104.

189. *In re Adoption of Robert Paul P.,* 63 N.Y.2d 233, 471 N.E.2d 424, 481 N.Y.S.2d 652 (1984).

190. Uniform Adoption Act § 5-103.

191. *Adoption Law and Practice, supra* note 21, § 4.06[2], at 4-121.

IX

"New" Families

Ours is by no means a tradition limited to respect for
the bonds uniting the members of the nuclear family.[1]

Family groupings other than the traditional nuclear family are not so much "new" as they are unrecognized, either by popular culture or the law. They are also not particularly rare. Almost one-third of American children are born to unwed mothers,[2] and one-third live with a single parent.[3] There are 3.5 million unmarried couples living together in the United States, over a third with children.[4] Another 2.5 million households comprise persons unrelated by marriage, blood, or adoption.[5] An astounding 23.6 million people, or almost one-quarter of all American households, are single persons living alone.[6]

Nonetheless, in many respects, the law continues to contemplate a married, heterosexual, two-parent family without cohabiting relatives as the norm from which all other family groupings represent deviations. Thus, rather than envisioning a comprehensive family law that would take into account the variety that is actually present in American society, courts and legislatures have developed the law piecemeal as challenges have emerged.

Perhaps not surprisingly, then, the law governing nonnuclear families is often contradictory, although there is a distinct movement toward recognition of alternative family groupings. For example, unrelated groups of people living together are considered a single household for eligibility for food stamps[7] but can nonetheless be constitutionally zoned out of certain neighborhoods.[8] Many states have passed civil rights laws that explicitly ban discrimination based on marital status yet have nonetheless upheld various distinctions between married and unmarried persons. As a result, these antidiscrimination laws arguably have little effect.

In other instances, courts and legislatures have made significant progress towards recognition of alternative families. Extended families have been accorded legal significance in housing and child custody cases; unmarried heterosexual partners have had their unions legally validated; and discrimination against children born out of wedlock has repeatedly been held unconstitutional. At least one commentator, however, has found such advances inadequate because they serve only to expand existing structures rather than allowing a fuller societal redefinition of "family."[9] According to this view, a more enlightened legal system would express a more open-ended recognition of self-determined family groupings, as did New York's highest court in *Braschi v. Stahl Associates Co.*[10] There the court, in finding that a gay male couple constituted a family for purposes of New York City's rent control laws, stated:

> The intended protection against sudden eviction should not rest on fictitious legal distinctions or genetic history, but instead should find its foundation in the reality of family life. . . . [I]t is the totality of the relationship as evidenced by the dedication, caring and self-sacrifice of the parties which should . . . control.[11]

Although the law governing nontraditional families is varied and complex, we have outlined below some of the major issues including the rights of unmarried couples, single parents, extended families, and other household groupings. For a more detailed analysis of some of these issues, readers should consult chapters 8 on adoption, 1 on child custody, and 2 on child support, and the ACLU handbook *The Rights of Single People.*

GRANDPARENTS AND OTHER RELATIVES

Do grandparents have any visitation rights?

Yes. At common law, grandparents had no rights to visitation or custody. However, since 1965, every state has enacted legislation granting grandparents the right to petition for visitation of their grandchildren under certain circumstances. Most of these statutes allow grandparents to petition for visitation only when the nuclear family has been disrupted in some way, for example, through divorce or death.[12] These states condition the grant of grandparent visitation on some triggering event because of the constitutionally mandated assumption that courts cannot infringe on a family's freedom from government interference absent some compelling reason, such as divorce or abuse.

Nonetheless, in some states, grandparent visitation statutes are open-ended, meaning that they allow grandparents to petition for visitation even in intact families.[13] These statutes may be vulnerable to constitutional attack, since they authorize government intervention into the family without a compelling reason.[14] Tennessee's highest court struck down the state's grandparent visitation statute as violating the state constitutional right to privacy when applied to intact families.[15] On the other hand, several state courts have upheld such statutes under the federal constitution.[16]

Even when grandparents are authorized to seek visitation, it will be up to a court to decide whether it is in the grandchild's best interests.

How do courts determine whether grandparent visitation is in the best interests of the child?

After a petition for visitation is filed, unless the parents consent to a visitation schedule, courts commonly will order some kind of investigation (usually by the court's own probation department; sometimes by social workers from a local child protection agency; in a few jurisdictions, by private investigators who will be paid by the parties). This investigation frequently includes interviewing the parents, grandparents, and children. Sometimes, forensic reports will be prepared by a psychologist or psychiatrist. Ultimately, unless the parties agree to a visitation schedule, a trial will be conducted at which all parties will have a chance to offer evidence and cross-examine witnesses called by the other side.

As in more traditional custody determinations, many states have statutorily mandated certain factors that courts must consider in determining whether visitation by a grandparent is in the child's best interests.[17] In most cases, however, only one clear pattern appears to emerge from court rulings on grandparent visitation: such petitions are more likely to be granted where grandparents have had extensive prior involvement in the child's life and especially where the child has lived with the grandparents for some amount of time.[18] Indeed, in some states, prior residence with the grandparents for a specified length of time (usually six months) is one of the triggers allowing a grandparent to petition for visitation in the first place.[19]

Moreover, different jurisdictions disagree on how to allocate the burden of proof on this issue: some require the grandparents seeking visitation to prove that such visitation would be in the child's best interest, while others require that parents opposing visitation prove that it would *not* be in the best interests of the child. Several commentators have argued that court-ordered grandparent visitation in an intact family represents a sufficiently significant diminution of parental rights to require placing the burden of proof that visitation is in the child's best interests on the grandparents.[20] However, courts have not always agreed. It appears that courts allocate this important burden of proof depending on the view the court takes of the role of grandparents. These views can vary dramatically. For example, the Missouri Supreme Court, in upholding a grandparent visitation statute, observed that "[the fact t]hat grandparents and grandchildren normally have a special bond cannot be denied."[21] The Tennessee Supreme Court, in striking down a grandparent visitation statute, expressly rejected this logic: "[W]e also seek to avoid the unquestioning judicial assumption that grandparent-grandchild relationships always benefit children, an assumption that overlooks the necessity of a threshold finding of harm before the state can intervene in the parent-child relationship."[22]

What rights do parents have when grandparents file visitation petitions?

Parents are normally granted broad discretion in deciding how to raise their children. State intervention is generally not permitted unless it is shown that some harm will come to one or more of the family members absent such intervention. When a court hears a petition for grandparent visitation, it is by definition considering an infringement on the parents' otherwise broad right to control their children's upbringing. For this reason, parents must be given an opportunity to oppose the grandparent visitation request. However, as discussed above, not all states place on the grandparents the burden of proving such visitation is in the child's best interests.

Do grandparents have a right to be notified that a petition for the adoption of their grandchild has been filed with a court?

Perhaps, at least in some circumstances. In most states, grandparents are not entitled to notice that a proceeding has been commenced for the adoption of their grandchild. However, the failure to give grandparents notice of such actions may violate the grandparents' constitutional rights to due process of law. In one Florida case, for example, an unmarried mother and her child had lived with the mother's parents, but the mother was killed in a car accident when the child was two years old. The grandparents continued to raise the child for another year and a half when the child's aunt sought and won custody of the child. Shortly thereafter the aunt filed a petition to adopt without notifying the grandparents. The grandparents first learned of the adoption after a court allowed the aunt to adopt. The grandparents sought to have the adoption voided because they did not have notice or an opportunity to participate in the proceeding. The Florida court agreed that the grandparents' constitutional rights to notice had been violated.[23]

Can biological grandparents seek visitation of children who have been adopted?

It depends. In most states, the rights of the child's biological grandparents do not survive an adoption. Almost invariably, when a child is adopted, the biological parents no longer have any rights in relation to the child. Most jurisdictions do not allow grandparents to seek court-ordered visitation once their own child's parental rights have been severed. Even in those states that give grandparents postadoption visitation rights,[24] most allow them to seek court-ordered visitation only when the child is adopted by another family member.[25]

When children are adopted by parents who are not biologically related to them, public policy in most states prefers that the new family be unencumbered by demands of so-called outsiders—even the children's biological grandparents—for access to the children. This reflects the further goal of giving adoptive families the same rights and responsibilities that biological families have. To accomplish this, the law commonly severs all ties between the adopted child and his or her biological family.[26] This means not only that grandparents through the adoptive relationship (the parents of the adoptive parents) have visitation rights but that they are usually the only sets of grandparents with these rights.

On the other hand, a minority of jurisdictions reason that the adoptive family relationship **is** different from a biological one in that a child does have extra sets of grandparents and may have had a strong relationship with biological grandparents before the adoption. This may be especially true for certain older foster children who are adopted by their foster parents or others. For this reason, these states permit greater intervention by the state into the privacy of the family in order to protect the child's emotional ties to certain members of their extended family.[27] For a further discussion of this issue, see chapter 8.

Can grandparents be required to provide child support?

Generally not. Traditionally, grandparents were not responsible for child support. Some states, however, have made grandparents and other relatives responsible for family members who become indigent.[28] In addition, where grandparents begin taking care of a child as if they were the child's parents, they may be held responsible for his or her support.[29] However, some courts have held that this obligation may be terminated at any time, provided the grandparents have not been appointed the legal guardians.[30]

Several recent welfare proposals at both the state and federal level have added a new twist to grandparent support obligations. Aimed at unwed minor parents, these proposals would require that mothers under twenty-one live with their parents in order to be eligible for Aid to Families with Dependent Children (AFDC).[31] Under existing AFDC law, the income of grandparents living in the same household as the recipient must be taken into account for purposes of determining eligibility and setting the grant level. Under these new proposals, grandparent income of all women under twenty-one receiving AFDC would in effect be deemed to the recipient, creating a de facto federal grandparent support obligation for poor families.[32]

Can other relatives seek visitation of children?

No, in the vast majority of states. Some states, however, including California and Connecticut, allow any interested parties (whether they are relatives or not) to seek visitation of children.[33] Courts have generally allowed such visitation only in cases where the child had previously lived with the person seeking visitation.[34] In many cases, however, courts have rejected requests for visitation, even by persons who had powerful claims that the child's best interests would be served by ordering such visitation, by concluding that the legislature had not given them standing to make visitation requests.[35]

Do family members have any duty of support towards parents and grandparents?

Absent a specific state statutory provision imposing such an obligation, no. However, several states have adopted such provisions, either imposing a general duty of support on close relatives of indigents[36] or, more commonly, rendering family members liable to the state for any public assistance paid to indigents.[37] These statutes have generally been upheld against constitutional challenges.[38]

SINGLE-PARENT FAMILIES

An increasing number of children are born to and raised by a single parent who has never been married. In some cases, both parents live together without marriage either by choice or because, as homosexuals, they cannot be legally married. The issues for couples and families in those situations are discussed both below in the section on unmarried couples and more extensively in chapter 10. Here we focus on the particular concerns of single parents, as well as the legal issues concerning out-of-wedlock births.

Are children born to unmarried parents still considered "illegitimate"?

Many states still have statutes that distinguish between "illegitimate" children—children born to unwed parents—and "legitimate" children—those born to married couples. The Supreme Court of the United States has held that classifications based on out-of-wedlock birth are subject to "intermediate" scrutiny, requiring the government to show that the classification is "substantially related to an important governmental objective."[39] This heightened scrutiny is required to prevent discrimination against children on the basis of the circumstances of their birth—a fact over which they have no control and for which they should not be held responsible.[40]

Laws that have withstood constitutional challenge include intestate succession laws that subordinate the inheritance rights of acknowledged out-of-wedlock children to those of other relatives[41] and immigration classifications excluding the relationship between an out-of-wedlock child and his or her biological father from the statutory definition of parent-child relationship.[42] On the other hand, states cannot completely bar children born out-of-wedlock from inheriting from their biological fathers[43] or from bringing wrongful death actions on behalf of their mothers.[44] From these and other cases, it seems that laws discriminating against children born out-of-wedlock are valid if they are narrowly tailored to avoid the risk of false claims of a father-child relationship and if any presumption against paternity is rebuttable.

Can children born out-of-wedlock become "legitimate"?

Yes. The harsh effects of most anti-illegitimacy laws can be mitigated in every state by the father's acknowledgement of paternity, by the biological parents' subsequent marriage, or both. In some states, if a child's custodial parent remarries and the new spouse adopts the child, the child will be considered the "natural" child of that marriage. In addition, most states have established a rebuttable presumption that children born to a married couple are the offspring of the mother's husband, regardless of the child's biological parentage.[45]

Can children born out-of-wedlock inherit from their parents?

In most states, yes. Children born out-of-wedlock can always inherit from their mothers and cannot constitutionally be completely barred from inheritance from their fathers.[46] However, states can establish procedures designed to establish paternity definitively, including presumptions that children are the offspring of their mother's husband, as long as there is a meaningful procedure whereby children can rebut that presumption. In addition, states can subordinate the inheritance rights of children born out-of-wedlock to those born during their parents' marriage.[47]

Do unwed fathers have any rights to custody or visitation?

Yes. If a noncustodial father acknowledges paternity, he has the right to petition for visitation or custody. As in postdivorce cases, courts make the custody or visitation determination based on the best interests of the child.

What are the child support obligations of unwed fathers?

All fathers—married or not—are presumed liable for the support of their children, once paternity has been established. (See chapter 6.)

Can the government deny welfare benefits to unmarried parents?

No. Children, not their parents, are considered the beneficiaries of AFDC (Aid to Families with Dependent Children) payments; consequently, to deny benefits to the child based on her parent's marital status is tantamount to unconstitutional discrimination on the basis of out-of-wedlock birth and is therefore prohibited.[48]

Nonetheless, recent proposals in Congress and state legislatures have sought to reduce or eliminate welfare payments to unmarried parents under twenty-one and their children.[49] As of this writing, it remains unclear whether any such proposals will become law; if they do, it is very likely these laws will be the subject of constitutional challenge in courts over the next several years.

Can an unmarried mother receiving AFDC be required to reveal the name of the child's father?

Yes. Federal law requires states participating in the AFDC program to take certain steps to find the father of any child on behalf of whom benefits are paid, to assist in establishing paternity, and to collect child support.[50] Mothers receiving AFDC for their children are required, pursuant to the federal provisions, to assist in these efforts as a condition for the receipt of benefits. Fathers of children receiving AFDC must make their support payments directly to the state, which then calculates the amount of the award due the family.[51]

UNMARRIED COUPLES

This section briefly covers some of the key issues for unmarried heterosexual couples. Many of these couples' concerns are covered more substantially in other chapters of this book, particularly in chapters 2 and 11. While some of the information below is relevant to both straight and gay couples, the latter should refer to chapter 10. A more detailed treatment of the issues touched upon below can be found in the ACLU handbook *The Rights of Single People*.

Is cohabitation by unmarried partners legal?

Generally, yes. Although twelve states retain prohibitions against cohabitation in their criminal codes,[52] these laws are seldom enforced.[53] Similarly, rarely enforced laws against fornication—sexual intercourse between heterosexuals who are not married to one another—are still on the books in several states.[54]

Even though these laws are not usually enforced, their existence sometimes influences judges in civil cases regarding unmarried partners. For example, a parent's cohabitation has been held to preclude an award of custody because it would not be in the best interests of the child to be exposed to such blatant illegality.[55] This, however, is no longer the view of most courts. For a full discussion of this issue, see chapter 1.

Is there any legal protection from discrimination against unmarried cohabitants?

The federal Constitution does not offer any special protection to persons based on their marital status. Rather, laws that discriminate against unmarried people are granted only a "rational basis" review. This means that if the discrimination is rationally related to any legitimate government purpose, the law will be upheld. Thus, for example, the Supreme Court has held that zoning laws prohibiting occupancy by unrelated persons are constitutional.[56] Some state courts, however, have held that their constitutions are more protective than the federal counterpart and have invalidated such practices.[57]

Several states have laws expressly prohibiting discrimination based on marital status in housing, employment, public accommodations, and other areas.[58] Unfortunately, these laws are inconsistently enforced. This inconsistency stems from a central contradiction: because the legal benefits attending marriage are themselves created by the government, the state finds itself in the awkward position of both practicing discrimination in favor of marriage and prohibiting discrimination on the basis of marital status.

In private discrimination cases, this contradiction is reflected in the courts' ambivalent treatment of marital status claims. For example, in housing, courts have split on whether antidiscrimination statutes prohibit landlords from refusing to rent to unmarried couples.[59] In one particularly tortured opinion, the court held that while unmarried individuals and married couples have a "marital status" (single and married, respectively), unmarried couples do not, and therefore discrimination against them cannot be based on that status.[60]

Can unmarried cohabitants be required to make contributions to offset one member's welfare grant?

No. Under federal welfare laws, if an individual is not actually contributing to the support of his cohabiting partner's child, his income cannot be considered as an offset in determining the family's grant level or eligibility.[61] This is because the cohabitant has no legally enforceable duty to support the child. However, welfare officials do take into account actual resources available to the child; thus if the cohabitant does in fact contribute support to the child, that amount will offset the grant.

The federal food stamps program works a little differently. The Supreme Court in 1973 held that for purposes of determining eligibility, the term *household* cannot exclude households of unrelated persons.[62] As a result, the subsequently amended federal statute requires consideration of the resources available to all members of the household in determining eligibility for the program.[63]

Can unmarried heterosexual couples take advantage of domestic partnership laws and policies?

Generally, yes. Most domestic partnership ordinances in fact allow for any two-person group to register as partners, once they have met certain requirements. For example, in San Francisco, domestic partners are defined as "two adults who have chosen to share one another's lives in an intimate and committed relationship of mutual caring, who live together, and who have agreed to be jointly responsible for basic living expenses."[64] Indeed, employers with domestic partnership policies have found that far more heterosexual than homosexual couples take advantage of the programs.[65]

Where domestic partnership policies in local governments or private companies provide benefits such as health insurance to the partners of employees, however, these benefits are sometimes only offered to gay couples. Companies reason that unmarried heterosexual couples have the option of marriage in order to qualify for the same benefits. Moreover, companies have financial incentives for restricting the availability of health insurance to unmarried heterosexual couples, since married partners receive these benefits at less cost.

Can single people and unmarried couples adopt?

Yes. Single people are expressly entitled to adopt by statutory provisions in every state. Similarly, no state prohibits adoption by unmarried cohabitants. However, judges and adoption agencies can make it more difficult for unmarried persons to adopt by giving greater priority to traditional married couples. In addition, a minority of courts remain reluctant to place children in family situations they deem immoral.[66] Often, only so-called hard-to-place children will be made available for adoption by unmarried individuals or couples.

In some states, a cohabitant may also adopt the children of her partner without marriage. Second-parent adoption grants the adoptor full parental rights and responsibilities, without terminating the rights of the biological parent. While courts have traditionally been reluctant to approve such adoptions, the more recent trend is to recognize second-parent adoptions. For a further discussion, see chapter 8.

Can a person lose custody of his or her child because he or she is cohabiting?

Yes. Ordinarily courts cannot remove a child from the parents' home absent a showing of actual neglect or harm to the child. However, the question of a parent's nonneglectful behavior may well arise when a court already has jurisdiction over the child's custody, as in postdivorce situations. In such cases, some judges have concluded that a parent's cohabitation with a nonmarital partner is not in the best interests of the child.

An increasing number of statutes and judicial opinions, however, mandate that cohabitation by a parent be considered legally irrelevant to the best-interests analysis, absent a showing of actual harm to the child.[67] This trend will likely increase in the future. As more couples raise children together without the legal sanction of marriage, fewer courts are likely to find such families detrimental to a child's best interests. So while some judges have held that cohabitation is evidence of an immoral and therefore improper setting in which to raise children,[68] other courts have held that cohabitation is only one of several factors to be taken into account in assessing the best interests of the child.[69] For a full discussion of this issue, see chapter 1.

Can a court place conditions regarding cohabitation on custody or visitation?

Yes. Indeed, some courts have placed express conditions on grants of custody forbidding overnight guests during visitation or custody periods.[70] At least one court has gone so far as to condition custody on the mother's either marrying or abandoning her lover.[71] On the other hand, various appellate courts have overturned such restrictions, finding them overbroad, difficult to enforce, or unrelated to any potential or actual harm to the child.[72]

Do former cohabitants have visitation or custody rights in children raised together?

Generally no, absent formal adoption or proof of paternity. Courts have most often found that persons unrelated to the child have no standing under state laws to petition for custody regardless of their prior involvement with the child's upbringing.[73]

Can unmarried partners own property together?

Yes. Unmarried and unrelated persons often own property together. Unmarried couples can own property either as *joint tenants with rights of survivorship* or as *tenants in common. Joint tenants* have equal undivided shares in the property. When one dies, the property passes to the other tenant, and does not pass to the deceased's heirs. *Tenants in common* own agreed upon shares of the property, which need not be equal. If one dies, his or her portion passes to the heirs or his or her estate, with none going to the other tenant. In every state, the law assumes that co-owners are tenants in common, unless the title provides specifically otherwise, in carefully drawn language. Unmarried partners seeking to own property as joint tenants should consult an attorney.

Can an unmarried couple enter into an enforceable contract setting forth their financial obligations toward each other?

Traditionally, courts have been reluctant to recognize agreements between unmarried persons that try to replicate the financial relationship that marriage entails, suggesting that such agreements undermine support for marriage. Some judges have gone so far as to compare such agreements to prostitution, since they can be interpreted to formalize a scheme whereby sex is exchanged for financial or material benefits.

In a well-known 1976 case, *Marvin v. Marvin*, the California Supreme Court made a dramatic departure from prior judicial convention and implied a contract of mutual support between two unmarried heterosexuals.[74] The Court indicated that only where an agreement explicitly relied solely on an exchange of sexual services would it be unenforceable. Moreover, an enforceable agreement for support need not be written but can be implied from the surrounding circumstances.

Since then, the courts in almost every state have had occasion to decide similar cases. Courts in most states have explicitly adopted the rationale of *Marvin,* and regularly entertain so-called palimony suits.[75] Only three states —Georgia, Illinois, and Tennessee—refuse to enforce contracts between unmarried cohabitants.[76] Most states will recognize express contracts, as long as sexual relations are not considered an indispensable part of the contract.[77] Some will imply such contracts after the fact from the surrounding circumstances,[78] although most choose not to do so in order to avoid fraud or because they believe that services performed by one cohabitant for the benefit of the other should be presumed to be gratuitous in the absence of contrary evidence.[79]

Unmarried couples wishing to protect their interests should draw up a contract, with or without a lawyer. To be safe, such contracts should make no mention of sexual relations.

Can an unmarried cohabitant inherit from his or her partner without a will?

No. When a person dies without a will, the estate is distributed according to the laws of the state where the decedent last had a permanent residence. These laws generally provide for distribution of various shares to spouses, children, parents, siblings, and more distant relatives, with any remainder going to the state.

Can an unmarried cohabitant recover damages for the negligent injuries to (or wrongful death of) his or her partner?

Probably not. Generally, only close relatives and spouses are entitled to recover damages for the death or injury of another person. *Loss of consortium* and other tort remedies normally available to spouses have only rarely been extended to cohabitants and then with conflicting results.[80]

HOUSEMATES, ROOMMATES, AND OTHER UNRELATED HOUSEHOLDS

What rights and obligations do housemates, roommates, and other unrelated members of the same household have with regard to one another?

Generally speaking, none. Although contractual duties may arise out of explicit lease and sublease arrangements or from specific agreements among members, absent these express provisions, unrelated household members have no duties of support toward one another. In addition, roommates have no rights to make emergency medical decisions for one another absent an explicit directive executed in advance.

There is one important exception to this general rule. On applications for food stamps, the income of all household members will be considered in determining eligibility for the program, provided they share meals together.[81]

Can a landlord refuse to rent to unmarried groups of people?

There is no constitutional bar to such discrimination. Indeed, the Supreme Court has held that municipalities may, through zoning laws, restrict housing in certain areas to families.[82] Nonetheless, in several cases, courts have found that statutes barring discrimination based on marital status protect potential housemates from refusal or eviction by landlords.[83] As noted above, however, because of the somewhat erratic application of the marital status statutes, some cases have held that such practices do not constitute discrimination.[84]

Notes

1. *Moore v. City of East Cleveland,* 431 U.S. 494, 504 (1977).
2. Barbara Vobejda, *Welfare Tie to Out-of-Wedlock Births Questioned,* Washington Post, January 21, 1995, at A6.
3. U.S. Dept. of Commerce, *Statistical Abstract of the United States* 66, 67 (114th ed. 1994).
4. Id. at 56.
5. Wetzel, *American Families: 75 Years of Change,* Monthly Labor Rev., March 1990, at 11–12.
6. *Abstract, supra* note 3, at 68.
7. *United States Dept. of Agriculture v. Moreno,* 413 U.S. 528 (1973).
8. *Village of Belle Terre v. Boraas,* 416 U.S. 1 (1974).
9. *See* Kris Franklin, *"A Family Like Any Other Family": Alternative Methods of Defining Family in Law,* 18 N.Y.U. Rev. L. & Soc. Change 1027, 1057 (1991).
10. 74 N.Y.2d 201, 543 N.E.2d 49, 544 N.Y.S.2d 784 (1989).
11. Id. at 53–54, 55.
12. *See, e.g.,* Ala. Code § 30-3-4 (1983), Alaska Stat. § 25.24.150 (1983), Ariz. Rev. Stat. Ann. § 25-337.01 (Supp. 1984), Ark. Code Ann. § 9-18-103 (1993), Cal. Fam. Code § 3103 (Deering 1994), Colo. Rev. Stat. § 19-1-117 (1994), Fla. Stat. Ann. § 752.01(1) (1993), Ga. Code Ann. § 19-7-3 (1994), Haw. Rev. Stat. § 571-46.3 (1994), 750 ILCS 5/607 (Ill. 1994), Iowa Code Ann. § 589.35 (1993), Ky. Rev. Stat. Ann. § 405.021 (Baldwin 1994), Me. Rev. Stat. tit. 19 §§ 1001 *et seq.* (1994).
13. *See, e.g.,* Conn. Gen. Stat. Ann. § 46b-59 (1992), Del. Code Ann. tit. 10, § 944(7) (1993), Idaho Code § 32-719 (1994).
14. *See, e.g.,* Michael J. Minerva, Jr., *Grandparent Visitation: The Parental Privacy Right to Raise their "Bundle of Joy",* 18 Fla. St. U. L. Rev. 533 (1991); Judith L. Shandling, *The Constitutional Constraints on Grandparents' Visitation Statutes,* 86 Colum. L. Rev. 118 (1986).
15. *Hawk v. Hawk,* 855 S.W.2d 573 (Tenn. 1993).
16. *Herndon v. Tuhey,* 857 S.W.2d 203 (Mo. 1993) (upholding grandparent visitation statute under federal constitutional "undue burden" standard); *King v. King,* 828 S.W.2d 630 (Ky.), *cert. denied,* 113 S. Ct. 378 (1992). *See also Spradling v. Harris,* 13 Kan. App. 2d 595, 778 P.2d 365, *review denied,* 245 Kan. 786 (1989) (upholding grandparent visitation under the federal constitution).
17. *See, e.g.,* Ariz. Rev. Stat. § 25-332 (1994); Cal. Fam. Code § 3011 (1994).
18. *See* Annotation, *Grandparents' Visitation Rights,* 90 A.L.R. 3d 222, and cases collected therein.

19. *See, e.g.,* Kan. Stat. Ann. § 38-129 (1994); N.M. Stat. Ann. § 40-9-2 (1994); W. Va. Code § 48-2B-5 (1994); Wyo. Stat. § 20-7-101 (1994).

20. Minerva, *supra* note 14, at 533–34 (arguing that grandparent visitation represents a substantial "stick" in the "bundle" of rights encompassing parental rights).

21. *Herndon v. Tuhey, supra* note 16, at 210 (quoting *King v. King, supra* note 16, at 632).

22. *Hawk v. Hawk, supra* note 15, at 581 (citations and quotations omitted).

23. *In re Adoption of a Minor Child,* 593 So. 2d 185 (Fla. 1991). *See also In re Interest of Brandon,* 179 Wis. 114, 507 N.W.2d 94 (1993); *In re Steven C.,* 169 Wis. 727, 486 N.W.2d 572 (Wis. App. 1992).

24. *See, e.g.,* Alaska Stat. § 25.24.150 (1993); *but see* Ga. Code Ann. § 19-8-14 (prohibiting postadoption visitation).

25. *See, e.g.,* Ala. Code § 26-10A-30 (1994); Ga. Code Ann. § 19-7-3 (1994).

26. *See, e.g., In Interest of Johnson,* 210 Kan. 828, 504 P.2d 217 (1972).

27. *See, e.g., In re Guardianship and Conservatorship of Ankeney,* 360 N.W.2d 733 (Iowa 1985).

28. *See* La. Civ. Code Ann. art. 229 (1994) (providing for support by grandparents where child cannot obtain basic necessities by any other means); *but see* Cal. Fam. Code § 3930 (1994) (prohibiting duty of support); Ky. Rev. Stat. Ann. § 405.021 (Baldwin 1994) (providing no support obligation if no visitation rights).

29. *See Franklin v. Franklin,* 75 Ariz. 151, 253 P.2d 337 (1953); *Austin v. Austin,* 147 Neb. 107, 22 N.W.2d 560 (1946).

30. *See Lipscomb v. Lipscomb,* 1993 Ala. Civ. App. LEXIS 474 (1993).

31. *See* Jason DeParle, *The 1994 Election: Issues; Momentum Builds for Cutting Back Welfare System,* N.Y. Times, Nov. 13, 1994, at 1.

32. 42 U.S.C. § 602(a)(39).

33. Cal. Fam. Code § 3040 (1994), Conn. Gen. Stat. § 46b-59 (1992).

34. *See, e.g., Gotz v. Gotz,* 274 Wis. 472, 80 N.W.2d 359 (1957) (aunts allowed to visit where estranged mother was too ill to visit, over husband's objection); *Rogers v. Trent,* 594 A.2d 32 (Del. Super. 1991) (great uncle and aunt allowed visitation where they had raised child for some part of his life); *Recknagel v. Roberts,* 465 So. 2d 844 (La. App. 1985), *writ denied,* 468 So. 2d 570 (1985) (grandmother, aunt, and uncle granted visitation where child had longstanding and close relationship with them); *L. v. G.,* 203 N.J. Super. 385, 497 A.2d 215 (1985) (adult siblings allowed visitation of minor child); *State ex rel. Noonan v. Noonan,* 145 Misc. 2d 638, 547 N.Y.S.2d 525 (N.Y. Sup. 1989) (half-sibling visitation allowed). *See generally Annotation, Visitation Rights of Persons Other Than Natural Parents or Grandparents,* 1 A.L.R. 4th 1270 (1993).

35. *See, e.g., People ex rel. Scalise v. Naccari,* 281 A.D. 741, 118 N.Y.S.2d 90 (1st Dep't 1953); *Acker v. Barnes,* 33 N.C. App. 750, 236 S.E.2d 715, *review denied,* 238 S.E.2d 149 (1977); *Wick v. Wick,* 266 Pa. Super. 104, 403 A.2d 115 (1979); *Ryan v. De Mello,* 116 R.I. 264, 354 A.2d 734 (1976); *Chavers v. Hammac,* 568 So. 2d 1252 (Ala. Civ. App. 1990) (finding that great-grandparent did not come within the grandparent visitation statute); *Huffman v Grob,* 172 Cal. App. 3d 1153, 218 Cal. Rptr. 659 (2d Dist. 1985).

36. *See, e.g.,* La. Civ. Code Ann. art. 229 (1993).

37. *See, e.g.,* Mass. Gen. L. ch. 273 § 20 (1994); Nev. Rev. Stat. § 422.320 (1973); Or. Rev. Stat. § 416.06 (1993); *but see* Cal. Fam. Code § 3930 (1994).

38. *See generally* Gregory G. Sarno, Annotation, *Constitutionality of Statutory Provision Requiring Reimbursement of Public by Child for Financial Assistance to Aged Parents,* 75 A.L.R. 3d 1159, and cases cited therein. *But see Swoap v. Superior Court of Sacramento Cty.,* 10 Cal. 3d 490, 516 P.2d 840 (1973) (striking California's then existing reimbursement requirement).

39. *Clark v. Jeter,* 486 U.S. 456 (1988); *Pickett v. Brown,* 462 U.S. 1 (1983).

40. *See Weber v. Aetna Casualty & Surety Co.,* 406 U.S. 164, 175 (1972).

41. *Labine v. Vincent,* 401 U.S. 532 (1971).

42. *Fiallo v. Bell,* 430 U.S. 787 (1977).

43. *Trimble v. Gordon,* 430 U.S. 762 (1977).

44. *Levy v. Louisiana,* 391 U.S. 68 (1968).

45. *See Michael H. v. Gerald D.,* 491 U.S. 110 (1989).

46. *Trimble v. Gordon,* 430 U.S. 762 (1977).

47. *Labine v. Vincent,* 401 U.S. 532 (1971).

48. *New Jersey Welfare Rights Organization v. Cahill,* 411 U.S. 619 (1973).

49. *See* Jason DeParle, *The 1994 Election: Issues; Momentum Builds for Cutting Back Welfare System,* N.Y. Times, Nov. 13, 1994, at 1.

50. 42 U.S.C. § 654 (1994).

51. 42 U.S.C. § 656 (1994).

52. Ala. Code § 13A-13-2 (1994); Ariz Rev. Stat. Ann. § 13–1409 (1994); Fla. Stat. § 798.02 (1993); ILCS 5/11-8 (1994); Mich. Stat. Ann. § 750.335 (1993); Miss. Code Ann. § 97-29-1 (1993); N.M. Stat. Ann. § 30-10-2 (1994); N.C. Gen. Stat. § 14–184 (1994); N.D. Cent. Code § 12.1-20-10 (1993); S.C. Code Ann. § 16-15-60 (1993); Va. Code § 18-2-345 (1994); W. Va. Code § 61-8-4 (1994).

53. *See* Note, *Fornication, Cohabitation and the Constitution,* 77 Mich. L. Rev. 252, 254 n.8 (1978).

54. Fla. Stat. Ann. § 798.02 (1994); Ga. Code Ann. § 16-6-18 (1994); Idaho Code § 18-6603 (1994); 720 ILCS 5/11-8; Mass. Gen. Laws ch. 272 § 18 (1994); Minn. Stat. § 609.34 (1993); Miss. Code Ann. § 97-29-1 (1993); N.C. Gen. Stat. § 14–184 (1994); N.D. Cent. Code § 12.1-20-08 (1993) (where act committed in public place); S.C. Code § 16-15-60 (1993); Utah Code § 76-7-104 (1994); Va. Code § 18.2-344 (1994); W. Va. Code § 61-8-3 (1994); D.C. Code § 22-1002 (1994).

55. *See, e.g., Jarrett v. Jarrett,* 78 Ill. 2d 337, 400 N.E.2d 421, 36 Ill. Dec. 1 (1979), *cert. denied,* 449 U.S. 927 (1980).

56. *Village of Belle Terre v. Boraas, supra* note 8.

57. *See, e.g., State v. Baker,* 81 N.J. 99, 405 A.2d 368 (1979); *City of Santa Barbara v. Adamson,* 27 Cal. 3d 123, 610 P.2d 436, 164 Cal. Rptr. 529 (1980).

58. *See, e.g.,* Alaska Stat. § 18.80.210 *et seq.* (1994); Cal. Gov. Code § 12940 (1994) (employment), 12955 (housing); Colo. Rev. Stat. § 24-34-502 (1992) (housing); Conn. Gen. Stat. § 46a-64c (1992); 6 Del. Code § 4502 (1993) (public accommodations), 4601 (housing); Del. Code tit. 19 § 711 (1993) (employment); D.C. Code § 1-2515 (1994) (housing); Fla. Stat. § 760.10 (1993) (employment).

59. *Hess v. Fair Employment and Housing Com'n,* 138 Cal. App. 3d 232, 187 Cal. Rptr. 712 (1st Dist. 1982) (finding practice to be unlawful discrimination); *Swanner v. Anchorage Equal Rights Com'n,* 874 P.2d 274 (Alaska), *cert. denied,* 115 U.S. 460 (1994) (same); *but see Prince George's County v. Greenbelt Homes, Inc.,* 49 Md. App. 314, 431 A.2d 745 (1981) (developer's refusal to sell to unmarried couple not illegal discrimination); *Mister v. A.R.K. Partnership,* 197 Ill. App. 3d 105, 553 N.E.2d 1152, 143 Ill. Dec. 324 (2d Dist.), *appeal denied,* 133 Ill. 2d 559, 561 N.E.2d 694, 149 Ill. Dec. 324 (1990) (same).

60. *Prince George's County v. Greenbelt Homes, Inc., supra* note 59, at 747–48.

61. 42 U.S.C. § 602; *King v. Smith,* 392 U.S. 309 (1968).

62. *United States Dept. of Agriculture v. Moreno, supra* note 7.

63. 7 U.S.C. §§ 2012(i), 2014(d)(1994).

64. San Francisco, Cal. Admin. Code ch. 62.

65. Jennifer Steinhauer, *Increasingly, Employers Offer Benefits to All Partners,* N.Y. Times, Aug. 20, 1994, at 25.

66. *See, e.g., Jarrett v. Jarrett, supra* note 55.

67. *See, e.g., Craig v. McBride,* 639 P.2d 303 (Alaska 1982); *In re Marriage of Moore,* 35 Colo. App. 280, 531 P.2d 995 (1975); *Cleeton v. Cleeton,* 383 So. 2d 1231 (La. 1979).

68. *See, e.g., Jarrett v. Jarrett, supra* note 55.

69. *See, e.g., Ahlman v. Ahlman,* 201 Neb. 273, 267 N.W. 2d 521 (1978).

70. *See, e.g., Drum v. Drum,* 263 Pa. Super.248, 397 A.2d 1192 (1979); *Palmer v. Palmer,* 138 Vt. 412, 416 A.2d 143 (1980).

71. *Krabel v. Krabel,* 102 Ill. App. 3d 251, 429 N.E.2d 1105, 57 Ill. Dec. 831 (4th Dist. 1981).

72. *Draper v. Draper,* 7 Fam. L. Rep. (BNA) 2208 (Fla. Dist. Ct. App. 1980); *Sorace v. Sorace,* 236 Pa. Super. 42, 344 A.2d 553 (1975).

73. *See, e.g., Alison D. v. Virginia M.,* 155 A.D.2d 11, 552 N.Y.S.2d 321 (2d Dep't 1990), *aff'd,* 77 N.Y.2d 651, 572 N.E.2d 27, 569 N.Y.S.2d 586 (1991).

74. 18 Cal. 3d 660, 557 P.2d 106, 134 Cal. Rptr. 815 (1976).

75. *See, e.g., Levar v. Elkins,* 604 P.2d 602 (Alaska 1980); *Mason v. Rostad,* 476 A.2d 662 (D.C. App. 1984); *Glasgo v. Glasgo,* 410 N.E.2d 1325 (Ind. App. 1980); *Heistand v. Heistand,* 384 Mass. 20, 423 N.E.2d 313 (1981); *Carlson v. Olson,* 3 Fam. L. Rep. (BNA) 2467 (Minn. 1977); *Dominguez v. Cruz,* 91 N.M.1, 617 P.2d 1322 (N.M. App. 1980); *Morone v. Morone,* 50 N.Y.2d 481, 413 N.E.2d 1154, 429 N.Y.S.2d 592 (1980); *Beal v. Beal,* 4 Fam. L. Rep. (BNA) 2464 (Or. 1978); *In re Estate of Steffes,* 95 Wis. 2d 490, 290 N.W.2d 697 (1980).

76. *See Rehak v. Mathis,* 239 Ga. 541, 238 S.E.2d 81 (1977); *Hewitt v. Hewitt,* 77 Ill. 2d 49, 394 N.E.2d 1204, 31 Ill. Dec. 827 (1979); *Rocah v. Buttons,* 6 Fam. L. Rep. (BNA) 2355 (Tenn. Ch. Ct. 1980).

77. *See, e.g., Levar v. Elkins, supra* note 75; *Poe v. Estate of Levy,* 411 So. 2d 253 (Fla. App. 1982).

78. *See, e.g., Kozlowski v. Kozlowski,* 80 N.J. 378, 403 A.2d 902 (1979); *Beal v. Beal,* 282 Or. 115, 577 P.2d 507 (1978).

79. *See, e.g., Morone v. Morone, supra* note 75; *Carnes v. Sheldon,* 109 Mich. App. 204, 311 N.W.2d 747 (1981).

80. *Bulloch v. United States*, 487 F. Supp. 1078 (D.N.J. 1980), *disapproved by Childers v. Shannon*, 444 A.2d 1141 (N.J. Super. 1982); *Sutherland v. Auch Inter-Borough Transit Co.*, 366 F. Supp. 127 (E.D. Pa. 1973), *disapproved by Rockwell v. Liston*, 71 Pa. D. & C.2d 756 (Pa. 1975); *Butcher v. Superior Court*, 139 Cal. App.3d 58, 188 Cal. Rptr. 503 (4th Dist. 1983), *overruled by Elden v. Sheldon*, 46 Cal. 3d 267, 758 P.2d 582, 250 Cal. Rptr. 254 (1988) (citing state's strong interest in privileging marriage relationship).

81. 7 U.S.C. §§ 2012(i), 2014(d).

82. *Village of Belle Terre v. Boraas, supra* note 8.

83. *See, e.g., Zahorian v. Russell Fitt Real Estate Agency*, 62 N.J. 399, 301 A.2d 754 (1973) (landlord's refusal to rent to two female roommates was illegal discrimination); *Loveland v. Leslie*, 21 Wash. App. 84, 583 P.2d 664 (1978), *review denied*, 91 Wash. 2d 1022 (1979) (same).

84. *See, e.g., Hudson View Properties v. Weiss*, 59 N.Y.2d 733, 450 N.E.2d 234, 463 N.Y.S.2d 428 (1983).

X

Gay and Lesbian Families

L esbians and gay men have historically found the family to be a less than welcoming environment. They have often been rejected by the families they were born into and are denied almost universally legal recognition for the families they later choose to form. Yet somehow, gay men and lesbians have come together to form loving homes and communities; indeed, they often refer to other homosexuals as "family."

In the 1990s, the rest of society is slowly coming to recognize, both socially and legally, the legitimacy of gay and lesbian families. Courts in an increasing number of states have granted approval to lesbian and gay adoption, childbearing, and childrearing. And while no state has yet sanctioned same-sex marriage, that prospect no longer seems so unimaginable.

It should be noted that the concerns raised by many of the questions below are common to other types of families and are covered more extensively in other chapters of this book. Thus, for example, more in-depth coverage of adoption and child custody issues can be found in chapter 8 on adoptive families and in chapter 1 on child custody. Conversely, issues of concern to unmarried couples—straight or gay—are discussed both here and in chapter 9; interested persons are encouraged to read both.

LESBIAN AND GAY RELATIONSHIPS

Are same-sex marriages legal?

As of this writing, no state recognizes marriages between two people of the same sex. Some states have express prohibitions against same-sex marriage;[1] all states have laws governing the issuance of marriage licenses, and these often make clear that only heterosexual couples need apply.[2] Even when statutes do not expressly contain such prohibitions, gay men and lesbians who have sought marriage licenses have been consistently refused. The gay civil rights statutes of at least two states provide explicitly that they should not be construed to authorize same-sex marriage.[3]

In almost every case ever brought, courts hearing challenges to the exclusively heterosexual interpretations of facially neutral marriage statutes reached the same conclusion: marriage is for opposite-sex couples only.[4] These courts applied tautological reasoning to reach these results. They defined "marriage" as including only heterosexual relationships and then found that same-sex marriages weren't within that definition.[5]

However, in 1993, the Supreme Court of Hawaii held that the state's refusal to grant marriage licenses to same-sex couples presumptively discriminates on the basis of gender in violation of the state constitution's equal protection clause. The court remanded the case to the trial court, requiring that the government show it has a nondiscriminatory compelling state interest in enforcing its ban on same-sex marriage.[6] Interestingly, the Hawaii court's holding is based on a finding of *gender* discrimination, not sexual orientation discrimination. A plurality of the court found that the existence of a homosexual relationship between two same-sex partners was "irrelevant" to the determination of whether the parties were entitled to a marriage license.[7] The plurality stated that the crucial element of the statute is that it excludes certain individuals from a marriage license—one-half of each same-sex couple—based solely on their gender. The plurality expressly rejected the logic of previous courts that had upheld same-sex marriage bans, calling those courts' reasoning "tautological" and "circular."[8]

In response to this holding, in 1994 the Hawaii legislature passed a law declaring same-sex marriages invalid and establishing a commission to study domestic partnership benefits for gay couples.[9] The law cannot, however, override the state Supreme Court's decision on the constitutionality of the same-sex marriage ban. As this book goes to press, the remand to the trial court is still pending.

What is the significance of the bans on same-sex marriage?

Although marriage is often thought of simply as the social recognition of a couple's romantic and loving commitment to one another, it confers a number of important legal benefits. These benefits include income tax reductions that accrue to married couples filing jointly, unlimited gift and estate tax deductions available for lifetime or testamentary transfers between married partners, mutual obligations of financial support for one another, automatic inheritance rights when one partner dies without leaving a will, the right to sue for injuries to the other partner, and the right to a protected realm of private sexual activity together.

In addition, there are several societal benefits that favor married couples, including employment-related health benefits, sick and bereavement leave, survivorship rights to pension and insurance plans, and a host of offers by private companies that only benefit married couples, from frequent flyer miles to "family" discounts.

If one or more states recognize same-sex marriages, will those marriages be valid in other states?

Perhaps. As a general rule, the Full Faith and Credit Clause of the United States Constitution requires that each state recognize laws and judgments that are valid under another state's laws.[10] However, judicial precedent has carved out an exception to this principle where the judgment sought to be enforced is against the "legitimate public policy" of the second state.[11] Moreover, it is well established that a state can refuse to recognize an out-of-state marriage that is against its public policy, such as an incestuous or polygamous marriage.[12]

Thus, it is unclear whether states opposed to same-sex marriages will refuse to recognize such marriages even when they were duly entered into in another state. At least in those states that expressly prohibit same-sex marriage, or that still retain sodomy statutes,[13] it is likely that state officials will refuse to recognize these marriages.

Would same-sex marriages authorized by a state be valid under federal laws, such as income tax and immigration laws?

It is unclear. On one hand, federal tax law recognizes any marriage that is valid under the laws of the state where it was entered into.[14] On the other hand, one federal court held that even though a gay male couple obtained a valid marriage license in Colorado, the pair did not qualify as spouses for immigration purposes, relying on traditional definitions of marriage and the then-existing statutory exclusion of homosexuals from immigration to the United States.[15]

Does any legal significance attach to private same-sex commitment ceremonies?

Generally, no. Although such ceremonies are often of great meaning to the persons involved and may entail religious import, they have no legal significance. Some states prohibit the joining in marriage of persons who have not obtained a valid marriage license,[16] but there are no reported cases enforcing such statutes. Arguments that a state's refusal to recognize a religious marriage ceremony violate the Free Exercise Clause of the Constitution are likely to be unavailing. The Supreme Court has consistently held that conduct that is otherwise proscribed by a state's legitimate public policy cannot be justified on religious grounds.[17]

Is same-sex marriage recognized in any other country?

Denmark, Sweden, and the Netherlands have all granted some form of recognition to same-sex unions, but all fall short of equating such unions with heterosexual marriage. In Denmark, for example, same-sex pairs may enter "registered partnerships" that confer most of the rights of marriage except the right to adopt or to obtain joint custody of children.[18]

Would a valid foreign same-sex marriage be recognized for immigration purposes?

It is unclear. There are no reported cases on this issue, but as noted above, even "valid" United States same-sex marriages are not recognized by the Immigration and Naturalization Service.[19]

Have courts granted any other kind of legal recognition to same-sex couples?

Yes. Several courts have interpreted existing statutes to protect gay and lesbian relationships. In a celebrated 1989 case, *Braschi v. Stahl Associates Co.*,[20] New York's highest court extended the protections of New York City's rent control laws to unmarried members of the same household, including gay and lesbian partners. In *Braschi*, a gay man sought protection from eviction after the death of his lover, in whose name the lease had been held. The relevant regulation prohibited landlords from dispossessing any "member of the deceased tenant's family who has been living with the tenant."[21] New York's highest court held that, for purposes of the statute, "family" should not be construed narrowly:

> The intended protection against sudden eviction should not rest on fictitious legal distinctions or genetic history, but instead should find its foundation in the reality of family life. In the context of eviction, a more realistic, and certainly equally valid, view of a family includes two adult lifetime partners whose relationship is

long term and characterized by an emotional and financial commitment and inter-dependence.[22]

A lower New York court relied on *Braschi* in deciding that a group of gay and lesbian teachers had the right to sue the New York City Board of Education to obtain the same health insurance benefits for their partners as their heterosexual counterparts' spouses received.[23]

In California, an intermediate court upheld the determination of the California Worker's Compensation Appeals Board that a gay man was entitled to death benefits after his partner's death, provided he could show that he had been a "good faith member" of his deceased lover's household.[24]

What is domestic partnership, and what rights and responsibilities does it entail?

Over twenty-five municipalities in the United States and Canada now offer some form of *domestic partnership* registration. Under domestic partnership ordinances,[25] unmarried couples file some form of declaration confirming, for example, that they "have chosen to share one another's lives in an intimate and committed relationship of mutual caring, . . . live together, and . . . have agreed to be jointly responsible for basic living expenses incurred during the Domestic Partnership."[26] Falling well short of marriage in terms of its legal significance, domestic partnership laws range in legal consequence from a mere public registry,[27] to sick and bereavement leave on behalf of a partner,[28] to extension of health benefits to unmarried partners,[29] to legal responsibility for one another's welfare.[30]

Laws that provide for mere registration confer no rights or duties. Rather, these laws have been passed in anticipation of a future extension of benefits to registered domestic partners, as a model for private industry, or for symbolic value.[31] Several companies rely on registry under local ordinances to determine which of their employees' partners will be granted benefits.[32]

Currently, gay and lesbian municipal employees in several cities obtain certain economic benefits extended by some domestic partnership ordinances. These include health benefits and sick and bereavement leaves. The domestic partnership ordinances in four California cities include a legal obligation of joint responsibility for debts incurred for shared living expenses.[33] These provisions are intended to be enforceable by third parties against either member of the partnership, but there have yet to be any reported cases brought under the laws.

In addition, a growing number of private companies and organizations—including Apple Computer, Lotus Development Corp., Levi Strauss, Greenpeace, New York University, and the law firm of Morrison & Foerster—have begun offering "domestic partnership" benefits to their employees.[34] These policies extend the health and other fringe benefits married employees already receive to unmarried workers. Some of these policies are restricted to homosexual couples, on the grounds that heterosexuals have the option of marriage, while most offer the benefits to all employees. Generally employers have found two surprises in implementing the benefit programs: far more heterosexual couples sign up than do gay and lesbians couples, and the costs are far below previous predictions.[35]

Finally, in California, lesbian and gay couples (as well as other nontraditional families) can now register as unincorporated associations.[36] Currently, no legal benefits are known to arise from registration but proponents hope it may have important symbolic value.

Can an individual create a legal bond with his or her partner through adult adoption?

As discussed more fully in chapter 8, it is usually difficult for sexual partners to create a legal bond through adult adoption, which is designed to establish a parent-child relationship, not to legitimize a sexual one. Florida and New Hampshire explicitly bar adoption by gay men and lesbians, a restriction that likely applies to adult adoption as well.[37] Other states impose age difference or other restrictions that make adult adoption difficult in practice.[38] New York's highest court held invalid the adoption of one gay middle-aged man by his lover who was only one year older, finding such a partnership "wholly devoid of the filial relationship that is fundamental to the concept of adoption."[39] Another New York court, however, approved an adoption of one elderly woman by another.[40]

Adoption has serious and irrevocable legal consequences. Adoption automatically disinherits the parents and siblings of both the adoptor and the adoptee, should either die without a will. In the absence of a will, the adoptee would become the intestate heir to the decedent's estate.

Can a lesbian or gay couple who intend to live together enter into an enforceable contract setting forth their financial obligations toward each other?

Yes, at least in a growing number of cases. For many years, courts were reluctant to recognize agreements between heterosexual unmarried persons that try to replicate the financial relationship that marriage entails because of the perception that these agreements undermine support for marriage. In 1976 the California Supreme Court decided *Marvin v. Marvin* initiating a dramatic reversal of this trend.[41] In *Marvin,* the Court went even further than enforcing a written agreement between unmarried heterosexual domestic partners. It *implied* a contract of mutual support where no written agreement existed. Under *Marvin,* when courts find evidence that domestic partners share expenses, or "hold themselves out as husband and wife," they can require one partner to pay the other an appropriate share of the income earned during the relationship. Courts in several other states have since adopted this rationale and regularly entertain so-called palimony suits.[42]

The reasoning in these cases is equally applicable to lesbian and gay couples, and several courts in California and elsewhere have applied the *Marvin* rationale to same-sex couples.[43] In one case, the court expressly noted, "[defendant] does not assert *Marvin* is inapplicable to same-sex partners, and we see no legal basis to make a distinction."[44]

This is not to say written agreements between same-sex partners will always be enforceable. It will depend on the particular jurisdiction and the facts of the case. The *Marvin* rule has not been adopted everywhere. Even in jurisdictions where it has been, there is no guarantee that courts will apply *Marvin* to lesbian and gay relationships.[45]

Because the law on this issue is still very much in flux, both with regard to these agreements in general and specifically for lesbians and gay men, same-sex couples should contemplate undertaking other measures to safeguard their relationships as well. For example, couples may want to execute wills, trust documents, and powers of attorney and establish joint ownership of property and bank accounts. Some of these measures are discussed below, but none should be undertaken without the advice of a lawyer, accountant, or investment counselor.

Can same-sex partners undertake joint financial obligations to others?

Yes, if the third party agrees to the arrangement. Couples seeking to undertake such obligations should make clear to a resistant creditor that joint arrangements actually benefit the third party. Persons who sign leases or enter contracts together are "jointly and severally" liable, meaning that each party can be held accountable for the entire debt. For creditors, this means doubling the chance of recovery of unpaid debts. Couples should understand, however, that depending on the nature of their agreement, payment by one partner does not necessarily erase the right of the creditor to collect from the other partner.

Same-sex couples should also be aware that, as noted above, registration as domestic partners in some cities entails a legally enforceable duty to be jointly responsible for each other's debts.[46]

Can same-sex partners make medical and other decisions for one another where one has become incapacitated by illness?

In most states, yes, but only if they make adequate preparations in advance. A *power of attorney* is a legal document that delegates the authority to take certain actions on behalf of another person. A *general* power of attorney confers the authority to take virtually any action on behalf of the person conveying the power, except the authority to execute a will. A *special* power of attorney is one limited to a specific purpose or transaction, for example, to find and rent an apartment or to run certain aspects of one's business.

Generally, a power of attorney becomes invalid if the person conferring the power dies or becomes mentally incompetent. Many states, however, provide for a *durable* power of attorney, which remains effective after the person executing it becomes mentally incapacitated. In some states, a durable power of attorney *only* becomes effective when the person conferring it becomes incapacitated. Durable powers of attorney can confer decision-making authority with regard to financial and business transactions and medical treatment. In several states, persons can execute *healthcare proxies*—powers of attorney limited to decisions regarding medical care.[47]

In some states, an individual can also appoint a *conservator*, someone who will assume the affairs of a person who has been declared incompetent. In most instances, such designations are not binding in courts; nonetheless, judges generally appoint as conservator the person so designated.

Living wills can serve as useful instruments for expressing an individual's wishes with regard to medical treatment should he or she later become mentally incapacitated. Rather than conferring authority on a specific person, living wills usually embody the individual's wishes regarding termination of life support. While not always legally enforceable, courts generally grant such documents great deference.

A power of attorney should not be executed without adequate reflection, since it legally binds the person executing it. Thus the person granting the power will be legally responsible for any action taken pursuant to the authority granted. Nonetheless, it remains an important means for lesbians and gay men to ensure that their partners are authorized to make certain decisions for them in the event of incapacity or illness. Absent a power of attorney or nomination of a conservator, courts generally appoint parents or siblings rather than a lesbian or gay lover.

Can same-sex partners inherit from one another without a will?

No. When a person dies without a will, his or her estate is distributed according to the laws of the state where he or she last had a permanent residence. These laws generally provide for distribution of various shares to spouses, children, parents, siblings, and more distant relatives, with any remainder going to the state.

Is a will naming a same-sex partner as an heir subject to challenge?

Yes. Generally, a person is entitled to dispose of her property by will in any manner he or she sees fit, as long as it is not illegal or contrary to public policy.[48] Nonetheless, a will is subject to challenge by anyone who would benefit if it were invalidated: either because they were named under the final or a previous will or because, as a blood relative, they would have shared in the estate if there had been no will at all. Most will challenges focus on technical irregularities or question the circumstances under which the will was written. Courts will invalidate a will if they find the deceased was not mentally competent when the will was written or that there was undue influence or fraud when it was made.

For lesbians and gay men, the most common challenge involves a claim of *undue influence.* These challenges typically allege that the deceased was unduly influenced by the surviving partner. Undue influence is defined as physical coercion, such as threats of physical harm, or mental duress so strong as to force the testator (the person executing the will) to bend to the will of another. In alleging undue influence, challengers to a will generally claim that the named beneficiary was not a "natural object" of the testator's affection, thereby implying some more sinister motivation for the bequest. For this reason, the longer the relationship between the deceased and the beneficiary before the will was written, the more likely it will be upheld.[49] Even so, one study has found that will challenges alleging undue influence are more likely to be successful where gay men or lesbians have left property to their lovers than where heterosexuals execute similar testaments.[50]

How can same-sex partners avoid subsequent will challenges?

The short answer is, consult a lawyer. Wills are subject to highly technical legal requirements, and often a small error in the execution of a do-ityourself will kit can invalidate the entire document. Moreover, the laws regarding handwritten (also known as "holographic") wills vary significantly from state to state, with many states refusing to probate them except in very limited circumstances. An experienced attorney who has no business or personal relationship with the beneficiary can help lesbian and gay couples execute wills that are relatively immune to challenge.

In addition, lesbians and gay men drafting their wills should take steps to provide evidence that the will represents the independent choices of the testator. One of the prerequisites for establishing competence to execute a will is proof that the testator knew the extent of her estate and the so-called natural objects of her bounty (i.e., the people to whom she would "naturally" want her property to go). Therefore, either alone or in consultation with an attorney, the testator should draft a memorandum detailing all her assets and the names and identities of any relatives excluded from the will.

If the testator was ever legally married, additional problems arise. If a divorce was never finalized, the former spouse may have a right to some share of the estate, regardless of any contrary will provisions. In addition, the divorce or separation decree may require certain distributions in the will. If the testator has children, those who are not mentioned in the will may have a right to a share of the estate under the laws of several states.

Lesbians and gay men who anticipate challenges to their wills can take other steps to make such challenges more difficult. These include videotaping the will's execution, executing the will outside the presence of any beneficiaries, bequeathing at least token amounts to biological relatives, and appointing as executor a nonbeneficiary who is willing to fight to uphold the testator's intent. In addition, the will can include a disinheritance clause whereby any unsuccessful challengers to the will forfeit any bequest they would have received had they not protested the testament.

What if the couple cannot afford a lawyer?

Unfortunately, there is not a large pool of attorneys knowledgeable about these issues who offer their services for free or at low cost. However, their numbers are growing. An increasing number of legal services and legal aid offices offer some kind of assistance in will preparation. For those who do not qualify for legal services, most local bar associations have referral lists for low-cost attorneys. In addition, Lambda Legal Defense and Education Fund keeps a regionally indexed referral list of "gay-friendly" lawyers.

Lambda also provides, at low cost, a handbook on the preparation of domestic partnership papers.[51]

Can a lesbian or gay man recover damages for the negligent injuries to (or wrongful death of) his or her partner?

Generally no. Most states allow spouses and other family members to sue to recover damages for the loss of the victim's companionship and economic support. Some states also allow suits for the emotional distress of witnessing a close relative's negligent death or injury. No state, however, has yet allowed such a suit by a lesbian or gay partner.[52]

Can lesbians and gay men name their partners as beneficiaries of their life insurance policies and pension plans?

Yes. Usually, individuals can name anyone as the beneficiary of a life insurance policy or pension plan. However, some policies and some employers restrict the range of potential beneficiaries to immediate family members or dependents. In addition, fearing excessive AIDS-related claims, many life insurance companies refuse to issue policies to adult males who name other unrelated adult males as beneficiaries. Such underwriting policies may violate state laws regulating insurance and employment or prohibitions against discrimination based on marital status. As an alternative, individuals can name the insured's estate as a beneficiary, reserve the right to change the beneficiary, and subsequently do so in favor of his or her partner.

Can lesbians and gay men include their partners in their health insurance plans?

Most people obtain their health insurance through their employers and receive coverage for their spouses and children at no or reduced cost to themselves. Few employers offer such coverage to the partners of their gay and lesbian workers. In fact, many states expressly prohibit the inclusion of unrelated persons in reduced family rate health insurance policies. Challenges to this practice on discrimination grounds (since gay and lesbian workers receive a lower overall wage and benefits package than their heterosexual counterparts) have not been successful. In rejecting these challenges, courts have suggested that whatever discrimination is involved is traceable to the marriage laws themselves, not to insurance company practices.[53]

Even where state insurance regulations allow such coverage, it remains largely unavailable: as of this writing, only about 10 percent of the insurance companies in the country offer coverage of unmarried partners as part of their reduced-rate family-benefits package.[54] In addition to simple reluctance to cover persons whom the insurance companies believe to be at high risk for AIDS, there are strong economic incentives: a couple who is refused a family-benefit package must purchase two individual policies at a higher aggregate premium.

Despite these obstacles, a rapidly growing number of state and local governments and private companies (and organizations) have begun making health insurance benefits available to the partners of their gay and lesbian employees. Vermont, New York State and City, San Francisco, Berkeley, Levi Strauss, Apple Computer, New York University, the Center for Reproductive Law & Policy, and the law firm of Morrison & Foerster are among those now providing such benefits.

Unfortunately, because of the limited number of insurance companies offering such coverage, employers who choose to provide domestic partner benefits often must either self-insure (i.e., establish their own pool of insurance money available to their employees) or purchase individual policies for each partner. These alternatives needlessly raise the costs of a company's fringe benefits expenditures. There are additional income tax expenses as well: the price of health insurance premiums paid for the families of married employees is excluded from income for tax purposes. But the Internal Revenue Service has indicated that such benefits for unmarried partners will only be excluded if the unmarried couple lives in a state that recognizes common-law marriage, and the partner is financially dependent on the employee.[55] It is unclear how this would apply to gay couples whose unions are generally not accorded even common-law status.

What tax disadvantages do same-sex couples suffer?

Married couples can file joint tax returns, thereby pooling their income, deductions, credits, gains, and losses. This is especially advantageous for couples whose partners have disparate incomes, since it allows them more joint income than an unmarried couple before they shift to a higher tax bracket. Unmarried couples cannot file jointly, no matter how long they have been living together.

In addition, unmarried couples are not entitled to the unlimited marital deduction under estate tax laws. A surviving spouse is not liable for any taxes on any portion of the decedent's estate that passes to him or her, while a same-sex partner would be subject to tax on the full amount. Similarly, under federal gift tax laws, spouses can transfer assets to one another of any amount without subjecting themselves to any tax liability; same-sex couples can only transfer tax-free to one another up to $10,000 in any one year.

Can same-sex partners be refused housing available to married couples, such as married-student housing?

In most states and localities, yes. Only the District of Columbia and eight states—California, Connecticut, Hawaii, Massachusetts, Minnesota, New Jersey, Vermont, and Wisconsin—and about one hundred localities prohibit discrimination on the basis of sexual orientation, and not all of these extend to housing practices. Even those that do often exempt owner-occupied and small multiple-unit buildings from compliance. Nonetheless, an increasing number of universities are making their married student housing available to same-sex couples, including New York University Law School and Stanford University.

Do same-sex partners have any entitlement to government benefits?

Yes. The food stamp program provides benefits to any "household" whose aggregate income satisfies the financial criteria.[56] In a 1973 case, the Supreme Court held that it would be unconstitutional to limit food stamp eligibility to those households consisting solely of blood relatives, since such a limitation is unrelated to the purpose of the program—to provide food at low cost to needy persons.[57] Congress subsequently amended the statute to include all households.

Although there are no cases directly on point, it would appear that lesbian and gay parents cannot be excluded from Aid to Families with Dependent Children (AFDC) on the basis of their homosexuality. In a landmark welfare case, the Supreme Court held that the state could not discontinue AFDC benefits for an unmarried woman simply because she lived with a man.[58] The primary goal of AFDC is to provide needy children with the basic necessities of life, and this goal would be frustrated if lesbian and gay parents were excluded. In any case, there are no reported incidents of such discrimination occurring. It should be noted that in determining eligibility for benefits, the government cannot assume that unrelated persons living in the same household contribute to the support of the otherwise eligible child or children. Rather, the government must prove either a legal duty of support or that the person is actually contributing.[59]

Other government programs discriminate against unmarried couples, including same-sex pairs. Social security, veterans' benefits, and some disability insurance programs pay higher benefits to married recipients. In addition, disability and survivors' benefits are only available to the surviving spouse and children of the primary beneficiary.

LESBIAN AND GAY PARENTS

Most of the issues surrounding custody and visitation, as well as the panoply of other legal concerns regarding parenting, are largely identical for homosexual and heterosexual parents and are amply discussed in chapter 1. Here, we have focused on those concerns particular to gay and lesbian parents.

Can a gay man or lesbian be denied custody or visitation of his or her child based solely on his or her sexual orientation?

In some localities, yes. Custody determinations take place in three types of dispute: (1) between biological parents; (2) between a biological parent and a third party, often another relative; and (3) between the biological parent and the state. While the governing standard for all three types of contest is "the best interests of the child," different burdens of proof apply in different situations. Between biological parents, there is no presumption in favor of one or the other; but between a biological parent and the state or a biological parent and a third party, there is a strong presumption in favor of the biological parent. This presumption must first be overcome by a showing that the parent is unfit before any inquiry into the best interests of the child is undertaken.

These presumptions are especially important for lesbian mothers, since a significant number of custody cases involve litigation between the mother and other family members.[60] Generally, because of the presumption in favor of the biological parent, a petition based solely on the mother's lesbianism should fail.[61] However, where other "contributing" factors can be shown to exist, courts are not reluctant to divest the mother of custody.[62]

As between biological parents, the best-interests standard has proven unpredictable at best. While some states delineate the factors to be considered in making these determinations, in practice judges are granted significant discretion in awarding custody.[63] Several states have adopted an irrebuttable presumption that a parent's homosexuality renders him or her unfit for custody, regardless of prior childrearing experience, or relationship with the child.[64] The majority of states, however, require a showing that the parent's homosexuality has a substantial and identifiable negative impact on the welfare of the child.[65]

Several unfounded myths about lesbians and gay men commonly constitute the rationale for denials of custody. The most frequent is a fear of harassment by the child's peers and by the community at large.[66] Several studies have found, however, that such harassment is less frequent than the fears would suggest, and that even when it occurs, the harassment does not appear to have a negative effect on the children.[67] Moreover, in 1984 the Supreme Court of the United States held that a custody dispute between biological parents could not be decided solely in anticipation of community fears and biases.[68]

Some courts suggest that lesbians and gay men are more likely than heterosexuals to sexually abuse their children, despite a complete lack of evidence to support such allegations. Indeed, judges have even rejected out-of-hand expert testimony to the contrary.[69] These rulings are particularly troublesome because studies consistently demonstrate that child sexual abuse is overwhelmingly committed by heterosexual men.[70]

Another common fear is that children raised by lesbian or gay parents will themselves be homosexual. This concern runs counter both to empirical studies—which have found no greater proportion of gay children in gay-headed households[71]—and common sense, since the vast majority of lesbians and gay men were raised in heterosexual households.

Finally, courts rely on the existence of sodomy laws and the absence of legal recognition for gay and lesbian relationships to justify denials of custody to homosexual parents. This kind of circular reasoning only serves to perpetuate the ingrained discrimination against lesbians and gay men.

How can lesbian and gay parents fight custody challenges?

A lawyer should be contacted immediately. Unfortunately, few lawyers—even among those specializing in family law—have experience in gay and lesbian parenting issues. Local lesbian and gay organizations often have referral lists of knowledgeable lawyers in the area. In addition, several national organizations provide referrals, assistance, and information to lawyers involved in such challenges.[72] If the parent cannot afford a lawyer, some courts will appoint one, or the parent can consult a local legal aid or legal services office or other community law project that offers free or inexpensive legal advice.

As in most custody hearings, the more expert testimony presented, the better. In addition to testimony by psychologists, teachers, clergy, and relatives familiar with both the parents and the children, lesbian and gay parents should present testimony that tends to refute some of the myths outlined above. Much of the prejudice involved in gay and lesbian custody determinations is the result of ignorance. To further their cases, lesbian and gay parents should take the opportunity to educate the court.

Are lesbian and gay parents who are denied custody entitled to visitation?

Under the best-interests standard, which also applies to visitation determinations, courts weigh heavily the importance of continuing contact between the parent and child. While some courts have denied visitation because of the parent's homosexuality,[73] most have been more liberal in their visitation determinations but have in some instances imposed certain conditions such as requiring that visitation be supervised or monitored.[74]

Can a court place restrictions or conditions on the grant of custody or visitation to a lesbian or gay man?

Yes. In fact, some courts have placed quite substantial restrictions on their grants of custody or visitation to lesbian and gay parents. In some cases, parents are prohibited from cohabiting with their same-sex partners during visitation or custody periods[75] and required to keep their children from meeting "known" homosexuals.[76] Other courts, including in New York and California, have struck down such restrictions, finding them unrelated to the children's best interests.[77]

Do former partners in same-sex couples have any rights or obligations with regard to any children they raised jointly?

Generally, no. Former partners who have sought custody or visitation of children raised jointly have usually seen their petitions denied.[78] Only one court so far has granted standing to a lesbian coparent to sue to continue her relationship with the child.[79] There are no reported cases of a gay or lesbian nonbiological coparent being favored over the biological parent in a custody dispute. Similarly, no gay or lesbian nonbiological coparent has ever been found liable for child support.

In addition, the Uniform Marriage and Divorce Act, adopted in several states, disallows custody actions by third parties when the child is in the custody of its biological parent.[80] While other statutes allow a broader class of persons standing to seek custody—"any person . . . who has established emotional ties creating a child-parent relationship with a child"[81]—some courts have denied visitation even where the couple had provided for it in a written agreement.[82]

Nonetheless, lesbian and gay couples contemplating joint childrearing should formalize their intentions with regard to custody, visitation, and support in a written agreement.[83] Even though courts are not bound by such agreements, in their absence a nonbiological parent will have a difficult time proving that he or she is the psychological or functional parent of the child and therefore entitled to some continuing relationship with the child.

In addition, lesbian and gay couples should indicate their preferences for the guardianship of their children in their wills. Again, such provisions are not binding on courts, but they are likely to be persuasive. At least one court has awarded custody to a nonbiological lesbian coparent after the death of her lover, the biological mother, over the objections of the child's blood relatives.[84]

Can lesbians and gay men adopt their partners' children?

In several states, yes. The highest courts of Massachusetts, New York, Vermont, and the District of Columbia have approved the adoption of children by their parents' same-sex partners.[85] In addition, lower courts in Alaska, California, Minnesota, Oregon, and Washington have all approved second-parent adoptions in same-sex couples.[86] Second-parent adoption grants the adoptor full parental rights and responsibilities, without terminating the rights of the child's biological parent. For a full discussion of this issue, see chapter 8.

Can lesbians and gay men adopt other children?

Two states, Florida and New Hampshire, expressly prohibit adoption or foster parenting by gay men and lesbians.[87] In every other state, gay men and lesbians are theoretically on the same footing as other unmarried persons when they seek to adopt. In New York, for example, regulations expressly prohibit rejecting an adoption application based solely on the applicant's homosexuality.[88] Even where not expressly prohibited, however, some courts have rejected adoptions by lesbians and gay men.[89] In one case, an Ohio judge wrote that "the so-called 'gay lifestyle' is patently incompatible with the manifest spirit, purpose and goals of adoption."[90] Of course, those states that automatically deny custody to lesbian and gay parents would prohibit adoption as well.[91]

Nonetheless, adoptions by lesbians and gay men are not uncommon.[92] Most adoptions take place under the auspices of adoption agencies, whose workers often either do not oppose gay and lesbian parents, or who do not know the sexual orientation of potential adoptors. When the adoption is unopposed by the agency, it is unlikely to be challenged by the court.

If the question of fitness arises, the prospective parent should insist that a hearing be held on the issue. Expert psychiatric testimony should be obtained after a psychiatric evaluation of the child to determine whether the adopting parent's homosexuality would have any adverse effects on the child.

Can lesbians and gay men be foster parents?

Some states have adopted laws and regulations prohibiting gay men and lesbians from becoming foster parents.[93] In general, state agencies have been less likely to place children with gay men than with lesbians. Nonetheless, lesbian and gay men have been permitted to become foster parents in a number of states.[94]

LESBIAN AND GAY YOUTH

Can parents force their gay or lesbian child to undergo psychiatric care to "treat" his or her homosexuality?

Tragically, young gays and lesbians face substantially higher rates of verbal and physical abuse from their parents than do heterosexual children. One report found that 33 percent of lesbian and gay adolescents said they had been verbally abused and 7 percent physically abused by relatives because of their sexual orientation.[95] Given this level of abuse, it is perhaps not surprising that 26 percent of young gay men in one study reported being forced to leave home due to negative parental responses to their sexual orientation.[96] Lesbian and gay youth also face higher rates of substance abuse,[97] and attempt suicide at two to three times the rate of heterosexual adolescents.[98] Studies consistently reveal that one-fifth to one-third of all lesbian and gay adolescents attempt suicide.[99]

Unfortunately, psychiatric treatment is frequently imposed on gay youth not to assist them in coping with the confusion, rampant discrimination, and abuse they face as homosexuals and as adolescents, but rather to "cure" their "deviance."[100] Indeed, professional counseling has been described as an additional risk factor in gay teenage suicide.[101]

Generally, parents are accorded great latitude in making medical decisions for their minor children, and the Supreme Court has held that this principle extends to parents who seek to commit their child to a psychiatric facility.[102] The Court held that while minors have an important liberty interest in resisting commitment, there is a strong presumption in law that parents act in their child's best interests.

Homosexuality has not been considered a mental illness by the American Psychiatric Association since 1973, and the American Medical Association recently adopted similar guidelines.[103] Nonetheless, many mental health workers persist in attempting to "cure" gay teens, despite ample evidence demonstrating that the depression, substance abuse, and suicidal tendencies found among gay and lesbian youth can be alleviated by helping young people come to terms with their sexuality.[104] Indeed, the Diagnostic and Statistical Manual of Mental Disorders (DSM-IV) still includes categories that arguably apply to gay youth.[105] Gay teens seeking to avoid parental abuse or forced treatment may have to consider taking steps towards emancipation.

Can high schools prohibit or refuse to sponsor gay and lesbian organizations?

No. If a federally funded public high school sponsors other student organizations—by giving them space to hold meetings, use of copy machines, or other types of support—the school is prohibited by federal law from discriminating against other students who wish to have meetings based on the "religious, political, philosophical or other content" of their speech.[106] Even without the statutory provision, such discrimination would be subject to challenge on First Amendment grounds.

Private schools, on the other hand, are free to prohibit such organizations, absent a local or state civil rights statute that protects persons from discrimination based on sexual orientation. Constitutional guarantees of free speech only protect individuals against government action, not against private censorship.

Do gay youth have a right to bring same-sex partners to school events?

Probably. Only one case has addressed this question: in 1980, a federal district court in Rhode Island held that a gay male high school junior could not be prevented from taking a male date to the prom.[107] The court reasoned that his act was "symbolic speech" and therefore entitled to the protection of the First Amendment.

RESOURCES

Lambda Legal Defense and Education Fund
666 Broadway, 12th Floor
New York, NY 10012
(212) 995-8585

6030 Wilshire Blvd., Suite 200
Los Angeles, CA 90036
(213) 937-2728

National Center for Lesbian Rights
870 Market Street, Suite 570
San Francisco, CA 94102
(415) 392-6257

ACLU Lesbian and Gay Rights Project
132 West 43rd Street
New York, NY 10036
(212) 944-9400, ext. 545

Hetrick-Martin Institute for Gay and Lesbian Youth
Two Astor Place
New York, NY 10003
(212) 674-2400

NOTES

1. *See, e.g.,* Md. Fam. Law Code Ann. § 2-201 (1984) ("Only a marriage between a man and a woman is valid in this State"); Tex. Fam. Code Ann. § 1.01 (1994) (providing that "[a] license may not be issued for the marriage of persons of the same sex"); Utah Code Ann. § 30-1-2 (1994) (marriage between persons of the same sex void).

2. *See, e.g.,* Cal. Fam. Code § 300 (Deering 1994)(defining marriage as "a personal relationship arising out of a civil contract between a man and a woman"); La. Civ. Code Ann. art. 86 (West 1993) (same); Minn. Stat. § 517.01 (1993) (same); Mont. Code Ann. § 40-1-103 (1990) (same); Ohio Rev Code Ann. § 3101.01 (Baldwin 1994) (male persons and female persons of requisite age may be joined in marriage). Others refer simply to "husband and wife" or "man and woman." *See, e.g.,* Colo. Rev. Stat. § 14-2-104 (1994); Ill. Comp. Stat. Ann. § 750 ILCS 5/201 (1994); Mich. Comp. Laws § 551.101 (1992); N.C. Gen. Stat. § 51-1 (1993).

3. Massachusetts and Minnesota both have the clause.

4. *See, e.g., Baker v. Nelson,* 291 Minn. 310, 191 N.W.2d 185 (1971), *appeal dismissed,* 409 U.S. 810 (1972); *Dean v. District of Columbia,* 653 A. 2d 307 (D.C. Ct. App. 1995); *Jones v. Hallahan,* 501 S.W.2d 588 (1973); *Singer v. Hara,* 11 Wash. App. 247, 522 P.2d 1187, *review denied,* 84 Wash. 2d 1008 (1974); *DeSanto v. Barnsley,* 328 Pa. Super. 181, 476 A.2d 952 (1984) (declining to recognize gay common-law marriage). *See also Anonymous v. Anonymous,* 67 Misc. 2d 982, 325 N.Y.S.2d 499 (N.Y. Sup. 1971) (granting dissolution petition of man who entered into marriage believing his partner was female).

5. *Jones v. Hallahan, supra* note 4, at 590; *see also Singer v. Hara, supra* note 4, 522 P.2d at 254–55 ("There is no analogous sexual classification involved in the instant case because appellants are not being denied entry into the marriage relationship because of their sex; rather, they are being denied entry because of the recognized definition of that relationship as one which may be entered into only by two persons who are members of the opposite sex").

6. *Baehr v. Lewin,* 74 Haw. 530, 852 P.2d 44 (1993).

7. *Id.* at 53 n.14.

8. *Id.* at 63.

9. 1994 Haw. Sess. Laws 217.

10. U.S. Const. art. IV, § 1; *Nevada v. Hall,* 440 U.S. 410, 421, *rehearing denied,* 441 U.S. 917 (1979).

11. *Nevada v. Hall, supra* note 10, at 422. *See also Pacific Employers Ins. Co. v. Indus. Accidents Comm'n,* 306 U.S. 493 (1939).

12. *See, e.g., Loughran v. Loughran,* 292 U.S. 216 (1934).

13. Twenty-three states still have criminal statutes banning sodomy. Ala. Code § 13A-6-65(a)(3) (1982); Ariz. Rev. Stat. Ann. §§ 13-1411 to 13-1412 (Supp. 1988); Ark. Stat. Ann. § 5-14-122 (1987); Fla. Stat. ch. 800.02 (1987); Ga. Code Ann. § 16-6-2 (1992); Idaho Code § 18-6605 (1987); Kan. Stat. Ann. § 21–3505 (1987); La. Rev. Stat. Ann. § 14:89 (1986); Md. Ann. Code art. 27, §§ 553–554 (1987); Mich. Comp. Laws §§ 750.158, 750.338–750.338(b) (1979); Minn. Stat. § 609.293 (1988); Miss. Code Ann. § 97-29-59 (1972); Mo. Rev. Stat. § 566.090 (1990); Mont. Code Ann. §§ 45-2-101, 45-5-505 (1987); Nev. Rev. Stat. § 201.190 (1987); N.C. Gen. Stat. § 14–177 (1986); Okla. Stat. tit. 21 § 886

(1992); R.I. Gen. Laws § 11-10-1 (1986); S.C. Code Ann. § 16-15-120 (1985); Tenn. Code Ann. § 39-2-612 (1982); Tex. Penal Code Ann. § 21.06 (1992); Utah Code Ann. § 76-5-403 (Supp. 1988); Va. Code Ann. § 18-2-361 (1988).

14. *Lee v. Commissioner*, 64 T.C. 552 (1975), *aff'd*, 550 F.2d 1201 (9th Cir. 1977).

15. *Adams v. Howerton*, 673 F.2d 1036, 1040 (9th Cir.), *cert. denied*, 458 U.S. 1111 (1982). The ban on homosexuals was repealed in 1990. Immigration Act of 1990, § 601, Pub. L. No. 101-64, 104 Stat. 4978 (Nov. 29, 1990).

16. *See, e.g.,* Miss. Code Ann. § 93-1-13 (1993); N.C. Gen. Stat. § 51-6 (1993).

17. *See Reynolds v. United States*, 98 U.S. 145 (1878) (polygamy); *Employment Div. Dep't of Human Resources of Oregon v. Smith*, 494 U.S. 872 (1990) (opium smoking).

18. *See Domestic Partnership: Issues and Legislation* § 1, at 8 (Lambda Legal Defense and Educ. Fund, Inc., Family Relationships Project, 1990).

19. *Adams v. Howerton, supra* note 15.

20. 74 N.Y.2d 201, 543 N.E.2d 49, 544 N.Y.S.2d 784 (1989).

21. N.Y.C. Rent and Eviction Regulations, 9 NYCRR 2204.6(d).

22. *Braschi v. Stahl Associates Co., supra* note 20, at 53–54.

23. *Gay Teachers Assoc. v. Board of Educ. of N.Y.*, 183 A.D.2d 478, 585 N.Y.S.2d 1016 (1st Dep't 1992). This case never went to trial, as then-Mayor David Dinkins issued an executive order granting domestic partner benefits to all city employees. Mireya Navarro, *New Choices in Care: New York Extends Health Benefits to Domestic Partners of City Employees*, N.Y. Times, Dec. 12, 1993, at B1.

24. *Donovan v. Workers' Compensation Appeals Bd.*, 138 Cal. App.3d 323, 187 Cal. Rptr. 869 (2d Dist. 1982).

25. No state has yet passed a domestic-partnership registration law, although such laws were debated in New York and Massachusetts during the 1993–94 legislative session. California's secretary of state has approved registration of families as nonprofit unincorporated associations under the state's corporations code. Such registration offers no legal or tax benefits, although it does provide for a public acknowledgement of the family's status.

26. San Francisco, Cal. Admin. Code ch. 62.

27. *See, e.g.,* Ann Arbor, Mich. Code, tit. IX, ch. 110 (1991); Ithaca, N.Y., Mun. Code ch. 7 (1990).

28. *See, e.g.,* Minneapolis, Minn., Ordinance 91-08-015 (Jan. 25, 1991); *Minnesota Domestic Partnership Plan Expands Sick, Bereavement Leave*, 29 Gov't Empl. Rel. Rep. (BNA) 131 (1991).

29. San Francisco, Cal. Admin. Code ch. 62.

30. *See id.*; *see also* Berkeley, Santa Cruz, and West Hollywood, California.

31. *See* Craig A. Bowman & Blake M. Cornish, *A More Perfect Union: A Legal and Social Analysis of Domestic Partnership Ordinances*, 92 Colum. L. Rev. 1164 (1992).

32. *Id.*

33. Berkeley, San Francisco, Santa Cruz, and West Hollywood.

34. *See* Jennifer Steinhauer, *Increasingly, Employers Offer Benefits to All Partners*, N.Y. Times, Aug. 20, 1994, at 25.

35. *Id.*

36. Tamar Lewin, *California Lets Nontraditional Families Register*, N.Y. Times, Dec. 17, 1990, at A15.

37. Fla. Stat. § 63.042(3) (1989); N.H. Rev. Stat. Ann. §§ 170-B:4, 170-F:6 (1989). The Florida law is the subject of a pending challenge, *Amer v. Johnson*, No. 92-14370 (17th Jud. Cir. filed June 1, 1992).

38. California, Connecticut, Massachusetts, and Nevada require only that the adoptor be older than the adoptee; in New Jersey, the adoptor must be ten years older, and in Puerto Rico, sixteen years older.

39. *In re Adoption of Robert Paul P.*, 63 N.Y.2d 233, 471 N.E.2d 424, 481 N.Y.S.2d 652 (1984).

40. *See, e.g., 333 East 53rd Street Associates v. Mann*, 121 A.D.2d 289, 503 N.Y.S.2d 752 (1st Dept. 1986) (allowing adoption of one elderly woman by another).

41. *Marvin v. Marvin*, 18 Cal. 3d 660, 557 P.2d 106, 134 Cal. Rptr. 815 (1976).

42. *See, e.g., Levar v. Elkins*, 604 P.2d 602 (Alaska 1980); *Mason v. Rostad*, 476 A.2d 662 (D.C. App. 1984); *Glasgo v. Glasgo*, 410 N.E.2d 1325 (Ind. App. 1980); *Heistand v. Heistand*, 384 Mass. 20, 423 N.E.2d 313 (1981); *Carlson v. Olson*, 3 Fam. L. Rep. (BNA) 2467 (Minn. 1977); *Brooks v. Kunz*, 637 S.W.2d 135 (Mo. App. 1982); *Dominguez v. Cruz*, 95 N.M. 1, 617 P.2d 1322 (N.M. App. 1980); *Morone v. Morone*, 50 N.Y.2d 481, 413 N.E.2d 1154, 429 N.Y.S.2d 592 (1980); *Beal v. Beal*, 4 Fam. L. Rep. (BNA) 2464 (Or. 1978); *In re Estate of Steffes*, 95 Wis. 2d 490, 290 N.W.2d 697 (1980). *But see Rehak v. Mathis*, 239 Ga. 541, 238 S.E.2d 81 (1977); *Hewitt v. Hewitt*, 77 Ill.2d 49, 394 N.E.2d 1204, 31 Ill. Dec. 827 (1979); *Rocah v. Buttons*, 6 Fam. L. Rep. (BNA) 2355 (Tenn. Ch. Ct. 1980), all refusing to adopt the *Marvin* approach.

43. *See, e.g., Whorton v Dillingham*, 202 Cal. App. 3d 447, 248 Cal. Rptr. 405 (4th Dist. 1988); *Richardson v. Conley*, 4 Fam. L. Rep. (BNA) 2532 (Cal. Super. Ct. 1978); *Cox v. Elwing*, 432 A.2d 736 (D.C. App. 1981); *Bramlett v. Selman*, 268 Ark. 457, 597 S.W.2d 80 (1980).

44. *Whorton v. Dillingham, supra* note 43, 248 Cal. Rptr. at 408 n.1.

45. *See, e.g., Jones v. Daly*, 122 Cal. App. 3d 500, 176 Cal. Rptr. 130 (2d Dist. 1981); *Barnett v. King*, No. C365232 (Cal. Super. Ct., L.A. County, Dec. 22, 1982); *Thornton v. Liberace*, No. C428492 (Cal. Super. Ct., L.A. County, Oct. 14, 1985).

46. Berkeley, San Francisco, Santa Cruz, and West Hollywood, California. *See* Bowman, *supra* note 31.

47. *See, e.g.,* Ark. Code Ann. § 20-17-202 (1993); Mass. Gen. L. ch. 201D, §§ 1 *et seq.* (1994).

48. *In re Estate of McBride*, No. 251 (Pa. C.P. Ct., Orphan's Ct. Div., Erie County, Sept. 20, 1984).

49. *Cf. Weekes v. Gay*, 243 Ga. 784, 256 S.E.2d 901 (1979) (finding existence of gay relationship reasonable basis on which to establish a constructive trust).

50. *See generally* Jeffrey Sherman, *Undue Influence and the Homosexual Testator*, 42 U. Pitt. L. Rev. 221 (1981).

51. Also of great assistance to practitioners is National Lawyers Guild Lesbian-Gay Rights Committee, *Sexual Orientation and the Law* (Roberta Achtenberg and Karen Moulding eds., 1993) [hereinafter *Sexual Orientation*].

52. *See, e.g., Coon v. Joseph*, 192 Cal. App. 3d 1269, 237 Cal. Rptr. 873 (1st Dist. 1987) (determining that a gay relationship was not sufficiently "close" to merit recovery for witnessing an assault against one's lover).

53. *See, e.g., Rovira v. AT&T*, 817 F. Supp. 1062 (S.D.N.Y. 1993); *Beatty v. Truck Ins. Exchange*, 6 Cal. App. 4th 1455, 8 Cal. Rptr. 2d 593 (3d Dist. 1992); *Hinman v. Dep't of Personnel Admin.*, 167 Cal. App. 3d 516, 213 Cal. Rptr. 410 (3d Dist. 1985).

54. *See* Steinhauer, *supra* note 34, at 25.

55. 1990 Lesbian/Gay Law Notes 63.

56. 7 U.S.C.A. § 2012(i), 2014 (1988 & West Supp. 1990).

57. *United States Dep't of Agriculture v. Moreno*, 413 U.S. 528 (1973).

58. *King v. Smith*, 392 U.S. 309 (1968).

59. *Lewis v. Martin*, 397 U.S. 552 (1970).

60. *Sexual Orientation, supra* note 51, at 1-12 to 1-13.

61. *See, e.g., Bottoms v. Bottoms*, 444 S.E.2d 276 (Va. App. 1994), *rev'd* 457 S.E. 2d 102 (Va. 1995).

62. *See, e.g., Bottoms v. Bottoms*, 457 S.E. 2d 102 (Va. 1995) (mother allegedly left child with grandmother for several days at a time and used "welfare funds to 'do' her fingernails before buying food for child"); *Bennett v. Clemens*, 230 Ga. 317, 196 S.E.2d 842 (1973) (mother smoked marijuana and left children with friends who had sex in front of them); *Chaffin v. Frye*, 45 Cal. App. 3d 39, 119 Cal. Rptr. 22 (2d Dist. 1975) (mother had criminal record and was unemployed and physically disabled); *Townsend v. Townsend*, 1 Fam. L. Rep. (BNA) 2831 (Ohio C.P. 1975) (mother had given media interviews and planned to raise children in home with lover); *Mathews v. Mathews*, 428 So. 2d 51 (Ala. Civ. App. 1982) (history of drug use).

63. Cases in which gay or lesbian parents prevailed include: *Conkel v. Conkel*, 31 Ohio App. 3d 169, 509 N.E.2d 983 (1987); *Stroman v. Williams*, 291 S.C. 376, 353 S.E.2d 704 (S.C. App. 1987); *S.N.E. v. R.L.B.*, 699 P.2d 875 (Alaska 1985); *Doe v. Doe*, 16 Mass. App. Ct. 499, 452 N.E.2d 293 (1983). Cases in which gay or lesbian parents lost include: *G.A. v. D.A.*, 745 S.W.2d 726 (Mo. App. 1988); *Bark v. Bark*, 479 So. 2d 42 (Ala. Civ. App. 1985); *D.H. v. J.H*, 418 N.E.2d 286 (Ind. App. 1981). *See Sexual Orientation, supra* note 51, at 1-11 to 1-12 and nn. 19–20.

64. *See Chicoine v. Chicoine*, 479 N.W.2d 891 (S.D. 1992); *Thigpen v. Carpenter*, 21 Ark. App. 194, 730 S.W.2d 510(1987); *Jacobson v. Jacobson*, 314 N.W.2d 78 (N.D. 1981); *S. v. S.*,608 S.W.2d 64 (Ky. App. 1980); *Dailey v. Dailey* 635 S.W.2d 391 (Tenn. App. 1981); *Roe v. Roe*, 228 Va. 722, 324 S.E.2d 691 (1985); *M.J.P. v. J.G.P.*, 640 P.2d 966 (Okla. 1982); *S.E.G. v. R.A.G.*, 735 S.W.2d 164 (Mo. App. 1987).

65. *S.N.E. v. R.L.B., supra* note 63; *In re Marriage of Birdsall*, 197 Cal. App. 3d 1024, 243 Cal. Rptr. 287 (4th Dist. 1988); *D.H. v. J.H.*, 418 N.E.2d 286 (Ind. App. 1981); *Bezio v. Patenaude*, 381 Mass. 563, 410 N.E.2d 1207 (1980); *DiStefano v. DiStefano*, 60 A.D.2d 976, 401 N.Y.S.2d 636 (4th Dep't 1978).

66. *See, e.g., Bottoms, supra* note 62 ("living daily under conditions stemming from active lesbianism practiced in the home may impose a burden upon a child by reason of the 'social condemnation' attached to such an arrangement.")

67. *See* Mary Hotvedt & Jane Mandel, *Children of Lesbian Mothers*, in *Homosexuality: Social, Psychological and Biological Issues* 282 (W. Paul et al. eds. 1982); Susan Golombok et al., *Children in Lesbian and Single Parent Households: Psychosexual and Psychiatric Appraisal*, 24 J. Child Psychol. and Psychiatry 551–72 (1983); Sharon Huggins, *A Comparative Study*

of Self-Esteem of Adolescent Children of Divorced Lesbian Mothers and Divorced Heterosexual Mothers, in *Homosexuality and the Family* 123–35 (Frederick Bozett ed., 1989).

68. *Palmore v. Sidoti,* 466 U.S. 429 (1984) (reversing removal of child from biological mother's home solely because she remarried a person of a different race).

69. *See, e.g., J.L.P.(H.) v. D.J.P.,* 643 S.W.2d 865 (Mo. App. 1982) (rejecting evidence that 95 percent of sexual molestation is committed by heterosexuals).

70. American Humane Association, Children's Division, *Protecting the Child Victim of Sex Crimes Committed by Adults* 216–17 (V. DeFrancis ed. 1969).

71. *See, e.g.,* Mary B. Harris & Pauline Turner, *Gay and Lesbian Parents,* 12 J. Homosexuality 101 (Winter 1985–86).

72. The National Center for Lesbian Rights (in San Francisco) and Lambda Legal Defense & Education Fund (in New York and Los Angeles) are the leaders on these issues. *See* the list of resources at the end of this chapter for additional contact information.

73. *See, e.g., Roberts v. Roberts,* 22 Ohio App. 127, 489 N.E.2d 1067 (1985).

74. *See, e.g., Miller v. Hawkins,* 549 So. 2d 102 (Ala. Civ. App. 1989); *In re Marriage of Birdsall, supra* note 65; *Stewart v. Stewart,* 521 N.E.2d 956 (Ind. App. 1988); *Irish v. Irish,* 102 Mich. App. 75, 300 N.W.2d 739 (1980).

75. *See, e.g., In re J.S.C.,* 129 N.J. Super. 486, 324 A.2d 90 (N.J. Super. Ch. 1974), *aff'd,* 142 N.J. Super. 499, 362 A.2d 54 (App. Div. 1976); *Gerde v. Butler,* No. 80-CI-2230 (Ky. Cir. Ct., Kenton County, Sept. 30, 1981).

76. *Gerde v. Butler, supra* note 75.

77. *In re Marriage of Birdsall, supra* note 65; *Gottlieb v. Gottlieb,* 108 A.D.2d 120, 488 N.Y.S.2d 180 (1st Dep't 1985).

78. *See, e.g., Alison D. v. Virginia M.,* 77 N.N.2d 651, 572 N.E.2d 27, 569 N.Y.S.2d 586 (1991); *Nancy S. v. Michele G.,* 228 Cal. App.3d 831, 279 Cal. Rptr. 212 (1st Dist. 1991); *Curiale v. Reagan,* 222 Cal. App. 3d 1597, 272 Cal. Rptr. 520 (3d Dist. 1990); *Kulla v. McNulty,* 472 N.W.2d 175 (Minn. App. 1991); *In re Z.J.H.,* 162 Wis. 2d 1002, 471 N.W.2d 202 (1991).

79. *A.C. v. C.B.,* 113 N.M. 581, 829 P.2d 660 (N.M. App.), *cert. denied,* 113 N.M. 449, 827 P.2d 837 (1992).

80. Unif. Marriage & Divorce Act § 401(d)(2), 9A U.L.A. at 550 (1987).

81. *See, e.g.,* Or. Rev. Stat. § 109.19(1) (1993).

82. *See Alison D. v. Virginia M., supra* note 78.

83. A sample written agreement can be found in *Sexual Orientation, supra* note 51, app. 1D at 1–105.

84. *In re Hatzopoulos,* 4 Fam. L. Rep. (BNA) 2075 (Colo. Juv. Ct., Denver County, 1977).

85. *In re Dana,* 660 N.E. 2d 397 (N.Y. 660 N.E. 2d 397, 1995); *In re M.M.D.,* 662 A.2d 837 (D.C. 1995); *Adoption of Tammy,* 416 Mass. 205, 619 N.E. 2d 315 (1993); *In re B.L.V.B.,* 628 A. 2d 1271 (Vt. 1993); *but see In re Angel Lace M.,* 516 N.W.2d 678 (Wis. 1994).

86. *See, e.g., In re J.M.G.,* 267 N.J. Super. 622, 632 A.2d 550 (N.J. Sup. Ch. 1993); *Matter of Camilla,* 163 Misc. 2d 272, 620 N.Y.S. 2d 897 Kings County Fam Ct. 1994); *Matter of Adoption of Evan,* 153 Misc. 2d 844, 583 N.Y.S. 2d 997 (N.Y. Sur. 1992); *but see*

In re Dana, 209 AD 2d 8, 624 N.Y.S. 2d 634 (1995), *appeal granted* 651 N.E. 2d 920 (N.Y. 1995); *see also* William B. Rubinstein, *Lesbians, Gay Men, and the Law* 536 (1993); *Sexual Orientation, supra* note 51, at 1–86, n.162.2.

 87. Fla. Stat. § 63.042(3) (1993); N.H. Rev. Stat. Ann. §§ 170-B:4, 170-F:6 (1989).

 88. *See* 18 N.Y. Comp. Codes R. & Regs. § 421.16(h)(2) (1992).

 89. *In re Adoption of Charles B.*, 1988 Ohio App. LEXIS 4435, No. CA-3382 (Oct. 28, 1988), *rev'd*, 50 Ohio St. 3d 88, 552 N.E.2d 884 (1990); *In re Appeal in Pima County Juvenile Action B-10489*, 151 Ariz. 335, 727 P.2d 830 (Ariz. App. 1986).

 90. *In re Adoption of Charles B.*, *supra* note 89.

 91. *See Sexual Orientation, supra* note 51, at 1-78 to 1-79.

 92. Note, *Developments—Sexual Orientation and the Law*, 102 Harv. L. Rev. 1508, 1643 (1989).

 93. *See, e.g.*, N.H. Rev. Stat. Ann. § 161:2 (1989); N.D. Admin. Code § 75-03-14-04(1) (1984) (restricting foster care placements to married couples).

 94. *See, e.g.*, Daniel Wise, *Lesbian Foster Mother Allowed to Adopt Child: Court Refuses to Permit "Prejudice" as Objection*, N.Y.L.J., June 21, 1993, at 1.

 95. Paul Gibson, *Gay Male and Lesbian Youth Suicide, in Report of the Secretary's Task Force on Youth Suicide* 3–110, 3–127 (U.S. Dep't. of Health and Human Services 1989).

 96. *Id.* at 3-112.

 97. *Id.* at 3-129.

 98. *Id.* at 3-110.

 99. *Id.* at 3-111.

 100. *Id.* at 3-129 through 3-130.

 101. *Id.*

 102. *Parham v. J.R.*, 442 U.S. 584 (1979).

 103. David Dunlap, *A.M.A. States New Policy on Sexuality*, N.Y. Times, Dec. 25, 1994, section 1, at 30.

 104. *See, e.g.*, A. Damien Martin & Emery S. Hetrick, *The Stigmatization of the Gay and Lesbian Adolescent*, 15 J. Homosexuality 163 (1988).

 105. *See, e.g.*, DSM-IV, 302.6-Gender Disorder in Children and 302.9-Sexual Disorder Not Otherwise Classified, (including "persistent and marked distress about sexual orientation.")

 106. 20 U.S.C. § 4071 *et seq.* (1982).

 107. *Fricke v. Lynch*, 491 F. Supp. 381 (D.R.I. 1980).

XI

Reproductive Rights

Children are central to the most common definitions of family; indeed, we tend to think of rearing children as a family's primary function. For this reason, the rights associated with choosing when and how to have children—referred to collectively as reproductive rights—are fundamental to an understanding of the legal structure of families.

In American law, the government's involvement in issues of abortion, contraception, sterilization, and pregnancy is of relatively recent origin. Only in the latter half of the nineteenth century did states and the federal government begin adopting laws regulating the availability of contraception and abortion.[1] As we near the end of the twentieth century, however, a complex and constantly evolving matrix of state and federal laws, regulations, and judicial opinions now define the rights of individuals to choose when and how to have children. This state involvement has not only insinuated the government into this most private realm of personal decision making but has also determined the rights of individuals within families to control one another's reproductive options.

This area of the law has proven itself subject to frequent and often dramatic changes, both at the state and federal levels, defying simple or lasting characterization of the rights involved. Thus, for example, it is no longer possible to state definitively that women have the right to choose abortion or that adults cannot be forced to use contraceptives or be sterilized against their will.

In addition, these legal developments are not the only determinants of the availability of reproductive options. New reproductive technologies, financial access to various options through Medicaid and insurance, the increasing harassment and violence at women's health clinics, and the level of an individual's basic health education often play far more central roles than the law in the availability of reproductive health care.

As a result, in this chapter we can do no more than provide a general lay of the land as of early 1996. To fully and intelligently understand the range of reproductive rights, continuing self-education is crucial.[2]

ABORTION

What is the status of a woman's right to an abortion?

Technically, women still have the constitutional right to obtain an abortion. This right, established originally in 1973 in *Roe v. Wade*,[3] was nominally upheld and reaffirmed in two of the Supreme Court's more recent abortion cases, *Webster v. Reproductive Health Services*[4] and *Planned Parenthood v. Casey*.[5] However, the Court's purported reaffirmation of the "essential holding of *Roe v. Wade*"[6] stands in sharp contrast with its upholding certain restrictive elements of the laws at issue in *Webster* and *Casey*.[7]

Moreover, in *Casey*, the Court formally changed the standard of review lower courts must apply when deciding the constitutionality of abortion restrictions. Previously, under the "strict scrutiny" standard established in *Roe*, virtually no restrictions on first trimester abortions were allowed.[8] According to the Court's new standard, only restrictions that place an "undue burden" on or a "substantial obstacle" in the way of a woman's access to abortion, prior to viability, will be found unconstitutional.[9]

Lower federal courts are still debating what this language means in practice. Outright bans on abortion and husband notification or consent requirements are clearly unconstitutional.[10] Restrictions that have been generally upheld in lower courts (with some exceptions) include mandatory delays, so-called informed consent provisions, prohibitions on public funding,[11] and parental notification or consent requirements (see below for more detail on each of these). However, each type of provision is currently the subject of ongoing litigation in several jurisdictions, and the Supreme Court has yet to enunciate a definitive statement as to which restrictions constitute an "undue burden." In addition, antiabortion lawmakers in most states propose new restrictions in every legislative session, each of which will likely be subject to further challenge in the courts. Finally, pro-choice advocates are increasingly challenging abortion restrictions under state constitutions in search of more rights-protective climates.

The result of all of the above is a dizzying patchwork of restrictions on the legal availability of abortion services, such that it is no longer possible to claim that there is uniform federal protection for a woman's right to choose abortion, except in the barest, most technical sense.

What are the problems with mandatory delay and so-called informed consent and laws?

Mandatory delay and "informed consent" laws are the most common type of new restriction passed by state legislatures since the Supreme Court in *Casey* approved them.[12] Eleven states—Idaho, Kansas, Louisiana, Mississippi, Nebraska, North Dakota, Ohio, Pennsylvania, South Carolina, South Dakota, and Utah—currently enforce some form of mandatory delay. These laws require that women seeking abortions receive specific information from a physician (or, in some cases, a nurse or counselor) including such things as alternatives to abortion, a description of the gestational stages of fetal development (sometimes with graphic depictions), the potential dangers of the abortion procedure to the woman, and advice that the father may be liable for child support and that state welfare funds may be available should the woman carry the pregnancy to term.[13] The laws then typically require that the woman seeking abortion services wait a specific amount of time, usually twenty-four hours,[14] before the abortion is performed. The waiting periods are expressly intended to ensure that a woman has had "adequate time" to fully reflect on her decision to undergo an abortion.[15] Violations of these provisions are usually punishable by both criminal and civil penalties.[16] It is clear, however, that these requirements have been imposed less to give women information about themselves and their pregnancies than to place obstacles in the path of women's access to abortion services.

The information that the laws require physicians give to patients is duplicative and unnecessary. General informed consent law and medical practice guidelines already require that physicians obtain voluntary and informed consent from patients before they perform *any* procedure, including abortion. States that have passed special informed consent rules specifically for abortion have done so without first finding that physicians failed to obtain informed consent from women. Indeed, there is no evidence to support such a contention.

The mandatory delay has a negative impact on women seeking abortion services. Currently, 51 percent of urban counties and 94 percent of rural counties have no abortion providers.[17] Women in many parts of the country often have to travel several hours to get to a provider and frequently must stay overnight. Moreover, providers usually perform abortions only one or two days a week; consequently, a theoretical twenty-four-hour delay can result in a week-long delay. Where laws require the initial counseling to take place in person, women must make two lengthy trips to the clinic, necessitating increased costs in lost work and related expenses. For young women and women who are further along in pregnancy, any delay increases the risk of complications from the procedure, as well as the cost. Antichoice activists have begun taking advantage of the two-visit requirement by copying down the license plate numbers of women, tracing their addresses and phone numbers, and harassing them at home about their decisions.

Can doctors be prohibited from giving certain information regarding abortion to women who seek it?

No. The First Amendment protects both the right of a private physician to give information and of a woman to receive it. The government is free, however, to limit the counseling provided in healthcare facilities that are federally funded. The Supreme Court upheld regulations promulgated by the Reagan administration that prohibited providers in federally funded family planning clinics from informing women about abortion options.[18] The Court thereby sanctioned an as yet undetermined range of conditions that the government can place on the receipt of state funding for healthcare.

Although the Clinton administration rescinded these regulations,[19] this issue is still very much of concern. As government involvement in the provision of healthcare increases, it is likely that legislators will make additional efforts to limit the availability of reproductive options through funding restrictions. Indeed, the Court's decision in *Rust v. Sullivan* essentially gives states and the federal government carte blanche to restrict any interactions between physicians and patients in government-funded facilities, not just those related to reproductive healthcare.

Prior to an abortion, can a state require the consent or notification of the woman's husband or boyfriend or of the putative father?

No. The Supreme Court in *Planned Parenthood v. Casey*[20] expressly held that a husband-notification requirement placed an undue burden on a woman's exercise of her constitutional right to choose abortion.[21] The Court reasoned that because the vast majority of women already involve the men in their lives in their childbearing decisions, the law must be considered in its application to those who do not. The Court found that a significant proportion of the latter group would be subject to abuse were they to notify their husbands of their decisions to seek abortions. For these women, the Court held that the law placed an undue burden on their access to abortion, since it would grant their abusive husbands an effective veto over their abortion choice.[22]

In addition, husband-notification or consent requirements clearly discriminate against women. A wife's consent could not be required for any medical procedure that a man underwent that might affect his reproductive capacity, including sterilization (see below) or surgery for prostate cancer. Further, pregnancy entails risks and burdens that only the woman will bear. Allowing a husband veto power over his wife's abortion would force her not only to undergo pregnancy and its attendant risks but to become a mother against her will.

The same logic would apply to a boyfriend or other unmarried putative father. The Court has repeatedly rejected attempts by unmarried partners to prevent a woman from having an abortion.[23]

Can a woman's husband or boyfriend or the putative father force a woman to have an abortion?

No. In general, no one—not the state, a doctor, a husband, or a boyfriend—can force a competent adult woman to undergo a medical procedure to which she does not consent.[24] This principle applies with additional force in the abortion context, given that the right to choose abortion itself emerges from the more basic right to make essential decisions regarding procreation.[25] Just as a woman cannot be forced to become pregnant against her will, she cannot be forced to terminate a wanted pregnancy.

Is the husband or putative father still financially responsible for a child he would have aborted?

Yes. The Uniform Parentage Act, passed in many states, explicitly adopts the general common-law rule prohibiting fathers from escaping liability for child support simply by offering to pay for an abortion. Establishment of paternity alone, through appropriate state procedures, is sufficient to determine the custodial parent's right to child support from the noncustodial parent (see chapter 1). A father may not escape this obligation by claiming that he did not want the child in the first place.

**Can the husband or putative father be held legally responsible
for paying for the abortion?**

Perhaps. A husband would be responsible for the costs of an abortion
only to the same extent that each spouse is responsible for any of the other's
medical expenses. Generally, an unmarried woman would be fully responsible for the cost of an abortion, as with any other medical procedure. However, one court in New York has held that where a woman, in deciding to
forego contraceptives, relied on her sexual partner's claim that he was sterile,
the man could be held liable for the costs of the subsequent abortion.[26]

Do poor women have the right to public funding for abortions?

The availability of public funding for abortion through programs such
as Medicaid (the federal-state medical assistance program for the poor) is
largely dependent on state law. The Supreme Court has held that neither the
federal nor state governments are required to fund abortions, even when
they fund all other medical services, including pregnancy-related services.[27]
However, under the Medicaid program, which is a joint state-federal program, states must fund all abortions for which federal funds are available.[28]
As of this writing, federal funding is available for abortions necessary to save
the life of the mother and where the pregnancy is the result of rape or incest.[29] Several states go beyond the federal mandate and fund abortions for
health reasons.[30]

Absent public funding for abortion services, low-income women simply
do not have the same access to abortion as other women. In many instances,
they are essentially prohibited from receiving an abortion, purely on financial grounds.[31] Although in practical terms this results in a two-tiered constitutional right—one for those who can afford abortions, and another for
those who cannot—the Supreme Court has held that this does not violate
the Constitution.

The abortion funding prohibition of federal Medicaid is not a permanent statutory provision. Passed anew each year in an annual appropriations
bill, it is regularly debated and subject to change more readily than many
other federal laws. On one hand this means that the availability of federal
funding for abortion services (such as it is) is on somewhat shaky ground;
on the other hand, it is an issue that is highly sensitive to pressure from
constituents and other lobbying efforts on an ongoing basis.

In the future, the issue of public funding of abortion will likely affect the healthcare of all women, not just those eligible for Medicaid. Recent congressional debate on healthcare reform has repeatedly touched on coverage for abortion services.[32] And although it is not clear whether there will ever be federal healthcare reform, there is a definite trend toward increased government involvement in the provision of healthcare. Thus the issue of abortion funding, including the judicially approved antiabortion conditions placed on recipients of federal funds,[33] is likely to remain at center stage over the next decade.

Can insurance companies refuse to provide coverage for abortion?

Yes. Insurance companies are private entities that, although heavily regulated by states, can choose those treatments for which they will provide coverage. Moreover, states can prohibit insurance companies from providing coverage for abortions altogether.[34] Indeed, the federal Pregnancy Discrimination Act expressly exempts from liability employers who refuse to provide health insurance coverage for abortion.[35] In addition, several states have attempted to require that insurance coverage for abortion be offered only in a separate, additional rider to the main policy, at an additional premium;[36] there is currently a split in the lower courts as to whether such requirements are constitutional.[37] Despite these various waivers and exemptions, over two-thirds of health plans in the United States provide coverage for abortion services.[38]

CONTRACEPTION/STERILIZATION

Do adults have the right to buy and use contraceptives?

Yes. In one of the first cases establishing a right to privacy under the federal Constitution, *Griswold v. Connecticut*,[39] the Supreme Court held that married persons have a fundamental right to make decisions regarding contraception, free of government intervention. This right was later extended to unmarried persons as well[40] and is now firmly established.

Does an individual need the consent of his or her spouse to use or not use contraceptives?

No. All individuals, including married persons, may use contraceptives without the consent or even knowledge of their partners or spouses.

Can the government force individuals to use contraceptives?

No. Individuals have the right to be free from government coercion in all facets of their reproductive decision making, including whether and when to use contraceptives.[41] However, two trends have arisen recently that threaten this basic freedom. First, in several states, legislators and other government officials have proposed cash incentives for welfare recipients who agree to use Norplant, DepoProvera, or another longlasting contraceptive method. For example, a bill proposed in Florida would have increased Aid to Families with Dependent Children (AFDC) payments to unwed mothers by as much as $150 per month if they used Norplant or DepoProvera. The same proposal would have reduced child support arrearages owed for children receiving welfare if the father obtained a vasectomy. Legislators in Colorado proposed mandatory family-planning counseling for AFDC recipients, with financial sanctions for failure to participate.

Federal law prohibits government agencies from conditioning welfare benefits on consent to sterilization but is silent with regard to contraception.[42] While none of these proposals has yet been implemented, they are being debated, and it is conceivable that such a proposal may be enacted in the near future.

The second trend involves judges around the country who have made sterilization or mandatory birth control (usually Norplant) either a condition for parole or part of a probationary sentence.[43] While these conditions have uniformly been overturned on appeal,[44] in cases where parolees do not have adequate legal advice the sentencing conditions may stand.

Is the father legally responsible for children born after contraceptives fail?

Yes. As noted above, the Uniform Parentage Act expressly mandates that adequate proof of paternity alone is sufficient to establish legal liability for child support, regardless of paternal use of contraceptives. (See chapter 9).

Is public funding available for contraceptives?

Generally, yes. Medicaid, Title X of the Public Health Service Act, and two federal block grant programs all provide federal funding for family planning services. Medicaid, the federal-state medical assistance program for the poor, makes "family planning services" a mandatory category of care, meaning that family planning services, including contraception, must be included in all state plans.[45]

However, the availability of Norplant as a publicly funded contraceptive has raised new legal issues. Several states, while providing funding for Norplant *insertion*, fail to reimburse the costs of *removal*.[46] Consequently, poor women who later change their minds about using Norplant are effectively forced to continue to use contraception against their will. In any case, Norplant must be removed approximately five years after its insertion. If it is not removed, a woman may suffer side effects, including infection, irregular bleeding, headaches, and weight gain.

Can individuals be sterilized without their consent?

Mentally competent adults generally cannot be sterilized against their will.[47] Federal regulations implemented in 1979 governing the use of public funds to pay for sterilizations prohibit involuntary sterilization.[48] Providers who perform sterilizations and seek Medicaid reimbursement must comply with a series of regulatory mandates, including obtaining informed consent from the man or woman in his or her own language, observing a thirty-day waiting period between consent and the operation, and providing information regarding the permanency and irreversibility of the procedures, as well as about possible alternatives. Consent obtained during an abortion or childbirth is invalid. No public funding is available for hysterectomies for sterilization purposes, sterilizations of persons under twenty-one, persons who are incarcerated, or those who have been legally determined to be incompetent.[49] In addition, by statute, receipt of welfare benefits cannot be conditioned on consent to sterilization.[50]

However, these regulations do not apply to privately funded sterilizations; the latter are regulated by state law. At least fourteen states still authorize the sterilization of those deemed mentally incompetent, with certain procedural safeguards.[51]

Does an individual need the consent of his or her spouse to be sterilized?

No. As with all medical procedures, an individual's right to determine the course of his or her treatment is not affected by his or her marriage. In some states, however, the inability to produce children may be grounds for divorce or annulment.

NEW REPRODUCTIVE TECHNOLOGIES

What technologies are available to assist women to conceive children?

For a variety of reasons, individuals and couples may be unable or unwilling to have children through sexual intercourse or by adoption. Infertile couples, lesbians, and unmarried women may seek to bear children through donor insemination or through in vitro fertilization (IVF). *Donor insemination* involves inseminating a woman with donated sperm either from a known donor or from a sperm bank (where the donor's anonymity is preserved). The procedure can be performed either in a physician's office or at home, with varying degrees of success. It has been estimated that 80,000 women are artificially inseminated each year in the United States.[52]

In vitro fertilization involves the fertilization of the woman's egg by a sperm outside the womb, with a subsequent implantation into the woman's uterus. Between fertilization and implantation, the embryos are frozen and stored. As with donor insemination, the sperm may be from a known donor (often the woman's partner) or from an anonymous donor.

What are the rights and responsibilities of sperm donors with regard to children conceived with their sperm?

The answer depends in large part on whether the donor was known or anonymous. Anonymous donors generally have no rights or obligations with regard to any children produced using their sperm. Most sperm banks require donors to sign away any potential parental rights; in any case, once they have donated sperm, their identity is generally not preserved. Identified donors, however, have been known to assert claims for visitation and custody.[53]

Over thirty states have adopted some sort of legislation addressing the rights of sperm donors, many of them modeled on the Uniform Parentage Act (UPA). The UPA provides that when a married woman is inseminated with physician assistance by a man other than her husband, the husband becomes the legal "natural" father, and the individual providing the semen has no parental rights or responsibilities at all.[54] Unfortunately, neither the UPA nor the laws of most states address the rights of the donor when the woman is unmarried or when a physician is not used.[55]

Courts have been divided in responding to these unanswered questions. Some have allowed sperm donors visitation and other parental rights,[56] while others have refused to recognize any rights of sperm donors.[57] There seems to be no correlation in these cases between the donor's involvement with either the woman or the child, on one hand, and the success of the petition for parental rights on the other. There are no reported cases of donees later seeking financial support from donors.

Donors and donees seeking to clarify their rights and obligations prior to insemination are advised to draft a written agreement. Although this agreement may not be binding when a dispute reaches a court,[58] it will likely be given some weight, since it clearly spells out the parties' intentions.[59]

What happens to previously fertilized frozen embryos after a divorce?

As noted above, fertilized embryos are frozen and stored for implantation in the future. In a celebrated case in Tennessee, a couple divorced after the man's sperm was used to fertilize the woman's eggs but before the eggs were implanted. The man sued to prevent the eggs from being used. The Tennessee Supreme Court held that neither party could implant the embryos or dispose of them without the other's consent. The Court reasoned that the right to privacy and reproductive choice under the state constitution encompassed the right *not* to become a parent against one's will.[60] On appeal, the United States Supreme Court declined to review the Tennessee decision. While no other state's highest court or any federal court have ruled on the issue,[61] the Tennessee decision appears consistent with prior federal precedent on reproductive decision making.

What is surrogate parenting?

Surrogate parenting is a form of donor insemination where a woman's egg is fertilized by her chosen partner's sperm and implanted in the uterus of another woman (the surrogate), who then carries the pregnancy to term. Alternatively, the first woman's eggs are not used at all: rather, the surrogate's own eggs are fertilized (usually in vitro) by the man, and she carries the pregnancy to term. In either case, the surrogate generally agrees to forfeit any parental rights she may have in favor of the couple (in some cases, some joint custody arrangement between the couple and the surrogate is contemplated), and the recipient mother adopts the child. Surrogate parenting commonly involves some sort of payment in exchange for the "service" of carrying the pregnancy.

Are surrogacy contracts legal?

About a third of the states have specific laws regulating surrogacy arrangements. Most of these laws refuse to recognize the legality of surrogacy
contracts involving the exchange of money for the willingness of the woman
to carry the pregnancy, making them unenforceable in court.[62] A handful of
states refuse to recognize surrogacy contracts even when no money is exchanged.[63] The remainder of statutes concerning surrogacy arrangements
recognize their validity provided the contracts comply with the details set
forth in the legislation.[64]

In most states, however, there are no laws specifically addressing the legality of surrogacy arrangements. In these states, courts considering surrogacy disputes must decide such cases by relying on common law and constitutional law. Commonly, this has involved balancing two legal principles.
On one hand is the constitutional right to bear and beget children free from
government interference; on the other are public policy proscriptions on the
exchange of money for babies. The results have not always been predictable:
some courts have found surrogacy contracts to be void as a matter of law,[65]
while others have held that they are only voidable,[66] meaning that they
are not illegal, but one party will be permitted to back out of the contract.
There are no reported cases of surrogacy contractors being arrested or convicted on "baby-selling" charges.

Where disputes have arisen between surrogates and couples or fathers, it
appears that courts have enforced surrogacy contracts against the surrogate
mother only if the egg used for conception was not her own.[67]

Does a surrogate mother have any rights if she changes her mind?

Generally, yes. Certainly in those states that void surrogacy contracts, a
surrogate mother has the same rights as any other mother. These rights include the right to compete for custody with the father (based on the child's
best interests) and to wait until after the child's birth to decide whether or
not to give up parental rights so that the child may be adopted.

Perhaps the most well known surrogacy case to date is *In re Baby M.*[68]
In that case, a New Jersey woman entered into a contract with a childless
couple and agreed, in exchange for money, to become impregnated in vitro
by the husband's sperm, carry the fetus to term, forgo parental rights, and
allow the baby to be adopted by the wife. When she gave birth, the surrogate
changed her mind and was unwilling to give up parental rights. Moreover,

she wanted custody of her child. The court refused to enforce the contract, concluding that under New Jersey law a parent could not relinquish parental rights until after the child was born (by which time the surrogate was unwilling to do so) and that there was no basis in law to cut off her parental rights because she had neither abandoned nor neglected her child. Finally, the court held that custody determinations must be based exclusively on the child's best interests. Accordingly, the court conducted an extensive best-interests custody inquiry in which the competing parents were the sperm donor and the surrogate. At the end of the hearing, the court awarded custody to the father; one of the factors the court took into account in determining the child's best interests, however, was the fact that the surrogate had initially agreed to give up the child to the couple.

What is the legal status of a child born as a result of a surrogacy arrangement?

Only one court has ruled directly on this issue, finding that a child born as a result of a surrogacy contract is "legitimate."[69] The court looked to the state's sperm donor statute for guidance and held that a child born to a legally married couple through any type of new reproductive technology should be considered the lawful progeny of that union.

The child's rights to support and inheritance from the surrogate raise different issues, however. If the contract is not void under the laws of the state, has not been contested by the surrogate, and all parties have fulfilled their obligation with regard to releasing parental rights and adoption, the child will be considered the lawful child of the couple. Once the surrogate has relinquished parental rights, she cannot be held liable for any child support, and there is no continuing legal relationship of any kind remaining between her and the child.

RIGHT TO DIRECT THE COURSE OF PREGNANCY

This area of the law, like many others, often operates on two planes. The first is theoretical or technical; the second is real or practical. Although women have many technical rights to control their own lives, in practice doctors commonly attempt to require women to do things that are not universally recognized as necessary. For this reason, we begin this section by discussing the limits of a doctor's authority to direct a pregnant woman's conduct.

Are women legally required to comply with their doctors' orders during pregnancy?

As a general rule, no. Traditionally, except in extreme cases, patients have been free to accept or reject their doctor's advice regarding treatment for a condition.[70] Doctors have few remedies available to them when patients refuse to follow their recommended course of treatment. The only way to attempt to force a patient to comply with the doctor's recommendation is to take the case to court and seek a court order against the patient. These actions are rarely successful.

However, pregnancy is sometimes regarded as different because the patient's actions will affect not only herself but also her fetus. Based on the assumption that a pregnant woman's interest may conflict with that of her fetus, doctors traditionally have been granted a prominent role in women's reproductive health decisions. Indeed, even *Roe v. Wade*, the Supreme Court decision that first recognized a woman's constitutional right to reproductive choice, focused predominantly on the doctor's rights and responsibilities: "[T]he abortion decision in all its aspects is inherently, and primarily, a medical decision, and basic responsibility for it must rest with the physician."[71]

Nonetheless, women retain the right to reject advice by their physicians during pregnancy and a doctor's attempt to compel a pregnant patient to comply with his or her advice by seeking a court order is rarely successful.[72] This does not mean that a woman's rejection of medical advice will never become the subject of litigation if there are problems with the baby after birth. In one California case, for example, a woman who gave birth to a seriously brain-damaged child was arrested and indicted for failure to provide necessary medical attention under a statute designed to enforce parental support obligations. Prosecutors alleged that the woman had ignored physician advice to remain in bed and refrain from sex with her husband (although the husband was never charged with any crime). The indictment was ultimately dismissed.[73]

Can a doctor force a woman to undergo a cesarean section?

Cesarean sections are one of the most frequently performed unnecessary operations in the United States. According to the United States Centers for Disease Control, 36 percent of the cesarean sections performed in 1991 were not medically necessary.[74] There are several reasons for this pattern: first, many obstetricians, fearful of medical malpractice suits, appear to engage in "defensive" medicine to ward off potential negative results of vaginal births. Second, many insurance companies reimburse the costs of cesarean sections but not of vaginal births. In addition, physicians charge on average one and one-half times more for cesareans than for vaginal births.[75]

Although several courts have upheld forced cesareans when a woman refused to consent to the operation,[76] the majority refuse to grant such orders. These courts prefer to defer to the patient's choice, and women accord a high level of autonomy in medical decision making.[77] As an Illinois court recently held, "a woman's competent choice in refusing medical treatment as invasive as a cesarean section during her pregnancy must be honored, even in circumstances where the choice may be harmful to her fetus."[78] Moreover, courts are increasingly aware that physician predictions of fetal outcome are frequently inaccurate.

Can a pregnant woman be forced by her husband or by the putative father to undergo a cesarean section against her wishes?

No. As with all other medical procedures, competent adults retain the right to determine the course of their treatment, regardless of marriage. Courts have consistently rejected applications by third parties (even when they are relatives) who attempt to intervene or be appointed as a "guardian" of a fetus in order to mandate a particular treatment.[79] Since fetuses are not legal "persons" under the Constitution, they have no rights that could be raised by a guardian or intervenor.[80]

Can a woman be incarcerated or otherwise punished for using drugs or alcohol while she is pregnant?

Law enforcement officials in several jurisdictions have attempted to prosecute pregnant women who test positive for drugs or whose newborns showed evidence of drugs in their bodies (which is indicative of maternal drug use during pregnancy). Between 1988 and 1992, more than 150 women in twenty-four states were arrested based on the discovery of trace elements of drugs or alcohol in their newborns' or their own bloodstream or urine. Of these, the vast majority ended in convictions or guilty pleas to charges ranging from child abuse and neglect to "delivery of drugs to a minor." However, every conviction that has been challenged on appeal has been overturned.[81]

In none of these prosecutions was the woman charged with violation of a statute specifically criminalizing various types of behavior during pregnancy; indeed, there are no such statutes. Instead, prosecutors have attempted to apply preexisting child abuse and drug trafficking statutes to behavior that is at base a public health concern, not a criminal violation.

The extent to which this is a serious public health concern remains unclear. Although there is some evidence of harm to children caused by a mother's drug use during pregnancy,[82] the extent of the problem may have been overstated initially. There has been very little research on the long-term effects on children from prenatal drug use, and some doubt has been cast on the widely held belief that prenatal drug use always entails grave harm to the child.[83] Unfortunately, drug treatment programs have paid less attention to this problem than have prosecutors. Most detoxification and rehabilitation programs across the country refuse to accept pregnant women for fear of liability arising from the potential effects of withdrawal and chemical drug treatments, such as methadone, on pregnant women and fetuses.

Finally, it is important to note that no men have ever been prosecuted for the effects their drug or alcohol use may have had on their sperm and subsequent children. Moreover, all the women who have been criminally prosecuted for their prenatal drug or alcohol use have been poor women, and almost all have been women of color, despite evidence that substance abuse patterns are stable across race and class lines.

Can a mother lose custody of her children due to her drug use during pregnancy?

In some states, yes. Courts in California, Michigan, New York, and Ohio have found that drug use during pregnancy (as evidenced by a newborn's positive drug toxicology at birth) was prima facie evidence of neglect, warranting removal of the children from the home.[84] Courts in some other states, including the Connecticut Supreme Court, have held that a positive toxicology result by itself is insufficient evidence of abuse or neglect.[85]

Because of the inconsistency in lower court rulings, the legislatures in some states have begun to address the problem. California has concluded that an automatic finding of neglect whenever children are born with positive drug toxicologies is not necessarily in the best interests of either the children or their mothers. In 1992 the California legislature passed a law specifying that a positive toxicology alone does *not* constitute prima facie evidence of neglect; rather, it should trigger only a more searching evaluation by government social workers into the conditions in the home to determine the level of intervention that is appropriate for both the mother and her children.[86]

The California legislature concluded that a positive toxicology may not indicate drug addiction or even frequent use; it can be evidence merely that the mother ingested drugs some time within the 24- to 72-hour period prior to the birth. Many women are known to take some sort of drugs to alleviate the pain of childbirth, and there is no evidence that such use so late in the pregnancy constitutes any harm to the fetus at all. Moreover, drug toxicologies produce many false positives.

Perhaps more important, use of a positive drug toxicology as the sole trigger for neglect proceedings short circuits preexisting child welfare statutes that seek to balance all the factors involved in making difficult custody decisions. Drug use alone is not sufficient evidence of neglect or abuse. The multifactored approach used in many states' neglect proceedings is designed to facilitate connections with social services that will enable families to overcome obstacles such as drug abuse without needlessly separating children and parents when the children may safely be kept at home.

Can hospitals and drug treatment programs divulge evidence of a mother's drug use to social workers, law enforcement officials, or her spouse?

Healthcare providers in most states are required to report evidence of child abuse to local child welfare authorities.[87] If hospital workers believe that a positive toxicology constitutes such evidence, then they may release the mother's medical records to government officials. The practice, however, may violate the patient's constitutional and statutory rights to confidentiality in their medical records. Federal and state constitutional guarantees of privacy and liberty, as well as statutory confidentiality requirements, may bar the practice of revealing addicts' medical histories to authorities.[88] Moreover, revelation of medical information without the patient's consent can undermine the patient-physician relationship, thereby discouraging women from confiding in their doctors or from seeking adequate prenatal and delivery care.

Finally, in practice, reporting policies may be enforced selectively, raising equal protection and discrimination concerns. For example, in a recent case in South Carolina, the Office of Civil Rights of the Department of Health and Human Services intervened to stop a hospital from reporting to law enforcement officials the names of women whose newborns tested positive for drugs. The hospital's policy appeared to have a disproportionate effect on African-American women, thereby implicating Title VI of the Civil Rights Act, the federal law prohibiting discrimination in federally funded healthcare facilities.[89]

Can drug treatment programs exclude pregnant women?

As noted above, many drug treatment programs exclude pregnant women because they fear that they will incur liability for any harm caused to the fetus by the withdrawal process or from chemical drug treatments, such as methadone. Such exclusionary practices arguably violate federal and state guarantees of equal protection, as well as state mandates to provide indigent care. In a challenge brought by the ACLU's Women's Rights Project, New York's highest court found that such exclusions violated the state's guarantees of equal protection in the provision of healthcare services.[90]

Discrimination against pregnant women in drug treatment occurs most frequently in detoxification programs, where mild sedatives are sometimes used and where providers fear the effects of withdrawal on both the fetus and on the pregnant woman. Such fears appear to be misguided for several reasons. First, it appears clear that the alternative potential harms caused by continued drug or alcohol abuse are greater than the risk from use of mild sedatives. Second, most healthcare providers agree that it is possible to provide detoxification services to pregnant women without harm to either the woman or her fetus, especially where adequate obstetrical care is provided. Third, traditional informed consent doctrines and laws should adequately insulate providers from unfounded malpractice claims. For these reasons, it appears that safe and effective drug treatment services can be made available to pregnant women with little or no risk of injury (or malpractice liability) if detoxification programs work cooperatively with prenatal care providers.

Can a child sue his or her parents for drug-related injuries he or she sustained in utero?

In most states the issue remains an open question. Courts in only three states have considered suits brought by children against their mothers for prenatal behavior, with two of them allowing such suits[91] and the third barring them.[92] Two trends in personal injury law seem to encourage these cases: the recognition of a cause of action for prenatal injuries (where a third party has injured both mother and fetus) and the partial abolition of the doctrine of parental immunity (which served to insulate parents from suits by their children).

Given the special nature of the relationship between a pregnant woman and her fetus, it is arguably unconstitutional to allow such suits to go forward. As one court stated, "Since anything which a pregnant woman does or does not do may have an impact, either positive or negative, on her developing fetus, any act or omission on her part could render her liable to her subsequently born child."[93]

Can government benefit programs limit benefits to recipients based on the number of children they have?

Federal law governing Aid to Families with Dependent Children (AFDC) currently requires that welfare recipients receive increases in their monthly benefits when additional eligible children are born. However, several states have sought waivers of this requirement in order to implement "family cap" or "child exclusion" programs, which would prohibit an increase in benefits for an additional child. Although New Jersey is the only state to implement such a measure as of this writing, waivers have been approved for family cap demonstration projects in Arkansas, Georgia, and Wisconsin, and waiver applications are currently pending for programs in several other states.[94] In addition, both the Clinton administration's welfare reform proposal and its more conservative Republican counterpart would permit states to implement child exclusion policies without going through the waiver process.

The New Jersey child exclusion law took effect on October 1, 1992 and applies to children born into families receiving AFDC as of August 1, 1993. The exclusion applies only to those families receiving AFDC at the time of conception. Since a woman applying for AFDC for the first time will receive benefits for all her children, two women with the same family size— one who has been on AFDC since before the birth of one or more of her children, the other just now entering the program—will receive different amounts of welfare assistance. Thus, one family will receive a smaller cash payment based solely on the timing of the child's birth in relation to the welfare application, even though the needs of the children are the same.

The evidence from New Jersey on the impact of the child exclusion program on birth rates remains inconclusive. New Jersey officials claim a 9 percent reduction in children born to AFDC recipients; however the accuracy of this number has been disputed. It is likely that many families are simply not reporting births of children to welfare authorities, since they will not receive increased benefits as a result. Even if the reported rate is accurate, it would represent a reduction of only one-quarter of 1 percent in the total case load of AFDC recipients.[95]

The New Jersey law is currently the subject of litigation alleging that it is invalid for several reasons.[96] First, the law arguably violates provisions of federal AFDC law that mandate that states provide benefits to all eligible individuals. But for the waiver provisions, the additional children excluded from receiving benefits would be otherwise eligible for AFDC. In a similar vein, the program may violate state and federal guarantees of equal protection, since similarly situated children are treated differently based on an irrelevant criterion over which the children have no control—the time at which their parents applied for welfare benefits. As a demonstration project, the New Jersey law also arguably violates federal regulations regarding experimentation with human subjects—the whole program is an "experiment" to determine whether welfare recipients will modify their birth rates in response to financial penalties.

Some of the proposed waivers would exempt from the "child exclusion" rule children born as a result of reported rape or incest or the failure of certain contraceptives (Norplant or DepoProvera).[97] However, these exceptions arguably interfere with poor women's reproductive decision making by coercing the use of certain contraceptives and undermining their privacy. A federal district judge has rejected these arguments, but the case is on appeal.

May an employer refuse to place fertile women employees in jobs that would expose them to dangerous materials that could adversely affect offspring?

No, at least not when the employer would permit fertile men to work in the same position, unless it could be shown that a man's exposure could not adversely affect offspring. In 1991 the Supreme Court declared that an employer's policy of only allowing women whose infertility had been medically documented to work in jobs where they could be exposed to lead levels exceeding OSHA standards violated the women's right to work.[98] The Court found that the policy discriminated on the basis of sex. Only women were required to produce evidence that they were infertile in order to perform certain jobs, even though lead exposure has damaging effects upon the male reproductive system as well. There was also no evidence that women could not perform the jobs as well as men because of the possibility that they may become pregnant at some future time.

May an employer refuse to hire employees with preschool children?

Yes, but only if there are actual conflicting family obligations that are demonstrably relevant to job performance. In addition, an employer's refusal to hire women with preschool children, while at the same time hiring similarly situated men, would be illegal and unconstitutional.[99]

May employers require pregnant women employees to take maternity leaves long before the expected birth?

No. The United States Supreme Court has held that "overly restrictive maternity-leave regulations" penalize women for deciding to bear children. This is impermissible because the Constitution protects freedom of personal choice in matters of marriage and family life. In the case decided by the Supreme Court, the employer required maternity leaves five months before the expected birth.[100] Less restrictive mandatory maternity leaves may be lawful if the employer has valid job-related justifications for the required leave.

Can doctors be sued for the birth of children with genetic defects?

Physicians are now capable of detecting the presence of a wide range of genetic abnormalities such as Down's syndrome in fetuses in utero through amniocentesis and other methods. Information regarding such abnormalities can be essential to women seeking to make intelligent decisions about the progression of their pregnancies. Genetic testing enables individuals, especially those with a history of genetic abnormalities, to become parents without the fear of passing on a disabling trait, to make special preparations for the birth of a disabled child, or to obtain in utero treatment for certain disabilities to enhance the child's health and chances for survival after birth. If a physician fails to inform a woman about the availability of genetic testing or fails to fully inform her of the results of testing that is performed, she will not be in a position to exercise her complete range of procreative choices. Normally, a woman in such a position would be able to sue her physician for medical malpractice for the costs of injury she suffered due to her lack of knowledge about any genetic abnormalities.

Several states have passed legislation prohibiting so-called wrongful birth or wrongful life suits,[101] believing that the availability of such actions devalues life generally, specifically the lives of people with disabilities, and encourages abortion.[102] However, the wisdom of barring such suits is open to question. It may result in denying parents the full range of reproductive choice. Because medicine is a self-regulating profession, the malpractice system, for all its faults, is an important means for aggrieved patients to obtain redress for conduct that falls below acceptable professional care.[103] Restricting malpractice claims of this sort arguably encourages behavior that would otherwise be actionable. Although the prohibitions on wrongful birth actions have been challenged in several jurisdictions on the grounds that they unconstitutionally interfere with a woman's right to choose whether to terminate her pregnancy, most courts have upheld such laws.[104]

HIV AND PREGNANCY

Are children of parents with HIV always HIV-positive themselves?

No. Only about 15 to 30 percent of American women with the Human Immunodeficiency Virus (HIV) give birth to children who remain HIV-positive.[105] At birth, all children born of HIV-positive mothers carry their mothers' antibodies to HIV and therefore test HIV-positive themselves (currently available tests detect only the presence of antibodies to HIV, not the virus itself). Thus an HIV test performed on a newborn only indicates the mother's serostatus, not that of her child. Only after the child is eighteen months old will she have completely shed her mother's antibodies and fully developed her own.[106] Researchers are still puzzled as to why some women transmit the virus to their children in utero while most do not. There is some evidence that early breastfeeding by an HIV-positive woman can result in seroconversion in the infant. To date, no studies have tracked the correlation between the father's HIV status and that of his offspring.

A recent controlled study of intervention with AZT (also known as zidovudine) in pregnant HIV-positive women showed a dramatic decrease in the rates of HIV transmission from mother to child, down to about 8 percent.[107] Because of the design of the trial, however, it remains unclear whether this decrease in transmission is the result of AZT therapy given to the woman during pregnancy or during delivery, of that given to the infant immediately after birth, or of a combination. Also unknown are the long-term effects of in utero AZT therapy on the child.

Can women giving birth, or their newborns, be tested for HIV without their consent?

In many localities across the United States, all newborns are tested for HIV anonymously for epidemiological reasons (i.e., to track the progression of the disease among women giving birth). Results are not matched up with specific mother-child pairs and are therefore not revealed to either the mother or to her physicians. Women typically give blanket consent to a series of routine tests, including HIV testing, when they enter the hospital for delivery.

Recently, due in large part to the dramatic results of the AZT study discussed above, the legislatures of several states have proposed mandating directive counseling and HIV testing of all pregnant women and newborns;[108] a similar bill has been introduced in Congress as well.[109] Such proposals would require that all women who seek prenatal care or who give birth be referred for HIV testing and that the results of such tests be reported both to the woman and to the state.

However, the wisdom and legality of mandatory HIV testing of pregnant women or newborn babies are open to debate. As a matter of policy, several prominent public health organizations oppose mandatory testing because of the combination of the difficulty of maintaining fully confidential HIV-related information and the reality that disclosure of one's HIV status can result in discrimination in the provision of healthcare, health insurance, employment, and housing.[110] In addition, it is unlikely that parents can be forced to treat their HIV-infected children in a particular manner over their objection. This is so because there are no lifesaving or curative treatments currently available for HIV-positive newborns. Prophylactic treatments available to adults to prevent opportunistic infections, especially pneumocystis carinii pneumonia (PCP), have been associated with a significant rate of serious side effects in children[111] and therefore do not offer the kind of unambiguously helpful intervention—such as blood transfusions— that have normally been thought to justify treatment without parental consent.[112] If treatment cannot be provided without parental consent, it is difficult to justify testing without such consent.

Moreover, mandatory testing would appear to violate a woman's constitutional and statutory right to confidentiality of medical information. Courts and legislatures have recognized the special privacy concerns that attach to the diagnosis of AIDS or HIV, noting that "the potential for harm is substantial."[113] Since HIV testing would at a minimum involve disclosure to other healthcare professionals and to the government in those states with mandatory reporting requirements, mandatory testing would result in important information about an individual being disclosed without consent. Even testing of newborns only reveals whether the mother is infected; neither prenatal nor postpartum HIV testing reveals any information about the HIV status of the fetus or child. However, it is firmly settled law that the constitutional right to privacy encompasses an individual's right to choose or refuse medical tests.[114] For this reason, most states require specific informed consent for HIV tests because of the serious implications of the results and the attendant often severe anxiety and trauma.[115]

Can women or their newborns be forced to undergo treatment for HIV?

No. Competent adults have the right to refuse medical treatment of any kind.[116] Under the laws of most states, parents have the right to refuse all but lifesaving treatments for their children.[117]

Can hospitals divulge the results of HIV tests to social workers or spouses?

Some states *require* that the results of all HIV tests be reported to the state or local health departments, generally for epidemiological reasons.[118] However, many states also have both general confidentiality laws protecting all medical records and specific laws regarding HIV confidentiality. These laws generally protect against involuntary disclosure of one's HIV status.

In several states, however, there is an important exception to this general rule for "emergency" situations, including notification of an "unsuspecting third party" who may have had sexual intercourse with the infected person. Persons who wish to inform potentially at-risk partners themselves should inform hospital personnel that they will do so.

Unfortunately, in practice confidentiality laws are not always a bar to unauthorized disclosure. Indeed, especially in many public hospital settings, HIV confidentiality is less than perfect.[119] Similarly, poor confidentiality records have been reported in homeless shelters and welfare offices.

Can a parent lose custody of his or her child because he or she is HIV-positive?

No. There have been no reported cases of a parent losing permanent custody of his or her child because of his or her HIV status. Indeed, several courts have specifically held that HIV infection is irrelevant to custody or visitation determinations.[120]

REPRODUCTIVE RIGHTS OF MINORS

What are parental consent and notification laws?

Parental consent and notification laws require a minor seeking an abortion to obtain the consent of or notify one or both of her parents prior to the procedure. In most cases, liability for failure to comply with notification or consent requirements falls on the physician who performs the abortion, subjecting him or her to civil and criminal penalties. Notification laws typically require that the physician attest that the parents have been notified, usually by phone; consent laws commonly require written consent of one or both parents, a guardian, or another "adult family member."[121]

For the vast majority of young women, there is often no practical difference between notification and consent. If a young woman has reason to refrain from discussing her pregnancy or abortion choice with a parent, it does not make a difference whether she is required to obtain their consent or to merely notify them. For most young women, mandatory notification poses the same dangers as mandatory consent.

In most instances, the law provides for a judicial bypass procedure, whereby a young woman who is unable to involve her parents can seek the consent of a judge for the procedure. In those cases, the judge must determine either whether the woman is mature enough to make the abortion decision on her own or whether obtaining the abortion without notice to her parents would be in her best interests.

These procedures, however, are deeply flawed. Despite requirements that the procedure be confidential, in small towns and rural communities, such assurances ring hollow. In addition, requiring a young woman to discuss her pregnancy and the personal details of her life before strangers in a courtroom can add unnecessary delay and further stress to an already tense situation. Many young women do not have access to transportation to get to the courthouse, and find it difficult to take time off from school or work in order to appear at a hearing. Finally, in some instances, judges arbitrarily reject such petitions based on their personal views of abortion.

In a handful of states, the physician may waive the requirement of parental consent or notification if he or she determines that such notification is not in the young woman's best interests. Such procedures are clearly preferable to judicial bypasses, since doctors are likely to be better able than judges to determine whether the parental involvement requirement is in the woman's best interests.

Are these laws constitutional?

The Supreme Court has held that one-parent consent and two-parent notification laws are constitutional only if they include an "alternative," such as judicial bypass, to waive the requirement for young women who cannot involve their parents.[122] Such alternatives must meet a four-part test: first, the procedure must allow the minor the opportunity to show that she possesses the maturity and information to make her abortion decision; second, the procedure must allow the young woman to show that even if she does not possess the requisite maturity, obtaining an abortion without her parents' consent is in her best interests; third, the procedure must ensure the minor woman's anonymity; and fourth, the procedure must be expeditious.[123] Where judicial bypass procedures violate any of these requirements, courts have prevented them from being enforced and allow minors to obtain abortions as if the laws did not exist.[124]

In addition, one state's highest court has found greater protection for minors' privacy under the state constitution. Florida's Supreme Court held that a parental consent law, even with a judicial bypass provision, violated a minor woman's right to choose abortion under the state constitution's explicit guarantee of a right to privacy.[125]

Which states have parental consent or notification laws?

As of September 1994, thirty-eight states had parental involvement laws of one sort or another on the books, but only twenty-eight states actually enforce the laws. The following laws are in effect.

1. *Consent of both parents with judicial bypass:* Massachusetts, Mississippi, North Dakota;
2. *Consent of one parent with judicial bypass:* Alabama, Indiana, Kentucky, Louisiana, Michigan, Missouri, North Carloina, Pennsylvania ("informed" consent), Rhode Island, South Carolina (parent or grandparent), Tennessee, Wisconsin (consent of an "adult family member"), Wyoming (with forty-eight-hour delay);

3. *Notification of "parents" without judicial bypass.* Idaho ("if possible"),Utah;

4. *Notification of both "parents" with judicial bypass.* Arkansas (with forty-eight-hour delay), Minnesota (with forty-eight-hour delay);

5. *Notification of one parent with judicial bypass.* Georgia, Kansas (with additional mandatory counseling), Nebraska (with forty-eight-hour delay), Ohio (with twenty-four-hour delay);

6. *Notification of one parent with physician waiver and/or judicial bypass.* Delaware (with twenty-four-hour delay), Maine, Maryland, West Virginia (with twenty-four-hour delay).

Can a minor's parents force her to have an abortion?

No. Although there is only one reported case on this precise issue,[126] it is well established that the realm of personal freedom accorded minors in reproductive healthcare decisions extends to the right to bear a child.[127]

Can a minor receive prenatal care without the consent of her parents?

Yes. Almost every state expressly allows minors to seek pregnancy-related services without the consent of their parents. In many states, minors who become parents are considered emancipated minors for all purposes.

May minors obtain over-the-counter contraceptives without prior parental consent?

Yes. Generally, over-the-counter birth control methods (condoms and spermicides) are available to anyone who wishes to buy them, regardless of age. In striking down a New York statute banning the sale of nonprescription contraceptives to minors, the Supreme Court in 1977 confirmed the constitutional right of minors to obtain over-the-counter birth control without parental consent.[128] The court held that

in a field that by definition concerns the most intimate of human activities and relationships, decisions whether to accomplish or to prevent conception are among the most private and sensitive. . . . Restrictions on the distribution of contraceptives clearly burden the freedom to make such decisions.[129]

If a store is permitted to sell nonprescription contraceptives to minors, there is no legal duty on the part of store owners or employees to inform the parents of a minor who purchases them.

May minors obtain prescription contraceptives without parental consent?

Most states have laws permitting minors access to prescription contraceptives—birth control pills, diaphragms, cervical cap, Norplant, and Depo-Provera—in some circumstances, though these laws are difficult to categorize. In a number of states, including Alaska, California, the District of Columbia, Maryland, Minnesota, and Oregon, minors of any age may obtain contraceptives from doctors willing to prescribe them. In Georgia, Louisiana, and Mississippi, any female regardless of age may obtain them. And in Arkansas, Idaho, Massachusetts, Mississippi, and Nevada, the minor, regardless of age, need only be of sufficient intelligence to understand the consequences to obtain birth control prescriptions. Other states use age as the criterion for consent: in Delaware, for example, a person must be twelve years old; in Alabama and Hawaii, fourteen years old; and in Kansas, Rhode Island, South Carolina, and Texas, the young person must be sixteen years old.

Several states (including Illinois, Maine, and Pennsylvania) permit doctors to give prescriptions whenever in their opinion there would be a serious health hazard if the minor were not treated. In these states minors do not have a clear right to obtain medical assistance, but if doctors are willing to cooperate, the minors will be able to be treated.

In the states that have no laws governing this issue, the question remains whether treatment for contraception falls under the general rule that prior parental consent is required for all medical care for children, or whether sex-related medical treatment (including prescription contraceptives) qualifies as an exception based on a child's right to privacy.

Does this mean states can distribute contraceptives to minors without parental permission?

Not necessarily. It is one thing to say that minors cannot be prevented from purchasing contraceptives in drugstores. It is another to say the state may actively distribute contraceptives to minors without parental consent. This issue has arisen in recent years in schools. One New York court recently held that a school-based condom distribution program could not be implemented without some mechanism for parental consent.[130] The court held that, absent a specific legislative directive authorizing the condom distribution without parental consent, the common-law rule mandating parental consent to a minor's receipt of health services remained in force. Any other result, according to the court, would interfere with the parents' rights to raise their children as they see fit. Because minors have access to contraceptives outside of school, the court held that applying the common-law rule requiring parental permission in school did not violate the young person's constitutional right to privacy. More recently Massachusett's highest court rejected this reasoning and upheld a high school condom-distribution program against a constitutional challenge by parents of students.[131]

May publicly funded clinics require parental consent before prescribing contraceptives to minors?

In most instances, no. In a number of states, local welfare departments are either required or permitted to distribute birth control information and prescriptions to minors of childbearing age without the consent of their parents.[132] In addition, under the federal Medicaid and AFDC statutes, states must make family planning services and supplies available to all recipients of childbearing age, including "sexually active" minors.[133] States cannot impose additional parental consent requirements in these federal programs.[134] Moreover, federal law prohibits the imposition of parental consent requirements for contraceptives in federally funded family planning clinics.[135] There are very few public clinics that are not subject to either federal or state prohibitions on parental consent. In those few, however, it remains unclear whether parental consent may be required, since the Supreme Court has never ruled on the constitutionality of such requirements with regard to prescription birth control.[136]

May parents insist that their child be sterilized over the child's objection?

No. Although there are no reported cases squarely addressing this issue,[137] it is well established that the realm of personal freedom accorded minors in reproductive healthcare decision extends to the right to bear a child.[138]

RESOURCES

ACLU Reproductive Freedom Project
132 West 43d Street
New York, NY 10036
(212) 944-9800

Center for Reproductive Law & Policy
120 Wall Street, 18th Floor
New York, NY 10005
(212) 514-5534

NOW Legal Defense and Education Fund
99 Hudson Street, 12th Floor
New York, NY 10013
(212) 925-6635

Planned Parenthood Federation of America
Legal Division
810 Seventh Avenue
New York, NY 10019
(212) 541-7800

National Abortion and Reproductive Rights Action League
1156 Fifteenth Street, NW, 7th Floor
Washington, DC 20005
(202) 973-3000

Women's Legal Defense Fund
1875 Connecticut Avenue, NW, Suite 710
Washington, DC 20009
(202) 986-2600

Women's Law Project
125 South Ninth Street, Suite 401
Philadelphia, PA 19105
(215) 928-9801

Fund for the Feminist Majority
1600 Wilson Blvd. No. 704
Arlington, VA 22209
(703) 522-2214

Notes

1. For a comprehensive history of abortion law in the United States, *see* James C. Mohr, *Abortion in America: The Origins and Evolution of National Policy 1800–1900* (1978).
2. A highly useful starting point is a free subscription to *Reproductive Freedom News,*

the biweekly newsletter of the Center for Reproductive Law & Policy, 120 Wall Street, New York, New York 10005.

3. 410 U.S. 113 (1973).

4. 492 U.S. 490 (1989).

5. 112 S. Ct. 2791 (1992).

6. *Id.* at 2840.

7. In *Webster*, the Court approved a law requiring fetal viability tests after the twentieth week of pregnancy, the concurrence of a second physician on second trimester abortions, and a prohibition on the use of public facilities for abortions. *Webster v. Reproductive Health Center, supra* note 4, at 492–93. In *Casey*, the Court upheld a mandatory waiting period, parental notification for minors, and so-called informed consent requirements (which mandate that women seeking abortions be given certain information regarding alternatives to abortion). *Casey, supra* note 5, at 2822–26, 2832.

8. In the second trimester, states could regulate abortion to protect a woman's health, and in the third trimester, abortion could be banned except in cases where the woman's life was endangered. *Roe v. Wade, supra* note 3, at 163–66.

9. *Planned Prenthood v. Casey, supra* note 5, at 2820–21.

10. *Id.* at 2831 (invalidating husband notification); *Sojourner T. v. Edwards*, 974 F.2d 27 (5th Cir. 1992), *cert. denied*, 113 S. Ct. 1414 (1993) (invalidating abortion ban); *Guam Soc'y of Obstetricians & Gynecologists v. Ada*, 962 F.2d 1366 (9th Cir.), *cert. denied*, 113 S. Ct. 633 (1992) (invalidating abortion ban).

11. Prohibitions on public funding were upheld even under strict scrutiny. *Harris v. McRae*, 448 U.S. 297 (1980).

12. In *Casey*, the Court held that such laws did not on their face unduly burden the abortion choice but did not decide their constitutionality as applied.

13. *See, e.g.*, Utah Code Ann. §§ 76-7-301, 305, 305.5.

14. *See id.* South Carolina recently passed a one-hour waiting period, 1995 S.C.S.B. 88, and a state court in Tennessee has struck down a 72-hour waiting period, *Planned Parenthood v. McWherter*, No. 92C-1672 (Tenn. Cir. Ct. Nov. 9, 1992).

15. *See, e.g., Planned Parenthood v. Casey, supra* note 5, at 2823 ("In attempting to ensure that a woman apprehend the full consequences of her decision, the State furthers a legitimate purpose.").

16. *See supra* note 13.

17. Stanley K. Henshaw & Jennifer Van Vort, *Abortion Services in the United States, 1991 and 1992*, 26 Fam. Plan. Persp. 100, 103 (1994).

18. *Rust v. Sullivan*, 500 U.S. 173 (1991) (approving 42 C.F.R. 59 (1989)).

19. Standards of Compliance for Abortion-Related Services in Family Planning Service Projects, 58 Fed. Reg. 7462 (1993).

20. *See supra* note 5.

21. The Court had previously held that a husband *consent* requirement is unconstitutional under the strict scrutiny standard. *Planned Parenthood v. Danforth*, 428 U.S. 52, 67–72 (1976).

22. *Planned Parenthood v. Casey, supra* note 5 at 2826–31.

23. *See, e.g., J.M. v. V.C.*, No. M-965 (N.J. Sup. Ct. Mar. 24, 1992), *cert. denied*, 113 S. Ct. 91 (1992).

24. *See Cruzan v. Director, Missouri Dep't of Health*, 497 U.S. 261 (1990).

25. *Roe v. Wade, supra* note 3, at 152.

26. *Alice D. v. William M.*, 113 Misc. 2d 940, 450 N.Y.S.2d 350 (N.Y. Civ. Ct. 1982).

27. *Harris v. McRae, supra* note 11 (federal funding); *Maher v. Roe*, 432 U.S. 464 (1977) (state funding).

28. This clear supremacy clause issue has been litigated in several lower courts, all of which have thus far supported this finding. *See Little Rock Family Planning Services, P.A. v. Dalton*, 60 F.3d 497 (8th Cir. 1995); *Elizabeth Blackwell Center for Women v. Knoll*, 61 F. 3d 170 (3d Cir. 1995); *Hope Medical Group for Women v. Edwards*, No. 94-1129, slip op. (E.D. La. July 28, 1994); *Planned Parenthood v. Engler*, No. 4:94:CV-49, slip op. (W.D. Mich. July 18, 1994); *Hern v. Beye*, 57 F. 3d 906 (10th Cir. 1995); *Roe v. Casey*, 623 F.2d 829 (3d Cir. 1980); *Zbaraz v. Quern*, 596 F.2d 196 (7th Cir. 1979), *cert. denied*, 448 U.S. 907 (1980); *Frieman v. Walsh*, 481 F. Supp. 137 (W.D. Mo. 1979), *aff'd in relevant part sub nom., Reproductive Health Services v. Freeman*, 614 F.2d 585, 592 (8th Cir.), *vacated on other grounds*, 449 U.S. 809 (1980); *Preterm v. Dukakis*, 591 F.2d 121, 134 (1st Cir.), *cert. denied*, 441 U.S. 952 (1979). To confirm this finding, on Dec. 28, 1993, the director of the Medicaid Bureau of the federal Health Care Financing Administration the U.S. Department of Health and Human Services advised state Medicaid directors that, effective Oct. 1, 1993, all Medicaid plans must cover abortions for which there is federal funding under current federal law.

29. Pub. L. No. 103-112 (1993), § 509.

30. Those states are Alaska, California, Connecticut, Hawaii, Idaho, Illinois, Maryland, Massachusetts, Minnesota, Montana, New Jersey, New Mexico, New York, Oregon, Vermont, Washington, and West Virginia.

31. The average cost of a first trimester, nonhospital, physician-provided abortion is $251. Stanley K. Henshaw, *The Accessibility of Abortion Services in the United States*, 23 Fam. Plan. Persp. 246 (1991).

32. *See* Robin Toner, *The Health Care Debate: The Abortion Issue*, N.Y. Times, July 14, 1994, at A1.

33. *Rust v. Sullivan, supra* note 18.

34. *Lehocky v. Curators of Univ. of Missouri*, 558 F.2d 887 (8th Cir. 1977).

35. 42 U.S.C. § 2000e(k) (1994).

36. *See, e.g.*, Idaho Code § 41-3439 (1991); Ky. Rev. Stat. Ann. § 304.5-160 (Baldwin 1988); Mo. Rev. Stat. § 376.805 (1986); N.D. Cent. Code § 14-02.3-03 (1991).

37. *See National Educ. Ass'n of R.I. v. Garahy*, 598 F. Supp. 1374 (D.R.I. 1984), *aff'd* 779 F.2d 790 (1st Cir. 1986) (invalidating Rhode Island's requirement under "strict scrutiny" analysis); *but see Coe v. Melahn*, 958 F.2d 223 (8th Cir. 1992) (upholding Missouri's similar requirement under "undue burden" analysis).

38. Alan Gutmacher Institute, *Uneven & Unequal: Insurance Coverage of Reproductive Health Services* 19 (1994).

39. 381 U.S. 479 (1965).

40. *Eisenstadt v. Baird*, 405 U.S. 438 (1972); *see also Carey v. Population Services Int'l*, 431 U.S. 678 (1977).

41. *Carey v. Population Services Int'l, supra* note 40.

42. 42 U.S.C. § 300a-8 (1992).

43. *See generally* Julie Mertus & Simon Heller, *Norplant Meets the New Eugenicists: The Impermissibility of Coerced Contraception*, 11 St. Louis U. Pub. L. Rev. 359 (1992).

44. *See, e.g., People v. Zaring*, 8 Cal. App. 4th 362, 10 Cal. Rptr. 2d 263 (5th Dist. 1992); *State v. Mosburg*, 13 Kan. App. 2d 257, 768 P.2d 313 (1989); *Thomas v. State*, 519 So. 2d 1113 (Fla. App. 1988).

45. 42 U.S.C. § 1396d(4)(C) (1992).

46. Oklahoma, South Dakota, and North Carolina.

47. *Skinner v. Oklahoma*, 316 U.S. 535 (1942).

48. *See* 42 C.F.R. §§ 50.203–50.205; 441.253, 441.257, 441.258 (1993).

49. *Id.* For more information on sterilization abuse, *see* Committee for Abortion Rights and Against Sterilization Abuse, *Women Under Attack: Victories, Backlash and the Fight for Reproductive Freedom* (Susan E. Davis ed., 1988).

50. 42 U.S.C. §§ 300a-5, 300a-8.

51. Ark. Code Ann. § 20-49-204; Colo. Rev. Stat. §§ 27-10.5-128 to 27-10.5-132; Conn. Gen. Stat. § 45-78r; Del. Code Ann. tit. 16, § 5702(a); Ga. Code Ann. § 31-20-3; Idaho Code §§ 39-3901 to 3910; Me. Rev. Stat. Ann. tit. 34 § 2474; Miss. Code Ann. §§ 41-45-1 to 41-45-19; N.C. Gen. Stat. §§ 35-36 to 35-50; N.J. Rev. Stat. § 30:60-5; Or. Rev. Stat. § 436.010 to 150; Utah Code Ann. §§ 64-10-1 to 64-10-13; Vt. Stat. Ann. tit. 18, §§ 8705 to 16; W. Va. Code §§ 27-16-1 to -5.

52. Judith Gaines, *A Scandal of Artificial Insemination*, N.Y. Times, Oct. 7, 1990, § 6, pt. 2 at 23.

53. *See, e.g., Jhordan C. v. Mary K.*, 179 Cal. App. 3d 386, 224 Cal. Rptr. 530 (1st Dist. 1986).

54. Uniform Parentage Act § 5, 9A U.L.A. 592–93 (1979).

55. Several states prohibit so-called turkey baster insemination, i.e., artificial insemination without physician assistance. *See* Ga. Code Ann. § 74-101.1(b) (1981); Okla. Stat. Ann. tit. 10, § 553 (West 1982); Idaho Code §§ 39-5491 to 39-5408 (1985 and Supp. 1986); Or. Rev. Stat. § 677-360 (1979); and N.Y. City Health Code, art. 21, § 21.01.

56. *See, e.g., C.M. v. C.C.*, 152 N.J. Super. 160, 377 A.2d 821 (N.J. Juv. & Dom. Rel. 1977) (decided before New Jersey adopted its current artificial insemination statute); *Jhordan C. v. Mary K.*, *supra* note 53; *Thomas S. v. Robin Y.*, 618 N.Y.S.2d 356 (1st Dept. 1994) (known donor entitled to order of filiation).

57. *See, e.g., McIntyre v. Crouch*, 98 Or. App. 462, 780 P.2d 239 (1989), *cert. denied* 495 U.S. 905 (1990).

58. *See Jhordan C. v. Mary K.*, *supra* note 53 (agreement held not binding).

59. A sample donor/recipient agreement can be found in National Lawyers Guild, *Sexual Orientation and the Law* 1–101 (Roberta Achtenberg and Karen Moulding eds., 1993).

60. *Davis v. Davis*, 842 S.W.2d 588 (Tenn. 1992).

61. In a similar case, a New York trial court disagreed with the Tennessee decision, finding no reason to distinguish between embryos in utero and in vitro. The court held that the woman had the absolute right to the embryos. *See Kass v. Kass*, N.Y.L.J., Jan. 23, 1995 at 34. The case has been appealed.

62. *See, e.g., Doe v. Atty. Gen.*, 194 Mich. App. 432, 487 N.W.2d 484 (1992) (upholding statute that refuses to recognize surrogacy contracts, but defining "surrogacy" as necessarily involving both gestation services and relinquishment of parental rights). Other states with specific statutory bans include Arizona, Ariz. Rev. Stat. § 25-218 (1994); District of Columbia, D.C. Code § 16-402 (1994); Indiana, Ind. Code Ann. § 31-8-2-1 (Burns 1994);

Kentucky, Ky. Rev. Stat. Ann. § 199.590 (Baldwin 1993); Louisiana, La. Rev. Stat. § 9:2713; Nebraska, Neb. Rev. Stat. § 25-21,200 (1993); New York, N.Y. Dom. Rel. Law § 122 (Consol. 1994); North Dakota, N.D. Cent. Code § 14-18-05 (1993), Utah, Utah Code Ann. § 76-7-204 (1994), and Washington, Wash. Rev. Code § 26.26.230 (1994).

63. *See* Ariz. Rev. Stat. § 25-218 (1994); La. Rev. Stat. § 9:2713 (1993); N.Y. Dom. Rel. Law § 122 (Consol. 1994); Utah Code Ann. § 76-7-204 (1994).

64. Ark. Stat. Ann. § 9-10-201 (1993); Fla. Stat. Ann. § 742.15 (1993); Nev. Rev. Stat. Ann. § 126.045 (Michie 1993); N.H. Rev. Stat. Ann. § 168-B:1 *et seq.* (1993); Va. Code Ann. § 20-156 *et seq.* (1994).

65. *See, e.g., Doe v. Kelley*, 106 Mich. App. 169, 307 N.W.2d 438 (1981), *cert. denied*, 459 U.S. 1183 (1982) (finding that the statute, as applied to surrogacy contracts, did not unconstitutionally infringe on the right to bear or beget children); *In re Baby M*, 109 N.J. 396, 537 A.2d 1227, *on remand*, 225 N.J. Super. 267, 542 A.2d 52 (N.J. Super. Ch. 1988); *In re Adoption of Paul*, 146 Misc. 2d 379, 550 N.Y.S.2d 815 (N.Y. Fam. Ct. 1990).

66. *See, e.g., Surrogate Parenting Assoc., Inc. v Commonwealth*, 704 S.W.2d 209 (Ky. 1986); *Matter of Adoption of Baby Girl L. J.*, 132 Misc. 2d 972, 505 N.Y.S.2d 813 (N.Y. Sur. 1986).

67. *See Johnson v. Calvert*, 5 Cal. 4th 84, 851 P.2d 776, 19 Cal. Rptr. 2d 494, *cert. denied*, 114 S. Ct. 206 (1993); *but see In re Marriage of Moschetta*, 25 Cal. App.4th 1218, 30 Cal. Rptr. 2d 893 (4th Dist. 1994) (disapproving *Johnson* analysis where surrogate's egg is fertilized).

68. *See supra* note 65.

69. *Syrkowski v. Appleyard*, 420 Mich. 367, 362 N.W.2d 211 (1985).

70. *See, e.g., Cruzan v. Director, Missouri Dep't of Health*, 497 U.S. 261 (1990); *Lane v. Candura*, 6 Mass. App. Ct. 377, 376 N.E.2d 1232 (1978) (upholding right of competent adult woman to refuse doctor-ordered amputation of gangrenous leg).

71. *Roe v. Wade, supra* note 3 at 165–66 (1973).

72. As one advocate has noted, allowing the government to demand that women comport themselves in the best interests of their fetus—as the government defines those best interests—would effectively create an adversarial relationship with the woman's own body that she could avoid only by aborting the pregnancy. Dawn Johnsen, *From Driving to Drugs*, 139 U. Pa. L. Rev. 179 (1989).

73. *See People v. Stewart*, No. M508197, slip op. (Cal. Mun. Ct. Feb. 26, 1987); J. Warren, *Infant Death Case: Mother Innocent of Prenatal Crime*, L.A. Times, Feb. 27, 1987, at 3.

74. *U.S. Says 349,000 Caesareans In 1991 Were Not Necessary*, N.Y. Times, Apr. 23, 1993, at A16.

75. *Id.*

76. *See, e.g., Jefferson v. Griffin Spalding County Hospital Authority*, 247 Ga. 86, 274 S.E.2d 457 (1981); *see also* Janet Gallagher, *Prenatal Invasions and Interventions: What's Wrong with Fetal Rights*, 10 Harv. Women's L.J. 9, 11 and n.16 (1987).

77. *See, e.g., In re A.C.*, 573 A.2d 1235 (D.C. App. 1990); *In re Baby Boy Doe*, 260 Ill. App. 3d 392, 632 N.E.2d 326, 198 Ill. Dec. 267 (1st Dist. 1994).

78. *Baby Boy Doe, supra* note 77, 632 N.E.2d at 326.

79. *See, e.g., In re Klein*, 145 A.D.2d 145, 538 N.Y.S.2d 274 (2d Dep't), *appeal denied*, 73 N.Y.2d 705, 536 N.E.2d 627, 539 N.Y.S.2d 298 (1989); *Woe v. Bear*, No. H-79-1866 (S.D. Tex. May 5, 1980); *Margaret S. v. Edwards*, No. 78–2765 (E.D. La. Oct. 2, 1978);

Akron Center for Reproductive Health v. City of Akron, No. C78–155A (N.D. Ohio May 16, 1978); *Zbaraz v. Quern,* No. 77-C-4522 (N.D.Ill. May 15, 1978) (subsequent history on merits omitted); *Ryan v. Klein,* 412 U.S. 924 (1973); *Doe v. Bolton,* 319 F. Supp. 1048, 1057 (N.D. Ga. 1970) (three-judge court), *modified on other grounds,* 410 U.S. 179 (1973). *See also* Susan Goldberg, *Of Gametes and Guardians: The Impropriety of Appointing Guardians Ad Litem for Fetuses and Embryos,* 66 Wash. L. Rev. 503 (1991).

80. *Poole v. Endsley,* 371 F. Supp. 1379, 1382–83 (N.D. Fla. 1974), *aff'd in part & remanded on other grounds,* 516 F.2d 898 (5th Cir. 1975). *See also Brady v. Doe,* 598 S.W.2d 338 (Tex. Civ. App. 1980), *cert. denied,* 449 U.S. 1081 (1981); *Rothenberger v. Doe,* 149 N.J. Super. 478, 374 A.2d 57, 58 (N.J. Super. Ch. 1977) (dismissing claim to enjoin woman's abortion brought by self-described guardian *ad litem* on behalf of the fetus); *In re D.K.,* 204 N.J. Super. 205, 497 A.2d 1298, 1302–3 (Ch. Div. 1985) (reversing appointment of guardian for the fetus as "unconstitutional and void").

81. *See, e.g., Johnson v. State,* 602 So. 2d 1288 (Fla. 1992); *State v. Gray,* 62 Ohio St. 3d 514, 584 N.E.2d 710 (1992); *State v. Osmus,* 73 Wyo. 183, 276 P.2d 469 (1954).

82. *See, e.g., Procopio v. Johnson,* 994 F.2d 325 (7th Cir. 1993).

83. *See* Linda C. Mayes et al., *The Problem of Prenatal Cocaine Exposure: A Rush to Judgment,* 267 JAMA 406 (1992); Katherine Greider, *Crackpot Ideas,* Mother Jones (July/Aug. 1995) at 52.

84. *See, e.g., In re Stephen W.,* 221 Cal. App. 3d 629, 271 Cal. Rptr. 319 (3d Dist. 1990); *Matter of Nash,* 165 Mich. App. 450, 419 N.W.2d 1 (1987); *In re Ruiz,* 27 Ohio Misc. 2d 31, 500 N.E.2d 935, (Ohio Com. Pl. 1986) (*but see Cox v. Ct. of Common Pleas,* 42 Ohio App. 171, 537 N.E.2d 721 (1988)); *In re Theresa J.,* 158 A.D.2d 364, 551 N.Y.S.2d 219 (1st Dep't 1990) (*but see Matter of Milland,* 146 Misc. 2d 1, 548 N.Y.S.2d 995 (N.Y. Fam. Ct. 1989); *Matter of Fletcher,* 141 Misc. 2d 333, 533 N.Y.S.2d 241 (N.Y. Fam. Ct. 1988)).

85. *In re Valerie D.,* 223 Conn. 492, 613 A.2d 748 (1992); *State ex rel. Juvenile Dept. of Marion County v. Randall,* 90 Or. App. 673, 773 P.2d 1348 (1989).

86. Cal. Penal Code § 11165.13 (Deering 1994).

87. *See, e.g.,* Ala. Code § 26-14-3 (1994); Ark. Stat. Ann. § 12-12-507 (1993).

88. *See, e.g.,* 42 U.S.C. § 290dd-2 (1994).

89. *Hospital Gives Up Notifying the Police of Cocaine Abusers,* N.Y. Times, Sept. 8, 1994, at A8.

90. *Elaine W. v. Joint Diseases North Gen. Hosp.,* 81 N.Y.2d 211, 613 N.E.2d 523, 597 N.Y.S.2d 617 (1993).

91. *Bonte v. Bonte,* 136 N.H. 286, 616 A.2d 464 (1992) (allowing child to sue mother for negligently crossing the street while seven months pregnant); *Grodin v. Grodin,* 102 Mich. App. 396, 301 N.W.2d 869 (1980) (allowing suit where mother used tetracycline while pregnant).

92. *Stallman v. Youngquist,* 125 Ill. 2d 267, 531 N.E.2d 355, 126 Ill. Dec. 60 (1988).

93. *Id.* at 359. In addition, such close scrutiny of a pregnant woman's behavior may impermissibly infringe on her right of bodily integrity.

94. *See* Center on Social Welfare Policy and Law, *Summary of AFDC Waiver Activity Since February 1993* 7 (Oct. 1994). In 1994 family caps were considered and rejected in several other states, including Alabama, Colorado, Delaware, Florida, Illinois, Maine, and Oklahoma.

95. Michael C. Larcy, *"The Jury is Still Out": An Analysis of the Purported Impact of New*

Jersey's AFDC Child Exclusion (aka "Family Cap") Law, Center for Law and Social Policy 2 (March 10, 1994).

96. *C.K. v. Shalala,* 883 F. Supp. 991 (D.N.J. 1995).

97. California (rape, incest, contraceptive failure), Maryland (same), and Arizona (rape or incest) have submitted waiver applications with these so-called good girl exceptions.

98. *International Union, United Auto., Aerospace and Agr. Implement Workers of America, UAW v. Johnson Controls, Inc.,* 499 U.S. 187 (1991).

99. *Phillips v. Martin Marietta Corp.,* 400 U.S. 542 (1971).

100. *Cleveland Board of Education v. LaFleur,* 414 U.S. 632 (1974).

101. "Wrongful birth" suits arise when a physician fails to advise a woman of the possibility of genetic testing, fails to discover diagnosable genetic or congenital disorders, or fails to inform a woman of this diagnosis, thereby preventing her from making informed choices regarding prenatal care and abortion. "Wrongful life" suits are brought on behalf of children for damages and costs resulting from his or her birth under similar circumstances.

102. *See, e.g.,* 42 Pa. Cons. Stat. § 8305 (1993); Me. Rev. Stat. Ann. tit. 24, § 2931 (1993); Minn. Stat. § 145.424 (1993).

103. The risk of medical malpractice actions has been recognized as a key factor contributing to proper medical practice. *See* Peter A. Bell, *Legislative Intrusions into the Common Law of Medical Malpractice: Thoughts about the Deterrent Effect of Tort Liability,* 35 Syracuse L. Rev. 939, 966–68 (1984).

104. *See, e.g., Sejpal v. Corson,* 536 Pa. 629, 637 A.2d 289 (1993), *cert. denied* 115 S. Ct. 60 (1994); *Edmonds v. W. Pa. Hosp. Radiology Assoc.,* 414 Pa. Super. 567, 607 A.2d 1083 (1992), *cert. denied,* 114 S. Ct. 63 (1993); *Dansby v. Thomas Jefferson Univ. Hosp.,* 424 Pa. Super. 549, 623 A.2d 816 (1993); *Flickinger v. Wanczyk,* 843 F. Supp. 32 (E.D. Pa. 1994).

105. Clara Gabriano et al., *Mother-to-Child Transmission of Human Immunodeficiency Virus Type 1: Risk of Infection and Correlates of Transmission,* 90 Pediatrics 369 (1992).

106. *Id.*

107. Richard D. Gelber et al., *Executive Summary of ACTG 076: A Phase III Randomized, Placebo-Controlled Trial to Evaluate the Efficacy, Safety and Tolerance of Zidovudine (ZDV) for the Prevention of Maternal-Fetal HIV Transmission* (1994).

108. During the 1993–1994 legislative session, such bills were proposed in Florida, Michigan, and New York, although none were passed. In addition, health department officials in North Carolina and Colorado have discussed instituting mandatory counseling and testing of pregnant women.

109. H.R. 4507, 103d Congress, 2d Session (introduced May 26, 1994).

110. Mandatory testing of newborns is opposed by the American College of Physicians, the Infectious Disease Society of America, the Institute of Medicine, the American Academy of Pediatrics, the American Medical Association, the American Public Health Association, and the American College of Obstetricians and Gynecologists. *See also* National Association of People With AIDS, *HIV in America: A Profile of the Challenges Facing Americans Living with HIV* (1991); ACLU AIDS Project, *Epidemic of Fear: A Survey of AIDS Discrimination in the 1980s and Policy Recommendations for the 1990s* (1990).

111. *See* Deborah Saunders-Laufer et al., *Pneumocystic carinii Infections in HIV-Infected Children,* 38 Pediatric Clinics of N. Am. 69 (1991).

112. *See, e.g., Guardianship of Phillip B.,* 139 Cal. App. 3d 407, 188 Cal. Rptr. 781 (1st Dist. 1983).

113. *Doe v. Barrington,* 729 F. Supp. 376, 384 (D.N.J. 1990); *see also Doe v. American Red Cross Blood Service,* 125 F.R.D. 646 (D.S.C. 1989); *Woods v. White,* 689 F. Supp. 874 (W.D. Wisc. 1988).

114. *See Whalen v. Roe,* 429 U.S. 589, 598–99 (1977); *Carey v. Population Services Int'l, supra* note 40.

115. *See* Suzanne Sangree, *Control of Childbearing by HIV-Positive Women: Some Answers to Emerging Legal Policies,* 41 Buff. L. Rev. 309 (1993); Institute of Medicine, *HIV Screening of Newborns* 1 (1991); A. S. Beevor & J. Catalan, *Women's Experience of HIV Testing: The Views of HIV Positive and HIV Negative Women,* 5 Aids Care 177 (1993).

116. *Cruzan v. Director, Missouri Dept. of Health,* 497 U.S. 261 (1990).

117. *Guardianship of Phillip B., supra* note 114.

118. *See, e.g.,* Ala. Code §§ 22-11A-14 *et seq.* (1984 & Supp. 1988); Md. Health-Gen. Code §§ 18-333 *et seq.* (1987); Mo. Stat. Ann. §§ 191.65 *et seq.* (Supp. 1989); Wis. Stat. § 146.025(7)(b) (1985).

119. Philip J. Hilts, *Many Hospitals Found to Ignore Rights of Patients in AIDS Testing,* N.Y. Times, Feb. 16, 1990, at A1.

120. *See, e.g., Doe v. Roe,* 139 Misc. 2d 209, 526 N.Y.S.2d 718 (N.Y. Sup. 1988); *Steven L. v. Dawn J.,* 148 Misc. 2d 779, 561 N.Y.S.2d 322 (N.Y. Fam. Ct. 1990); *Stewart v. Stewart,* 521 N.E.2d 956 (Ind. App. 1988).

121. *See, e.g.,* Miss. Code Ann. §§ 41-41-51 through 41-41-63; Pa. Cons. Stat. Ann. § 3215.

122. *See Planned Parenthood v. Casey, supra* note 5 at 2832; *Ohio v. Akron Reprod. Health Center,* 497 U.S. 502, 510-14 (1990); *Hodgson v. Minnesota,* 497 U.S. 417 (1990).

123. *Ohio v. Akron Reprod. Health Services, supra* note 122 at 511–14; *Bellotti v. Baird,* 443 U.S. 622 (1979).

124. *See, e.g., Planned Parenthood of So. Ariz. v. Neely,* 804 F. Supp. 1210 (D. Ariz. 1992); *Foe v. Vanderhoof,* 389 F. Supp. 947 (D. Colo. 1975); *In re T.W.,* 551 So. 2d 1186 (Fla. 1989); *Planned Parenthood v. Miller,* No. 93-3033, 1994 U.S. Dist. LEXIS 11972 (D.S.D. Aug. 22, 1994); *Wicklund v. Salvagni,* No. 93-92-BU-JFB (D. Mont. Dec. 21, 1993); *Wynn v. Carey,* 599 F.2d 193 (7th Cir. 1979) (enjoining Illinois' notification requirement); *Glick v. McKay,* 616 F. Supp. 322 (D. Nev. 1985).

125. *In re T.W.,* 551 So. 2d 1186 (Fla. 1989). *But see American Academy of Pediatrics v. Lungren,* 912 P. 2d 1148 (Cal. 1996).

126. *In re Smith,* 16 Md. App. 209, 295 A.2d 238 (1972).

127. *See Carey v. Population Services Int'l, supra* note 40.

128. *Id.*

129. *Id.*

130. *Alfonso v. Fernandez,* 195 A.D.2d 46, 606 N.Y.S.2d 259 (2d Dep't 1993), *appeal dismissed* 637 N.E.2d 279 (1994).

131. *Curtis v School Committee of Falmouth,* 420 Mass. 749, 652 N.E. 2d 580 (1995) *cert. denied,* 116 S. Ct. 753 (1996).

132. *See, e.g.,* N.Y. Soc. Serv. Law § 350 (1)(e)(1992).

133. 42 U.S.C.A. §§ 602(a)(15)(Supp. 1994), 1396d(a)(4)(c)(Supp. 1994).

134. *T.H. v. Jones,* 425 F. Supp. 873 (D. Utah 1975), *aff'd mem.,* 425 U.S. 986 (1976).

135. 42 U.S.C. § 300a; *Jones v. T.H.,* 425 U.S. 986 (1976); *Planned Parenthood Assn. of Utah v. Dandoy,* 810 F.2d 984 (10th Cir. 1987).

136. A number of Supreme Court justices have indicated that minors have a constitutional right to obtain prescription contraceptive devices. *See Carey v. Population Services Int'l, supra,* note 40 at 691–99 (1977)(Justices Brennan, Marshall, Stewart, and Blackmun). But one justice stated that he would describe as "frivolous" the "argument that a minor has the constitutional right to put contraceptives to their intended use." *Id.* at 713 (Justice Stevens).

137. *In re Smith, supra* note 129.

138. *See Carey v. Population Services Int'l, supra* note 40.

APPENDIX
The Legal System

Appendix

The Legal System

For many persons, law appears to be magic—an obscure domain that can be fathomed only by the professional initiated into its mysteries. People who might use the law to their advantage sometimes avoid the effort out of awe for its intricacies. But in fact the main lines of the legal system, and of the law in a particular area, can be explained in terms clear to the layperson. The purpose of this short chapter is to outline some important elements of the system.

What does a lawyer mean by saying that a person has a legal right?

Having a right means that society has given a person permission—through the legal system—to secure some action or to act in some way that she or he desires. For example, a woman might have a right to an abortion, a minority person the right to employment free from discrimination, or a person accused of a crime the right to an attorney.

How does one enforce a legal right?

The concept of *enforcing* a right gives meaning to the concept of the right itself. While the abstract right may be significant because it carries some connotation of morality and justice, enforcing the right yields something concrete—the abortion, the job, the attorney.

A person enforces her or his right by going to some appropriate authority—often, a judge—who has the power to take certain action. The judge can order the people who are refusing to grant the right to start doing so, on pain of going to jail if they disobey. The judge can also order the people to pay money to compensate for the loss of the right. Sometimes other authorities, such as federal and state administrative agencies or a labor arbitrator, can take similar remedial action.

The problem with the enforcement process is that it will often be lengthy, time-consuming, expensive, frustrating, and may arouse hostility in others—in short, it may not be worth the effort. On the other hand, in some cases you may not need to go to an enforcement authority in order to implement your right. The concerned persons or officials may not have realized that you have a right and may voluntarily change their actions once you explain your position. Then, too, they may not want to go through the legal process either—it can be as expensive and frustrating for them as it is for you.

Where are legal rights defined?

There are several sources. Rights are defined in the statutes or laws passed by the U.S. Congress and by state and city legislatures. They are also set forth in the written decisions of judges, federal and state. Congress and state and local legislatures have also created institutions called administrative agencies to enforce certain laws, and these agencies interpret the laws in written decisions and rules that further define people's rights.

Are rights always clearly defined and evenly applied to all people?

Not at all, although this is one of the great myths about law. Because so many different sources define people's rights, and because persons of diverse backgrounds and beliefs implement and enforce the law, there is virtually no way to uniformity. Nor do statutes that set forth rights always do so with clarity or specificity. It remains for courts or administrative agencies to interpret and flesh out the details; and in the process of doing so, many of the interpreters differ. Sometimes two different courts will give completely different answers to the same question. Whether or not a person has a particular right may depend on which state or city he or she lives in.

The more times a particular issue is decided, the more guidance there is in predicting what other judges or administrative personnel will decide. Similarly, the importance of the court or agency deciding a case or the persuasiveness of its reasoning will help determine the effect of the decision. A judge who states thoughtful reasons for a decision will have more influence than one who offers poor reasons.

Law then is not a preordained set of doctrines, applied rigidly and unswervingly in every situation. Rather, law is molded from the arguments and decisions of many persons and institutions. It is very much a human process of trying to convince others—a judge, a jury, an administrator, the lawyer for the other side—that your view of what the law requires is correct.

What is a decision or case?

Lawyers often use these words interchangeably, although technically they do not mean the same thing. A case means the lawsuit started by one person against another, and it can refer to that lawsuit at any time from the moment it is started until the final result is reached. A decision means the written opinion in which the judge declares who wins the lawsuit and why.

What is meant by precedent?

Precedent means past decisions. Lawyers use precedent to influence new decisions. If the facts involved in the prior decision are close to the facts in the present case, a judge will be strongly tempted to follow the former decision. She is not, however, bound to do so and, if persuasive reasons are presented to show that the prior decision was wrong or ill-suited to changed conditions in society, the judge may not follow precedent.

What is the relationship between decisions and statutes?

In our legal system, most legal concepts originally were defined in the decisions of judges. In deciding what legal doctrine to apply to any case, each judge kept building on what other judges had done before him. The body of legal doctrines created in this way is called the common law.

The common law still applies in many situations, but increasingly state legislatures and the Congress pass laws ("statutes") to define the legal concepts that judges or agencies should use in deciding cases. The written decisions of individual judges are still important even where there is a statute because statutes are generally not specific enough to cover every set of facts. Judges have to interpret the meaning of statutes, apply them to the facts at hand, and write a decision; that decision will then be considered by other judges when they deal with these statutes in other cases. Thus it is generally not enough to know what a relevant statute defines as illegal; you also have to know how judges have interpreted the statute in specific situations.

What different kinds of courts are there?

The United States is unique for its variety of courts. Broadly speaking, there are two distinct court systems: federal and state. Both are located throughout the country; each is limited to certain kinds of cases, with substantial areas of overlap. Most crimes are prosecuted in state courts, for instance, although there a number of federal crimes prosecuted in federal court. People must always use state courts to get a divorce (except in the District of Columbia and other federal areas), but they must sue in federal court to establish rights under certain federal laws.

In both federal and state court systems one starts out at the trial court level, where the facts are "tried." This means that a judge or jury listens and watches as the lawyers present evidence of the facts that each side seeks to prove. Evidence can take many forms: written documents, the testimony of a witness on the stand, photographs, charts. Once a judge or jury has listened to or observed all the evidence presented by each side, it will choose the version of the facts it believes, apply the applicable legal doctrine to these facts, and decide which side has won. If either side is unhappy with the result, it may be able to take the case to the next, higher-level court and argue that the judge or the jury applied the wrong legal concept to the facts, or that no reasonable jury or judge could have found the facts as they were found in the trial court, and that the result was therefore wrong.

What are plaintiffs and defendants?

The plaintiff is the person who sues—that is, who *complains* that someone has wronged him or her and asks the court to remedy this situation. The defendant is the person sued—or the one who *defends* herself against the charges of the plaintiff. The legal writing in which the plaintiff articulates her or his basic grievance is the *complaint*, and a lawsuit is generally commenced by filing this document with the clerk at the courthouse. The defendant then responds to these charges in a document appropriately named an *answer*. Some states use different names for these documents.

One refers to a particular lawsuit by giving the names of the plaintiff and defendant. If Mary Jones sues Smith Corporation for refusing to hire her because she is a woman, her case will be called *Jones v. Smith Corporation* (v. stands for versus or against).

What is an administrative agency?

Agencies are institutions established by either state or federal legislatures to administer or enforce a particular law or series of laws and are distinct from both courts and legislature. They often regulate a particular industry. For example, the Federal Communications Commission regulates the broadcasting industry (radio and television stations and networks) and the telephone and telegraph industry, in accordance with the legal standards set forth in the Federal Communications Act; and the Interstate Commerce Commission regulates trucking and railroads.

These agencies establish legal principles, referred to as rules, regulations, or guidelines. Rules are interpretations of a statute and are designed to function in the same way as a statute—to define people's rights and obligations on a general scale, but in a more detailed fashion than the statute itself. Agencies also issue specific decisions in particular cases, like a judge, applying a law or rule to a factual dispute between particular parties.

How does one find court decisions, statutes, and agency rules and decisions?

All these materials are published and can be found in law libraries. In order to find the item desired, one should understand the system lawyers use for referring to, or citing, these materials. Some examples will help clarify the system. A case might be cited as *Watson v. Limbach Company*, 333 F. Supp. 754 (S.D. Ohio 1971); a statute, as 42 U.S.C. § 1983; a regulation, as 29 C.F.R. § 1604. 10(b). The unifying factor in all three citations is that the first number denotes the particular volume in a series of books with the same title; the words or the letters that follow represent the name of the book; and the second number represents either the page or the section in the identified volume. In the examples above, the *Watson* case is found in the 333rd volume of the series of books called *Federal Supplement* at page 754; the statute is found in volume 42 of the series called the *United States Code* at Section 1983; the regulation is in volume 29 of the *Code of Federal Regulations* at Section 1604.10(b).

There are similar systems for state court decisions. Once you understand the system, all you need do is find out from the librarian where any particular series of books is kept, then look up the proper volume and page or section. It is also important to look for the same page or section in the material sometimes inserted at the back of a book, since many legal materials are periodically updated. A librarian will tell you what any abbreviations stand for if you are unfamiliar with that series.

Given this basic information, anyone can locate and read important cases, statutes, and regulations. Throughout the book, such materials have been cited when deemed particularly important, and laypersons are urged to read them. Although lawyers often use overly technical language, the references cited in this book can be comprehended without serious difficulty, and reading the original legal materials will give a deeper understanding of their rights.

What is the role of the lawyer in the legal system?

A lawyer understands the intricacies and technicalities of the legal system, can maneuver within it efficiently, and, is able to help other people by doing so. Thus the lawyer knows where to find out about the leading legal doctrines in any given area and how to predict the outcome of your case, based on a knowledge of those doctrines. A lawyer can advise you what to do: forget about the case; take it to an administrative agency; sue in court; make a will; and so on. The lawyer then can help you take the legal actions that you determine are necessary.

How are legal costs determined and how do they affect people's rights?

The cost of using the legal system is predominantly the cost of paying the lawyer for his or her time. Since this has become prohibitive even for middle-class individuals, many people are not able to assert their rights, even though they might ultimately win if they had the money to pay a lawyer for doing the job.

Is legal action the only way to win one's legal rights?

By no means. Negotiation, education, consciousness raising, publicity, demonstrations, organization, and lobbying are all ways to achieve rights, often more effectively that through the standard but costly and time-consuming resort to the courts. In all these areas, it helps to have secure knowledge of the legal underpinning of your rights. One has a great deal more authority if one is protesting illegal action. The refrain "That's illegal" may move some people in and of itself; or it may convince those with whom you are dealing that you're serious enough to do something about the situation—by starting a lawsuit, for instance.